UNRECONSTRUCTED

CONFLICTING WORLDS

New Dimensions of the American Civil War

T. Michael Parrish, Series Editor

UNRECONSTRUCTED

SLAVERY
— AND —
EMANCIPATION
— ON —
LOUISIANA'S
RED RIVER
1820–1880

Carin Peller-Semmens

LOUISIANA STATE UNIVERSITY PRESS

BATON ROUGE

Published by Louisiana State University Press
lsupress.org

Designer: Michelle A. Neustrom
Typefaces: Sentinel, text; Job Clarendon, display

All interior photos are copyright © Carin Peller-Semmens.

Cover photograph: Adobe Stock/Fotoluminate LLC

Library of Congress Cataloging-in-Publication Data

Names: Peller-Semmens, Carin author
Title: Unreconstructed : slavery and emancipation on Louisiana's Red River, 1820–1880 /
    Carin Peller-Semmens.
Other titles: Conflicting worlds
Description: Baton Rouge : Louisiana State University Press, [2025] | Series: Conflicting
    worlds: New dimensions of the American Civil War | Includes bibliographical references
    and index.
Identifiers: LCCN 2025018568 (print) | LCCN 2025018569 (ebook) | ISBN 978-0-8071-8467-7
    (cloth) | ISBN 978-0-8071-8511-7 (epub) | ISBN 978-0-8071-8512-4 (pdf)
Subjects: LCSH: White supremacy movements—Red River Region (Tex.-La.)—History—
    19th century | Slavery—Red River Region (Tex.-La.)—History—19th century | Violence—
    Red River Region (Tex.-La.)—History—19th century | Reconstruction (U.S. history, 1865-
    1877)—Red River Region (Tex.-La.) | African Americans—Red River Region (Tex.-La.)—
    History—19th century | Massacres—Red River Region (Tex.-La.)—History—19th century |
    Red River Region (Tex.-La.)—Race relations | Red River Region (Tex.-La.)—History—
    19th century
Classification: LCC E185.93.L6 P45 2025 (print) | LCC E185.93.L6 (ebook) |
    DDC 306.3/6209763609034—dc23/eng/20250716
LC record available at https://lccn.loc.gov/2025018568
LC ebook record available at https://lccn.loc.gov/2025018569

In loving memory of my Grandma, Muriel Peller.
For David, with love, always.

History ... does not refer merely or even principally to the past. On the contrary, the great force of history comes from the fact that we carry it within us, are unconsciously controlled by it in many ways, and history is literally *present* in all we do.

—James Baldwin, "The White Man's Guilt"

CONTENTS

Photographs follow page 110.

ACKNOWLEDGMENTS

This book is the product of many years of work and dedication. It is a great privilege to reach the end of the project and have the opportunity to list the institutions, funding bodies, fellow historians, family, and friends who have come on this journey with me and have assisted in its completion in diverse ways. No historian is an island, to borrow John Donne's phrase, and this historian is grateful for the network of support that has followed and sustained this project and its author from the beginning.

I've always been intrigued by history, but my first engagement with the historian's craft came from the peerless mentorship of Joseph Ellis at Mount Holyoke College. Mount Holyoke's proud tradition of encouraging women to ask probing questions and challenge accepted narratives instilled in me the confidence to critically analyze the world, which has proved invaluable. Joe showed me how to harness that tradition and taught me to always approach historical actors on their own terms, without modern assumptions. His mentorship and his own work established a model for digging deeper into history, seeing what drove people and events, and finding good handles to grab and approach a topic.

My luck with mentors continued at Rutgers-Newark, where I studied with the larger-than-life Clement Price. Through his own involvement as a public historian, Clem showed the importance of history and public engagement in communities and community dialogue. Clem encouraged my passion for historical scholarship written for the education of the general public as well as for fellow historians. He taught me to listen closely to the voices of people disadvantaged in racial power structures and to look for the ways that marginalization impacts people's daily lives.

At the University of Sussex, Richard Follett pushed me to refine my historical analysis and to rely on the evidence to construct a complex but compelling argument that pushed the historiography further. His incredible knowledge of southern history and his focus on Louisiana history taught me the importance of a powerful narrative that critically but assertively grapples with the past. He encouraged boldness in my investigations with arguments that supported and promoted the long-lens approach taken in this work. I became a better historian under his mentorship, and his enthusiasm for my work has never wavered.

Many fantastic institutions underwrote the archival research for this book. The Mount Holyoke Alumnae Association's Mary Hazen Fellowship funded large portions of two research trips to Louisiana. I also received two separate sets of grants from the Royal Historical Society, the University of Sussex, and the School of History, Art History, and Philosophy at the University of Sussex. Additionally, I received funding from the Society for the Study of Labour History. A Louisiana State University Libraries Special Collections Research Grant helped make another trip to Hill Memorial Library's fantastic repositories possible.

I enjoyed the most wonderful time in the archives in no small part because of the generous individuals at each of the archives I've visited. Over the course of six years, I visited LSU's Hill Memorial Library five times. I relished my time at Hill because of the extraordinary documents I read and because the archivists freely shared their insights and knowledge. They provided access to LSU's extensive library and microfilms, and speedily processed a new acquisition for my use. For these kindnesses and countless others, I am extremely grateful to Germain Bienvenu, Tara Zachary Laver, Judy Bolton, Leah Wood Jewett, Jennifer Mitchell, and Mark Martin. I also thank Mary Wernet and Nolan Eller at the Cammie G. Henry Research Center at Northwestern State University for having all of my requested collections waiting for me when I arrived in Natchitoches. Sean Benjamin at Tulane's Louisiana Research Collection kindly sent digital copies of letters I required after my visit. In addition, the archivists at Noel Memorial Library, LSU Shreveport, the Historic New Orleans Collection, Tulane's Louisiana Research Collection, and Prescott Memorial Library, Louisiana Tech University, were all incredibly helpful and accommodating throughout my research trips.

My participation in panels on Reconstruction violence expanded my thinking and strengthened my arguments. Panels at Waging Peace, the Organization of American Historians, and the American Historical Association provided wonderful intellectual experiences that underscored the vibrancy of the historical profession. Many thanks to Brad Proctor, David Williard,

Michael Fitzgerald, Elaine Frantz, Crystal Feimster, Justin Behrend, Aaron Astor, and Greg Downs for being panelists with me. David Silkenat graciously invited me to the University of Edinburgh American History Workshop, and I appreciate the opportunity to workshop the Civil War chapters with Edinburgh's thriving American History department. The discussions and comments were insightful and beneficial. Thanks as well to Catherine Clinton for her unwavering support of female historians and her guidance, generosity, and friendship over the years.

Friends and family have encouraged, supported, and sustained my spirits throughout the writing process. Erin has been my closest friend and confidante for over half my lifetime, and her friendship, understanding, and presence have never wavered. She graciously read multiple chapters and offered incisive comments that have improved this work. Lauren has always been an indispensable friend and vocal champion, offering both levity and brevity at the precise moments they are required. She can always find the silver lining in every situation, which has proved cathartic. Kaete deserves plaudits both for her friendship and invaluable assistance in listening to my arguments over the years as I honed and sharpened their clarity. Erin, Lauren, and Kaete also visited me in Louisiana while I conducted research, and they transported countless books across the Atlantic for me in their luggage. Their positive outlooks on this work as it has progressed to a monograph have empowered and focused me. For their gifts of friendship and steadfast support and our shared adventures, I am immeasurably grateful.

I have been fortunate to have the support and cheerleading of friends, neighbors, and colleagues while writing this book. I am so thankful for the conversations, encouragement, and support over the years. Aoife and Sue, my dearest friends in Edinburgh, have enriched my life with their friendship and have always known just the right time to suggest extended dog walks. My dog, Byron, was my constant companion as I wrote this book. He excelled at being the most excellent writing partner, an ever-ready listener and spirit lifter, and champion cuddler. My son joined as this book entered the final publication phase, writing the perfect conclusion to this chapter of my life.

My sister, Michelle, my brothers-in-law John and James, and my sisters-in-law Amanda and Samantha have always given their love and encouragement but also knew when I needed to talk about topics other than this book. My parents-in-law, Jane and Kim, are two of the kindest and most generous people. They have showered me with love and celebrated every accomplishment. Some family members have been with me in spirit. My grandmother-in-law, Klare, shared my love of classical music, literature, and history. It would have been a privilege to share this book with her. My father, Arthur, deeply respected intellectual curiosity. Although his specialty in electrical engineering diverged from my interests, we shared a love of history and research. I know he would have enjoyed reading this book.

This book is dedicated to the two most important people in my life. My grandma was the definition of a strong woman. Grandma was determined, smart, quick-witted, generous, thoughtful, funny, and unbelievably elegant. She was vivacious and unwavering in her support and urged me to dream big and grab hold of every opportunity. I miss her every day in countless ways. This book is dedicated to Muriel Peller with boundless love.

My husband, David, has illuminated my life with constant love and the gift of complete emotional security. No matter life's challenges, David is right by my side as we take on the world together. He has never doubted my ability and has always encouraged my ambition. He never stops making our dreams a reality, planning our next adventure, making me laugh, being thoughtful, or celebrating everything we are fortunate to share together. I adore each of our shared traditions, creating lasting memories, and the strength of our bond. This book is for David, my soul mate, with infinite love.

A NOTE ON LANGUAGE AND SOURCES

Readers should note that the spelling, punctuation, and emphasis present in the original archival sources have been maintained in the quotations utilized in this book. This keeps the tenor, construct, and feelings of the time period and the individuals studied herein intact and unfiltered.

Regional African American first-person voices are scarce during the antebellum period. Solomon Northup's *Twelve Years a Slave* is the only narrative from an ex-slave. Northup was abducted from New York and sold into slavery in Louisiana in 1841. What is gleaned about enslaved people's lives before his narrative comes from tabulations in plantation ledgers, enumerations on the 1850 and 1860 slave schedules, and slaveholders' letters. Whenever appropriate, Northup's voice is included alongside glimmers of statements from the formerly enslaved to show the contours of the enslaved experience.

Slaveholders on the Red River infrequently talk about enslaved people by name or in detail, except when they discuss the management of cotton production, the use of violence against the enslaved population, or the sale or purchase of enslaved people. As a methodological technique to invoke for readers the oppressive, violent, and dehumanizing nature of enslavement in the Red River region, there are portions of chapters 1 and 2 that intentionally use the noun *slave*. The intent is to impart for a short span of time the crushing environment under which enslaved people toiled, how they held productive monetary value but were denied humanity, and the violent foundation that undergirded their daily existence.

To seize and utilize the tracks left in the archives about Red River African Americans, I have compiled demographic information by counting the number of enslaved people listed in the census for each parish. Census takers mostly looked at a group of enslaved people, broke them down into a tripartite color scheme, and allocated a sum total. Heartbreakingly, this is the entire record available for the African Americans who toiled in the Red River region. It is nonetheless important to include this evidence to mark the existence of the numerous Black individuals held in bondage in northwest Louisiana. The names of the enslaved are used whenever they are present in the available plantation ledgers.

Readers familiar with Reconstruction will know of the Works Progress Administration interviews with the formerly enslaved in the 1930s. This is a rich source, widely used by historians to hear from Black southerners about enslavement in their own words. The Louisiana interviews are compiled in a now out-of-print volume titled *Mother Wit: The Ex-Slave Narratives of the Louisiana Writers' Project* by Ronnie W. Clayton. Unfortunately, no recollections or interviews from the Louisiana narratives discuss the Red River region.

The words of African Americans from Red River do enter the historical record through their testimonies in *Use of the Army in Certain of the Southern States,* which captured Black voices and experiences during the violent years of Reconstruction. *Use of the Army* is rich with accounts from Louisiana freedpeople, with more than half of the testimony coming from Red River parishes. Sometimes, the only record left of a Black person—often only a short sentence in the sources—is from another family member recounting the murder of that freedperson who never spoke into the historical record. By including the testimony of the brave Black individual(s) who recounted the pervasive violence as well as the details of the murder of that Black person, the existence and humanity of multiple individuals is recorded for posterity.

UNRECONSTRUCTED

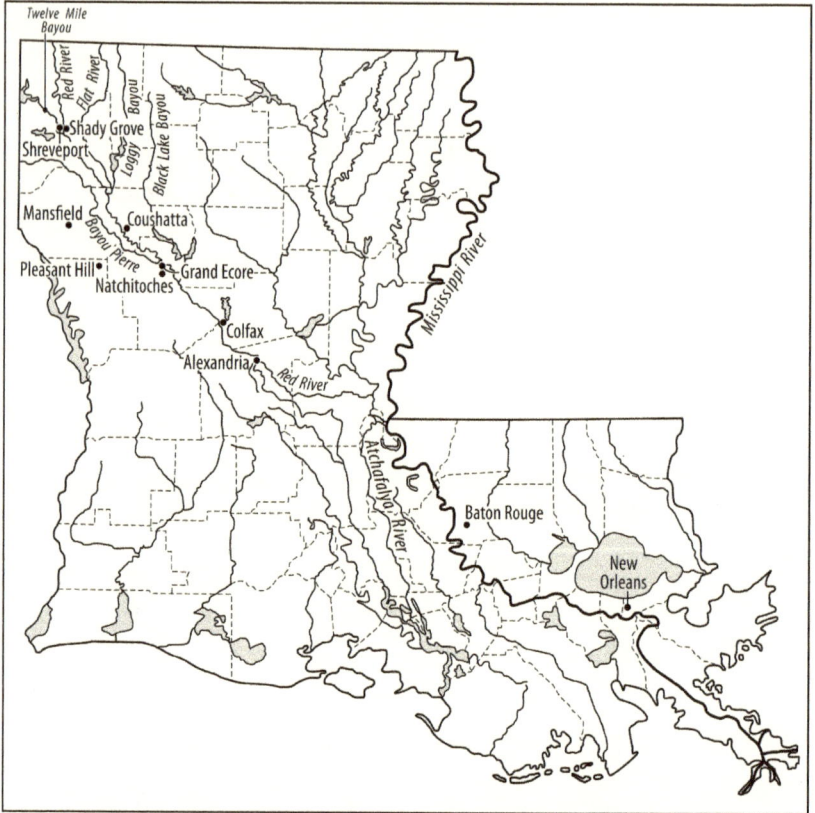

Map of Louisiana, highlighting discussed cities or communities and rivers.
Parish divisions are indicated with dotted lines. Map by Mary Lee Eggart.

INTRODUCTION:
"RED RIVER IS SO GRAND"

The Long Arc of Mastery

> I swear to the Lord
> I still can't see
> Why Democracy means
> Everybody but me.
>
> —Langston Hughes,
> "The Black Man Speaks"

Henry Adams was twenty-two when the Civil War ended. He had been enslaved near Shreveport, Louisiana, and he enlisted and served in the U.S. Army after emancipation, from 1866 to 1869. There, he learned to read and write, skills he then used in the struggle to protect freedpeople's rights in northwest Louisiana. In 1870, he organized Black veterans from Shreveport into a committee to campaign for Republicans and encouraged Black voting, political involvement, and labor rights throughout the Red River region. Through this work, he witnessed countless acts of violence, bigotry, mistreatment, debasement, cheating, and barbarity committed against freedpeople. He testified before a United States Senate committee in 1875 as part of the federal investigation of Louisiana's astonishing levels of violence. Addressing the chamber, he prefaced his speech with the pressing need to testify despite great personal risk:

Gentlemen: Let me say to you and to the good people of the North, I did this with no fear. I did it with honesty, and did it because I thought that such things should be reported to the people at large; but I [say] to you, and to you, gentlemen, and to the officers of the military service, to the world at large and my name signed to them, I cannot live no longer in the Southern States, because I would be killed by the white people of the Southern States and never allowed to travel through the South no more. But if it is necessary for to publish my name at the world at large, publish it, sink or swim, live or die.[1]

Testifying about white supremacist vigilante violence was a dangerous undertaking, and Adams's bold, clear statement transcends time to underscore the incisiveness and necessity of Black testimony that elucidated the violence they endured during Reconstruction. Freedpeople like Adams who courageously entered their experiences into the historical record understood the significant risk inherent in shedding light on the entrenched, systemic violence in northwest Louisiana.

This book recovers northwest Louisiana's violent nineteenth century, seeking to better understand why it was so hostile, discriminatory, and deadly toward formerly enslaved Americans like Henry Adams. The resulting story of Black subjugation and white domination connects three significant epochs in American and southern history. Beginning with antebellum settlement, it chronicles the aggression and curtailment of Black freedom sustained throughout the Civil War and reaffirmed during Reconstruction. Examining the connective cords binding enslavement with emancipation in this understudied region deepens our understanding of how racial subjugation and violence shaped white and Black identity. It informed demographic dichotomies and sentiments, curtailed political engagement and access, and ingrained racial views and behaviors.

The effectiveness of white supremacists' aggression and vigilantism during Reconstruction entrenched systemic racism and structures of inequality in the Red River region. Violence was a commonplace feature of enslavement, and its effectiveness as a tool of white racial dominance made it a crucial component of restricting Black freedom and citizenship. Events and actions from this region directly supported southern white vigilantism. Federal failures to protect against violence, uphold Black citizenship rights, and enforce laws meant to scaffold freedom underpinned broader trends and shortcomings of Reconstruction. These highlight this region's relevance to the complex national story of violence, capitalism, and systemic racism.

White racial domination enforced by violence suffused regional ante-bellum settlement and propelled market-focused cotton cultivation. After the Civil War, this durable connective creed and core manifestation of white supremacist ideology cemented race relations, racial attitudes, community composition, and the regional political landscape. Indeed, 45 percent of all homicides during Reconstruction occurred in the Red River region, with 85 percent of those victims being Black.[2] The daily experiences of Black individuals remained grounded in racial prejudices that anchored themselves deeply in the national psyche; they are burrs with thorns that resist being pulled from the fabric of the nation.[3] Racism defined how opportunities, identity, and citizenship were accorded, and it determined which portions of the populace were deemed worthy of rights, protections, and power. Hierarchical racial attitudes split Americans into a binary. The ideology of whiteness—including who was classed as white at particular junctures—coalesced around definitions of white personhood, in juxtaposition to those whom whites dominated, controlled, and denigrated.[4]

Nestled at the heart of the Red River region's white regional character was the centrality of violence to white personal and collective identity. Regional white slaveholders performed, understood, and defined mastery for themselves as being able to control enslaved bodies, exert violence to emphasize racial subjugation, and maintain profit-focused market dependence that reaped financial rewards. Like other southern regions, sustained and omnipresent violence was critical to expressing mastery along the Red River. Violence—including violent acts, rhetoric, and accepted social mores—created a durable communal white identity founded on domination, violence, and racial subjugation. By dehumanizing Blacks, equating them with animals, and describing them in terms wholly oppositional to white descriptors, whites created a society and an unshakeable mindset grounded in racist thought, strengthened by economic gains, and maintained by violence.

Mastery was a malleable and diuturnal construct that adapted as slavery expanded its structural boundaries, when new laws protected and strengthened slaveholding rights, and as politics crescendoed into the secession crisis. Its evolving capacity for violence transmits a continuous presence throughout the nineteenth century, while under the surface, the ideology of mastery was recalibrated alongside national and regional laws to enforce racial hierarchies and prejudices. Abolitionists helmed attacks on slavery, and hotly contested questions about extending slavery. This ideology was not only adaptive; its inclusion of white southerners who joined the slaveholding class throughout the 1850s solidified a commitment to racial hierarchy, prejudice, and domination that manifested as mastery. Thus, mastery was a way of thinking, acting, and being for white southerners that transcended the idiosyncrasies of southern regional slaveholding. It united slaveholding and nonslaveholding white southerners behind a creed steeped in racist ideas and actions that were alive and respondent to any attack on white supremacy, the rights of slaveholders, or the commodification of African Americans.

The critical position of violence as an emotional and psychological tool for social control and an enforcer of white southern male dominance—gendered and racial—cemented its significance within the language and ideology of mastery. Whites in the Red River region understood themselves within this context, and they constructed a world in which their self-worth, privileges, freedom, citizenship, and authority were founded on the denial of those things to an entire group based on race.[5] Violence was a self-reinforcing facet of this ideology, inculcated as a learned behavior. Violence begot power and power violence, in a perpetuating closed system.[6] Power reinforced a rigid hierarchy that indoctrinated whites within a superiority framework that rewarded the fortification of a racially bifurcated society.[7] Violence served as a mechanism to affirm membership and position within white society and to create institutions and structures that bolstered racial inequality while also unifying whites across the slaveholding spectrum.[8] This created an enduring rubric that informed postbellum racial, political, labor, and social relations and constricted the pathways out of slavery for regional Blacks.

The endurance and flexibility of violence defined the cadence of a brutal slave regime with the same deftness that it catalyzed the persistent assaults of Reconstruction. This legacy and pervasiveness of violence, deployed through a wide range of methods for an array of changing circumstances, affected how Blacks conceptualized freedom and the visceral regional white reaction to Black political, labor, and economic efforts during Reconstruction.[9] It was a key driver behind the massacres at Shady Grove, Colfax, and Coushatta while also undergirding the sustained labor-related violence as market-focused, capitalistic ex-slaveholders rushed to lock in laborers.

In northwest Louisiana, violence was the response to Blacks' political participation, efforts to vote, wanting the freedom to travel without a pass, working contracted hours for agreed-upon wages, desiring education, and controlling access to and ownership of their bodies. The Civil War and post-war Red River region carried the same social, economic, racial, and labor ideologies as the antebellum. The embedded, resolute, profit-driven, and brutal white regional identity forged during settlement continued to buttress regional commitment to white power and white supremacy that was strengthened and reaffirmed during Reconstruction. The enduring legacy of slavery ensured that from slavery to freedom, the Red River region remained completely unreconstructed. As Henry Adams stated in 1874, it was "utterly impossible to live with the whites of Louisiana."[10]

— — —

There is no comprehensive history of slavery, emancipation, or Reconstruction along Louisiana's Red River. Focused on a small corner of the South, this sustained investigation addresses that geographic lacuna and provides an opportunity to parse adherence to systems of racial power and violent subjugation that created a postwar world rooted in white supremacy and violent control. This chronological investigation deepens our understanding of slavery and emancipation in Louisiana and outside the plantation belt while generating discussion about the impact of violent white supremacy on African American personhood, citizenship, and identity.[11]

Undertaking a continuous examination of the period from 1820 to 1880 demonstrates how the long arc of domination, control, and violence shaped and defined the Red River region. History does not occur in a vacuum, with delineated periods of study halting the lives and events unfurling for historical actors, leaving them neatly packaged for later scholarly reflection. Hence, this multidimensional articulation of the centrality of violence provides a fuller appreciation of the extent of the horrors endured by African Americans. It enters the dialogue with recent investigations into white supremacy—including acts of terrorism, vigilantism, and the memorialization and commemoration of Reconstruction violence.[12] This approach moves beyond lists of gruesome brutality to contextualize, unpack, and portray violent acts as precise indications of regional ethos and postwar southern ideology, demonstrative of the manifold ways that violence shaped and reconstructed northwest Louisiana. Violence is not used as a summative catchall for Reconstruction events and the steady diminishment of African

American freedom. Instead, it offers an analytical lens to examine the cacophony of assaults on African Americans and to explain its ramifications. It provides an opportunity to grapple with the psychological drivers of these attacks and to incorporate violence as a means of understanding the postwar landscape.

Recent scholarship has discussed capitalism and slavery to stress the exploitative thrust of American slavery and the centrality of enslaved laborers and the cotton complex to the emergence of a modern, capitalist American economy. These works investigate and reexamine arguments from earlier generations of economic scholarship on slavery.[13] This book joins the conversation about the economic implications of slavery and defines capitalism as widespread and systematic market dependence.[14] It demonstrates capitalism's key role in shaping the plantation sphere and manifestations of Confederate fealty, including the impressment of enslaved people and the focus on securing labor for cotton cultivation postwar. The argument advanced herein is that regional slaveholders were capitalist because they acquired land and slaves through markets, focused on productivity and profitability, and were compelled to maintain productivity levels to stay afloat financially.[15] Red River slaveholders were capitalist and part of a capitalist network. They depended on the market for survival and relied on the most productive techniques to keep costs low, with scant attention paid to subsistence crops.

Red River region slaveholders were rapacious entrepreneurs, informed and genuinely embedded in the global marketplace. Slaveholding was crucial to regional white identity and the elastic, encompassing parameters of whiteness. Indeed, slavery brought these capitalist motivations into reality at the "value-making periphery."[16] Northwest Louisiana thrived economically, driven by commodity production, because of sustained and close alignment among slaveholders, market dependence, and profit. Since enslaved people were purchased through markets, every regional slaveholder remained dependent on those same markets and was compelled to sell cotton to maintain their access to the marketplace. Reliance on market forces translated into adopting practices that minimized expenditures and leveraged the most productive agronomic techniques.[17] Significantly, regional slaveholders found lasting durability in capitalism that outlived slavery's market usefulness. Ex-slaveholders replicated the market-focused plantation system, with profitability as the sole economic goal, as much as possible following the Civil War. Conditions strikingly similar to enslavement were maintained, violence persisted, and Black mobility was controlled.

This argument builds on the work of economic historians Alan Olm-stead and Paul Rhode—mainly their focus on productivity growth due to fertile land and the increased ease with which hybrid seed varietals could be picked, in addition to their efficiency argument—and the modern, profit-able, and capitalist argument of Robert Fogel and Stanley Engerman. This contrasts with Ed Baptist's take on efficiency and productivity rates. How-ever, Eugene Genovese's paternalism argument is ultimately rejected be-cause paternalism is conspicuous by its absence. Genovese's argument that paternalism was the byproduct and connective glue between the mode of production and the social relations of production is not borne out by the ar-chival evidence for slaveholders in the Red River region. Additionally, since the region's slaveholders did not distrust capitalism—on the contrary, they were galvanized to continue large-scale cotton production because of their dependence on market behavior—attempts to view slaveholders' motiva-tions through a paternalistic lens eradicate the violence that surrounded en-slaved life.[18] Instead, concern centered on profit, markets, and productivity. Profit was what enticed slaveholders, drove continued settlement, shaped enslaved life, cemented staple crop cotton cultivation, and embedded vio-lence within racial relations.

The most significant overlap between this book and the works of Walter Johnson, Ed Baptist, and Sven Beckert is the agreement that slaveholders were profit-motivated, and in the case of the Red River region, that rapid and continuous productivity growth made this manifest. The commodifi-cation of enslaved people by the region's slaveholders, slave traders, and the entire slave trading industry was dually driven by racial attitudes and profit, and it reduced Black human beings to productive, wealth-generating prop-erty. Stripped of their personhood in the white mind, enslaved people were placed in the same category as livestock and household items; they were often described as "moveables." Their labor and financial value defined the enslaved; they produced incomes and were easily maneuvered physical, fi-nancial assets. Market competition drove increased owner violence, which was flexible and deployed whether yields were high or pickability low. Not-withstanding Johnson's and Baptist's stance, while Red River slaveholders had no value or respect for the life of Black people as individuals, slavehold-ers did protect their investments in human property—because they were concerned with their property.

Slavery made regional wealth and market growth possible, enabling regional slaveholders of all sizes to slide into and benefit from the dynamic capitalistic marketplace. Red River cotton fed the already present demand for this raw good. Cotton cultivation shaped every aspect of enslaved people's work rhythms and constructed a crushing world of sunup-to-sundown labor. Enslaved people turned undeveloped Red River land into functional, productive, thriving cotton fields. They cleared the land, broke the soil, chopped or thinned out the young cotton plants, picked the cotton, manned the gin that separated seed from fiber, packed the crop into bales, and lastly, lugged the heavy white bales to the riverfront before steamboats transported it to market.

Booming cotton production redefined the United States as a slave society and reconfigured politics, and the mobility of enslaved people was crucial to slavery's survival and dynamism.[19] The opening of the Red River raft, a dense and mercurial logjam, connected this cotton region with the commercial entrepôt of New Orleans. The value of raw cotton produced by the United States in 1820 was $22 million. In 1831, the United States produced about 350 million pounds of cotton—just under half of the world's raw cotton—rising to 500 million pounds by 1835 and 800 million pounds in 1839.[20] By the late 1850s, the southern states had produced nearly all 374 million pounds of cotton used within American borders, and 77 percent of the 800 million pounds produced were processed in Great Britain. By 1860, the southern states produced more than 4.5 million bales of cotton, and the value of cotton exported was $192 million.[21] On the eve of the Civil War and at the apex of the cotton boom, three-quarters of the South's slave population labored in cotton fields.

— — —

Slaveholders migrated to the alluvial soil of northwest Louisiana—the land comprising the parishes of Bienville, Bossier, Caddo, Claiborne, DeSoto, Grant, Natchitoches, Rapides, Red River, and Sabine—driven by the expansion of the cotton South, the vociferous demands of the global cotton empire, and insatiable desire for profit. Aggressive land settlement was aided by the forceful removal of local Native Americans before 1820, allowing unencumbered land acquisition. Caddo Parish's name gestures at the Native nation that called this their homeland, but there is no discussion of Native peoples in the papers of regional slaveholders. In slaveholders' rendering, the land had lain fallow until market-savvy white cotton planters realized its inherent potential. While the tapestry of the United States is woven on Native destruction, the forceful removal of Native people, and the seizure of their lands, the section of the tapestry under examination in this book is told in Black and white.[22]

The records available in public holdings do not provide a vastly rich cache of information on enslaved life or slaveholders' inner thoughts and daily pressures. This emphasizes the emotional rawness and heaviness of this regional story. It is one full of violence endured by Blacks and is substantiated by reams of sources that distill Black mortality down to the violent acts that ended their lives. Documents written or capturing Black perspectives and experiences are sparse, with the most complete antebellum Black voice from the region being that of Solomon Northup. His narrative is a significant resource, though it was written for a white abolitionist audience and thus incorporates numerous tropes and stereotypes that resounded with that audience.[23] African Americans who escaped to freedom were able to speak of the brutality of enslavement, but many needed to rely on the assistance of white writers, publishers, and supporters to put those experiences on paper. Thus, as Saidiya Hartman notes, Black recollections remained delimited and bounded by historical permissions and prohibitions. Reconstruction similarly restricted opportunities to recollect enslavement, and Blacks might have felt uncomfortable or unable to recount their experience and feelings during Works Progress Administration interviews. It should also be recognized that the WPA interviews were written and edited by white individuals, who may have removed or failed to include significant recollections and experiences. The collected Louisiana WPA narratives contain no reminiscences of regional enslaved life.[24]

Regional slaveholders left little information about enslaved life in their private and business papers. For example, the birth or death of an enslaved person might be news written down by a record-keeping slaveholder. It was noteworthy because it impacted slaveholders and their position within the market economy, and the diary or ledger entries reflect that stance. Beyond that abrupt ledger line, little attention was afforded to Black life. Perhaps such callous inattention was compounded by limited literacy or less desire to write for posterity. In this nonpaternalistic and emotionally bleak plantation world, enslaved people were assets and essential productive resources within an economy dependent on their labor. In their writings and business dealings, slaveholders reduced Blacks to instruments of labor that did not necessitate detailed records.[25] As Stephanie Jones-Rodgers has shown, this included slaveholding women, who were devoid of paternalism in their correspondence and in the management and investment of their enslaved property.[26]

Here, there is a similarity with the behaviors of slaveholders from other southern areas. Whereas the slaveholders in Piedmont, North Carolina, were affectionate, concerned, and forgiving in correspondence with their children and family, they dehumanized their enslaved Blacks, referring to them using market terminology. Omitted from the documents that comprise the historical record from the start, the slaveholder documents' silence about enslaved people is only punctuated by tabulations, inventories, cotton picking numbers, and occasional remarks about ill Black individuals.

Whether field hand or skilled laborer, enslaved Blacks also faced the ignominy of being denied an individualized name. Naming practices on large-scale, densely populated cotton and rice holdings of the seaboard states connected kin, indicated kin obligation, and enshrined family history. Names embedded social obligations within the community and carried deep-rooted significance, although Blacks had little say over the official names of their children, which were chosen by slaveholders.[27] Names, however, also connote personality and humanity. Slaves on the Red River were property with a price.[28] It is therefore important that enslaved people's names are used whenever they are recorded, and their testimony incorporated, to allow us to recognize the lives of people who are only given a number on census sheets or plantation ledgers or whose deposition is the only mark left behind. Respecting the personal, private selfhood each Black person possessed is equally essential; historian Daina Ramey Berry eloquently calls this "soul value." The records of enslaved life are patchy in this region, but each enslaved person had a soul value, they claimed their personhood, and they reacted and pushed back against their commodification.[29]

Additional source limitations are rooted in the slaveholder mindset alongside environmental and social factors. This region experienced flooding throughout the nineteenth and twentieth centuries, which damaged archival holdings and reduced documentation. For literate whites who maintained correspondence (which does not represent the majority), it was also common practice to burn letters after a loved one's death. Conversely, many slaveholders would not have wasted time and paper to write about human property in an era where immediate family members and relations might see one another only a handful of times over a lifetime. Letters took a long time to reach recipients and the contents were often devoted to matters concerning the white family: health, business, and aspirations. For Red River slaveholders, their bondspeople were a means to achieve wealth but did not deserve lines in a letter. The same is true of other extractive, market-focused southern slaveholders, who routinely omitted Black people from their correspondence and diaries.[30] This harks back to and reinforces Michel-Rolph Trouillot's statement that those who manipulate and hold power produce the collective understanding of the past.[31]

The lopsided racial power dynamic renders this a story told primarily through the unfettered words of white sources and white action until Reconstruction. Then freedpeople enter the historical record with their powerful, stark testimonials of white supremacist violence during Reconstruction. The dynamics and tenor of the region created a world that restricted the opportunities to hear Black voices. The presence of African American voices in the Red River region's historical record is limited to attestations directly related to occasions of violent reassertion of mastery or instances when freedpeople pushed back at the obstacles to freedom. Agency, in the "canonical way to frame an argument," which Walter Johnson rightly indicates is used as shorthand to humanize and empathize with the enslaved, must not be engaged as a trope or to show in starker relief the closed boundaries of African American personhood.[32] Enslaved and freedpeople's voices provide the vantage point to understand the violent relationships that supported slave and postemancipation societies, where racial power literally and figuratively erased Black speech from the archival record. The extensive Reconstruction era testimonies mark the entrance of regional African Americans into the historical record on a large scale, with their own voice. It is important to recognize the strength it took to provide these testimonials and to internalize that a whole life is encapsulated within a short declaration. Their statements—often detailing violence enacted on a murdered loved one, or personally experienced—expose the violent, contested, and charged nature of freedom along the Red River.

— — —

The powerful, inescapable, destructive, capricious, wealth-giving Red River itself played a significant role in shaping regional experiences, particularly during the Civil War. The Red River shaped and preserved the region's distorted racial dynamic, while environmental factors were central to the unfolding of history for inhabitants.[33] Copious funds and labor were devoted to clearing the morass of driftwood and silt that formed the Red River raft in order to easily link the region to the cotton and slave markets of New Orleans. During the Civil War, the raft and the high waters of the Red hermetically sealed the region. The river was impassable for most of the war, which increased the Confederacy's reliance on northwest Louisiana as a source of food and medicine for the army. The river—and the atypical experience of the war it proffered—strengthened and solidified regional commitment to the tenets and aims of the Confederacy, while the region's limited experience of combat redoubled its stalwart dedication to the cause well after fighting concluded. However, just as the Red River provided lifeblood to the cotton economy and served as a protective shield during the war, the mercurial waterway also carried destruction and disease. Leveraged as a weapon by white vigilantes, it frequently served as a disposal site for murdered freedpeople. The Red River's environment played a significant role in white supremacy's domination and shaped the lived experience of enslavement and freedom.

Slaveholders' overarching ideology and identity were sustained because of relative geographic isolation combined with their unmitigated adherence to mastery and white racial domination. Ardent regional commitment to the Confederacy was built firmly on the embedded yet elastic ideology of mastery and the market-dependent capitalist ecosystem made tangible by commodified enslaved laborers. The power dynamic of slavery remained extractive and violent, while the regional white identity of racial hierarchy, white mastery, and white superiority was responsive to wartime changes and fluctuations of fortune. It regulated racial hierarchies and prejudices through pervasive racial violence. The relatively spare firsthand Civil War experience afforded by the indomitable Red River revealed a white population unapologetic in its dedication to racial supremacy and confident in the durability and responsiveness of mastery as an encompassing, dynamic ethos for white southerners. The unique unfolding of the war shaped attitudes in a wholly singular fashion that brought white slaveholders into Reconstruction feeling justified in the righteousness of the Confederate cause.

Black emancipation further hardened their deeply entrenched racial views. The invulnerable river created a geographic barrier that cushioned the racist attitudes of the region's slaveholders.

During Reconstruction, regional white supremacy adapted antebellum iterations of violent control into an efficacious method to subjugate freedpeople, with tangible, undeniable results. Violence and racial authority were utilized in explosive and visceral post–Civil War events to hobble freedpeople's civil and political rights, to realign and reassert white identity, and to maintain the regime of white control and mastery. When the former slaveholders found themselves without slaves, forced to take an oath of allegiance and to enter into labor contracts with their former chattel, they relied on racial hierarchy and power to redraw the lines of control and dominance. The prolific use of violence was the most straightforward of progressions because violence was so honed, so perfected, and so enmeshed in the very fabric of the region.

Violence is a foundational element of the Red River regional dynamic and identity, which was strengthened during the Civil War. When the South lost the war and was occupied by federal troops, the presence of the military allowed for the exercising, implementation, and physical manifestations of the rights outlined in the Emancipation Proclamation. Any modicum of realization of those rights was because the U.S. military occupied the southern states and this occupation provided the platform to bring in legislation that further enraged southerners.[34] In northwest Louisiana, the loss of property and ownership of human beings dismantled white identity and societal structures, and former slaveholders relied on violence to rebuild that lost world. Whites could utilize violence in so many different permutations because they were so adept at using it. Violence was second nature, something done without needing to think, easy to fall back on, and a common denominator among all whites.

The metamorphosis of violence as a deft political instrument was a natural extension of its antebellum usage, and regional whites applied it with surety, alacrity, and visible results. What makes violence stand out beyond its omnipresence is the myriad ways it was used to chip away at Blacks' daily expressions and exercise of freedoms, in addition to seismic incidents of racial violence that permanently altered African American rights at the local, state, and national levels right up to the present day. Violence controlled political involvement and curbed labor and mobility. It was used with profound mutability and flexibility in northwest Louisiana, and the undeniable results became a blueprint for behavior statewide and a clarion call for southerners. The pliability and applicability of violence as an effective method to generate desired results ensured its continued usage for a wide array of reasons, to limit a range of social, political, and economic rights. Violence was the most reliable and guaranteed tool in the arsenal of northwest Louisiana's whites, and its dependability and precision in delivering desired results cemented its position at the forefront of race relations, politics, and civil rights.

It is precisely because violence produced visible, undeniable results that this methodology was further ingrained regionally while its popularity and profusion extended across the breadth of the South, and as the nineteenth century drew to a close, it jumped across the Mason-Dixon line. The events of extraordinary violence and vigilantism that occurred in the Red River region had a broad and long-standing impact on legislation and racial relations. A perfect example is the 1876 Supreme Court ruling in *U.S. v. Cruikshank,* the case that stemmed from the Colfax Massacre, the bloodiest single Reconstruction attack. In the ruling, the court stated that it was the federal government's obligation to provide remedies to state actions that violate specific rights guaranteed by the Constitution. The Colfax case was a question of whether the brazen murder of freedpeople because of their political affiliation and desire to participate in politics was a violation of a constitutional right or merely an ordinary crime. The massacre was ruled an ordinary crime because the court held that the vigilantes needed to declare that this act of terrorism was carried out for racially motivated reasons.

This decision and its blueprint for future legal recourse reverberated across the country. There was no judicial recourse or military safeguard to ensure that African Americans could access the voting booth. The franchise might be a civil right, but this was the state's prerogative and not the federal government's responsibility to ensure access to voter registration and the vote. *Cruikshank* cut to the core issues of Reconstruction and signaled a shift away from equal rights and civil liberties. This decision laid the groundwork for other landmark Supreme Court cases and continues to play a significant role today in issues like gerrymandering, voter registration, and voting accessibility.

In the aftermath of the Colfax and Coushatta massacres, White League violence continued, bolstered by institutional support alongside widespread political and moral validation. This extended not only across class

and wealth backgrounds but knitted together rural and urban white communities in a narrative that neatly divided Republicans and African Americans from Democrats and whites.[35] Violence remained the connecting
creed and core manifestation of white supremacist ideology throughout the
nineteenth century, and it continued to prove malleable and effective as a
unifying force to catalyze activity and moderate the boundaries of freedom
during the twentieth century. Reliance on violence as a framework for action and control is further demonstrated by widespread Civil War commemorative work and the adoption of the Lost Cause narrative as the definitive
southern story. Confederate veterans and former enslavers wielded authority and control that entrenched the postwar world in systemic racism and
social, political, and economic structures of inequality that have not only
endured but also proven robust, evolving, and durable more than 150 years
after Appomattox.

The legacy of regional white identity, violence, and racial hierarchy explored in this book continues to define the political sentiments, political
ideology, and institutional disparity along racial lines in northwest Louisiana. As insightful recent work from Avidit Acharya, Matthew Blackwell,
and Maya Sen demonstrates, the persistence of political and demographic
attitudes endures across generations, and these historical patterns predict
current attitudes. In the Red River region, the shaping of every aspect of life
is affected and informed by antebellum and Reconstruction era ideology.
These legacies deeply influence voter suppression and voting outcomes.
These institutionalized attitudes of segregation and racial violence are entrenched in areas such as northwest Louisiana, where reliance on Black labor remained during Reconstruction and where white hegemonic views and
identity focused on restricting Black access to the body politic. Indeed, the
self-reinforcing and lasting results of the widespread racial violence, White
Leagues, and the vigilantism of Reconstruction in this region underpins the
framework that promotes anti-Black sentiment and conservative practices
on race and racial issues across economic, cultural, social, and institutional
channels.[36]

America still grapples with these same issues of violence, mastery, and
racial domination that continue to color all aspects of political, social, legal,
and economic life. African Americans and nonwhite members of American
society profoundly feel the impact of the legacies of mastery, racial hierarchy, and violence in myriad ways. Incidents of racial violence—those that

dominate the news and those that never reach outside a small community—bear striking similarities to and echoes of their nineteenth-century counterparts. From the unbending parameters to access civil rights, the preconceptions about personal autonomy and access to health care, incarceration rates, and the abundant use of violence toward Black people to the pervasiveness of racial stereotypes that inform the political, civic, economic, and educational opportunities available to African American and nonwhite citizens, many events of the twenty-first century share an eerie similarity to those of the nineteenth. Engaging with the effect of these racial legacies in shaping and defining present-day America is essential. The centrality of a white identity built upon the subjugation of African Americans, and the knee-jerk, habitual reliance and dependence on violence—both verbal and physical—to maintain the rigid parameters of citizenship, equality, and accessibility, is the heartbreaking reality of America, and it is through direct and unfettered engagement with our blemished past that we can strive to build a more perfect union.

"THE RED RIVER BOTTOMS ARE NEARLY THE BEST COTTON LANDS IN THE WORLD"

Settlement and Slaveholding

D. B. Allen arrived in Shreveport, Louisiana, in November 1851. Like many slaveholders from the Upper and Lower South, Allen traveled from Wilson County, Tennessee, to one of the richest and fastest-growing cotton regions. Effusive with optimism, Allen wrote to his mother, "Speaking of the Red River, I never knew until I saw the lands upon its banks what good lands were." "I had heard of the immense cotton fields that grow in this country," he enthused, "but they never gave me an idea . . . When I beheld the cotton I was perfectly amazed, and what was stranger to me than all was the colour of the soil it is almost perfectly red resembling very much the very purest clay banks that you see in wilson county." This exuberant reaction to the rich soils and the prospects of the country was common among white slaveholding settlers to the Red River region and embodied their zeal toward expanding both the cotton frontier and slaveholding territory. This thirsty, determined, and continuous migration to northwest Louisiana began after the War of 1812 and did not diminish until the mid-1850s. Those settlers sought what Allen encountered: "immense fields of cotton higher than my head on my horse."[1]

The terrain defined by the Red River captivated slaveholding settlers. A major alluvial waterway, the Red originates in northwestern Texas and divides into two forks at the Texas panhandle, one of which delineates the Texas-Oklahoma border. The river meanders and turns decidedly southward to form the Texas-Arkansas border, curling around the town of Texarkana before entering northern Louisiana near Ida. Passing through Shreveport and Bossier City, it then descends toward Alexandria, Louisiana, where it joins the Atchafalaya River, a tributary of the Mississippi. Named for the fertile, ruddy soil stretching from the river's banks, the Red River made northwest Louisiana a valuable economic corridor. Removal of the raft, a densely wooded tangle in the Red River, beginning around Natchitoches, ignited frontier–market integration and created a commercial avenue connected to New Orleans. Centered on the burgeoning market town of Shreveport, the Red River cotton region incorporated a lengthy zone of agricultural productivity from Alexandria to Shreveport and stretched into eastern Texas and southwest Arkansas.

The raft was dynamic and mercurial, which added further complexity to relocation and regional development. Growing from the raft, which was "so close and compact as to be walked over without wetting the feet" was "broom-straw, willow, and other small bushes" that lent the river the appearance of "an old worn-out field."[2] This barrier had assumed a permanent form in many places and forced the river to divert itself, which created various bayous, channels, and lakes.[3] The river often rose to levels not conducive to river traffic, and local newspapers reporting on river conditions frequently commented on its erratic nature. The *Caddo Free Press* noted that in "the higher portion of Red River . . . navigation can never be depended on with any degree of certainty," and agricultural publication *De Bow's Review* wrote of the raft, "such a mass of decaying wood is malarious in the extreme," proving a health hazard and an impediment to settlement.[4]

Ensuring that the Red was navigable for easy transport of cotton to New Orleans was paramount to the livelihood of slaveholders and the regional economy throughout the antebellum period. Captain Henry Shreve, an inventor and the namesake of Shreveport, helmed the Army Corps of Engineers' work to clear the raft. Clearing began in 1833 but was not finally completed until 1873, after Shreve's death. Shreve's July 1835 update discussed six months of work clearing a new formation in the raft near Coushatta Chute, which presented a "formidable obstruction to the navigation of the river." Escalating costs presented a further challenge, and Shreve requested additional funds.[5] When regular steamboat traffic began in 1838, river bottomland became more attractive, concurrently accelerating cotton cultivation along the river and its tributaries.[6]

Steamboat traffic became central to a panoply of networks, including those providing news, letters, and market information; food and supplies; and transportation of enslaved people and cotton. Steamboats, including the *Belle of Red River, Live Oak,* and *Yazoo,* maintained regular schedules following Shreve's clearing.[7] This dependable river transport also signaled progress and stability to enslavers relocating to the region. Newspaper advertisements for steamboats promised "the traveling public and mercantile community" a "safe, expeditious and above all regular communication with New Orleans" and published departure times from all ports.[8] Removal of the raft was crucial to the Red River cotton boom. The regular availability of steamboats ensured the transport of staple crops and enslaved labor, all of which enhanced the region's desirability.[9]

Allen belonged to the contingent of slaveholding settlers who moved in chain migrations from the established plantations of the Upper and Lower South to claim land for cotton cultivation along the Red River. Irrespective of their holding size, the number of enslaved people they owned, or their economic stature, these slaveholding settlers were both capitalist and modern. From settlement through the antebellum period, these white southerners were fully immersed in the South's dual economy. The region's transformation into a profitable epicenter of cotton production exemplified a commitment to extractive commodity production and a reliance on enslaved laborers.[10] These were market-oriented slaveholders who not only strove to extend the cotton South, and thus the portion of the country with slaveholding, but also aimed to ensure the viability and profitability of large-scale, integrated cotton plantations. Slavery and the productive output of enslaved labor formed the crux of the regional determination to operate within a market economy and led to the establishment of plantation holdings with an incredibly brutal, oppressive slave regime. The advantageous position of the Red River relative to the Mississippi reinforced white, southern convictions that enslaved labor was optimally suited to prosperity.[11]

Regional slaveholders leveraged their power to "command people as property" to relocate their chattel and to organize this labor resource to reap maximum results. Slavery advanced agricultural growth and propelled the movement of enslaved labor and cotton-fueled profitability.[12] As the area progressed into a settled plantation region, small and midsize slaveholders exerted control over the land that turned the soil profitable through the unceasing toil of enslaved people on sprawling cotton plantations. The establishment of profitable integrated cotton plantations and slaveholders' environmental mastery formed a core component of a regional white identity firmly grounded in extraction from the land and commodification of Black labor. The dehumanization of enslaved people entwined with the investment potential of enslaved labor and their intrinsic value as property to establish distinct, unshakeable racial identities. The persistence of these proscribed racial identities throughout the postbellum period fueled racially motivated events that both set this region apart and made it significant for understanding racial violence in the American South.

The Red River region's slaveholders eschewed the manifestations of established plantation society, including large, decadent homes and slavery glossed with a veneer of gentility. They focused instead on establishing integrated plantations for cotton cultivation and forming a strong, white identity grounded in unbridled racial dominance. As this chapter will demonstrate, these slaveholders were distinguished by their racial identity as masters, by their market motivation, derived from a combination of profit seeking and environmental transformation, and by their mobility. Driven by the promise of profit, they invested their resources—financial, familial, and enslaved—in the more direct and immediate promise of financial returns from the fertile soil. They were market-oriented, extractive, enterprising, and modern; capitalism was intrinsic to regional slaveholding and defined the regime's profitability, cruelty, and legacy.[13]

The strong concentration of market-oriented commodity crop production and the entrenched enslaved labor behind the explosion of cotton-derived wealth underscores the core composition of this dynamic region, alongside the dependent, exploitative relationship of slavery and capitalism. Significantly, slaveholders, particularly small and midsize, continued to settle in the Red River right up until the Civil War and retained focus on the expansion of cotton profitability. Continued settlement meant that northwest Louisiana retained a rough edge and did not have the solidified gentility present in most other similarly profitable areas of the cotton South. Regional white slaveholders were distinctive in their almost singular drive toward extractive cotton cultivation, informed by a high degree of market awareness and market-driven adaptation of all plantation resources.

Palpably connected to national and transatlantic commerce and market forces, slavery along the Red River etched an indelible foundation that embedded ideological, racial, political, and material identities firmly within white identity. These elemental aspects of the dominant white identity shaped the contours of regional freedom and defined the violent tenor of Black life from the antebellum period through Reconstruction. This chapter examines why slaveholders moved to the Red River region to expand or rebuild their wealth and how cotton cultivation and enslaved labor made their wealth possible. Settlers migrated from already settled, often soil-depleted plantation districts along the eastern seaboard to this region's alluvial soil. Their migration was spurred because they sought the financial rewards afforded by large-scale cotton plantations run with maximum extraction and with a market-oriented outlook as the catalyst. The transatlantic demand for cotton concentrated the attention of these slaveholders on profitability, and at the crux of this realized market prowess was a brutal form of enslavement. Exploration of the demand for cotton and its close relationship with regional migration unearths why the Red River became a significant antebellum region, notable for its connectivity with the New Orleans marketplace and its immense productivity.

The extractive cultivation replicated on holdings across the region was viewed positively by the white slaveholder settlers. It reinforced a racial dynamic that predicated not only white economic success but also white self-worth and identity on the financial remunerations reaped from Black labor. The ultimate monetary success within the region for nearly all white slaveholding settlers further strengthened this duality and rendered white identity inextricable from Black subjugation, dehumanization, and domination. While the driving forces behind migration for economic success held similarities to other parts of the expanding South, the hyper focus on pulling profit from land and enslaved labor was distinctive. Added to this was the decisive, rigid racial binary enforced by racial violence that formed the cornerstone of regional white identity. This bifurcated view of racial interactions, attitudes, and hierarchy endured, passed down from generation to generation, irrespective of the size of the slaveholder's property. The solidity of this generative, white identity proved elastic and unifying, particularly during the postwar period, and because its core composition revolved around racial domination and deployment of violence, this identity was remarkably adaptive and resilient in the face of change.

— — —

The Red River region's expansion was defined and marked by mobility alongside a dynamic economy and capitalistic core.[14] Many regional settlers crisscrossed the South to expand familial wealth, using various relocation methods. The Flournoy family, for example, followed the classic chain migration pattern and sent eldest son, Alfred, westward from Pulaski,

Tennessee, to settle the fertile ground just north of Shreveport in 1836. He established the family's western cotton plantation while the Tennessee holding remained in his brother's care. After 1838, with an overseer installed at Pulaski, Alfred's brothers fanned out along the Red River, following the contours of a typical second family wave of regional migration. Similarly, James and Tabitha Fullilove moved from Mississippi to Caddo Parish and established Four Forks plantation. James built his first home of logs in the two-room dogtrot style, adding rooms to the rear and a gallery to the front over time. He acquired more land as funds permitted and only built a new home once he was prosperous, two hallmark practices that differentiated Red River region settlement. His son Thomas would establish Preston plantation, two miles from Four Forks and northeast of Keachie.[15]

The expansion of the Red River plantation district was emblematic of more profound economic transitions that mirrored the southern reliance on cotton as the central staple crop. Transatlantic demand for cotton spurred an explosion in settlement and necessitated enslaved people's labor to meet mounting demand for commodities. The entwined dependence of wealth on productive labor and, as will be discussed later, the tangible value of the bodies of enslaved people was stark and palpable. The movement of enslaved people from other plantations or through the internal slave trade to new cotton lands increased production from "1.2 million pounds in 1790 to 2.1 *billion* in 1859." By the 1830s, American cotton dominated the British textile industry. At the same time, the Natchez and New Orleans branches of the Bank of the United States (BUS) lent a full third of the total capital of the BUS, much of it to purchase thousands of enslaved people.[16]

Slaveholders began amassing wealth by actively investing in more humans than ever before, a wealth accumulation pattern without a counterpart in nonslaveholding societies and one that vanished when slavery ended. Slavery rapidly became a reasonably secure method of holding and transferring individual wealth. The federal system of taxation protected wealth and rights vested in slave property, while financial institutions were founded and funded on enslaved bodies and the cotton extracted from them.[17] Slavery was a core element of American foreign trade, and its commercial influence on banking, insurance, and shipping ensured that slavery was peculiar to the South but also a national institution.

Throughout the antebellum period, migration followed the rise and fall of cotton prices. Slaveholding settlers like the Flournoys and Fulliloves in-

tertwined the Jackson era land-grabbing ethos with territorial manifestations of economic growth. Their settlement focused on land and enslaved
people and was integral to strengthening the national dependence on a
commodity-based southern economy.[18] Booming cotton prices from 1815
to 1819 heralded the opening of the frontier. The 1815 price of cotton was
21 cents, double that of the prior year, and it rose to 29 cents in 1816. The
price of cotton halved in 1820 from the 1819 rate, to 17 cents, and continued to fall until 1824, when cotton was worth 14 cents. The oscillations of
cotton prices created three pulses of westward settlement tied to the high
prices and heavy cotton trading. Relatively affordable credit accessibility in
the 1850s yielded another wave of migration as high cotton prices restored
property values. The confluence of available land and the cotton revolution
solidified southern importance in the booming world economy.[19]

As with planters in other frontier locations, including Florida, Missouri,
and Texas, Red River immigrants were looking for alluvial land that would
either restore or increase their wealth. The financial backing for relocation
might be borrowed from wealthier family members, and small, midsize, and
large-scale planters often relied on kin already present in the Red River region to select, secure, and purchase choice tracts.[20] Older males, either heads
of households or eldest sons, spearheaded moves to the Red River region
following an initial relocation to the interior sections of the southeastern
states. They would then bring their family westward after establishing cotton crops. Their correspondence portrayed the newly inhabited region in
glowing terms while disparaging eastern homes, a tactic that helped promote relocation.

As male progeny settled across the cotton belt, the congested nature of
most small to midsize slaveholding households dissolved. Moreover, as relocation to remote areas became commonplace, significant changes occurred
among households as individual families became more isolated and spread
out.[21] Families splintered; some members remained on already established
properties in cotton-rich areas—such as the Alabama Black Belt, western
Georgia, and Mississippi—while others continued the arc of settlement
across the southern states. Black enslaved families were notably impacted,
as their families, relationships, and communities were shattered, often irrevocably, to fulfill the ambitions of slaveholders.[22]

The Flournoy, Fullilove, Hutchinson, Marshall, and Powell families,
who all became well established, arrived as part of a chain migration after

the initial relocation of one family member. This practice ensured that land was purchased, temporary housing was built, and enslaved people were relocated to break the ground for planting before the larger migration. The Fullilove family's relocation narrative is representative of Red River chain migration. The eldest brother, James, was born in Georgia around 1809, and during his childhood the family relocated to Oglethorpe, in central Georgia. James married Tabitha in 1831 and moved to Columbia, in central Kentucky. At this time, he owned two slaves and in all probability toiled alongside them as a small slaveholding farmer. James began to transition from small slaveholding farmer to planter in 1850 when he relocated from Noxubee, Mississippi, to Four Forks—their Blossom Hill holding, south of Shreveport. Ten years later, James, Tabitha, and four children were an established slaveholding family with twenty-six enslaved people.

Enticed by James's success, his brothers John and William followed a similar migration arc to Caddo Parish. John, the middle child, was born in 1811. He married Almeda and had two children on Georgia soil before 1847. The family of four relocated to Blossom Hill in 1850 with fourteen slaves. Their youngest brother, William, completed the family chain migration. Born in 1822, he moved to Caddo Parish before his 1848 marriage to Elizabeth. In 1850, William was twenty-eight and owned thirteen slaves on a farmstead near his siblings. By 1860, he had moved to Shreveport.[23] James Fullilove's brother-in-law, Robert Holmes, followed suit and laid down roots in Caddo Parish, further expanding the familial migration pattern.

The plentiful and rich Red River soil remained incredibly alluring to migrants from within the cotton South until the start of the Civil War. German travel writer Friedrich Gërstacker noted that the banks along the Red were so densely planted with cotton that it seemed "covered with snow." A traveler to Natchitoches wrote that flourishing cotton plantations rose "almost without interruption on both banks" of the Red.[24] In 1838, siblings Bennett Dickson and Margaret Dickson Whitworth decided to move from Alabama to northwest Louisiana. Bennett and eldest nephew, Benjamin, set out for Greenwood to survey and select land for settlement. The two families relocated in the spring of 1839, and Margaret Whitworth quickly established Forest Park.[25] One daughter, Isabella Whitworth, became mistress at Forest Park while son Samuel moved just over the Red River into East Texas. Writing to Isabella in 1855, Samuel exemplified the market-oriented mindset of slaveholding migration to the Red River. He wrote that he lacked "interest in fixing things nice as I don't expect to live here long," before he boasted, "we are getting along verry well with our crop our corn is coming up verry nice and now prepairing our cotton land."[26]

Like other settlers, Samuel encountered both the promise of the soil and the dangers inherent in living alongside the powerful Red River. Three years later, he reported that flooding and bad weather had damaged the crops, adversely affected valuable enslaved people, and hindered transportation. For two months, he moaned, "we have had a wretched wet muddy time, water courses up, roads almost impassable," and the situation worsened, because "only a few days ago we lost a valuable negro man of typhoid pneumonia."[27]

Eager to profit from the newly dredged rivers, steamboat packets, and larger upriver vessels, settlers were not awed by the river or its dense mass of snags.[28] Instead, regional slaveholders set about controlling this valuable tributary and the surrounding natural environment. The Red River raft—a one-hundred-sixty-mile morass of tangled driftwood, detritus, and silt—clogged the channel beyond Natchitoches and made navigation upstream difficult and hazardous.[29] Clearing the naturally occurring logjams constituting the raft targeted southern zeal for settlement and influenced regional settlement patterns. Breaking the raft, which had impeded settlement and reliable trade, enabled planters and settlers to realize the region's full cotton potential. Five years before the raft was cleared, one Louisiana resident predicted the centrality of a cleared waterway to regional growth, noting, "a mine of trade would in a few years come down the Red River!"[30]

Migration accounts detail struggles with the surroundings. In an 1836 letter, Henry Marshall, who arrived in the Red River region at peak settlement, informed his wife that while his railroad money had arrived, "I shall move my negroes to town to be ready for the first boat. The river is very low and I may be detained." Three weeks later, he had cleared another obstacle—the raft—and wrote, "We arrived . . . through the raft, literally as in one place they were obliged to remove the logs in order to get the boat through."[31]

Throughout the antebellum period, the physical journey to the Red River region was an arduous trek for white and enslaved members of migrating families. However, improvements to transportation meant greater ease and efficiency. Before the early 1820s, the Red River region contained two trails instead of full-fledged roads, which suggests that wagon travel was difficult and underscores the reliance on river transportation. Settlers from the East often traveled through Tennessee, descended the Cumberland

and Mississippi Rivers by keelboat to the Red River, and then traveled upstream through the raft.[32] A combination of changes ameliorated the state
of transportation during the antebellum period. Turnpike mania gripped
the nation and led to the rapid building of quality toll roads, which allowed
swifter travel with fewer mishaps and better rural connectivity. These toll
roads laid the foundation for a biphasic transport improvement that facilitated the steady transport of people and goods.[33]

Bartholomew Egan's 1850 instructional letters to his son James regarding relocation from Virginia to their holding in Bienville Parish detail road
and waterway travel. Though it was "tedious and tiresome," Egan suggested
traveling by horse to Augusta, Georgia, where James could enjoy respite
with his uncle. Then he could board the stagecoach to Montgomery, Alabama, followed by three separate river journeys to Mobile, New Orleans, and
Minden. On arrival at Minden in northern Louisiana, the elder Egan would
send horses to complete the journey to their plantation. Although it utilized
numerous transportation methods, Egan assured his son this would be "expeditious," though perhaps "more expensive than by horse all the way."[34]

In his 1835 travel diary, New Hampshire native James Burns Wallace
noted that forty miles passed without him seeing another person, emphasizing the remote nature of northwest Louisiana.[35] As late as 1854, Frederick
Law Olmsted described Natchitoches, Shreveport, and Fulton as the three
main arrival points, with the latter two locations being the most popular.
Shreveport garnered wagons and traffic from Alabama and Mississippi; Fulton, Arkansas, attracted travelers from Arkansas and Tennessee.[36] Fulton,
located between present-day Texarkana and Hope, Arkansas, gained popularity because of the prominent southwest trail or "military road" that connected Saint Louis to the Red River. George Featherstonhaugh, who traveled
through the Red River district in November and December 1834, stayed on
the military road, though he wrote that it was filled with rocks, stumps, mud,
and felled trees and was often missing bridges. Even so, this road accom-
modated wagons, was better maintained, and was wider than many trails.
Despite the difficulty in navigating the potholes, thousands of slaveholders
and their households used the road, especially after the raft's clearance.[37]

When her family moved near Colfax from South Carolina in the mid-
1850s, Dosia Williams Moore's father traveled to the Red River with most
of their enslaved population. Dosia, her sister, her mother, and her "negro
nurse" journeyed by steamboat to New Orleans, followed by an overland

journey from Alexandria.[38] Although wealthier families like Moore's might have arrived by steamboat, the costs of relocation and land redevelopment prevented most small and midsize slaveholding families from using this method. Until 1824, the Red was navigated almost entirely by keelboats, flat-bottomed boats later supplanted by steamboats. Steamboat travel became less expensive and more frequent after the raft was cleared; thirty-five boats made regular journeys up the Red River from 1835 to 1840.[39] It was a cost-effective way to get cotton to market, but it remained relatively expensive for relocation. James Laroe, for instance, began the trip to the Red River region from New Jersey in 1846 to scout out his plantation. His three-week steerage steamboat passage to New Orleans cost seven dollars. The nine-day journey from New Orleans to Shreveport cost five dollars. The impediment of the raft and the fluctuating conditions of the river no doubt added to the immense cost of traveling "up the Red River about 700 miles."[40] Even so, the high price of one steerage ticket from New Orleans to Shreveport made the cost prohibitive for an entire family and their slaves and seemed re-served for wealthier or female settlers.

Like Moore, Ellison Adger's family utilized water and land travel to reach Bossier Parish from South Carolina. Adger, whose family owned Chicora and Caroline Bluff plantations in Bossier Parish, recounted the taxing journey as it had been imparted to him by old "Ma Jane," an enslaved woman who made the 1846 journey with an earlier generation of Adgers. Ma Jane, who was just a year older than Ellison's great-grandfather and had toiled for five generations of Adgers, remembered "the horses, mules and cattle, as well as the negroes all came over land, a trip that took weeks if not months." As the elderly enslaved woman recalled, it was a long period un-til "they at last reached the Mississippi River on Christmas Day." Ma Jane noted that "after leaving Natchez or Vicksburg they started across the great swamp between there and Monroe," evidently crossing northern Louisiana by foot before finally reaching Bossier.[41]

— — —

The flush times of the 1830s proffered a palpable feeling that a limitless pool of money was available and accessible to anyone. This bred both a unique culture of speculation and a feeling of invulnerability among slaveholders like the Fulliloves and Whitworths.[42] This does not mean that the ubiquity of large-scale cotton production in tandem with steady migration was not a concern for nonslaveholders and yeomen in northwest Louisiana and across the South. The fact that many migrating slaveholders had access to more significant resources and chose to focus them on migrations to alluvial land along the Red River perfectly encapsulated the contradictions and complexities of southern society.[43] But it does relegate this part of the southern narrative to the edges of this study, since a hallmark of Red River settlement and slaveholding was the widespread, entrenched dependence on enslaved labor and the centrality of racial domination to the region's white identity. While small and midsize slaveholders might have worked alongside their enslaved population during the first year or two, this did not remain a feature of regional slaveholding. In the Red River area, all slaveholders shared a common approach to exerting control over enslaved people. Regional planters upheld the mastery and social standing of white slaveholders with smaller plantations, thereby creating a monolithic, self-perpetuated planter identity in this corner of the South.[44]

Small and midsize slaveholders formed the majority and were particularly ambitious in their quest for more land, more slaves, and more status.[45] For these enterprising members of the slaveholding class, the vast swaths of available land along the Red amplified the appeal of relocation and spurred their migrations. An 1839 article in the *Caddo Free Press* ascribed the undeniable pull and surging settlement to regional desirability combined with the complete domination of land and labor emphatically embraced by regional settlers. The local paper observed, "The tide of Anglo Saxon population is setting steadily and with no ebb to the west. Wave will follow wave until the towers and palaces of Mexico shall be submerged, the Rocky Mountains swallowed up and the stream of life flow uninterruptedly from the Atlantic to the Pacific."[46] Settlers to the Red River embodied this antebellum culture of expansion, one that privileged white mastery and extractive cultivation, and they wove these characteristics into the fiber of regional and white identity.

Henry Marshall exemplified these traits, and his letters to his wife, Maria, tell a familiar story. Hailing from Columbia, South Carolina, Marshall discovered that the profits he desired were not feasible from his overworked mid-Carolina land. This catalyzed his numerous trips across the breadth of the South to secure new, fertile land. He wrote to Maria that only his quest to find profitable land triggered his "absence of two months a year." Once out of debt and with a reasonable income, he promised "to devote the other ten entirely to my wife."[47]

The enormous decision of where to settle weighed on Marshall. An ambitious man, he followed the typical contours of chain migrations, first scoping out property near his brother in Mississippi and then near his brother-in-law in Alabama. His November 1, 1833, letter detailed the risk and beauty of land in Yazoo County, Mississippi. Marshall outlined to Maria the relative merits of Mississippi: "The risk in cotton is bad for a purchaser, but I feel confident of being able to do better than I did in Carolina . . . the crops are indeed beautiful—so much so that if I owned them I should be tempted to spend a great part of my time upon it . . . so much rich land must make society." After deliberation, he determined he was not willing to settle in Mississippi and informed his wife that he would investigate prospects along the Red River "before I make up my mind where to settle." Hesitant about Alabama and Mississippi, Marshall saw great potential along the Red River. He acquired land in DeSoto Parish for his plantation, fittingly named Land's End, which was established in 1857 with enslaved people valued at $6,100. At his death in 1864, Marshall's Louisiana enslaved property was valued at $170,121. The one tract of land whose title had not been moved to Texas for safekeeping during the Civil War was valued at $37,000, and he owned $54,504.45 in moveable property and $37,200 in immovable property.[48]

Like Marshall, William Hutchinson and his family moved westward in stages. Hutchinson, whose grandsons would become prominent Red River slaveholders, first moved to Alabama in 1825. His 1829 land grant for a large tract in Montgomery County, Alabama, signed by Andrew Jackson, signaled the first step of the migration.[49] When Hutchinson died, this tract passed to his two sons, Haley and John. Following the sale of this land, the brothers continued acquiring land and enslaved people in Alabama. The 1830 census indicates that John and his wife, Matilda, resided in Lowndes County, Alabama, with two male children under five and four enslaved people. The historical record is silent on Haley Hutchinson's activities after 1834, but John advanced westward with his family to Bossier Parish, Louisiana, in 1843, settling a tract near Rocky Mount. John Hutchinson amassed land and continued plantation expansion until he died in 1846. He left a Bossier Parish estate of more than 1,349 acres with improvements valued at $7,018, fifty-seven enslaved people valued from $125 to $600 each, and a total estate valued at more than $50,000.[50]

Joseph Graham, his wife, Isophena, seven children, and twenty slaves moved to northwest Louisiana with the Hutchinson family in 1843. After John Hutchinson's death, Graham was appointed administrator to minors William and Robert Hutchinson. Graham, along with William and Robert, continued expanding their plantations and enslaved populaces. They purchased eleven enslaved people from Mobile, Alabama, for $5,200 and five more enslaved people from New Orleans for $3,460 in 1849 to work the Hutchinson holdings.[51]

Ever attentive to their prospects, settlers like the Hutchinsons and the Grahams recognized that their immediate and long-term financial success rested squarely with the cotton economy. Enslaved people provided a constant labor source to break new land; drain, clear, and plant fields; and build levees in the Red River region. It was their work that turned slaveholders' prospects and dreams into reality. Enslaved people held a dual role in the economic vitality of the South, as the labor that powered the cotton boom and as a form of liquid currency essential for the growth and expansion of the cotton complex.

The brutality, dislocation, and commodification of enslaved people in this region continued a long tradition of turning Africans, and then African Americans, into property. As Stephanie Smallwood has demonstrated, the ongoing trauma of dislocation for Africans sold in the transatlantic slave trade was physical and psychological. The complete rupture and loss of community informed integration once they were on American plantations, and the rebuilding of personhood.[52] The alienating process by which people were transformed into property continued with gusto in the antebellum South, and it was particularly vituperative and dislocating in a market-focused area like the Red River. The forced relocation, sales, and breakage of family and community ties for enslaved people brought to northwest Louisiana extended this rupture to new generations of Blacks moved to new geographies.[53] Louisiana, along with Alabama and Texas, were notorious among enslaved people as foreboding, violent places to be sold or relocated.

The antebellum southern economy rested on the idea that the physical bodies of the enslaved had an inherent, measurable monetary value, whether that monetary worth was exercised in sale or not.[54] Recent scholarship has depicted the complex, interconnected multiplicity of being an enslaved person stripped of personhood in the eyes of the slaveholding class yet possessing a physical body that held tangible, saleable financial value. For enslaved women, this was doubly compounded, as masters owned not just the individual woman but also her "future increase." Her unborn children rendered her both an object and a producer of desired goods. Enslaved people were distilled into commodities by the web of white people who bought, sold, controlled, and profited from their bodies and labor throughout their lives. As Daina Ramey Berry's scholarship has shown, slaveholders and members of the slave trade continued to profit from and trade Black cadavers, still viewed as saleable merchandise even postmortem. The financial values attached to enslaved bodies served a broad range of purposes, including their use in tax assessments, probate settlements, and legal depositions, and these valuations were taken at numerous stages of life.[55]

The previously held assumption that white southern mistresses were either removed from the realities of slaveholding or were kinder, less violent slaveholders is untrue. White slaveholding women, like those residing along the Red River, were wholly invested in the economics of slavery, and as Stephanie Jones-Rodgers has elucidated, their economic investment unearths the triumvirate relationship among gender, slavery, and capitalism. Female slaveholders were often masters of their own enslaved people, whose ownership they retained separately from their spouses. Southern white women were frequently gifted enslaved people to mark special life occasions, including baptisms, birthdays, holidays, and marriage, and enslaved people were often bequeathed in wills. As we will see in chapter 2, because enslaved people held secure financial value that rarely fluctuated down, slaveholding parents favored gifts and bequests of enslaved people to daughters to solidify a stable financial future.[56]

Wealth held in slaves was an integral component in the complex financial system that supported a debt load in the hundreds of millions of dollars throughout the South.[57] Enslaved people were collateral in credit transactions, loan security, valued when estates were divided, and often sold off to pay outstanding debt. The Consolidated Association of the Planters of Louisiana, a state bank, created leverage for slaveholders at less cost and on longer terms by securitizing slaves. These bonds converted slaveholders' largest investment—other human beings—into multiple income streams, all under the control of borrowers, each of them a stockholder. The mortgaging of slaves was "essential lubricating credit" in the expanding South.[58] The value that enslaved people held abstracted from their bodies was a critical component of planter mobility. It allowed planters to establish credit pred-

icated on the valuation and understood liquidity of slave property as a tradable, market-rated asset. As in Louisiana's sugar regions, this was prudent
economically because these capital investments in land, labor, or machinery
could be liquidized and the collateral moved.[59]

Enslaved people held value as moveable assets. Slaveholders regularly
leveraged chattel assets to fund further settlement and land purchase or
transported them to areas of high demand to maximize their value.[60] In April
of 1824, for instance, Alfred Flournoy sold three enslaved women—Celia,
Judy, and Pamelia—in exchange for sixty mules. His letter to his wife states
that he viewed this as a favorable bargain and perhaps even a profitable disposal of his enslaved property since "I have sold the girls for two hundred
dollars more than I could have had for them in cash, the mules I purchased
at cash price." Eager to establish his Red River plantation, Flournoy quickly
sold these enslaved women to purchase goods necessary for settlement.[61]

Converting enslaved human capital into animal power, Flournoy revealed how interchangeable these commodities were in the slaveholder
mindset and how slave pricing sometimes appeared in transfer markets.
The use of human collateral in mortgage arrangements, among many other
financial transactions, drove the easy circulation of resources central to expanding local and regional economies. This movement of enslaved people,
goods, cash, or credit was essential on agricultural frontiers like northwest
Louisiana because it provided a repository of credit and moveable collater-
alized assets alongside rural banking systems.[62] During the 1830s, lenders
deemed loans backed by slaves to be risk-free.[63] Regardless of the number of
slaves held, slaveholders needed the ability to change their slave property in
whatever permutation would maximize profits. For Flournoy, that calcula-
tion converted women into mules, but for others, mortgaging slave property
underpinned land purchases.

Slave mortgages—or the income accrued from slave rentals—were essential components of the process of migration. Private mortgage contracts
using enslaved people allowed slaveholders to borrow from one another
and to endorse the debt contracts of friends or family. Purchases using slave
mortgages could be faster because having the entire purchase price ahead of
the acquisition was unnecessary. Conversely, slaves might also be liquidated
in times of personal or national economic distress. Many families that chose
to move did not have liquid funds or the means to finance their journey, so
they took out loans or lines of credit. Others used credit to purchase additional slaves or to move their enslaved people with them. Consequently, en-

slaved people were often hired out near the plantation of origin to pay for the slaveholder's relocation costs. Henry Marshall, for instance, hired out nine slaves in Atlanta in 1835 to underwrite his Louisiana relocation in 1836.[64] He also hired out his slaves in 1833 to cover his land-scouting trips.[65] Marshall recognized that his enslaved property helped maintain credit relationships extending across the South.

Enslaved people were also utilized as collateral to raise significant cash and credit through informal networks that operated in parallel but not directly with the emerging banking system. Slave property formed the nexus that linked antebellum credit relations, and most banking in Louisiana happened directly with factorage firms instead of banks. These firms were integral in purchasing and selling enslaved people and cotton and in servicing the needs of farmers, who availed themselves of every source of capital and credit. Small merchants in rural and small towns served as the small farmer's business factor and forwarded essential credit and cash advances for daily estate operations. These merchants frequently deducted a 10 to 25 percent interest fee from the small farmer's final crop sales. Although local furnishing merchants came to dominate postbellum credit relations, cotton and slavery firmly underpinned the cash and credit antebellum economy, especially in relatively isolated portions of the cotton kingdom, such as northwest Louisiana.[66]

The steady expansion of the cotton frontier fueled formal and informal banking systems that made credit readily available. The Consolidated Association allowed slaveholders to monetize enslaved people by securitizing and then leveraging them multiple times across markets. The state of Louisiana chartered its Union Bank in 1832 and issued $7 million in state bonds.[67] The lack of actual currency and the use of slaves as leverage to extend credit limits to purchase more slaves, cotton, and land would come to a head with the banking crisis of 1837. Louisiana purchasers also insisted on warranties, and local courts borrowed from the Roman buyer's protection policy to hold the seller legally responsible for "defective" slaves. Louisiana also remained unique among the southern states because of its redhibition laws, which regulated the terms of warranty for the sale of enslaved people and the terms under which a sale of human property could be challenged. These laws shielded enslavers against an immediate loss of slave labor.[68]

During the 1820s and 1830s, the capital raised by mortgages that used enslaved people as collateral rose from 67 percent to 88 percent.[69] Armed with available slave-based credit, many Red River planters preferred investments directed at expanding their plantation's productivity. William Hutchinson reinvested his handsome 1859 returns into a mill on his Caddo Parish holdings.[70] The prosperous Mathews family began to regularly ship enslaved people and goods from New Orleans to their Cocobend and Chaseland plantations, while concurrently paying off the mortgage held on eight enslaved people at 8 percent interest.[71]

— — —

As westward expansion continued during the antebellum period, the superb quality of Red River land enticed relocation into the late 1850s.[72] Peripatetic journalist Frederick Law Olmsted passed through the Red River region thrice. In 1853, he noted that "the Red River bottoms are nearly the best cotton lands in the world" and that land on the river "is now worth from $15 to $40 an acre. Improved plantations average, perhaps, $20 in value."[73] Irrespective of the land's appeal, once in Louisiana, many slaveholders—especially those with small slaveholdings—found the price of land steep. Numerous newcomers squatted on the land to circumvent this obstacle, and this pervasive practice led to a series of preemption laws in 1841.[74]

Though Red River settlers snapped up land at two dollars an acre before preemption, the government found squatting palatable because it raised the value of public domain lands.[75] John Texada squatted to settle a large Rapides Parish lot by "preemption . . . in the public lands" before gaining official ownership by land grant. Preemption was a response to trespassing on public lands that gained popularity after 1812 and remained consistently popular throughout the 1830s despite the opposition of land officials. Preemption allowed people who lived on their improved land to buy that land before public sale at the minimum price of $1.25 an acre. It appealed to a broad range of settlers but was also widely used by relatively well-off slaveholders like Texada.[76] Settlers who purchased land via preemption were given one year to pay off the debt. Early claiming of land was important, giving first right to natural resources, but it was not the only method used to stake a land claim; neither was outright purchasing. By 1839, land in Caddo Parish was still considered reasonably priced at ten dollars per acre in the woods, though it was more expensive along the river.[77] Riverside land prices remained high, as indicated by Texada's June 8, 1836, purchase of fifty-nine acres on Bayou Rapides, adjacent to his property, for $73 an acre.[78]

As boom-phase cultivation took hold and commercial agriculture advanced, immediate land purchase became the norm. Land improvements remained an important feature of claiming and controlling the wilderness, and a cleared field, a well-maintained levee, or a planted crop signified ownership and mastery of the land.[79] Private property ownership encouraged farmers to break the squatting cycle and incentivized land development and improvement. John Texada, for instance, squatted on his land in the first stage of his family's migration, but his son Lewis formally purchased the large tract of 1,900 acres—extending on both sides of Bayou Rapides—in 1852 for the sum of $12,000.[80] River proximity presented a trade-off between the health of white and Black inhabitants residing along the malarial waterway and the prospect of immense financial gains from the enriched soil. Like many other settlers, land and cotton won out for the Texada family.

Lewis Texada's attention to river frontage was sound. Plantations positioned on the river possessed several benefits, not least of which was the ease of getting cotton to market. Like others, William Powell headed west and snapped up valuable riverfront property. He received a land grant in 1843, moved his wife and six children from Tuscumbia, Alabama, to Caddo Parish (later part of Red River Parish), and established Mount Flat plantation. The family would continue to expand their holdings over the antebellum period to include Slate Place plantation in Red River Parish. Letters written by Powell's daughters shed light on the land's quality and the region's adversarial conditions for the early inhabitants. In a June 1, 1845, letter to her aunt, the eldest Powell child, Jane, intertwines the profits to be reaped from the land with the peril of residing alongside the Red River. "The river is very high but is falling," she observed. "We are in hopes the water will not overflow the land this year for our crops are finer than they ever have been our cotton is very large and in bloom."[81] Jane did not state explicitly whether their property's levees were reinforced, which would have shifted the potentially destructive power of the river into a force to improve the land, but given their location on the river and their recent settlement, it is likely some levee protection and water drainage system was used.

In 1828, an intricately maintained levee system extended continuously along the Mississippi, some 195 miles from New Orleans to Red River Landing. As Red River migration boomed, so did attention to the levee system. One early historian of river navigation noted that these levees extended from the Red to the mouth of the Arkansas River. Collectively, Louisiana's river protections were immense, with calculations in 1860 estimating that the enslaved-built Louisiana levees cost $12.5 million to construct and maintain.[82] Levee systems were essential for the commercial development of the plantation system. Every northwest Louisiana resident knew the Red River possessed the power to provide a bountiful crop, but it could easily flood and wipe away all profit for at least a year. The river dictated inhabitants' livelihood during the entire nineteenth century, and slaveholders kept a vigilant watch. As Jane Powell knowingly wrote to her aunt, if the river remained high but not overflowing, the Powell crop would render "about a hundred and seventy five bales of cotton" that year.[83]

Thus, the lure of the Red River was strong, but the ensuing physical and monetary hardships often gave settlers pause. Before settling near Shreveport, Henry Marshall's letters were tinged with regret for not purchasing in Alabama, where land was profitable. He lamented that acreage was too "dear" in Yazoo County and that the "risk in cotton is bad for a purchaser." He was not risk averse but wished to do "better than I did in Carolina" and absolve himself of debt.[84] Ultimately, Marshall was pleased with the Red, writing that it "has exceeded my anticipations" and that "this river is a Nile." He was enthralled by the prospects of the land where "the crops have been good" and felt relocation opportune because "settlers are coming in rapidly."[85] Egan concurred that it was a propitious time to relocate and told his son that an "improved population" was advancing rapidly to the area because "this country . . . is destined to furnish homes to a teeming population of an energetic and thrifty class of farmers." He underscored that "great estates may not abound here," but the region's magnetic appeal was the bounty promised by the "fine land."[86]

Exhilarated by the alluvial region's potential, Marshall established slave quarters and a temporary residence in 1837.[87] He swiftly drew parallels between his new region and his home state. Marshall observed that "slaves are treated pretty much alike in this country when they are managed by overseers. They are fed well, have sufficient clothing and are worked all day. They are usually fed better than in S. C." Marshall settled closer to Shreveport and indicated from the outset that easy transportation of the staple crop formed an essential factor in plantation location: "I should prefer a place near Alexandria on account of the convenience of getting to it."[88]

For Marshall and others, completing the migration process took time and the accumulation of funds. For instance, in an 1857 letter from J.

Prestuge to established DeSoto Parish planter William Benson, Prestuge outlined the steps already taken to facilitate his move from Virginia: "I brought out from Richmond 36 negroes. This fall I have sold a few . . . I have a good blacksmith and waggon maker." Toward the close of the letter, he summed up his goals and gauged the average time necessary to move a plantation across the southern states: "I intend to sell out all very fair property as soon as I can and go to planting somewhere in the west, to do this . . . it will take me two or three years."[89]

Gathering capital, enslaved people, and credit were not the only preconditions for migration. Family migrations frequently provided a network of relations that stabilized the uncertainties of nineteenth-century life and alleviated a measure of loneliness for white slaveholders. Men often chose spouses from within their social milieu, and marriage was a frequent precursor to westward migration. With few single women in the Red River area, marriage before migration was often commonplace. The urgency to marry before relocation is underscored by the average female marriage age hovering around the late teens and early twenties while the male age remained closer to thirty.[90] Some men, like Henry Marshall, left their wives behind on established holdings while they ventured westward. For young women accustomed to established society and the proximity of kin, the isolation of frontier life remained less than appealing. As in other parts of the expanding South, white women ordinarily moved to the Red River because of marriage. The comfort and support of proximate families presented an acute pull that resulted in pressure on husbands to follow chain migrations to maintain kinship networks.[91]

White women seldom found migration to be an easy process. Indeed, female settlers commonly compared migration to death and found the new landscapes and homes insipid, vacant, and often repulsive. Since white women defined their world in terms of proximity to family, letters from frontier women, including those in the Red River region, were peppered with imploring pleas for family members to relocate.[92] Jane Powell recounted a lonely inhabitance on the edge of the Louisiana wilderness. In her letters, Jane remarked that a movement of settlers from the river to the hills left the neighborhood "very dull" and noted that "society is very indifferent," in large part because "there are no young ladies within fifty miles of our house either up or down the river." She detailed a summer tour visiting kin and female friends to compensate for the lack of female company near their plantation. Many men lived in the area, which was in keeping with the rapid, male-oriented bent of western settlement, and Jane earnestly awaited the improving of society "as some of our old batchelors have married lately and intend on bringing there families to the river."[93]

The improvement and civilizing of the region became a staple talking point in newspapers and letters. "Civilization" was a coded term to express stability, a settled society, and importantly, a shift away from a primitive frontier. For instance, the Powell plantation vicinity was booming by the late 1840s, and pressure increased to establish a local post office. Post offices played a critical role in mediating political messages, and steamboat packets delivered the private letters and commercial correspondence vital to the fiscal success of the region's slaveholders.[94]

The clamor for a post office highlights the region's dramatic development and societal growth. For many local settlers, post offices and regular postal service symbolized the region's relative modernity, urban development, and political connection, and the requirement for geographic connection indicated the extent of regional development. "Civilization" was also deftly used by slaveholding men to entice their wives into relocation and by women hopeful that kin would join them in the region. Greenwood, an enclave a few miles west of Shreveport, captured particular attention for its civilized aspects. The *Caddo Gazette* published an article boasting that "our village has four horse stage coach passing through it twice a day." Greenwood featured Caddo Parish's first brick home; the Whitworth plantation—later known as the Howell plantation—stood from 1839 and "became the scene of many gala social functions."[95] When writing to his wife back in South Carolina, Henry Marshall detailed the gradual "filling up with respectable people and an episcopal clergyman from Tennessee" to induce his wife to relocate.[96]

The Powells' early settlement in northwest Louisiana allowed them to reap financial benefits from the subsequent rise in the value, desirability, and productivity of their holding.[97] But for all their wealth, settlers like William Powell still privileged business interest over luxury. "Comfort could wait," noted a contemporary about settlers like Powell. Slaveholders were not devoid of taste, but "it is their principle to make it yield to interest."[98] Powell began making his holding more palatable by building a more permanent residence three years later. His daughter Pirella wrote, "The dwelling in which we now reside is not worthy of a name[.] it was built for an overseers house . . . now preparing to build a brick house which I hope will be worthy of a name."[99] Her statement captures the type of frontier settlements along the Red River and their gradual transformation. In conjunction with building a more prestigious home, Powell steadily expanded his plantation and its cotton growing potential by purchasing more slaves in 1847.

A proud Silas Flournoy described in detail the layout of his property to his wife, Elizabeth. His letter was designed to whet her appetite for relocation, and he detailed the "excellent spring, the best in the whole country around" that stood on his land. He pointed out that his plot was adjacent to his brother Alfred—highlighting that kinship proximity would remain intact for Elizabeth—and that their property was healthy because it was "elevated and dry." Though the home was simple, the surroundings constituted "the prettiest section," with woods and high grass, set off by a "grove of trees" connecting the Flournoy brothers' properties with a "beautiful avenue."[100]

Large-scale slaveholding existed in the Red River region, but small and midrange planters stood at the fore of regional transformation. Even with the expansion of personal fortunes, the entrenchment of slavery, and strengthened commercial routes from the Red River downriver to New Orleans, census records show that most Red River slaveholders were small to midsize. Like their forefathers in the eastern seaboard slave states, these slaveholders understood and internalized slaveholding as an escalator of personal progress. While the Red River region produced vast wealth from cotton, the aim was not to re-create the luster and grandeur of the sugar parish homes in the southern part of Louisiana or to transplant the polish of Upper and Lower South plantation homes. Investment in the Red River coalesced around land and enslaved labor. The slaveholders who relocated to this region were fueled by the goal of expanding and building personal wealth, and the international need for cotton informed their plantation establishment. This demand rendered slavery a lucrative, modern, export-driven enterprise in which enslaved people and cotton were traded indeterminately as human and agricultural commodities. Removal of the raft cemented the importance of this region to the cotton South. It meant Red River slaveholders like Powell, Marshall, the Hutchinsons, and the Flournoys were fully immersed in the market economy by the close of the antebellum era. Slavery lay at the crux, and enslaved people lived a brutal and extractive existence to bring to fruition slaveholders' dreams of prosperity.

– 2 –

"FARMING HERE IS A SURE ROAD TO A FORTUNE"

The Cotton Complex and Enslavement

Life for white settlers and enslaved Blacks on the Red River was organized and defined by the transatlantic appetite for cotton. All aspects of life—from the violence that punctuated cultivation productivity to the rhythm of Black existence, the investment in new seed varietals, and slaveholders' economic and trade relationships—were shaped by cotton. Red River region slaveholders maintained a concentrated focus on maximum profit from both the soil and enslaved people. These modernizing planters adroitly harnessed the cotton boom's agricultural, social, and economic mobility to transform northwest Louisiana into a leading cotton-producing region. Fertile land drove settlement, but slavery advanced southern agricultural development and allowed slaveholders to position their enslaved labor force responsively to the growing demand for cotton.[1]

The ability to move enslaved laborers quickly, to organize their labor to meet specific needs, and to focus investment decisions around labor, land, and technology provided slaveholders with an element of microeconomic control.[2] Enslavers demonstrated, enacted, and delineated mastery as the control of enslaved bodies through violence and racial subjugation for financial gain and maintaining the boundaries of whiteness. This control underpinned and defined a particularly brutal and dehumanized form of slavery that concurrently deployed violence to regulate each facet of enslaved life and to solidify mastery as an inclusive regional white identity.

Regional slaveholders were exploitative, focused on productivity, and deeply invested in the commercial world. The demand for cotton from cotton brokers known as factors, from manufacturers, and from consumers in growing worldwide metropolitan centers transformed cotton from a regional crop with derivative goods produced locally to an entire industry in which cultivation and material production occurred in different locations. This enterprise changed the marketplace and expanded many financial institutions and trading infrastructures that are familiar today. This commodity's trade, production, and consumption relied on large-scale industrialization, rapid economic growth, and incredible productivity increases. Red River slaveholders' ability to respond rapidly to rising prices, expanding markets, and increased demand for affordable textiles lent the global cotton network fluidity and elasticity.[3] This chapter examines the agricultural advances adopted on regional plantations and details both the enslaved experience and the process by which Blacks were commodified and dehumanized by white slaveholders.

According to the *American Cotton Planter*, cotton was the "controlling influence of commerce, but it is emphatically, the barometer of commerce."[4] Two related technological advancements contributed to and supported expanded cotton production. Widespread access to the cotton gin after 1793 ensured swift processing and cleaning of large volumes of cotton, while the introduction of short-staple or upland cotton further expanded the geography of American cotton. Growing the valuable fibers of this commodity structured every facet of how enslaved people labored and lived. This makes understanding the botany of cotton, the agronomic changes introduced by slaveholders, and the means by which cotton was cultivated and harvested critical to appreciating the cadence of work and the pressures experienced by Blacks enslaved in this region.

Cotton is a remarkably hardy plant that requires only warmth, rainfall, and fertile soil for growth. Its environmental needs and growth requirements differ from other commodity and staple crops. Unlike rice or sugar, cotton requires no specific environmental conditions, and unlike wheat, cotton needs no sustained care or maintenance during the entire growing season, and especially during planting.[5] Short-staple and upland varieties can grow in a wide range of locations, which enabled agronomists to cross plant varieties and create robust and adaptable new plants with easily picked bolls. The quick adoption of agricultural innovations, especially seed varietals, by Red River area slaveholders led to the introduction of the short-staple and upland varieties to boost output to market, and this introduction, particularly of upland cotton varietals, extracted additional labor productivity from enslaved people. The viability and adaptability of robust upland cotton ensured good profits for slaveholders but intensive labor for enslaved people in northwest Louisiana.

People today rarely understand how cotton is planted, grown, and harvested. A compressed summary of the commodity that dictated Black enslavement is thus required. A cultivated cotton plant has a prominent, monopodial main stem with secondary branches that are both monopodial and sympodial.[6] The sympodial branches are fruiting branches composed of bolls, a segmented pod containing immature seeds from which cotton fibers grow. Though cotton is not a true annual plant, certain frost-free varieties were adapted to a growing season that included growth, fruit, and maturation. The most conspicuous part of the large, bell-shaped open flower is the corolla, which ranges from a creamy white to light yellow cream in upland varieties to a deep yellow color in Sea Island cotton. For upland cotton—the most prevalent variety in the antebellum South—the time from flowering to open boll is forty-five to sixty-five days.[7] Cotton plants are harvested three to five weeks after the boll opens, producing a dense mat of roughly inch-long fibers.

Cotton is labor- and time-intensive year-round, but unlike rice and sugar it does not demand overly specialized or skilled labor. Even so, cotton was finicky in its consumption of labor, especially on new ground, where it had an appetite for fit laborers.[8] Although Red River area slaveholders favored prime-age enslaved people as their principal workforce, all ages could cultivate cotton. Enslaved people in the Red River region consequently came into a work regime that was defined by cotton—necessitating nimble, dexterous, quick fingers—and the need to clear land, which required immense physical strength. Gang labor was used on cotton plantations, establishing labor patterns that were distinct from practices on rice and sugar plantations, where tasking prevailed. Tasking afforded a modicum of independence because enslaved people set their own work pace and established a clear division of labor time, which encouraged Blacks to supplement food and clothing through an internal economy.[9] This sliver of work autonomy and ability to supplement food sources was absent in the Red River region.

Picking did not require task specificity but it did require stamina and manual dexterity in equal parts.[10] Solomon Northup, who was enslaved in northwestern Louisiana and whose narrative, *Twelve Years a Slave,* provides the bulk of recollections of the enslaved in the region, remembered that the average picking requirement was two hundred pounds. Each enslaved person was required to pick at least this amount, and those who failed to match the previous day's weight were whipped. The same picking weight was demanded daily; dropping below the prior day's amount resulted in punishment, while picking more set a new target to reach the next day. This cycle of fear required enslaved people satiate picking demands under pain of violence while also mustering the technique, dexterity, and stamina required to pick cotton in hot and humid climes, with little sustenance and without respite. Northup noted that enslaved people's approach to the "gin house is always with fear and trembling."[11]

There were some positions with more authority among the field hands, including driver, but skill specificity and task diversity were substantially reduced.[12] The demographics of the enslaved on the Red River skewed toward young and prime-age individuals. Field hands completed the same tasks, and there is scant indication of delineation between household and field slaves, which was rare on large-scale entrenched plantations. Cotton did not require extensive technology or labor-saving innovations to yield a profitable crop, so enslaved laborers and cottonseed varietals were slaveholders' most reliable and succinct technology investments. Enslaved people provided an elastic labor source that facilitated the indefinite expansion of plantation agriculture, allowing the region's slaveholders to maximize profits accrued from bondage and to set a grueling work pace defined by their agricultural expectations.[13]

Securing fertile land was essential, but planting cotton swiftly was paramount. The popular southern periodical *American Cotton Planter* advised that all lands designated for cotton needed to "be broken deep, close and soft" and long enough before planting to allow rainwater to settle.[14] January and February were designated for soil preparation, and regional slaveholders were anxious to ensure a bountiful crop. Publications advised laying manure in thick, even layers across the entire field and in the furrows to a depth of three inches before demarcating cotton rows with a scooter plow. Cotton stalks were also plowed up so the beds would have ample time to settle before opening them in April.[15]

Breaking and plowing ground was very important for Sarah Hunter, who managed her Rapides Parish plantation while her husband served in the Louisiana senate. She wrote to her husband that Mr. Trent, the overseer, "is uneasy about getting so little ploughing done. The fact is, he has not been able to plough more than three days in any week since you left, without killing up the teem, and negroes, which he had judgment enough not to wish to do."[16] Her concerns echoed the vast body of guidance on agricultural practices, advancements, and preservation accessible to Red River slaveholders. Although current agricultural advice was available regionally, there is no record of the execution of this advice. However, because the region's slaveholders balanced their desire to maximize cotton production with protecting soil fertility, they would have been interested in agricultural developments and preservation techniques, particularly around soil nutrients.

When not effusing about the rich soil, slaveholders were writing about geographic concerns, precautions, and climate woes that presented particular circumstances to overcome for profitable cotton cultivation. The Red often flooded and required engineering expertise—predominantly garnered from enslaved knowledge and skill—to construct floodgates, undertake levee maintenance, and plow diagonally to minimize runoff and dislodged cotton seeds. Many enslaved people would have learned this engineering knowledge from earlier generations captured in Africa, who had deployed it when enslaved on rice, indigo, and cotton plantations throughout the Carolinas and Georgia.

Flooding was a grave concern. Intense rains or rising river levels could flood fields, wash away fertile topsoil, uproot cotton plants, and destroy cotton bolls. At Willow Point in Red River Parish, enslaved women leveed the bayou from mid-February through March 1859. Though the plantation ledgers do not record this activity in previous years, it is logical to conclude that prior years with high river water levels would have required similar leveeing expertise from these women.[17] Floodwaters often resulted in a bad crop and a depreciated amount of cotton fit for market, making water management hugely significant, and this was facilitated by enslaved people's labor and knowledge. John Houston noted in an 1858 letter to his brother-in-law that land along the Red River tended to overflow when the river rose, and all those planters who wished to plant early "throw up a levee from one to three feet high."[18] Pirella Powell was very concerned about the rising river in June 1845, which threatened to "overflow our lands" in a year with particularly fine crops that were "very large and in bloom." The year before, Joseph Olcott was a "large sufferer" after the Red River overflowed and wiped out one-third of his crop. He described the flood as a calamity that had "befallen our devoted and beloved country ... distroying all the crops."[19]

Water issues were not solely down to flooding; too much or too little rainwater presented different problems. George Mathews wrote that too much water, combined with excessive winds, had damaged his 1830 crop, reducing it to three hundred bales, and that he suffered "considerable injury" from storms in 1831.[20] Twenty-four years later, his son Charles received letters from the overseer at Chaseland, one of four regional family plantations, discussing rainfall. In mid-May, the overseer was vexed by the lack of rain, which was drying out the cotton crop—a situation going on for more than six weeks—but he assured Mathews that his crop was in the same condition as others in Rapides. A jubilant letter written a month later told of "two good rains" that would secure bountiful crops at Chaseland. Henry Marshall was affected by drought in 1839. However, he reckoned the crop would net three hundred bales minimum, and a few weeks later his spirits had buoyed sufficiently for him to describe his prospects as "so good" and to consider buying more river-facing land.[21]

Maintaining soil fertility was necessary, as indicated by Chaseland's overseer, who wanted to refertilize the soil after harvest to ensure the continuation of good crops.[22] Such concerns were commonplace because all growth occurs within this "layer of black loam just two feet deep," which was easily leached during floods.[23] DeSoto Parish slaveholder William Sharp chronicled this situation in an 1850 letter. Due to a flood the previous July, his crop was one-third that of 1849 and the Red threatened further damage.[24]

Sharp and his contemporaries recognized that soil erosion and flood damage posed a severe problem and strove to preserve the land's natural fertility. In the 1840s, agricultural innovators introduced drainage ditches to "take off water from horizontal furrows and thus prevent them from overflowing." Drainage and water management systems proved especially important to slaveholders who hoped to benefit from early planting while also instituting recovery measures against a ruined and waterlogged crop. William Dunbar's system of horizontalizing was one prevalent preventive method because "it reduced loss of valuable topsoil by erosion."[25]

Hillside ditching, a practice involving laying level, horizontal rows near the apex of the field, was also popular. Guide rows on either side of the furrow served as governing rows, creating a uniform inclined plane with orderly rows above and below. The first furrow was plowed on the lower side so that the furrow slice could be turned into the open furrow, a tactic that allowed the dirt to be turned more advantageously and often translated into better aerated cotton shoots. Hillside ditching ensured that alluvial soil was not lost to runoff but was retained and turned into the cultivated furrows.[26] Such pertinent advice clearly bore fruit, for, as Henry Marshall observed, the resulting crop was so abundant after manuring his cotton fields that all the cotton could not be gathered.[27] Despite the environmental mastery demonstrated by clearing the Red River raft to enable river traffic, water presented a particular challenge. Effective plantation management required a careful balance of environmental and soil control.

Frost and frozen ground presented major concerns during winter months, despite the humidity and heat of spring and summer in northern Louisiana. Short-staple cotton required a growing season of two hundred frost-free days.[28] As Mrs. Hunter relayed to her husband, "the ground was frozen hard, and the icicles hung on the house for days last week," halting essential crop preparations.[29] Cold weather endangered the cotton plant, leaving the seed prone to pathogens and cessation of cellular processes. Frost and temperature fluctuations were a threat because autumn frosts early in the germination cycle determined crop yield and quality. Excessive moisture—from flooding, drain runoff, or melted ice—changed the soil salinity and left the plant vulnerable to soil-borne diseases, most notably boll rot.[30] Boll rot, seed rot, and other bacterial blight diseases could decimate a crop and strike fear in planters' hearts. The 1853–1854 ledger for Pre Aux Cleres plantation chronicles the insect damage inflicted on the crop. That year, the crop was hit by lice and rust in the bolls, and it was infested with caterpillars, leaving the cotton very thin.[31]

Cotton required long hours and a tremendous amount of labor from enslaved people, alongside their soil management capabilities and flood mitigation experience. A typical workday began at four in the morning, and except for hurried breaks for breakfast and lunch, enslaved people toiled well past dark. During ginning and bagging time, the gin would run nonstop; the overseer at Willow Point noted in 1854 that the gin was in constant use from "9 oclock till 4 in the evening without seesing."[32] During the winter, when the ground was hard and frost enclosed the topsoil, the enslaved felled trees, split logs, hauled and repaired rails, tended to the barns, cleared underbrush and briars from the established fields, and broke new ground. Northup wrote, "ploughing, planting, picking cotton, gathering the corn, and pulling and burning stalks, occupies the whole of the four seasons of the year."[33] Cotton commanded enslaved people's time and labor year-round, and the cadence of cotton cultivation underscored the demanding requirements placed upon them to enable the success of large-scale, market-focused cotton plantations.

When soil dried and weather warmed in early spring, the enslaved spread fertilizer in preparation for sowing cotton alongside corn. Red River slaveholders did not comment profusely on planting staple food products except to briefly mention vegetables and potatoes. Northup recollected that "garden products . . . are cultivated for the use of the master and his family" while the enslaved were allowed only "corn and bacon." He continued that the hogs on Epps's plantation were "fed on *shelled* corn—it was thrown out to his n——s in the ear." Epps thought that the hogs would "fatten faster by shelling" but that Blacks treated in the same fashion "might grow too fat to labor."[34]

Though the focus remained on extracting maximum cotton from land and slaves, plantations operated as safety-first holdings and thus grew enough food to remain largely self-sufficient. George Mason Graham wrote proudly about his fine 1848 cotton crop in the same sentence as he mentioned "a very heavy one of corn," estimated at one hundred bushels to the acre. George Mathews had cultivated five thousand barrels of corn in 1831. Henry Marshall had grown "plenty of corn," plus peas and potatoes so abundant that consumption before rotting would prove challenging. He boasted to his wife that there were enough hogs to "give you sausages all next winter" because of his foodstuff production in 1839.[35] Regional slaveholders grew adequate corn, supplemented by imported pork and molasses, to feed both enslaved people and livestock.[36]

Breaking up the soil and beating down the old plants were important, carefully timed steps for a new crop. Enslaved people used a heavy plow pulled by two mules to break up the land. As the previous crop wound down in December, *De Bow's* agricultural magazine urged a method called ridge husbandry, which required the formation of "four or five furrows through together with a leading furrow run first," with ridge placement "varying from six to three feet" depending on soil density.[37] Cultivation implement preferences varied throughout the South, but northwest Louisiana slaveholders eschewed labor-saving tools because they had already invested in enslaved labor, negating the need for large-scale technological advancement. The early reliance on the hoe shifted as planters used horse-drawn tools, a transition that led to the adoption of the scraper, skimmer, and sweep; the latter two items greatly economized cultivation labor because they covered a wider width furrow than other plows. These new implements were particularly well suited to planters along the Red River because they were better adapted to loamy soils, and they were widely used across Louisiana, Mississippi, and Arkansas.[38]

The drive for maximum profit and extraction yielded a keen interest in seed varietal diversification. As agronomists devised ways to breed seeds with specific traits, Red River planters purchased seeds with easy picking properties, high lint quality, and improved immunity to rot or frost. This alleviated many anxieties and offered a measure of profit security. When the price of cotton fluctuated in the 1840s, planters increased the cotton output to the uppermost quantity enslaved people could harvest, and they planted an improved grade of product. Seed hybridization enhanced production, and the significance to these planters of specially engineered varietals underscores their focus on increased profit.[39]

Various cotton diseases plagued plantation fortunes and informed planters' choice of new varietals. The diseases popularly called "rust" and "blight" were very serious, while the cotton caterpillar—colloquially called "army worm"—remained the most dreaded of insect enemies. Experiments to find the sturdiest cotton varieties yielded engineered varieties with a longer staple, less proclivity for disease, larger and more numerous bolls, or highly dense yield.[40] One varietal, Petit Gulf, particularly suited the region's improvement-minded slaveholders. It was adapted to the dexterity of human hands and was the easiest cotton to pick, which maximized enslaved labor while diminishing requirements for expensive, additional technological innovations. Petit Gulf grew prolifically in various soils and climates, bloomed two weeks earlier than any other strain, and allowed for an elongated picking season. It also produced long, fine cotton fibers that were desirable and exceptionally marketable.[41] Continued refinement of the Petit Gulf resulted in large bolls with wooly white seeds, ideal picking characteristics, and immunity against rot.[42] The Creole, another popular choice, was an annual varietal that always fell victim to the first heavy frost but produced very good quality lint, while the Petit Gulf, created in response to the demand for an improved upland variety, boasted a longer staple and higher lint quality than the Creole.[43] The Petit Gulf's exceptional picking qualities allowed for three- to fourfold picking output, which overshadowed the key drawback: uncomplicated access to the lint also meant that it easily fell to the ground or was swept away by the wind.

As agricultural historians Alan Olmstead and Paul Rhode indicate, biological innovations and continued investment in engineering the ideal cotton varietal drove a 49 percent higher picking rate in the South by 1862.[44] Since these new varietals were more accessible to pick and the rich regional soil led to higher per-acre yields, enslaved people were driven harder and expected to pick more cotton each day to realize the investment in new seed varietals. The ingrained violence inherent in enslaved life, combined with the callous, profit-focused mindset of white slaveholders, created an environment in which whippings and gruesome physical punishment were doled out when crop productivity or profitability were low, but also when they were high. Violence was not the sole catalyst of high picking rates, nor was it prevalent only when a crop struggled. Instead, enslaved Blacks dealt with terrible violence whether their fingers whizzed through a bountiful field picking cotton at lightning-fast speed, as Patsey did on the plantation where Northup was enslaved, or they picked quickly on a field blighted by rot.[45] The increased picking rates during the late antebellum period resulted from a confluence of speed picking from enslaved laborers, the soil maintenance work and expertise of enslaved Blacks, and new seed varietals that flourished in the region and featured larger bolls for swifter pickability alongside immunities to rot.[46]

— — —

The regional goal of reaping maximum cotton from the land defined the year-round work of the enslaved and the violent timbre of their life. Since cotton required constant attention, with cotton picking lasting from August to February, enslaved people labored in a self-contained system wherein masters dictated the degree and severity of work.[47] Chattel bondage provided a flexible labor system that allowed planters to stretch enslaved labor for economic benefit and to enact agronomic alterations in response to weather or crop disease. Slavery as a labor model also made sense in a world wherein the staple crop required constant attention and planters sought maximum financial gain. The "allocative efficiency" of slave work gangs on individual regional farms allowed slaveholders to combine production factors with efficiency in accordance with prices and marginal productivities.[48] By dint of slave ownership, slaveholders also had the ability to mobilize labor throughout the cultivation and harvesting period. The flexibility of the plantation labor force was advantageous when planters expanded their crop or had a bumper crop. All of these elements influenced the daily life and work patterns of the region's commodified enslaved population.

Cotton cultivation started with breaking ground in the winter, after which Blacks would "list" the ridge to raise rows and beat down the remnants of the prior cotton crop. The Willow Point plantation journals record ten days during which the enslaved broke one hundred acres.[49] Then, three groups of enslaved people began planting cottonseed. One group would drill into the ground, creating a furrow into which the next group would carefully drop the seed. This usually commenced during the first week of March, as was true on Henry Marston's Ashland plantation and on the Epps plantation, where Solomon Northup toiled.[50] Careful hands would place the seeds from fourteen inches to three feet apart. Another group followed behind with their hoes to turn the earth. Four gangs completed this process at Willow Point, and these small gangs formed the most common regional plantation work unit.[51]

Gang labor was a particularly efficient labor system of intense, exhausting, and routinized work. Though Red River planters left no record indicating gang size preference and no enslaved recollection details this, smaller units were likely used to enforce control and ensure peak productivity. It also enabled planters and overseers to supervise the work strictly. Gang labor created work units that labored at the pace of the fastest worker, allowing overseers to monitor the gang's progress directly and to accelerate the pace through targeted punishment. Emphasis was also placed on routine and precision in work quality from the laboring enslaved.[52] Northup remembered that the "fastest hoer" took the lead row, usually "a rod in advance of his companions." Anyone who passed that individual was whipped, and anyone who fell behind was whipped. Thus, "the lash is flying from morning until night, the whole day long."[53]

Willow Point utilized four gangs, and Pre Aux Cleres had five gangs, with no skill levels delineated.[54] George Marshall of Rapides Parish divided the 102 enslaved people on his Crescent plantation into twenty-one families in his only full record concerning them. He did not specify if kinship networks or work groups determined these families. The plantation diary lists twenty-four men, twenty women, and their progeny.[55] Slaveholders broke each gang into *full, half,* and *quarter hands* and employed these terms to delineate the amount of work expected and to track individual productivity.

Northup recalled that on the first picking day in the field, the enslaved were "whipped up smartly" and then made to "pick as fast as he can possibly." When the cotton was weighed at night, the individuals' "capability in cotton picking is known." They were subsequently required to pick the same amount consistently.[56]

After enslaved Blacks planted the cottonseeds, crop care and maintenance commenced. From mid-February to June, enslaved people labored in the field, plowing, picking weeds, and skimming. The Willow Point plantation book tabulates the plowing and skimming of the gangs that worked from morning to night "without seesing."[57] In midsummer, slaveholders tasked their bondspeople with thinning or "chopping" cotton, a laborious process wherein the enslaved used hoes to create foot-wide intervals between growing plants, chopped weeds, plowed, and concurrently tended corn and sustenance crops.[58] Usage of a drill in planting cotton made it necessary to thin out the rows, and enslaved people did this by "chopping out," a tedious and delicate procedure that required cutting through the drill with hoes while keeping a minimal distance of twelve inches between plants.[59] In mid-June, following thinning, enslaved people "molded" the crop, using a plow with a mould board through the rows to free the plants of grass and weeds and ensure the success of the strongest plants.[60] Finally, late summer and autumn brought the cotton harvest. Some Blacks continued to pull and stack fodder and tend the corn alongside their work in the cotton fields, but the focus of plantation operations shifted to the demanding and time-consuming harvest work. Demands on enslaved labor increased during the harvest and workdays were more oppressive, longer, and more taxing. Moreover, there was a significant rush to collect and prepare cotton as a saleable product in a compressed period, both for financial reasons and to outwit the potentially tempestuous northern Louisiana weather.

During the harvests at Willow Point and Pre Aux Cleres, enslaved people consistently picked approximately the same weight each day while one or two of the enslaved manned the gin stand. George Mathews told his wife that one enslaved person picked 326 pounds daily. Walter Moore wrote to his brother Thomas, who later served as Louisiana governor, about their plantation's prolific 1830 crop and the quantities of daily picking. Most of their enslaved picked an average of 180 to 220 pounds of cotton per day, while the "best pickers" averaged 430 pounds. This mirrors what Northup writes about picking rates on the Epps plantation, including his statement that when she picked cotton, Patsey was equal to two people and "five hundred pounds a day was not unusual for her." Two months later, after his nuptials, Moore outlined his goals for his new plantation. He rested his financial success and the first repayment of the $7,500 plantation purchase price on the continual labor of ten Blacks and "remarkably fine" crops with an average of "twelve and fourteen bales to the hand." Thinking of profit and maximum extraction, he boasted that some of his slaves "frequently to pick 500 bales . . . as high as 620 bales in one day."[61]

It was customary practice to pick the field three times, with each round of picking designated successively as bottom, middle, and top crops. The middle picking bore the largest product and was often the highest quality.[62] Except for a small enslaved group on larger holdings tasked only with household duties, or those manning the gin, the enslaved workforce entered the fields to pick cotton. Some large slaveholders like Henry Marston brought enslaved people from their other holdings to assist with picking. In 1858, Marston transported ten enslaved people from his Clinton, East Feliciana Parish, holding to Ashland, his plantation on the Red River, to plant and pick.[63] Picking slaves tied a voluminous sack about the waist for picked cotton. Overseers or drivers weighed the full sack—those individuals who did not meet the required daily poundage were immediately whipped—before emptying the contents into a basket. After each enslaved person's cotton picking was weighed and recorded, the gathered cotton dried out on temporary scaffolds in a large barn before transportation to the gin house. This practice allowed the cotton fibers "to 'sweat' for a few days before ginning."[64] Then the cotton was ginned, pressed, and formed into giant bales to send down the Red River to the cotton warehouses of New Orleans. There, wrapped in a protective woven cotton covering, cotton entered the marketplace.

Good quality cotton determined a slaveholder's success, leaving them anxious about the outcome of the yearly crop. Successful, profitable crops triggered boasting and slaveholders were unabashed in their enthusiasm, particularly in correspondence. After harvesting began on the 1855 Chaseland crop, Charles Mathews's overseer wrote that the "cotton is very fine inded the crop on the uper place is said to be the best in the cuntry."[65] In 1854, Willow Point's overseer charted the weight of all 263 bales of cotton, each weighing between 320 and 480 pounds. The following year, the cotton bales at Willow Point swelled and produced less bottom grade, or trashy, cotton.[66] At Pre Aux Cleres, in Natchitoches Parish, the enslaved gathered "37000 seed cotton" for the 1852 harvest that they ginned into "275 bales of 400 lb each of 110000 lint."[67]

A notable rhetorical element within letters was the erasure of the enslaved people from the cultivation process; the amount and quality of cotton gathered was discussed in detail but the people who made the crop possible were absent. In other letters, the slaveholder attributed the cultivation success solely to himself, appropriating enslaved people's expended labor in a pen stroke. George Mason Graham, a prominent Rapides Parish slaveholder and influential figure in antebellum Louisiana, indicated his exuberance for a good crop. He wrote to his sister in October 1848, with harvest in full swing, and reflected on the imminent change occasioned by a bumper harvest. His 1848 crop was "very heavy one of corn, having gathered 100 bushels to the acre . . . I am picking over 10,000 wt of cotton a day." He was finally pleased with the outcome of his crop and declared that he had "less annoyance with my plantation this year than I have ever had before."[68]

Enslaved people were the engine that drove regional success and individual profit but they were not included or credited in correspondence. This poignantly captures how slaveholders, possessing power and the ability to silence the people they dominated, manipulated the production of history and recorded narratives.[69] Silas Flournoy captured planters' sentiments regarding economic success in an 1838 letter to his wife in Tennessee. Very pleased with his Pleasant Point, Caddo Parish, crop, he wrote, "As to making money, there can be no doubt about it. Nothing is wanting but a start and then a little perseverance and farming here is a sure road to a fortune."[70] In truth, it was the unceasing toil of Flournoy's enslaved Blacks in the cotton field that paved that road to fortune. The "little perseverance" that Flournoy referenced bore scant resemblance to the lives of the enslaved on regional plantations.

Crop success proved to be the determinative influence on every aspect of plantation life. It affected the quality of slave life in the coming year, the procurement of more land and more hands, and the purchase of clothing. It decided the quantity of foodstuffs that would be grown on the plantation, external purchases, and hiring out practices. The success or failure of a crop composed the total factor productivity—or the ratio of output value to a weighted average of inputs such as land, labor, and capital—of the plantation for that financial year.[71] Each year, the outcome of this ratio determined the movement of resources from output to inputs and whether slaveholders would dole out items or make choices that visibly altered enslaved life.

Planter preference for cottonseed that was "most healthy and of stoutest stamina" mirrored their laborer requirements and determined who was purchased through the internal slave trade.[72] The unvarnished nature of many holdings, the remote regional location at the edge of the cotton belt, and the profit-maximizing predilection of masters added up to a desire for hardy prime-age hands. The 1850 and 1860 censuses are unique because the brusquely named "Slave Schedules," documents that tallied enslaved people and estimated their ages, accompanied the survey. These schedules allow for the existence of each enslaved person to be acknowledged—often their only trace—and for a broad-stroke re-creation of the region's total slave population. The schedules indicate that the enslaved population steadily increased from 1830 to 1860, with a significant increase from 1850 to 1860. Decennial census numbers show that enslaved people totaled 38,919 in 1850 and jumped to 63,926 by 1860, an increase of 39 percent. During the first decade of settlement, the enslaved population grew 59 percent, then swelled 43 percent from 1840 to 1850. Aggregate data from 1830 to 1860 shows that the enslaved population increased by 86 percent during the antebellum period. These numbers highlight the visible Black majority, cultivated for maximum cotton extraction.

The slave schedules also outlined a population with an evenly balanced male-to-female ratio clustered around twenty to thirty-nine years of age. Younger Black people populated regional plantations, a trend that enabled slaveholders' rigorous extraction of labor and progeny from their property. Slaveholders only saw the market value of Blacks, as "flesh and blood value," to trade, purchase, or appraise; they did not recognize the self-worth or self-conception of Blacks.[73] The distinct lack of older Black enslaved between the ages of forty and forty-nine (and a minuscule population over fifty) underscores slaveholders' exploitative, extractive, and market-oriented focus. These older individuals were from the initial settlement generation, in the 1830s and 1840s, but as the plantation complex was embedded, slaveholders were not acquiring older enslaved people.

By 1860, the enslaved population had grown further and had changed its contours. A notable child population across the parishes substantiates planter preference for youth and concentration on brawn. Female Blacks were valued for their fecundity, and their auction value was linked with their fertility; enslaved women were called "breeders," and their children, when discussed prospectively by slaveholders, were called "increase," employing the same value terminology as livestock.[74] However, just as the prime age population dramatically increased, the number of enslaved people ages thirty to thirty-nine plummeted sharply. For example, the 1860 report indicated only 581 male enslaved and 309 female enslaved in Caddo in that age bracket, with the population of both genders starkly diminishing in older age brackets.

Census data and slave schedules indicate that regional slave population composition was overwhelmingly of prime age. The conscious choice to augment this category of hands through the slave trade is indicative of profit-minded targets of regional planters wanting a nimble, strong, and self-perpetuating population. Enslaved women on the slave market were sold as both laborers and producers of laborers, and slaveholders frequently chose to purchase Black women because they were already pricing in unborn children. Black women's reproductive value played a central role in the expansion of chattel slavery, and slaveholders viewed them as catalysts for economic growth. Forgetting completely the humanity of Black enslaved women, slaveholders and traders put high prices on female enslaved because of their reproductive promise.[75] Purchasing an enslaved woman meant a slaveholder gained more hands without an additional financial outlay, and it allowed for a swell in wealth that could be further leveraged or mortgaged to serve as collateral to buy appurtenant land, goods, and slaves.

The lure of fertile land and the need for enslaved labor to meet plantation requirements turned the interregional slave trade into a mainstay of commerce that represented nearly half a billion dollars in human property from 1820 to 1860. Between 60 and 70 percent of Black movement resulted from interregional trade and created regional spheres of slave exporting and importing.[76] Generally, the price of enslaved people correlated with cotton prices and planter demand, with traders shipping prime slaves to New Orleans's profitable market to satisfy consumer demands.[77] Slaveholders in the Red River region used the slave trade in response to their labor needs, contributing to the transference of enslaved people from the Upper and Lower South across the South in unprecedented numbers, dwarfing the numbers imported through the transatlantic trade.[78] Robert Gudmestad notes that the interstate slave trade, in combination with the migration of slaveholders across the Deep South, forcibly relocated approximately one million slaves from 1790 to 1860.[79]

The domestic slave trade firmly cemented regional commitment to slavery as an institution and labor supply. It was highly lucrative and was the largest economic sector in the South after plantation agriculture.[80] It also bound the southern states together in a mutual dependence that shattered Black families, cut Black familial ties, and transported isolated individuals to areas where they had no ties or community. Enslaved migrants to the Red River region often needed to rapidly acquire the agricultural skill set and endurance mandated by the cotton districts, particularly if they were transplanted from the Upper South. This adjustment to a ferocious workday and pace while processing the layered trauma of sale gave relocation to Louisiana a reputation within the enslaved community as a death sentence.

New Orleans and Natchez boomed as slave trading centers from the 1820s, with large dealers operating alongside small interstate traders and local slaveholders in the business of buying and selling human beings. Most Blacks brought to the New Orleans market were sold in the six months between November and April; in other words, they were acquired by new owners to plant or pick a cotton crop. Louisiana's redhibition laws were unique among the slaveholding states because they regulated the terms of warranty. Other states had commercial laws concerning the sale of slaves, but Louisiana's laws specifically protected the buyer of a slave from "defects"— whether physical, mental, or moral—and offered a sort of guarantee to purchasers concerning the quality and vitality of their human acquisition. The redhibition laws for human property were identical to those for the sale of animals.[81]

Slaveholders typically bought enslaved people immediately upon relocation to the Red River area or shortly after plantation establishment. Slaveholders whose prospects and fortunes expanded after arrival turned to the slave trade to populate growing plantations or additional holdings. Enslaved people might come from large firms operating slave markets in New Orleans and Natchez or from local slave traders. While larger trading operations often advertised in antebellum newspapers and broadsheets, local or rural traders relied on community connections and word of mouth to ascertain demand or potential purchasers. Since these dealings transpired verbally or within personal correspondence or interactions, there is less in the historic record to help reconstruct how large a role or how grand a scale local, small slave trading played in regions like the Red River basin.[82]

The diaries of Zack Howell, who moved to Caddo Parish from Chester, South Carolina, in the twilight years of the antebellum period, indicate that not only was there demand for a local trader but also slaveholders along the Red River incorporated slave trading to diversify their income portfolios. His entries detailing round-trips from the Red River back to South Carolina record sales and purchases and provide another lens through which to view the centrality of slaveholding to northwest Louisiana's white community.

Howell married Isabella Whitworth, whose mother and uncle had relocated from Alabama in 1839, and he resided at her plantation, Forest Park. In addition to operating the plantation, Howell trafficked enslaved people across the region, and his trading peaks coincided with crop preparation. This phase of the agronomic cycle was less demanding of his physical presence and was a popular business period with individual slave traders throughout the South. This entrepreneurial diversity was bolstered by seasonal specificity in trading and the complementary nature of slaveholding, slave trading, and cultivation—particularly for mid- to large-scale planters. Local traders like Howell solicited their own business and often had regular recruitment areas within a county or two of their homes. Proximity made these traders familiar with their customers, and local sales proved advantageous.[83] As Howell's correspondence reveals, slave trading was viewed by slaveholders as a part of the regional economy.[84] The bulk of white regional identity was grounded in slave ownership, domination of Blacks, and profitable cotton, and thus slaveholders concentrated on buying slaves to cultivate cotton—and cultivated cotton to purchase more slaves.[85]

September through February was considered prime slave-selling season. Like other traders, Howell returned to Louisiana in September 1860 to oversee the crop and to sell enslaved Blacks, without relying exclusively on the slave trade for his "principle or steady income." The first entry in his 1859 diary states that he "left home this day for Charleston to take charge of some negroes belonging to E. D. Golfraith," though his diary does not disclose whether these slaves were ultimately sold in Charleston. Howell brought a coffle of thirty-six slaves, consisting of twelve men, eighteen women, and six children, to Charleston for Golfraith, totaling $25,600 of slave property. Like other slave traders, Howell listed names and prices in a ledger, with little other information. His operations hinged on the success of self-funded slave-purchasing trips. Rarely did Howell bother to learn an enslaved person's name, further commodifying them through repeated names or nouns. In an 1859 entry, for instance, he lists "woman + five kids $4200" and is selling three Black women named Mary and two sets of enslaved women named Nancy and Martha.[86]

Howell traveled extensively with the enslaved people he traded. He left for Texas with slaves on November 8, 1859, and arrived home after four months, on March 8, 1860, before leaving "for the west to sale negroes," on April 10, 1860.[87] He traversed the country again to sell Jane, an enslaved woman, in Charleston on August 22, 1860, where he "expect[ed] to buy one and then leave for Arkansas." Howell sold Jane to A. G. Cary, a Desha County, Arkansas, planter, on September 26, 1860, for $1,350, having purchased her a month earlier for $955. Howell recouped his expenses and often turned a profit with interstate slave sales. Interestingly, on the same day that Howell sold Jane, he also hired her out for fifty cents per day to one Mr. Kay of Monticello, Arkansas. This is emblematic of small and midholding, market-centric enslavers who used every opportunity to make money. He wrote, "She worked one day and I sold her for $1350."[88]

Throughout 1860, Howell trafficked enslaved people in and out of the Red River region, importing groups ranging in size from fourteen to twenty-four. He sold $27,925 of human property—or twenty-four individuals—to various slaveholders in southwest Arkansas. Human tradesmen like Howell filled a void in the region's slave-driven economy by providing an essential local service that enabled smallholding slaveholders, both male and female, to buy and sell their chattel with relative ease and with less expenditure, within the immediate locale. Howell's diary indicates that he catered regularly to slaveholders in the Red River region—extending into Arkansas and westward into Texas.[89]

Howell's business operations suited the rapidly growing needs of Red River slaveholders. He provided a regular supply of enslaved people and responded swiftly to the flexible market of opportunities prevalent in northwest Louisiana. His diary, like the lists that enumerated enslaved people on Red River plantations, reduced enslaved Blacks to saleable commodities. The bulk of his diary is filled with lists titled "cost of the following negroes," and his mercantile language is proof positive that enslaved African Americans were viewed only as tradable commodities, people with a price.

Howell was not the only itinerant regional slave trader. Some slaveholders reinvested wealth or purchased slaves on credit from major New Orleans operators to expand plantation size and production capabilities. John Hutchinson's sons, Robert and William, purchased $10,950 worth of bondspeople—nine slaves in total—from a trader in New Orleans in 1852. The slaves purchased included six males—ages 24, 18, and 15, and three 19-year-olds—and three females, ages 17, 18, and 20. The Hutchinsons purchased prime-age slaves, including a blacksmith, to increase output on their plantations. The brothers added acreage and enslaved people to their main plantation, Rocky Mount Place, and cleared new land in south Caddo Parish for a small cotton crop. They purchased this land, which would become William's main plantation, in June 1852, paying $11,324.88 for 944 acres.[90]

Likewise, William Powell invested in his future by purchasing four slaves on May 5, 1843. Powell purchased outright a slave family of five, consisting of parents, about thirty-five years old, and three young children, for $1,500. Powell purchased five young male hands from a Maryland trader two years later for $3,875.[91] Powell's receipts show that he bought slaves approximately every two years until 1852, when he made successive yearly purchases. Powell favored purchasing complete families, which slaveholders did not always prioritize. This may have occurred out of convenience, a desire to keep fertile enslaved couples together, or because his local traders delivered according to his preferences.[92] The Hutchinson brothers and Powell expanded their slave populations as they expanded their holdings. These purchasing habits show that Red River slaveholders acquired their chattel in diverse ways, from local agents or large slave markets, and always in response to labor needs.

— — —

Historian Dale Tomich writes that slavery represented a "generalized form of commodity production effected through specific relations of domination."[93] Enslaved people in the Red River area were instruments of production—the engine and fuel that drove cotton plantations and cotton entrenchment. Throughout the antebellum period, planters shaped their enslaved populations to fulfill dual demands for more cotton and for nimble, quick-fingered laborers. When operations expanded, slaveholders purchased land and additional slaves. An efficient prime hand could clear approximately one-eighth of an acre per day, and in four months they would clear the twelve acres they would then cultivate as a full hand.[94] Regional planters were devoid of paternalism and reactive to production demand, and this type of market awareness enabled them to maintain lean expenditure but effective work crews, drawing upon the slave markets to build out or reduce their property portfolio as required.

The silence from slaveholders about enslaved people and the scarcity of first-person African American recollections from this region speaks volumes about whites' disregard for Black personhood. Slaveholders and their families left behind documentation on the importance and centrality of successful cotton crops to their livelihood but little concerning their daily lives, and even less about their slaves. Similar to eastern and Piedmont North Carolina planters, there was no evidence of paternalism, and sources remain free of paternalistic language or pretext. Instead, slavery was cold and detached, and slaves were distilled into numbers. Making the land productive was the central focus, and planters used their commitment to slavery as an economic and racial system to reduce slaves to simplified objects that could maximize profit. As the demographic data indicate, many regional slaveholders resided on small to midsize holdings, leaving little time to record plantation activities. It is significant that Red River slaveholders exhibited little interest in the lives of the humans they enslaved; they were not curious about the people who labored to generate wealth and whose bodies were repositories of personal wealth.

The demographic records from the 1850 and 1860 slave schedules demonstrate that the enslaved population in the Red River region remained exceptionally young throughout the antebellum period. The minuscule numbers of elderly Blacks recorded are likely from the first waves of settlement and represent the survivors of harsh regional enslavement. Older and elderly enslaved people occupied an interesting position in a plantation's social structure. Among their fellow enslaved, they were overwhelmingly treated with respect and represented a living link with the past, while slaveholders viewed elderly enslaved negatively, as burdensome and less productive field-workers. Older enslaved people, still capable cotton pickers, labored in the fields, as Abram did alongside Solomon Northup on Epps's plantation south of Alexandria. Though sparse information remains in plantation ledgers about the work of elderly Black women, they were often responsible for child care for both the slaveholder's children and enslaved children, alongside cooking and producing clothing for the enslaved.[95] Ellison Adger, whose family settled in Bossier in 1846, wrote about Ma Jane in his memoirs, primarily regarding her care for the Adger children. Allegedly 102 at the time of her death, Ma Jane's life was distilled into a few lines centered on her labor in the fields in her prime and her service rearing five generations of Adgers.[96]

The two surviving plantation journals for this region are for Pre Aux Cleres and Willow Point plantations. These record-keepers listed only enslaved people's names and the corresponding amount of cotton picked, leaving out ages, family connections, and personal descriptors. We know their productivity in the field but nothing to sketch a biography. The 1859 journal at Willow Point noted that of the estate's seventy-four enslaved, only five people were over forty-five, with the eldest only age fifty-six. Only two people over forty-five were female, and the following year, Veronique, the eldest Black woman, was no longer listed in the plantation ledger.[97] There is no notation of Veronique's death; she, like many other Blacks, slips off the page abruptly, leaving behind only a record of cotton picked.

Minimal ledger details coupled with a lack of parish-level detail within the slave schedules presents a hurdle to highlighting the nuanced composition of enslaved populations, including physical and mental disabilities that affected enslaved Blacks in the Red River region.[98] Blindness was the most commonly noted affliction, though numerous debilities affected the enslaved community. The absence of reported disabilities may derive from a lack of interest by census takers, deliberate resale of debilitated enslaved people elsewhere, or the fact that not all disabilities present as a physical impairment that would inhibit contribution to labor productivity.[99]

What we can deduce from extant records for the enslaved population remains heavily shaped by morbidity and mortality rates. Numerous diseases plagued the health of all southerners, and infectious epidemics significantly contributed to mortality rates.[100] Both Blacks and whites residing in humid, low-lying, swampy regions like Louisiana perpetually feared yellow fever and malaria.[101] Nineteenth-century people lived with many forms of "the fever," but most Americans saw epidemic yellow fever as entirely southern. Malaria was often lumped together with yellow fever and typhus under the vague rubric of "remittent" fevers. Hubbard Bosley of Telegram plantation in Bossier received a letter from a friend in Pleasant Hill, near Shreveport, describing the dreaded "Louisiana chills" that had rendered him and his sister "dangerously sick" for two weeks.[102]

This lack of distinction and treatment protocols ensured high fatality rates throughout the South and meant that immunity was highly coveted.[103] Those who made it through a yellow fever epidemic or survived a bout of the disease were "seasoned." Slaveholders prized immunity, whether acquired or from genetic predisposition. Many enslaved people, particularly those of West African origin, enjoyed a degree of genetic immunity to malaria because of a lack of Duffy antigens. Additional protection might come from two genetic hemoglobin conditions: sickle-cell disease and sickle-cell trait. People with the disease usually died young, but those with sickle-cell trait lived normal lives, with added protection against malaria, and passed the sickling gene to their children. Slaveholders, ignorant of this genetic factor, assumed that Blacks were predisposed to harsh laboring and used this as further justification for the suitability of Black people to plantation labor in hot, environmentally challenging, and disease-prone regions.

Alongside the health hazards presented by the Louisiana climate, enslaved people suffered from a high incidence of tetanus, rheumatism, pneumonia, cholera, and eye complaints, including partial and total blindness. Additionally, poor diet triggered anemia and calcium, magnesium, and/or iron deficiencies. Cholera had hit George Mason Graham's Tyrone plantation in 1833—when the floor of his cabin was covered with the pallets of sick enslaved—and again in 1849, when he lamented the lack of quarantine in nearby Alexandria. Mary Sibley lived at Mount Elon plantation in Alexandria and corresponded regularly with her daughter, whose plantation was outside Shreveport. In May 1855, cholera broke out near Mount Elon "among the lower class, and negroes badly fed." Framing the outbreak in terms of race and class, she wrote that the town's cisterns were entirely exhausted, forcing inhabitants to pay "two dollars a barrel for water from across the river." Dr. Sullivan, a nearby neighbor, "lost three negroes with cholera," all of whom "drink river waters."[104]

Slaveholders in this region, like many of their southern counterparts, noticed enslaved health only when it impacted plantation productivity.[105] Just as storms rolled in, so too did illness and death. However, these slaveholders only found aberrant events, widespread illness, or the death of productive enslaved people noteworthy, expunging everyday health and medical concerns from the record. Mary Sibley noted the cholera outbreak precisely because it impacted daily plantation life and impinged on required labor at affected plantations. Sibley and her slaveholding contemporaries reduced enslaved illness and death to productivity impediments. Economic impact overshadowed human loss.

Enslaved women and men were subjected to further trauma and exploitation when it came to matters of sex, procreation, and marriage. Black women were especially exploited, assaulted, and violated by slaveholders, who viewed their fertility as a surefire path to economic growth, a larger workforce, and further profit. This is why, as indicated earlier, Black women's bodies were valued highly within the slave trade and at valuations, and it underscores why many slaveholders frequently purchased women of childbearing age. Enslaved women's bodies were not only under attack for procreation; they experienced astonishing levels of sexual assault and rape from male slaveholders and white family members. White men of all ages sexually abused, raped, and coerced sexual relationships with Black women. Black women were denied sexual virtue and were viewed as hypersexual by whites, a convenient construct that permitted white men to sexually assault Black women.

Enslaved women were thus property that reproduced, which meant a high involvement of white men in bondwomen's sexual lives, while these women were left with limited control over their bodies. The latter greatly affected the choices Black women could make about relationships and familial life.[106] Like slaveholders throughout the South, Red River enslavers made themselves decision-makers in Black procreation, using practices and terminology that mirrored animal husbandry—like *breeding, buck,* and *stock*—to determine which women and men had forced sanctioned sexual relationships.[107] The connection between sex and profitability for slaveholders is palpable, as is the negation of Black sexual autonomy, desire, and personhood.

For the enslaved community, the institutions of marriage and family were impacted by forced relationships and breeding-centered pairings, a failure to recognize enslaved marriages, and the dismantling of families. Stress, marital strife, and disharmony were all present within the Black family. The fact that slaveholders controlled the destiny of family units, overwhelmingly selected spouses, denied Black couples marital rights, broke families apart, and determined visitation for spouses abroad removed autonomy within these relationships. Enslaved people had to fight for a semblance of normalcy in their committed intimate relationships, including but not limited to those defined as slave marriages. The attitude of slaveholders and white society that Black marriages were ephemeral gravely affected the meaning Blacks themselves ascribed to these relationships.[108] Black men, attuned to this lack of familial authority, also strove to fulfill the contemporary southern vision of manhood, and finding this circumscribed, they at times resorted to violent behavior to fill the void.[109]

Like other holdings with a young population, Willow Point plantation had eighteen women of childbearing age in 1859. There were ten children ages five and under, seven children between the ages of six and ten, and four adolescents ages eleven to fifteen. The number of children in 1859 had grown from ten (no discernment made with regard to age) in 1856.[110] Enslaved children nevertheless died at high rates from "nine-day fits" (neonatal tetanus) and had fatal difficulties with teething. Worms, diphtheria, and whooping cough also killed many infants and contributed to child morbidity regionally. The nutritional deficiencies of enslaved mothers affected their children. Slaveholders' complete disregard for prenatal care, an intensive work pace throughout pregnancy, and nutritional deficiencies in diet combined to make Sudden Infant Death Syndrome more prevalent among enslaved babies and likely added to the number of stillborn births. Children were nutritionally deficient when weaned and then were introduced to a diet even higher in carbohydrates and lower in protein than that of Black adults, resulting in a very anemic and mineral-deficient child population. Black children experienced growth depression and recovery, and this pattern suggests that most planters limited nutritional intake.[111]

The single-minded concentration on cotton cultivation had long-term adverse effects on nutrition and hobbled an internal enslaved economy. Without the framework to supplement Black diets—and perhaps slaveholders' diets as well—most enslaved people consumed a diet severely lacking in vitamins and minerals. The diet of the region's slaveholders, particularly small and midsize slaveholders during early settlement, was likely more restricted and coarser than in many gentrified plantation sections of the Mississippi Valley. However, the protein sources, diversity and quantity of foods, and preparation styles utilized by slaveholders were better than those available to the enslaved, especially as the region became a settled plantation area. Fatty cuts of meat paired with corn and the occasional molasses ration created a high caloric diet for enslaved people, but one deficient in protein, vitamins C and D, essential amino acids, calcium, and iron.[112] The Louisiana slave codes only required that slaveholders give enslaved people one barrel of Indian corn, or its equivalent, per month. In marked contrast, an 1814 law required white prisoners be given a per diem allowance of "one pound of beef or three-quarters of a pound of pork, one pound of vegetables, one pound of potatoes or a comparable portion of rice, four quarts of vinegar, and a small salt allowance."[113]

In contrast to other slaveholding areas, little evidence indicates that enslaved people in this region supplemented their diet with vegetables grown on personal garden plots or with fish and game. The 1854 Willow Point plantation journal contains scattered mentions of slave gardens but no further record of their proficiency or impact. Slaveholders believed that salt pork was the best meat for the enslaved, and as on Willow Point plantation, they attributed to it nourishing properties that made it the "fuel upon which the efficiency of labor depended."[114] Slaveholders raised corn alongside cotton, due to corn's wide availability and low production costs. Planters also planted field peas, cowpeas, and beans among the corn, which would have provided additional nutrition for the enslaved.[115] This nutritionally inadequate diet, coupled with quantities disparate to the labor expended, led to high rates of infections and contributed to higher morbidity and mortality rates in the enslaved community.[116]

Willow Point's plantation journal and Northup's book both recorded weekly rations. Northup received 3.5 pounds of bacon and a peck of corn (equivalent to two gallons, or eight dry quarts). Master Epps fed his hogs on shelled corn but threw corn to his slaves by the ear. The ten children at Willow Point collectively received five pecks, while each full hand got a peck of corn per week; the overseer received four pecks per week.[117] This average allowance of meat and corn was the accepted standard among southern slaveholders, who did not adjust the allowance in accordance with extended work hours or heat during peak cultivation and picking periods.[118]

Children ages nine and under were perilously exposed to a host of mortal infections. Black children died from convulsions, teething, tetanus, lockjaw, suffocation, and worms at more than four times the rate of white children.[119] Rickets posed a significant problem and remained a persistent issue for adult women, who suffered from deformed and small pelvises. In addition to health issues stemming from pregnancy, pregnant women toiled without alteration in type or reduction in workload. Approximately 80 percent of Black women were field laborers, with the highest numbers of stillbirths occurring in November or December. This is consistent with continued hard work and an overall net nutritional deprivation during the preparation and planting season.[120] In southern locations that promoted population growth, nursing women received extra rations to supplement their poor diet; sometimes they might feign illness to gain a respite from or alter the nature of their work.[121] In the Red River region, pre- and postnatal accommodations for work and diet were conspicuous by their absence. Feigning illness, often noted with irritation by planters in other regions, does not appear from the historical record to have been an oft-used method in this region, and pregnant or nursing women labored in the field.

Young enslaved children might have been spared fieldwork, as was Polly Mason on her owner's Alexandria plantation. Polly carried out tasks such as bringing water and picking weeds. However, once they were old enough to pick cotton, children like Polly entered the fields—a clear departure from childhood.[122] Generally, young Blacks tended to do the same work as their parents and continued this their whole life.[123] Unlike on eastern seaboard plantations or in more gentrified portions of the Deep South, there is no evidence to support work differentiation in the Red River region. On most regional estates, enslaved people worked without particular distinctions, though there were some slaves with specialized skill sets. Willow Point's 1854 plantation book lists twenty-seven field-workers, five children, a blacksmith, a hog minder, a carpenter, a teamster, a cook, a ferryman, and two gin drivers.[124] However, the plantation manager did not elucidate whether specialized laborers also worked the cotton fields, and with no similarly detailed list for the prior or following years, no firm conclusion can be made about rigid distinctions in specialization. Since few enslaved people worked solely in the house and these distinctions existed only on the largest regional plantations, it is likely that every enslaved person at Willow Point picked cotton during peak harvest.

Red River slaveholders put little premium on additional skills and adopted gang labor as the preferred method of organizing production.[125] Though Henry Marshall's Land's End, Henry Marston's Ashland, and Willow Point utilized overseers, there is scant documentation regarding the use of Black drivers within the gang labor structure on Red River holdings. Drivers were popular enforcers of white domination and control in other sections of the South, and some Blacks held this role. Solomon Northup, for example, was made a driver during his enslavement, while the Willow Point's plantation book lists a Black overseer and driver in 1854. The ledger provides no further information about this role or its duration at the plantation.[126] Nevertheless, overseers dragooned enslaved labor, even if the relatively modest size of operations in northern Louisiana precluded regular employment of drivers.

Enslaved people toiled in sprawling cotton fields from sunup to sundown, with the rhythm of their work punctuated by short meal breaks and the slicing sounds of the overseer's whip. Nature dictated the workday structure and length, with a shortened day during the winter cultivation period and markedly longer hours on summer days. Planters eagerly adopted the clock as a useful regulatory and disciplinary device because clocks satisfied planters' drive for both profit and discipline. Clocks were used to regulate work times and the duration of breaks, and to time work rates.[127] This mechanized management added an additional sound to the aural landscape. Though slaveholders often imagined and recollected antebellum life as one of quietude and singing slaves, plantation life was ordered by clocks, bells, whips, and horns.[128]

Charley Williams, enslaved in the Red River region, remembered the regimentation and cacophony of noise that accompanied each workday, which began before daybreak. Even before the bells rang out, slaves were rushing to prepare victuals. Bells at nearby plantations could be heard on windy mornings, but "old Master's old ram horn wid a long toot and den some short toots" daily prefaced the overseer "hollering right and left" down the row of cabins. The bells and horns signaled the choreography of the plantation routine as Williams recalled "bells and horns! Bells for dis and horns for dat! All we knowed was go and come by de bells and horns!" Bells and horns were present on the Epps plantation as well. Northup remembered that the horn was blown an hour before daylight, and the offense of tardiness was "invariably followed by a flogging."[129]

Slaves roused from their slumber by the morning bells awoke in rudimentary wooden shacks. These living quarters were generally uniform in construction throughout the South, with the main variation being their form as a single or double cabin, though there is no indication which was more popular in the Red River region. However, double cabins, with their shared chimney and built-in front roof overhang, would probably have been more common on larger holdings and a more likely edifice on those plantations where some of the enslaved worked in the big house. In the Natchitoches area, the Creole cottage architecture prevailed, but there is little evidence that similar structures existed along the upper Red River. Overwhelmingly, enslaved people lived in single cabins, approximately sixteen feet by twenty feet, of paltry wood construction. Planters erected such single-room dwellings some distance from the slaveholder's home.[130]

Bill Homer, enslaved near Shreveport, remembered that his former plantation had "fifty one-room cabins and dey was ten in a row and dere was five rows." He noted that the dwellings were "built of logs and had dirt floors" and the window was a hole in the wall. A stone fireplace provided a heat source and cooking area.[131] The overseer at Willow Point plantation was fastidious about neatness in the quarters and held Sunday inspections. Dwellings not meeting his expectations resulted in punishment for the inhabitants.[132] Elsewhere, cabins for the enslaved were swiftly assembled, with little thought given for their inhabitants. For example, Northup stated that his cabin was constructed of logs but lacked the window hole present in Homer's cabin, though the gaping crevices between the logs admitted both light and rain. Northup's floorless cabin possessed a "rude door" on wooden hinges and was furnished with a narrow plank bed, a stick of wood for a pillow, and a coarse blanket.[133] These crude cabins provided little respite or comfort for the beleaguered enslaved people who resided in the hastily constructed structures.

For some enslaved people, fieldwork made up most but not all of their labors. Most plantations tasked one male with the job of ginner, which became their full-time chore once picking was in full swing. York served as ginner at Willow Point, alongside Morer, the driver. At Pre Aux Cleres, Jeff was ginner and Bazell was wagoner. While ginners pressed bales, all other people picked cotton, as was the case during the 1856 harvest at Marston's Ashland plantation.[134] Occasionally, greater task delineation and more complex structures emerged on larger regional estates like Willow Point. In addition to York and Morer, Harkins worked as a teamster and Hardy served as carpenter and corn minder. Francoise was both cook and gardener in addition to her fieldwork, while Cherry—subsequently hired out in 1859—doubled as house servant. Henry and Charlotte cared for the plantation livestock, feeding the hogs and milking the cows at early light and at the close of the day in addition to their field duties. During the cultivation period, many women and children were also sent into the house to perform household chores, including spinning, food preservation, and sewing. Other laborers, usually male, chopped wood, repaired fences, and undertook building maintenance, although the plantation's 1859 journal notes that females had been reinforcing the irrigation structures by "leeving basin bayou" from mid-February through early March.[135] Come harvest, most enslaved people on regional plantations of all sizes were in the fields picking "white gold."

The historic record is silent regarding the type of community the Red River area's enslaved people created or the contours and interactions of that private world. From the white vantage point, the enslaved were interchangeable laboring commodities. Indeed, as Olmsted noted during his visit to the Calhoun plantation at the site of present-day Colfax, "each laborer is such an inconsiderable unit in the mass of laborers, that he may even not be known by name, or personally recognizable by his master."[136] The repetition of names and use of terse descriptors to differentiate among individuals underscores this interchangeable, faceless aspect of slave identity from the planter perspective. Enslaved people were distilled into numbers and made invisible, so there was no need to deliberate on names.

There is scant oral or written testimony from the Red River enslaved regarding their established naming practices. While names bestowed upon children in other plantation districts were chosen with roots in the developing Afro-American culture, regional plantation journals indicate that most children were merely listed as "infants," a demarcation sometimes made alongside the mother's name.[137] As evidenced earlier by Zack Howell, local slave traders listed mothers and small children only as saleable units.[138] In this lonely plantation world, Blacks carried out their lives in a nameless and brutally controlled system.

Like Solomon Northup, who was known as "Platt" throughout his twelve-year enslavement in Natchitoches Parish, other slaves brought to the region through purchase were likely given new identities upon arrival. Enslaved people's original identities and personalities were immaterial to slaveholders.[139] Available regional records indicate that names were often recycled and bestowed upon multiple individuals. The repetition of names, frequently applied childlike diminutives, or references to geography or past statesmen racially marked and demeaned enslaved individuals. At Willow Point, individuals with duplicate names were distinguished by using their associated numbers. Henry #1 and Henry #2, for instance, worked alongside Johns 1, 2, and 3; Joe #1 and Joe #2 toiled next to Eliza 1 and Eliza 2. Two women, also named Eliza, enslaved at Pre Aux Cleres, were called Eliza Georgia—indicative of where she was brought from—and Eliza Strader—descriptive of a past owner. Planters George Marshall and William Hutchinson used descriptive nouns to differentiate. Marshall's Crescent plantation was home to Big Joe, Little Joe, Big John, John, Washington, and Big Washington. Hutchinson's Caspiana plantation housed Washington, Wash, Big Gunie, Little Gunie, Big Bill, Little Bill, Big Sam, Little Sam, Big Henry, and Little Henry. At Henry Marshall's Land's End plantation, most monikers were repeated at least twice, but some as many as four times.

The multiplicity of names reduced individuals and was another manifestation of the replaceable, brutal, and bleak nature of enslavement. Sometimes slaveholders selected objects, places, or occupations as monikers, calling their slaves by a wide variety of appellations, including Binky, Tuba, Brass, March, Unity, Buff, Monday, and Handy at Land's End plantation; Shepherd, Past Angel, Farmer, and Florida at Crescent plantation; Hasty, Barbary, Lettuce, and Green at Caspiana; and Easter at Willow Point.[140] Some of these names, such as Tuba and Buff, might be adapted from older Afro-American names. However, other names seem an arbitrary selection and a byproduct of a world in which enslaved people were seen as brutish animals or childlike appendages, listed alongside animals and furniture in household inventories, and completely divorced culturally and racially from whites.[141] One Alexandria mistress exposed her racially dismissive views in an 1851 letter, writing that Lucinda was "a perfect curiosity," fit for a circus, and was so comical that "if barnum would buy Lucinda and exhibit her he would make a fortune."[142]

At Willow Point, skin tone was used to differentiate between two of three women named Susan. They were known as Susan (Black), Susan (Yellow), and Susan (Stallings); the latter descriptor was likely that of a former owner.[143] Terminology that indicated an enslaved person's physical appearance applied to prime-age hands of both genders but was particularly prevalent when describing the appearance of young, attractive Black women.[144] These descriptors were used in the internal slave trade and in common parlance. The most popular term was *fancy,* and it served as an umbrella term to indicate a woman's appeal and desirability to white men looking to commodify, in more than one sense, a female house slave.[145] Some slaveholders and traders referred to these women as "custom." This label, with its eerie air of specificity, appeared on slave sale receipts such as that for the 1859 sale of "a custom negro girl—mulatress—named Jenny aged about 12 years," to a Bossier Parish slaveholder.[146]

When not using skin tones to individualize enslaved people, Red River slaveholders likened their chattel to livestock. Eliza Powell, wife of William

Powell and mistress at Mount Flat plantation, drew up her will in 1860. In one section, she set out to delineate which slaves were the property of her deceased daughter and which had always been her own property. Five slaves are listed by name, then by complexion, and lastly by value. When describing Sarah, age fifteen, Powell estimates she is "the value of a fine horse, say two hundred and fifty dollars."[147] Human property was conflated with animal property in the minds of the Red River region's slaveholders. Formerly enslaved abolitionist Frederick Douglass recalled the degrading process of being valued alongside his enslaver's livestock. He recalled "horses and men, cattle and women, pigs and children, all holding the same rank in the scale of being," and that people were subjected to "the same narrow examination" as livestock. For Douglass, and no doubt for Sarah, this crude racial reductionism highlighted the nameless, interchangeable tenor of this rough-hewn enslavement.[148]

Slaveholders viewed enslaved people as producers and sources of income, so if it was advantageous, they were hired out. Regional enslavement was a highly controlled, insular system, but these pragmatic slaveholders were flexible when it came to hiring out or moving the enslaved to maximize assets and realize income.[149] Hiring out was a practice whereby a slaveholder retained ownership but for multiple reasons—usually financial—hired an enslaved person to labor for another person. This arrangement was popular in the Red River region because it maximized opportunity for profit and ensured complete productivity of enslaved populations. Various arrangements abounded, but common practice involved the hirer paying a set fee plus maintenance, which included shelter and food, to the slaveholder. For periods of longer hire, such as a year, a set of clothing and shoes was normally provided. For example, the agreement between Benjamin Cuny and J. B. Knapp for Ann's yearlong hire stipulated that Knapp provide Ann with two suits of summer clothes and one for winter.[150] Though hiring out was common in the urban South, it retained broad popularity because of labor dynamics. Some slaveholders needed to augment ranks for projects or discrete time frames, such as harvest or picking, while others desired enslaved labor but lacked the monetary means for purchase. Regional slaveholders with larger populations did not want to lose money on their chattel, and at a minimum wished to avoid incurring debt in their maintenance. Hiring out safeguarded against loss, even during a productive year.

Henry Marston hired out numerous enslaved people throughout 1857.

He leased out four men to R. H. Draughton on varied contracts. His slaves Bill and George were hired out together for June, each at sixteen dollars per month. He also hired out Jim for June at the same rate. Additionally, he hired out Brown Joe from April until June 16 at a cost of forty-eight dollars, and the infantilized "Boy Dangerfield" from April 1 until July 1 at a fee of sixteen dollars a month. Within three months, Marston had made ninety-six dollars from the labor of four enslaved people from Ashland, his Red River holding. Draughton again hired a Marston slave in July.[151]

Hiring out meant reliable additional money could be made. Marston began 1857 by hiring out "Boy Ben" for the month at twenty dollars, although Boy Ben was brought back to Ashland six days earlier than originally agreed. Then Marston hired out Nat for three months and Charity for two, and garnered ninety-five dollars for their rentals. Draughton had commenced the year by hiring "Boy Bill" for a full year at $185 and a barrel of potatoes. Marston also hired out Moses at a fee of twenty dollars for October and leased out George from October for a three-month contract at the same monthly cost.[152] Charles Mathews had to wait on the purchase of a slave because that slave was already hired out for a three-week period.[153] In 1844, Henry Marshall's friend, P. M. Butler, wrote with concerns about his Caddo Parish plantation. There had been flooding in the vicinity and a nervous Butler was away in South Carolina. He asked Marshall to advise his overseer and to "hire out the hands to the best advantage" to curb the financial impact.[154]

Mary Sibley reflected matter-of-factly on slave rentals. She wrote to her daughter that hiring out her enslaved females in Alexandria kept them from idleness. She repeatedly hired out Chaney since "she can get a plenty of work in town." In Sibley's estimation, her plantation's 1855 crop was subpar, and "if it does not rain" shortly, "three or four of my negroes down next week" would get hired out.[155] In Sibley's case, renting out enslaved women in local towns was another method utilized to maximize assets or make ends meet. Chaney, who was both field hand and cook at Willow Point, was again hired out in 1859, for $150 per annum.[156] Steamboat captains who transported cotton to market also hired enslaved labor. The region's integration into the wider market economy ensured that multiple outlets were available to slaveholders with extra laborers who desired additional profit from their chattel or to deploy them to advantage when plantation operations slowed.

— — —

Violence permeated the field and the plantation household. Persuasive works by Thavolia Glymph and Stephanie Jones-Rogers expose the prevalence of extreme brutality within the household domain, detailing mistresses' familiarity with violence and their confidence in demonstrating their control as enslavers. White slaveholding women used violence to reinforce power structures. For women and men alike, violence was integral in shaping their identity as slaveholders.[157] It was used in the fields to secure "efficient use of labor" from enslaved persons, who were viewed by slaveholders as "ignorant and indolent vicious negroes." Slavery's rigid power structure, in tandem with the southern obsession with honor and individual defense, bred a dependence on violence and its excessive application.[158] Violence rested at the crux of the interactions among white southern men as well as between slaveholders and the enslaved. In the latter relationship, subjugation solidified the conventional use of violence to enforce racial stratification and control.

The comfort and ease that antebellum and postbellum southern whites exhibited in deploying violence was part of a long tradition of violent control, traced back to the cruel treatment of white indentured servants—many of whom became overseers after the sudden end of indentured servitude—and of enslaved Black people in the British colonies. Men who served in Britain's standing armies would not have found plantation violence unusual or shockingly harsh. Planters were violent people and employed more violent underlings to manage integrated plantations. This desensitization toward and normalization of gruesome acts of bodily torment was integral to a process of learning to use a particular kind of violence to control African Americans in slavery and in freedom.[159] African American bondage in the South, like African bondage in British America, possessed the crucial features of being both heritable and perpetual. These features secured the plantation economy and simultaneously articulated discrete, white-only opportunities and privileges.[160]

Violence, and especially race-based violence, was a taught behavior.[161] Men and women learned the violent contours of the regional tenor from a young age. Slaveholding parents watched with approval as their children played at being overseers or doled out punishment—which often was physically inflicted by the youth.[162] Northup recollected two poignant examples of how inflicting and carrying out violence was taught to white children. When Patsey was tied facedown to four stakes and whipped until she passed out and blood "flowed down her sides and dropped upon the ground," Mistress Epps and her children stood on the piazza, watching with "heartless satisfaction." Master Epps encouraged his twelve-year-old son to "play the overseer" and took pride as the child called Old Abraham "to account . . . [and] sentence[d] him to a certain number of lashes," then allowed his son to whip the enslaved "without discrimination."[163]

Violence inflicted on Blacks by whites was assumed, customary, and frequent. Northup, tied to a high tree and bound for a whole day when his cotton picking pace lagged in the field, stated that the crack of the lash could be "heard from dark till bed time" on the region's plantations.[164] The Red River region was an aggressive, brutal, crushing place to be enslaved, and violence—especially meted out to Blacks—was so commonplace that it was rarely considered noteworthy. Thus, letters frequently discussed cotton prospects but not the welfare or punishments inflicted on Black laborers cultivating the crop. White settlers, in describing the region to kin, noted the ferocious tenor of daily life. One woman wrote to her sister that white inhabitants of Alexandria were "bad enough for <u>anything</u>," while everyone "goes armed" and altercations were "met with certain death." When Friedrich Gërstacker passed through Shreveport, he likewise described the rough, vitriolic city as a locale in which one was likely to receive "a knife wound or pistol bullet."[165]

In most instances, monstrous punishment did not result from a large transgression or a significant decrease in picking amount. On some holdings, drivers cracked their whips while hurling insults. Other slaveholders and overseers maintained an aura of calm composure while whipping slaves, while some required that other slaves mete out punishments as masters watched.[166] Indeed, Olmsted remarked in his journals on the frequent and severe punishments in the region. Olmsted never learned of any set rules for punishment. It seemed overseers and drivers "used the whip whenever they deemed there was an occasion." Whenever an instance arose, the severity and manner of punishment remained at the discretion of the overseer or driver. Violence permeated Red River slavery and served as the remedy for "all wrong-doing, whether of indolence or indiscretion." Brutality proved so prevalent that one Red River overseer declared to Olmsted, "I wouldn't mind killing a negro more than I would a dog."[167] This violent penchant and proclivity was deeply ingrained regionwide, and it would influence the extent of racialized violence throughout the nineteenth century.

The Louisiana slave codes detailed the punishment for numerous infractions, including thirty-nine lashes for trespassing, twenty-five lashes for riding a horse without permission, and twenty lashes for traveling without a pass. The codes also included punishments for anyone who taught enslaved people to write (twelve months in jail); a sentence of hard labor, life imprisonment, or death for publishing items to "produce discontent"; and fixed rewards for capturing runaways. Despite the codes' stipulations for certain slave transgressions, owners were largely free to deal with their property how they liked. Slaveholders had unfettered control and rights over the enslaved—an aspect upheld by individual states—and often pressed bondspeople into the capture of fugitive slaves, forcing enslaved people into the unenviable quandary of obeying the enslaver and maintaining community cohesion while betraying one of their brethren.[168]

Despite a lack of regulation of severity or form of punishment, the number of lashes was usually exponentially higher the more severe the transgression. For example, Northup recalled that twenty-five lashes were "a mere brush," inflicted when a piece of boll or a dry leaf was found in the cotton; fifty served as the ordinary penalty, while one hundred lashes was a severe punishment used for the "serious offence of standing idle in the field." The most severe punishments, infrequently administered by slaveholders interested in keeping everyone vigorously employed in the field, included between 150 and 200 lashes.[169] Pregnancy did not check the frequency or severity of whipping. Instead, an overseer or slaveholder who wanted to whip a pregnant woman had a hole dug "an' made her lay acrost in an' her han's and foots were tied."[170] This punishment was employed even during the late stages of pregnancy, with no easement in ferocity, since slaveholders claimed that burying the belly protected the fetus.

Whipping remained the preferred day-to-day punishment method, though there was a wide range of possible violent acts at the slaveholder's disposal. A penchant for whipping arose because the lash did not generally lead to an extended loss of labor time. The representative power of the whip transformed the threat of whipping from just the violence itself to an internalized power tool to discipline the flesh.[171] Throughout the South, but particularly in profit-focused regions like the Red River region, productivity outputs were exceptionally important, and punishment was aimed at driving maximum performance with minimal loss of labor in the fields. In the main, masters desired painful and brutal punishments with minimal damage to the functionality of their human capital.[172] The scattered notations of punishments in the 1859 Willow Point journal are in keeping with that assertion.

Daily whippings formed the mainstay of plantation management as standard daily picking rates jumped to 150 pounds by the 1830s, and up to nearly 300 pounds in the 1850s.[173] Northup's final enslaver, Edwin Epps, used the lash regularly and often appeared in the field without warning and began whipping. At the close of daily picking, the cotton would be weighed, a procedure that caused "fear and trembling" in every approach to the gin house. If too little cotton had been picked, Epps had the enslaved person whipped; if the amount exceeded expectation, then the picking amount for the next day was established. Epps's practices and setting of picking amounts were replicated at holdings across the region.[174] Whether there was too little or too much cotton in the basket, enslaved people across the region lived under constant threat of violence.

Slaveholders believed that enslaved Blacks became uncontrollable, troublesome, and too independent without frequent punishment to reaffirm the hierarchies of racial bondage. They felt, as Mary Sibley described, that public retribution served "infanet advantage" to quell the "entirely too boisterous and defying" behavior of their enslaved.[175] Progeny resulting from forced sexual encounters and assault often were penalized or subjected to specialized brutality. Hatred of these offspring could originate from the father himself or from slaveholding women, resulting in a torturous existence for the child. One DeSoto Parish slaveholder relentlessly mistreated his slave son, J. W. Terrill, requiring him to wear a bell "strapped 'round my shoulders with the bell about three feet from my head in a steel frame" until he was twenty-one. He was unable to lie down, and his father often chained him to a tree. On one occasion, Terrill's father strapped him to a tree and whipped him "like a beast" until he was unconscious. Treated like a captured animal, Terrill was left tied to the tree for the entire night. This brutal practice remained popular with Master Terrill, who often instructed the overseer to accrete an additional "39 licks" for not working fast enough.[176]

On Terrill's holding, as on countless others, violence prevailed in multiple forms, and its frequent occurrence made it commonplace. The paucity of Black sources and firsthand accounts makes it impossible to re-create Black life beyond broad strokes. The lack of material is particularly acute when reconstituting slave community relationships and kinship networks, and the corollary of intraracial violence. Since African Americans enslaved in this region endured an intensely detached, commodified, violent, and profit-driven bondage, it is reasonable to assume that the enslaved community experienced a degree of tension and personal circumstances that resulted in intraracial and self-inflicted acts of violence.[177]

Enslaved people who attempted flight were punished to the satisfaction of the slaveholder within the private fiefdom of the plantation. Records do not elucidate the frequency of runaways, the punishment administered, or whether there were public instances of punishments by the slave patrols. Under the Red River regional power structure and embedded culture of violence, there were fewer successful runaways than in other parts of the South. Deduction suggests that attempted escapes were stifled with alacrity and through pointed punishment, or that instances in which detainment and restriction proved unsuccessful and insufficient were rare. Silence in the historical record about enslaved neighborhoods and communities in this region also hinders any sure conclusions about the role of neighborhood and kinship networks in assisting runaways or efforts to escape. Enslaved people may have stolen away or attempted to run away as a "redemptive figuration," to feel ownership and control of their own bodies and destinies, if only briefly. It is likely that, as in other areas of the South, enslaved women chose truancy for a week or so instead of full escape, because of their children.[178]

Those enslaved who successfully escaped the confines of the plantation faced slave patrols that hunted them down. J. P. Flournoy recalled that large slaveholders had "overseers and they rode the public roads at night" in search of Blacks without the requisite travel permit from a slaveholder. Individuals found on the road were "sent home and punished," and Flournoy states that such people were then not permitted to travel for several months.[179] The patrols included either individuals paid by a slaveholder to quickly recapture a specific bondsperson or a group of local whites drawn from the community and appointed as patrollers for a limited time. Patrols were not a nightly occurrence but were mobilized when the alarm was raised or at the community's discretion. Slave patrols often would sweep through plantations to search slave quarters and break up anything that might constitute a slave gathering. These patrols also safeguarded the area around plantations and towns by riding or walking the roads and demanding passes from any slave found off the plantations.[180] The 1850 Fugitive Slave Act further reinforced the patrols by providing constitutional provisions, with the full backing of the federal government, to assist slaveholders in recovering fugitive enslaved property. The new fugitive slave law built on the existing 1793 act and a bevy of associated personal liberty laws to enforce the constitutional guarantee that runaways would be returned; it also catalyzed antislavery activists in the decade leading up to the Civil War.[181]

Most runaways who eluded the initial patrols were found and brought to local jails for collection by owners. In 1853, Nilson ran away from Pre Aux Cleres. The plantation overseer later retrieved him from jail at the cost of ten dollars.[182] When an enslaved man escaped William Powell's Mount Flat plantation in August 1854, he wrote to the local jailer to locate his lost property. The man—about forty years old, "very black, rather slender made, had large whiskers"—had been found, and Powell was eager to reclaim his chattel.[183] Slaveholders in Caddo and Bossier Parishes frequently advertised runaways in the local newspapers whenever slave patrols failed to recapture escapees. Bold advertisements crammed with details about a runaway ran briefly but produced the desired result—the return of the slaveholder's property—rather quickly because repetitions of announcements were few.[184] Indeed, recaptured enslaved people faced violent repercussions for depriving slaveholders of their labor. In the highly controlled and self-contained world along the Red River, the brutal nature of racialized enslavement and the unforgiving regional landscape deterred escape and limited the possibility of successful flight. Tragically for the enslaved, little could ultimately direct the region away from its vehement commitment to racial bondage.

Cotton cultivation defined and buttressed life in the Red River region, and the increased global demand for cotton drove the region's market-oriented slaveholders. The clearing of the Red River raft allowed frequent and more reliable traffic between the economic hub of New Orleans and northwest Louisiana, enabling expansion and solidifying cotton's significance. Slaveholders concentrated on maximum gain from the bountiful soil and the commodified land and labor in pursuit of financial success. Like the cotton they raised, enslaved Blacks were commodities, and as laboring objects, they were required to extract maximum productivity from each holding. Although slaveholders like Mary Sibley believed dependence on slave labor made them "the Slave of Slaves," the contours and legacy of slavery, slaveholding violence, and racial control remained deeply embedded in the region's ideology and political allegiance.[185]

Mastery in the Red River region was an active manifestation of social standing and power as well as being a critical component of white identity. Imbued with and sustained by racial notions of white supremacy, mastery would remain part of post–Civil War conceptions of white selfhood and power. Simply called white supremacy after the Civil War, this durable ideology would respond to different social, economic, and political pressures. Regional slaveholders' deep market dependence and extractive focus worked in tandem with the lack of elite planter manifestations of wealth and privilege to cement mastery as a structural construct with staying power. Red River mastery was defined by slavery but also by the firmly held belief in racial hierarchy and by perpetuating a social framework that permitted and promoted systemic racism. Built into this ideology was the use of violence to control and reaffirm racial boundaries while also demonstrating that white southerners believed Blacks were racially inferior. As the nation moved steadily to the outbreak of the Civil War, whites along the Red River leaned heavily on the ideology of mastery and racially motivated violence as they rallied to the Confederate cause to maintain their interests in slaveholding, which was threatened by the election of Abraham Lincoln.

– 3 –

"THEY WILL HAVE YANKEE MASTERS AS WELL AS US"

Secession and Confederate Commitment

Slaveholders from across the South continued to move to the market-dependent and profit-focused Red River region throughout the 1850s, while the long-standing fractures over slavery's reach deepened between North and South. Regional slaveholders viewed measures to curtail the expansion of slavery into new territories as a direct assault on their rights. As in other plantation regions, slavery remained the lens through which regional slaveholders viewed the world. The regional ideology of mastery, with its self-reinforcing rubric of racial hierarchy and embedded violence, and the region's reliance on enslaved labor fit in lockstep with states' rights and popular sovereignty as the means to protect the institution of slavery. The acceleration of events and heightening of tensions following the Kansas-Nebraska Act convinced the region's slaveholders that the foundation of their livelihoods, the generator of their wealth, and the critical component of their racial identity was under attack. While the nation grappled with and divided over slavery, its expansion, and its protection by the federal government, Red River slaveholders saw the 1854 creation of the Republican Party and the nomination of Abraham Lincoln as proof positive that their rights were in peril.

The question of how far slavery would extend within the geographic bounds of the United States had taken center stage since the nation's founding. Though the word *slavery* is absent from the Constitution, the document contains dozens of instances that recognized and protected slavery within the states, even acknowledging the right of slaveholders to recapture enslaved runaways.[1] Slavery's legality was decided within state boundaries, while nonslaveholding states were required to respect and enforce the rights of property bestowed on slaveholders by their individual state, which presented a tangled web for abolitionists and progressive politicians. This fueled the political machinations and debates that designated slave and free state boundaries, hashed out in the Missouri Compromise of 1820 and the Compromise of 1850, which included the strengthened Fugitive Slave Act of 1850 and shaped the sectional conflict that intensified following the passage of the Kansas-Nebraska Act in 1854. These were landmark decisions that punctuated decades of congressional wrangling and court cases that determined slavery's reach and the power wielded by the southern states.[2] Whether debated in Congress or practiced at the slave market, slavery was a charged topic that permeated and entwined political, economic, and societal aspects during the antebellum era.

The new Republican Party gained momentum and congressional seats because the Kansas-Nebraska Act, the upshot violence in Kansas, Democratic support for the proslavery faction, and the 1857 *Dred Scott* decision angered northerners.[3] Southern economic reach sat alongside a boosted presence in the House of Representatives and in the Electoral College, which was long supported by slavery. While the enslaved population was considered property and not citizens, three-fifths of them were nonetheless counted for representation. This lopsided overrepresentation of slaveholding interests also resulted in social stratification, with limited opportunities for ordinary, poor whites nationwide. The Republican Party's foundational belief in equality, particularly in the right of any man to work and to earn a livelihood from that work, effectively grounded the Republican platform in the Declaration of Independence.[4]

The *Dred Scott* decision, handed down a month after violent attacks by proslavery men in Kansas against settlers who opposed slavery in the territory, was a gilt-edged answer to slaveholders' dreams. It declared that African Americans were not citizens, with "no rights which the white man was bound to respect," while also prohibiting Congress from blocking the spread of slavery to new territories because the Constitution protected property, which included slaves. The Missouri Compromise was thus unconstitutional because it had forbidden slavery in the Northwest.[5] Slave owners now argued for slavery's expansion with the federal government's protection. Abolitionists found the most important premise of their politics—that enslaved property was different than other property—rendered obsolete.[6]

More than ever for southerners, the flow of allegiance was local and then national, and most southerners came to value their state citizenship above the national.[7] From a legal standpoint, the concept of citizenship was under-developed before the Civil War. No specification spelled out the privileges and immunities of citizenship, and citizenship did not include the privileges of sovereignty; hence, questions like why women were citizens but not eligible to vote, or exactly what rights were enjoyed by free Blacks, further complicated any discussion. White men who were able to vote could do so only for state legislators and congressmen; it was left to the planter-dominated legislatures to appoint all other officials.[8] States, not the national government, determined citizenship, and they used a series of requirements that limited not only eligibility for citizenship and voting but also who constituted an antebellum citizen.

While Lincoln and Douglas debated in the 1858 congressional election, proslavery southerners forced the calling of conventions to consider secession, evidence that political differences among southerners and southern slaveholders were hardening. Secessionists were displeased that they did not gain undivided support from nonslaveholders, and younger slaveholders wanted the older generation to be more forceful and vocal in defending slavery as an unqualified good. The 1860 Democratic convention in Charleston saw the split of the national Democratic Party, with the South Carolina radicals helming the group that pushed fervently for secession and states' rights.[9] There were four candidates in the 1860 election: John Bell for the Constitutional Union Party, John Breckinridge for the southern faction of the Democrats, Stephen Douglas for the northern faction of the Democrats, and Abraham Lincoln for the Republicans.

The Whig Party had traditionally maintained a strong following in Caddo Parish before 1850, but the Democrats gained traction following the ratification of the 1852 state constitution. This saw the Whigs' foremost state-level issue, and main differentiating feature from Democrats, ratified: constitutional revision of representation, giving greater representation to slaveholding parishes.[10] Consolidation of wider Democratic Party aims was so successful that after the 1855 gubernatorial election, Louisiana politicians agreed on most issues, irrespective of party affiliation.[11] As was the case in new southern plantation areas, Breckinridge was the candidate of choice in regions with higher rates of economic growth and with a larger proportion of younger, more radically minded slaveholders. On the other hand, slaveholders of the older guard in the mature plantation areas, and city-based bankers and merchants who benefited from cotton infrastructures, favored Bell.[12]

Lincoln's selection as the 1860 Republican candidate crystallized regional opposition to the Republican Party. As the collective feeling within
Louisiana moved swiftly toward secession following the 1860 election, the
northwest parishes led the push for immediate secession. Throughout the
region, there was an extreme confidence in slavery and its power demonstrated through action and decisive sentiment regarding secession. Right
until the 1861 secession convention, slaveholders were moving to the region,
and established slaveholders continued to invest in enslaved laborers and
land. The letters of regional slaveholders are populated with discussions of
crops, crop management and expansion, rainfall and environmental management, plans for expansion, and enslaved output. In years when the crop
was less fruitful, these market-oriented slaveholders wrote about hiring out
enslaved Blacks to generate additional income and to cover plantation costs.
Letters from the latter portion of the decade speak to continual land scout-
ing and the unbridled confidence of regional slaveholders in cotton and the
institution of slavery.

— — —

There is little engagement with the 1860 presidential race, and no mention
of the Republican platform, in the existing correspondence of the Red River
region's slaveholders. Discussions of national politics fleetingly mention
support for Breckinridge. Dislike for abolitionists and their cause peppers
letters, but there is a profound sense of assurance in the longevity of slavery and of politics "faithful to the south and its institutions."[13] In Louisiana,
as in many of the slave states, Lincoln was omitted from the state's 1860
presidential election ballot papers. Though Lincoln won a solid 54 percent
of the northern popular vote, he only won 2 percent of the southern vote.[14]
Louisiana's electoral return gave states' rights southern Democrat Breckinridge 45 percent of the vote, cooperationist and Constitutional Unionist
Bell 40 percent, and northern Democrat Douglas just 15 percent of the vote.
Breckinridge polled strongest in north Louisiana, with nearly 55 percent of
the vote. Veteran politician and large slaveholder John Slidell summed up
the political transformation thusly: "Louisiana will act with her sister states
of the South. I see no probability of preserving the Union, nor indeed do I
consider it desirable to do so if we could."[15] For white Louisianans, Lincoln's
election threatened the equality of the individual states within the Union and
marked the culmination of the long-feared political isolation of the South.

With South Carolina turning secession from threat to reality, Louisiana Unionism crumbled and Louisiana's state and congressional delegates quickly reconsidered their state's future within the Union. Louisiana governor Thomas Overton Moore, a Rapides Parish slaveholder, had previously opposed immediate secession in private—a position amended shortly after Lincoln's election. He declared, "I do not think it comports with the honor and self-respect of Louisiana, as a slaveholding State, to live under the Government of a Black Republican President." Red River slaveholders overwhelmingly upheld Moore's conviction. He pushed for a southern conference to decide the secession issue, and a special legislature was swiftly convened on December 10, 1860, that approved an election on January 7, 1861, to determine whether Louisiana would send delegates to a secession convention.[16] Moore's secession speech neatly summarized key catalysts for "manly action" against a government "lodged in the hands of a Party whose avowed principles are in antagonism to the interests, the well being, and the dignity of Louisiana." He highlighted the "fanatical hostility to slavery" evinced by Lincoln and the Republicans, the perversion of government purpose by "purely section vote" in complete opposition and contempt "of the other section of the country," and the emboldened and increasing strength of abolitionists to "attack our system of labor as a sin and a crime." He believed that the institution of slavery emerged from the scrutiny of the slavery debates fully vindicated, and like other slaveholders in the Red River region, he did not want the slavery question "assuaged or dissipated by any new compromise, or by bartering away any of our constitutional rights." Louisiana used the secession election to take control of its sacrosanct economic and social institution back from the dangerous grasp of Lincoln, Republicans, and northern interests.[17]

The January 7 election was conducted on the same basis as a regular legislative election, with each senatorial and representative district allotted the same number of seats in the convention as in the legislature. Louisiana voters could choose between immediate, unconditional secession or secession later if other states also seceded. The election was a staggering victory for the secessionist forces, with a majority of the delegates agreeing on a radical, straight-out secession platform and expressing "intolerance for anyone who continued to object to their actions."[18] Remaining Unionist strongholds—New Orleans merchants and pro-tariff sugar planters—collapsed under the weight of secessionist support. Pro-secessionist planter

Henry Marshall, who would serve in the Confederate senate, received a letter from his factor in New Orleans two days after Lincoln's victory that encapsulated the merchant dichotomy in the capital. The factor believed that Louisiana would secede only out of necessity and not by choice—in contrast to the sentiments in the Red River region—but also felt that the South needed to "take a bold stand for her rights" because if "she submits now we may prepare to see our slaves worthless before the end of Lincoln's administration." This fear of declining worth for slave property and cotton prices at market spurred a sea change, and by late December New Orleans emerged as a "hotbed of secession."[19]

The turn of events enthused north Louisiana slaveholders. In a letter to her cousin in Caddo Parish, one slaveholder remarked, "I much prefer this state of affairs to the Abolition terrors that we had to contend with all summer."[20] Along the Red, secession provided a clear opportunity for slaveholders to protect the profit-driven cultivation of land and the extraction of labor that undergirded regional prosperity. Since Lincoln and his election encapsulated the abolition terrors, this turn toward political independence highlighted the quick shift of many former cooperationists into a more radical stance toward secession.[21] Published secessionist votes totaled 20,448 votes out of 37,733, and these elected delegates adopted an ordinance of secession at the January 23 convention.[22] Three days later, Louisiana officially seceded from the Union.

The Red River cotton parishes emerged as the stronghold of secessionist sentiment. Regional enthusiasm for the cause soared as votes were cast at the secession convention. Indeed, the senatorial district returns indicate that secessionists outpolled cooperationists 2 to 1, with 2,123 secession votes in Caddo, DeSoto, Natchitoches, and Sabine Parishes, 961 secession votes in Bienville and Bossier Parishes, and 933 votes in Rapides. Only the left bank of Orleans Parish possessed more secession votes than the Red River region.[23] The total returns statewide show the secessionists with 20,214 votes to 18,451 cooperationist votes. It was not a landslide election, but the immediate secessionists won the majority.[24]

Secession candidates were elected on a wave of support in DeSoto Parish, though votes were tighter elsewhere. Henry Marshall, of Land's End plantation in Caddo, led a mobilizing force in northern Louisiana for secession. He was elected with 747 votes as a delegate to the state secession convention, one of four senatorial representatives from Caddo, DeSoto, Natchitoches, and Sabine Parishes. Lewis Texada, an enslaver with a sprawling riverfront plantation whose father settled in Rapides in 1832, was elected parish representative.[25] Small and medium-size slaveholders elected to the secession convention constituted the largest percentage who voted for immediate secession. Delegates with one to nine slaves represented 17.5 percent, those with ten to nineteen slaves made up 25 percent, and officials with twenty to twenty-nine slaves constituted 15 percent of the immediate secession vote. Most of these slaveholding delegates grew cotton, owned improved land in 1860, and held more slaves and more land, on average, than cooperationists.[26] Across northern Louisiana, the gamut of slaveholders, those from smallholdings to large plantations, translated their adherence to slavery and slave-based cotton cultivation into a vote for secession.

Red River slaveholders' fealty to the Confederate cause manifested in bountiful military volunteering enthusiasm, in alignment with other southern plantation districts. Mere days after official secession, Henry Marshall received a detailed roll of volunteers and oaths of the captains for the newly created Pelican Rifles of DeSoto.[27] Marshall used his wealth to finance a regiment commanded by his cousin. Both of his sons joined the Confederate forces in early 1861 and perished during the war.[28] Samuel Hyams, son of Natchitoches planter Henry Hyams, joined the Pelican Rangers on January 21, moving to the Third Regiment of Louisiana Volunteers a few months later.[29] Some exuberant men, many of whom had grown up hearing about the military escapades of their older male kin, did not wait for Louisiana's formal secession to form a military company. Though they didn't leave for war until April 16, 1861, the Shreveport Greys were founded on January 1, 1861. Shreveport and its vicinity—including the plantation districts of Greenwood, Keachie, and Mooringsport—furnished around two thousand men for the Confederate forces.[30]

A slaveholding friend of Marshall's wrote to him that determination to sustain the Confederate cause permeated the regional marrow. For them, the "great war question" would "open to the world the principle that the great American idea of the right to make their own government was right—and that this is the last time this right will be questioned . . . there is no dissension here all support the war."[31] Impressive enlistment numbers were commonplace in the region, and John Houston, a resident of Springhill, Bossier Parish, noted that the militias "are drilling in nearly every parish," a claim substantiated by the 980 military companies quickly organized by

Louisiana communities.[32] Caddo Parish slaveholder Alfred Flournoy noted that "never before have volunteers enlisted with more promptness. Every parish is doing her duty." Flournoy, who began his family's migration to Caddo in the 1830s, wrote to his enlisted sons, "Glorious old caddo has raised three more companies. Two have started and one will leave next week."[33] John Houston detailed plans for his participation and chronicled the Red River region's volunteer spirit. Northern Louisiana "answered nobly to the call for troops," he observed. Locally mustered units such as the Coushatta Rifles had left in early September 1861. Houston continued apace with cotton production, but because the "war excitement does not abate in this country," and although the current crop was "the finest ... I ever saw in this country," he would defend Louisiana with no hesitation "if our state is invaded this winter." Expectations of Yankee arrival on Louisiana's doorstep drew strong volunteering. Like Henry Marshall's sons and numerous unrecorded others from established Red River families, Flournoy's children joined the first companies, mustered into service, and remained devoted to the cause until the bitter end.

The Confederate government summoned three thousand volunteers from Louisiana for a twelve-month tenure in April 1861, and shortly thereafter requested a further five thousand troops. The overwhelming response forced Governor Moore to request that units wait at home until another enlistment call enabled their dispatch. Militia units reported to New Orleans, and the first Louisiana regiments left for Virginia on April 28, 1861. Many individuals received their authority to organize units directly from the Confederate government, resulting in volunteer units mustered into service without falling under state jurisdiction. However, bureaucracy did not hinder volunteer enlistment in northwest Louisiana.[34] The gregarious enthusiasm for enlistment was not confined to fighting-age slaveholders or the first months of the war. Pineville's Louisiana State Seminary of Learning and Military Academy—the precursor to Louisiana State University—suspended classes in the spring of 1861 and ultimately closed in April 1862 because so many cadets had enlisted. When the seminary shuttered its doors, it gave all the bedding to General Edmund Kirby Smith and expected all remaining cadets to take up arms.[35]

Even after the Confederate government, on May 15, 1861, advised that all volunteers would be required to muster for the duration of the war, Flournoy noted that volunteering continued with "such enthusiasm" as "I never witnessed . . . at any time prior to this." He wrote to his enlisted son that Caddo and its residents were "fully aroused to the dangers that threaten us." This commitment to the Confederacy translated into widespread enlistment, which quickly left many parishes depleted of fighting-age men. Flournoy observed that after successive rounds of enlistment, "all our arms and all our men are gone."[36] Less than a month after the Confederate bombardment of Fort Sumter, H. G. Hargis declared that "the people arose as one man" in the cotton parishes.[37]

Potent enthusiasm for enlistment arose because southern whites, and particularly slaveholders, felt that the Confederacy best served their personal and economic interests and better protected their families. For them, the Confederacy and the Confederate cause aligned most closely with their individual needs, identity, and aspirations.[38] Regional slaveholders agreed with the racial sentiments and worldview set out by Confederate vice president Alexander Stephens in his Cornerstone Address. They were defending a world founded on the "great truth that the negro is not equal to the white man" and emphatically believed the ideology and rationale of the Confederate government was to uproot the "sandy foundation" of the U.S. Constitution and to instate one "based upon this great physical, philosophical, and moral truth."[39]

Like numerous other families from the Red River settler generation, the Flournoy family became thoroughly enmeshed in Louisiana's military contribution to the new Confederate nation. William Flournoy, brother to Alfred, founded the Greenwood Guards for service as Company 1 in the Second Regiment of Louisiana Volunteers. The Greenwood Guards was one of nineteen state-commissioned units that left Caddo Parish during the first year of the war. Volunteer units, of which there were plenty, were generally recruited for transfer to Confederate service. Units that entered the service of the state only, like the Greenwood Guards, fell under the jurisdiction of Confederate officers by order of the Louisiana governor. As state regiments, the Greenwood Guards, Shreveport Greys, and the Caddo Rifles were mustered one month after the fall of Fort Sumter and remained in service for the duration, engaged in almost every major battle. The latter two units departed Shreveport on April 16, 1861—four days after the bombardment at Fort Sumter—amid great fanfare.[40]

In a letter to his son Alfred Jr., a lieutenant in the service of the Greenwood Guards, the senior Alfred underscored the soldiers' fervent commitment to protect home and hearth. If William, serving as captain, and Alfred Jr. and their "noble greenwood guards, who were among the first to leave their homes to drive back the invader of their country, were to return from the face of the enemy they would feel ashamed to walk among the old men of their parish and find all their young friends gone to the war." Southern honor intertwined with a soldier's attachment to family and home to both buoy enlistment and imbue service with deep significance. As Flournoy made clear, "no company in the service stands higher in the estimation of their countrymen."[41] The Greenwood Guards were not alone in receiving such accolades. Across the country, locally recruited units emerged, often to the acclaim of residents who derived pride and enthusiasm for the war effort from the service of their Confederate soldiers.

Enlistment was one of the most visible and tangible aspects of Confederate nationalism and a nationalistic ideology based on white male unity. C. B. "Brack" Johnson, newly married to Louisiana Powell, daughter of planter William Powell of Mount Flat and Slate Place plantations, had not volunteered by the fall of 1861. Brack's enlisted friends wrote that Louisiana, and most especially Caddo, had "responded nobly" and "more are willing to go." They sent him numerous enthusiastic letters that balanced the manly fun of camp with the importance and benefit of military service. It was, his friend implored, "better to meet the enemy at the threshold than to wait for him to penetrate the breach of the country," and while service contracts were "for three years or the war," Brack could "expect to complete it soon." Brack duly enlisted in 1862 and died in 1863 near Chattanooga. This abiding bond with the Confederate cause inspired loyalty and commitment from regional citizens.[42]

This loyalty was evident in Brack's battlefield correspondence to his wife, wherein he vowed that despite the need "to fight now several years first," the southern cause "must succeed at the end."[43] Natchitoches resident David Pierson understood the long duration of his enlistment and did not join to "gratify an ambition." Instead, his reasons for fighting echoed those of other Red River slaveholders, especially small and midsize holders: he fought "in the defense of our common country and homes which is threatened with invasion and annihilation." Initially hesitant regarding secession, Pierson experienced a change in political stance and a strengthened bond with Louisiana after the state decided to secede. Like many of his Louisiana brethren, Pierson believed secession presented two alternatives, "to take up arms against the south or in her defense." White identity—inextricably tied to slavery and supported through mastery as an active manifestation of white power and standing within a rigid racial hierarchy—was the Red River region's identity. Now, with both white southern manhood and the embedded regional identity under clear attack, fighting was essential. Committed northern Louisianans like Pierson, the Marshalls, and the Flournoys were "not slow to choose," and once committed, they were quickly devoted to the "sacrifice which destiny impels every patriot to make at the alter of his country's glory."[44]

Numerous prominent slaveholders and senior household heads continually pledged their support through verbal and written endorsements alongside monetary sponsorship of militia companies. Henry Marshall organized and equipped the Marshall Guards, served as a signatory for the constitution of the Confederate States of America, and was a representative in the Confederate Congress. In March 1861, he wrote to his daughter about his outlook regarding the severity of battlefield engagements and volunteering. Though he underestimated the bloodiness of the war, he was quick to pledge his own service if volunteers were called from Louisiana, and "let somebody else do the legislating."[45] While selection for service in the Confederate Congress denoted his regional prominence, Marshall's eagerness to pledge his life indicates the outward demonstration of fidelity prevalent throughout the region.

Alfred Flournoy was simultaneously proud of his sons' service and of the overall representation of Caddo Parish among volunteers. The exuberant "prompt ness" of volunteering left Caddo "one of the most defenceless portions of the world," but the esteem in which the Greenwood Guards were held was common knowledge on the home front and was "duly appreciated." Flournoy Sr. boasted of newly enlisted and created companies from Bossier, DeSoto, and Caddo and relayed his financial support in another letter to his son.[46] From the scions of planter households to the young men constituting the Confederate army's rank and file, whites from the Red River region were fully committed to the ethos of invincibility and southern superiority that buoyed convictions during wartime and permeated and shaped postwar white identity and memory.[47] John Houston encapsulated slaveholders' sentiments when he identified Lincoln's election and new federal government policies as the moment when southerners "drew our swords and placed them upon the altar of our country and pledged our lives, property and sacred honor" to the protection of the South "from the bondage of the north."[48]

Houston's letters also acknowledged the sensibilities and inclinations of the region's women. Dosia Williams Moore recalled that the women "were all ardent rebels," and this dedication was manifested most pervasively in provisioning military companies; sewing uniforms and battle banners; an expanded, politicized purview of traditional domestic duties; and the practical daily management of plantations. Female dedication and involvement in the Confederate cause were clearly displayed, alongside war effort enthusiasm that mirrored that of their male kin. Confederate women, particularly slaveholding women, demonstrated their nationalism and patriotism through a framework that drew upon and reflected prewar notions of femininity and family honor.[49] The war opened avenues for expanding women's roles and authority, but within decidedly traditional parameters that reinforced antebellum gender roles. This, in turn, quietly underscored the commitment to slavery and social order, including gender relations, as a crucial component of the Confederacy.[50]

At the onset of the war, patriotism manifested in outpourings of public support and material war provisions. Brack Johnson's sister, studying at Wesleyan Female College in Macon, Georgia, wrote to him in Caddo two weeks after Fort Sumter. Her letter overflowed with excitement for the war, earnest nationalism, and profuse determination. She contrasted the reality that the "prevailing excitement in our city is war" with the profound sadness surely to be felt by families after "five hundred men left macon last week" for Virginia.[51] Even in the early days of war, she indicated how southern women could sacrifice their personal feelings for the "abstract and intangible 'Cause.'"[52]

The stalwart commitment of regional women to the war—ideologically, materially, and personally—despite the dramatic changes it heralded, neatly encapsulated the friction between the necessary unity and the prescribed change inherent in Confederate nationalism. Though the Confederacy inspired a nearly instantaneous loyalty and commitment from its white citizenry, the nation needed to quickly construct a foundation and culture to inform, guide, and instruct citizens. Nationalist and patriotic rhetoric created a common vocabulary that drew upon iconography, honor, and southern exceptionalism while simultaneously weaving slavery, racial hierarchies, and the Confederate cause together. Letters from Red River's slaveholding women showcase devotion to the war alongside a deeply rooted fealty to Confederate ideology and nationhood.[53] Women's home front letters asserted citizenship and crafted their identity throughout the war. These letters and diaries often contained religious overtones that buttressed southerners' belief in a victorious outcome, combined with the righteousness of the Confederate cause.[54] As mothers, sisters, lovers, and daughters parted from the newly enlisted, Johnson's testament that "every day some of the girls fathers stop" en route to war for a last farewell, "perhaps forever," underscores the sacrificial element of Confederate nationalism.[55] The theme of sacrifice reverberated strongly on Red River plantations.

Female contributions to the Confederacy included the production of clothing and provisions, with women of the Red River region fiercely committed to domestic patriotism. Slaveholding women, particularly the elite, undertook to clothe the men in gray, extending the patriotic female sacrifice from strictly benefiting family to encompass all Confederate soldiers. Throughout the war, white women used the labor, sewing, and weaving skills of enslaved women to clothe soldiers who fought for the institution of slavery.[56]

Sidney Harding, who fled from her family's plantation in southern Louisiana to their Keachi, DeSoto Parish, holding in late 1863, knitted items for particular officers stationed in Shreveport.[57] Alfred Flournoy Jr. and his wife, Theodosia, maintained regular correspondence during his military service. In her first letter to him, she wrote that southern women were steeling themselves for the war—though she didn't think they would ever be conquered. Despite being relegated to the home front and plantation management, Theodosia actively involved herself in a local society dedicated to supporting all members of Alfred's—and her uncle-in-law William's—Greenwood Guards. A summer 1861 letter remarks that one hundred drawers were made in one week and would be sent with the one hundred shirts made the prior week. Theodosia beseeched Alfred to "tell the boys we have a great deal of fun making their clothes, and have cryed over them too." This ladies' society did not confine its efforts to sewing; they also were busy drying peaches for soldiers who "will want something besides pork and beans." Although she was busy with these contributions and plantation management, Theodosia made her husband special food parcels with preserves, condiments, and "good ole home whickey [sic]," which displayed her devotion and patriotism to her fellow mistresses and his company members.[58]

Annie Jeter Carmouche met and married her husband, Emile, during the war and recalled that he had to leave shortly after their nuptials. Though saddened by the parting, she was "proud of him in his uniform going to fight the Yankees." She met regularly with other women to sew and knit for the soldiers and fondly remembered giving concerts and frolics "to help them [soldiers] on." For one particular concert, Carmouche sewed "small confederate flags to be worn as aprons" and all the ladies wore cotton bolls in their hair. Though she was cognizant in her memoir that she and her compatriots did not comprehend the depredation of war, she recalled that "everyone was proud to say they had someone in the army" and all were "eager for the fray."[59]

In their correspondence, women of the Red River region voiced the wish to be of more use to the Confederacy. Oftentimes, this connected with visceral outbursts that conveyed white women's familiarity and facility with pervasive violence. Trained to exercise violence to regulate and control enslaved people, white women knew violence as an efficacious framework to dominate and assert power. Indeed, for regional slaveholding women, the Civil War connected their comfort with violence—inculcated through years of mastery, participation in the slave marketplace, and involvement with the punishment of enslaved people—into intense feelings of hatred toward northern men.

Brack Johnson's sister enumerated in a plucky letter her active steps to fight the Union. She had decided to learn how to shoot so "if the Yankees whip our men the ladies will be ready to take their place." She took additional consolation that "the ladies of the southern confederacy can lash any yankee with their tong," while she lamented that the fine Confederate men "have to fight such a degrading set of northerners." Here, the southern societal mainstays of honor and violence sat hand in glove with regional pride and Confederate patriotism, within a rhetorical device that positioned the whip, the ubiquitous disciplinary tool of the plantation South, in discussions of military success. Then she declared that she hoped Washington and "old abe" would be the first burned. Her loyalty to the CSA was irrefutable, and northern aggression—evinced by Lincoln's call for volunteers—stirred a new "feeling of revenge" and resulted in the declaration that "I never would be contented until I killed a yankee."[60]

Women's dedication to the Confederacy and contributions to the war effort were synonymous and tightly entwined with their home front experience. White women along the Red River exhibited steadfast patriotism throughout the war, even under challenging circumstances.[61] However, this does not mean that life was easy, unchanged, or without significant sacrifice for white women, children, non-enlisted men, and enslaved people in the region. The most noticeable alteration to white slaveholding women's lives was the near-total responsibility for daily plantation management, in addition to their usual household remit. Some were well versed in plantation management, but it was the first foray into field management for others. Mistresses assumed all head-of-household responsibilities. Depending on their holding size and situation, they relied on overseers, their husband's advice in letters, and the assistance of older male kin.

While Theodosia Flournoy had overseers' assistance, she had ultimate responsibility for managing crops, enslaved people, and the household. She continued regular sewing with the ladies' society and fulfilled many far-ranging requests sent by her husband. Her letters to Alfred regularly updated him on the health of his cotton and subsistence crops and her competent handling of plantation affairs. In June 1861, she wrote about a fine crop, with "corn 14 foot in height" and indications that "there has never been such a prospect for a crop." However, she needed to reassert her authority regarding ownership and punishment of the enslaved. Rufe—an enslaved man who, along with Godfrey, was charged with interplantation tasks—had gone to another holding, presumably on Theodosia's orders, where a group of whites had threatened to hang him. Mr. Daniels, the Flournoy overseer, had knocked Rufe down while Theodosia was at her brother-in-law's home. On her return, she "sent for mr d and informed of one thing that Ruf was no free negro" and then reaffirmed her mastery, stating, "He belonged to me as much as Godfrey, and he had no more right to whip him than other of my house servants." It was *Theodosia's* right to whip her enslaved property, and she would not let Mr. Daniels subsume that power in her husband's absence.

Subsequent letters from Theodosia relay predictions and progress reports for the crops—"if the wormes don't come you can pay your dets without any trouble"—as well as news of unfortunate crop failures. Despite a "magnificent prospect for a crop" in 1861, for instance, a lack of rain meant that the cotton crop was only satisfactory, matching rather than surpassing the previous year under Alfred's management. The food crops had thrived with "pease and pottoes, lots, plenty of corn and fodder," and Theodosia believed her husband "ought to be perfectly satisfied." The Flournoy pea crop had been a bumper one, and a proud, patriotic Theodosia planned to ship them to New Orleans because "peas will be so nice for our soldiers."[62] Alfred shared a similar view; disappointed by the static cotton outcome but aware that provisions would be important for sustenance and trade for his family, he wrote, "We have so much to rejoice over . . . we can't well starve as long as we have an abundance of those things."[63] In the first year of the war, Theodosia epitomized the ideal Confederate woman: unerringly patriotic and enthusiastic for the war effort, committed to providing for the troops, and competent in managing the plantation and her enslaved property.

Elizabeth Ann Scofield had a contrasting wartime experience in Cheneyville, outside Alexandria. Her husband worked as a foundry agent until it was shut, later in the war, and her eldest son, Walter, joined the army at seventeen, where he served until Appomattox. Her daughter left school after 1861 and her younger sons never attended. They had lived without "many of the comforts and necessaries of life" and the entire family was ill most of the war. Her 1862 crop of "growing well fifteen acres of corn that looked very fine," along with sundry subsistence crops, was utterly ruined by flooding that began June 7. The home was only four feet above ground and there was "one little spot of dry land . . . near our corn crib" where she kept any remaining livestock. As the flooding worsened, she fell ill with "hard chills," alongside her daughter, husband, and enslaved people, "excepting Clara the cook." Writing of her experience in a postwar letter to her father that summarized all four years, Elizabeth specifically mentions the drowning of Clara during the flood, indicating the extent of the financial and labor loss presented by her death. Elizabeth remained in Cheneyville until early 1863, when she and her family became caretakers at Oakland plantation in Natchitoches. Many slaveholders would refugee their slaves to Texas and sought "respectable families owning few or no slaves to occupy their homes" as caretakers. With few enslaved people and requiring a watertight abode, the Scofields became caretakers, first of Oakland and later Catalpha Grove.[64]

Through wartime writings, we are privy not only to the passion of regional commitment but also to the astounding desire to keep enslaved people's productivity rates at prewar standards. Regional slaveholders remained market-focused capitalists confident of international buyers' demand for southern cotton. Throughout the war, they maintained cotton outputs and leveraged enslaved labor to maximize profitability while producing essential goods for the Confederacy. They kept mastery and racial domination central to their daily interactions. They were, after all, fighting for slavery's unrestricted existence and African Americans' perpetual domination by whites. This continued cotton cultivation underscores the extent of regional confidence and sentiment but also illuminates the unique, commodified situation of the region's enslaved population.

Older, non-enlisted men often assumed managerial roles on plantations and were tasked with market-facing, monetary, or unsavory aspects deemed unsuitable or beyond women's abilities. Alfred Flournoy wrote to his son concerning issues with the overseer, who had taken to drinking and was not keeping up standards in the field, meaning Flournoy Jr.'s presence was required for any resolution. While Flournoy Sr. and Theodosia were in charge day to day, they were not the embodiment of authority on the plantation. Father and son also had more open exchanges regarding finances. Alfred wrote to Theodosia with instructions for selling crops, but he relegated to male correspondence discussions of money scarcity, the demise of the credit system, the fact that "one man in fifty has the money to pay his Taxes," and issues with New Orleans–based cotton factors, as well as a frank acknowledgment of dependence on cotton that cannot be "sold at any price," resulting in the inability to purchase necessities.[65]

Similarly, Charles Mathews received a letter from his brother-in-law detailing the dereliction of duty by Chaseland plantation's overseer. The overseer had taken to the woods, leaving Mathews's human property and land, "with not a white man on it," to fate. The following year, following Charles's death, his brother-in-law and his mother corresponded about sickness at Chaseland and Cocobend and the persistent issue of enslaved people running off. Left with twenty-four men, of which "14 are over 50 years of age and are not efficient," Mrs. Mathews was advised to make do with growing corn and "some cotton."[66]

Joseph Texada, who led a Louisiana State Guard battalion he hoped would become a proper regiment, frequently wrote to his wife, Margaret, about plantation management and instructions on what livestock or crops to sell with his father's assistance. One of his letters splits its contents between recounting battalion recruitment efforts and instructing Margaret. Joseph wanted her to inspect the entire holding, scrutinize the crops, and "write me about every particular." If the crops "should be in the gross," she needed to secure someone trustworthy to sell the excess and bring him the money. Failing that scenario, she should have his brother or father purchase a horse for their son and "a fine horse for me." In another letter, Joseph acknowledges that he has failed to "give you any advice respecting plantation affairs" and instead has relied on "your own good judgment to look ahead" to take care of their property.[67]

John Coleman Sibley—a small slaveholder from Many, a town west of Natchitoches and south of Pleasant Hill—joined Company E, commanded by Samuel Furman of DeSoto, and part of Breazeale's Battalion, in late August 1862, and served for the war's duration. Members of this cavalry company came from slaveholding families already discussed here, including Henry Marshall's two sons, three other Marshall relations, four Furman men, and Sibley's three brothers. Sibley's wife, Nancy, managed their land and received frequent instructional letters from her husband. In November 1862, he worried about the cotton and requested that she "gin and pack it and hoop it so as to take care of it." Though he was unsure what should be done immediately with the cotton, Sibley wanted Nancy to take precautions. The following month, Sibley recommended that she hold on to the corn crop and not sell "a bushel before next spring." Serving in south Louisiana, he was uncertain whether the Union would take the rivers, but he conjectured that if they did, corn would be worth "five dollar before next gathering time." Perhaps because of his officer ranking or thanks to his market-oriented mindset, Sibley explored all avenues for diversification and familial preservation. In January 1863, he instructed Nancy to purchase cattle if they were reasonably priced. He knew that the army would need food and that northwest Louisiana's environmental situation made it ideal for provisioning. He cautioned her against buying cattle at the high prices she'd received, as they needed to save money to "make better use of it in paying some debt."[68]

Home front morale remained very high during the first half of the war. It dipped slightly in the second half because of increased pressure from the army, difficulty in selling cotton, the Red River campaign, and the death toll sustained by southern troops. This does not mean that Red River Confederates lost faith in the Confederacy or the war, but it does signify a tempering of unrealistic expectations for a quick victory with limited casualties. The actual, sobering casualties of war, combined with the extended timescale, realigned regional expectations for military resolution and ignited these market-focused slaveholders toward entrepreneurial enterprises that would maximize the labor of enslaved people for slaveholders' gain. It also promoted the belief that all hardships and impressment of goods were part of the sacrifice necessary for victory. Patriotism, support of and for the Confederacy, and commitment to slavery remained unshaken but was recalibrated for slaveholders as the war continued.

William Chase wrote to his daughter from Chaseland plantation in February 1862 to relay how personal deprivation would ultimately benefit the

South. Acknowledging his comfortable living situation heretofore, Chase thanked "the good cause of secession and the present noble struggle for our defense of the confederate states" for demonstrating how little in the way of material possessions and comforts was necessary. Chase closely related his individual forfeit of amenities with political and military consequences when he declared the abnegation worthwhile with respect to "how amply our people . . . will be compensated for present sacrifices by the good in store for us!" Chase continued to write to his daughter letters of a similar ilk that year. He utilized pioneer imagery to strengthen the revolutionary and sacred nature of the Confederate cause, calling it akin to the "french and other great revolutions." In the Red River region, as elsewhere across the South, planters and their families believed in individual and collective sacrifice for the Confederacy. They remained committed to the war and felt that, like their Revolutionary-era forefathers, their armed kinsmen were engaged in a battle to protect liberty.[69]

— — —

While regional cotton cultivation continued apace, northwest Louisianan slaveholders discussed enslaved people and slavery sparsely in their correspondence. In part, this was because racial slavery formed the cornerstone of the Confederacy and regional identity, rendering discussion needless. The rich reservoir of nationalistic imagery downplayed discussion of slavery while spotlighting virtue, faith, and the constitutional states' rights of southerners. Also, since the private correspondence of Confederates echoed the contours of public Confederate sources, letters between servicemen and kin on the home front did not focus on the machinations of slavery.[70]

For slaveholders on the Red River, discussions about slavery revolved around how enslaved people were employed, the expense incurred by enslaved people as supplies became scarcer, and how to secure enslaved populations from federal reach. A letter from Hubbard Bosley's sister, who solely managed her holding, detailed typical frustrations for small to midsize slaveholders. Her correspondence highlights that food and clothing supplies were in short supply for both whites and enslaved people. The one suit of clothing given to enslaved people was now homespun, as was the cloth needed by white family members. This permutation made doling out minimal provisions for enslaved people more arduous. Opportunities to make extra money, usually by hiring out enslaved labor in order to purchase additional cloth and food, were diminished.

However, the contributions of enslaved people to staple and subsistence crop cultivation and household production were minimized throughout the letters to Bosley. His sister had limited access to cloth and "no one to help me spin but lelora and she a slow chance." She wanted to follow antebellum precedent and hire out her enslaved people to pay expenses, certain that at the very least "Primas and Horis labor ought to pay our board."[71] The difficulty she faced in finding a plantation to hire them was part and parcel of the isolated nature of the region, the scarcity of cash, and the effect of the trade blockade.

Elizabeth Samford Fullilove faced similar frustrations on her larger holding. Though her plantation continued to utilize the labor of fifty enslaved people, "there was nothing to buy," and so all clothing and previously purchased sundries were made "from the place." She recollected that "these negroes had to be clothed," and to that end they grew cotton and raised sheep from which "the women spun the thread from the cotton and wool." John Sibley's cousin Letitia wrote of similar tribulations, recounting her success in hiring out enslaved people and in spinning. Since "everything is heigh" and access to goods limited, they were required to "spin everything we ware." Letitia underscored the commonplace nature of this production and wartime adaptation by remarking, "I don't cear where you go you can see spinning a going on," and she linked a desire for the war's conclusion with a desire for less spinning. The Willards, living on a smallholding in Bossier, noted that the constant spinning had left their area without looms and sleighs.[72]

Feeding the enslaved was the primary concern for Charles Mathews's cousin, who beseeched Mathews to send molasses for his Shreveport-area plantation. He asked for the provisions to be good quality "as molasses will be my main dependence to feed my negroes." He was nearly out of pork, and his merchant could no longer procure provisions.[73] The arduous and onerous nature of procuring clothing and victuals was emblematic of regional hardships faced during the war's latter years. The region did not undergo privations commensurate with more battle-worn and heavily traversed portions of the South, but there were notable restrictions on accessible goods and a lack of currency to buy and sell items. Hunger was also a regional issue, and white slaveholders did request aid from the Confederate government as the war progressed. From 1861 to 1862, there was no food shortage in north Louisiana because food crop cultivation continued, but food resources became more limited in 1863.

Armies and civilians competed for food, especially once hard and sustained fighting began in 1862. While stragglers from both armies would steal from civilians, the pressure on the food supply exerted by regular uniformed troops affected availability for civilians and soldiers, and led to a variety of additional requests from soldiers for foodstuffs. Dosia Williams Moore remembered the inability to get flour or coffee, even as scores of Red River soldiers wrote home beseeching family members to send items to supplement and diversify their rations.[74] John Sibley's wartime journal and letters home track the fluctuations in troop provisions and encapsulate the concerns of enlisted men. Sometimes, in the aftermath of a skirmish or when setting up camp, his company received "bacon & four and plenty of nice beef"; other times they were fed by local families or hunted, and most often the troops were "living very hard . . . nothing in the way of rations but a little fresh beef."[75] Sibley's letters to his wife, Lizzie, focused heavily on food. He wrote about food shortages—particularly lack of bacon and beef—and foods he craved, a vast list running from peaches to buttermilk. However, he also detailed delicious dinners hosted by families he quartered with or hospitality given him by relations living near his encampments. He invoked the image of dining at his own table to demonstrate how he yearned to be reunited.[76]

Food was not the only common element in home front and soldiers' letters. A deep dislike of the Union, in tandem with anger at the loss of white southern male lives, permeated letters and diaries of Red River whites, with vehemence toward the Union deepening as the war progressed. Alfred Flournoy's younger brother Alonzo crammed news, crop updates, and hatred of Yankees into one telling letter. His recounting of recent battles described Yankees as dogs. He wrote that hearing of Confederate victories with "the dogs piled up and run to death from fright" gave him intense satisfaction. Alonzo was disappointed to miss the Battle of Manassas, since "the fight come off with a good pack of dogs," but pledged his readiness and his militia's eagerness to respond to the call for troops.[77] Alfred Sr. wrote to Alfred Jr. underscoring that despite the "incalculable damage" the civil war would inflict upon "our country," the virtuous goal of this "horrid war you are engaged in" was seizure "at last" of southern independence. For him, his sons, and his fellow slaveholders, that trade-off was worthwhile, and the result was overdue.[78]

John T. Sibley, kinsman to John Coleman, wrote to a friend from camp in Vicksburg. Sibley wished they could meet and discuss this "ungodly war that is drenching our Country in the best blood of the land." Foreshadowing the idyllic Lost Cause reimagining of antebellum life, Sibley lamented the barriers to a return "to the peaceful pursuits of domestic life" and the increasing savagery of the war.[79] For the Willards, the nightmare of Union victory encapsulated the termination of "our prosperity," the emancipation of enslaved people, and the imposition of outside laws. Invoking a religious element and the righteousness of the Confederacy, Willard worried that the South was being tested through "trials" for "the faithful" that would cause suffering and "weare us out."[80]

Letters from the Red River region's soldiers mentioned various aspects of the military experience alongside their thirst for crushing the enemy. William Tamplin detailed sickness in camp, the fluctuating spirits of the army, the difficulty of securing a furlough, and the tenure of enlistment terms in letters to his sister Betincia. The conscription law distressed William because it confined him to the infantry for three years, and he desperately wanted to transfer to a company of cavalry belonging to "Wals legion" that was the "best field ever opening for me" and would bring him near the enemy line to "see and know" their activity. The conscription law rankled him further because he was "willing to serve my country without being forced." His Red River campaign letters detail wide-ranging experiences, including long marches between engagements, as well as boastful recollections of "whipping the yankeyes on every side" and the shock of witnessing the company captain shot "in five foot of him" during combat near Camden.[81]

John Harris captured the despair and despondency of war in his letter home from the Corinth battlefield. He questioned southern ability to "ever whip the yankeys" when Union gunboats sustained no damage from Confederate cannon. He was baffled that the cannon "hardly ever leaves the dent of the ball."[82] Alfred Flournoy Jr. wrote to his wife about harsh conditions and meager protection from the elements at Camp Moore. He declared "Virginia a cold country indeed," and he slept under five blankets and wore "one flannel, one linen and my red shirt with a big heavy vest" to stave off the chill. Many of his fellow soldiers were sick with the flux and a measles outbreak frightened Flournoy. Other letters to Theodosia detailed preachers' sermons in camp, the resignation of Colonel DeRussy, and the instatement of General Magruder—a soldier his company initially did not like but who now "is the great man with us. He is truly a great soldier."[83]

John Coleman's diary discussed not only clothing and food provisions but also the movement of goods through Natchitoches, women assisting Confederate troops, the 1864 election, exorbitant prices, and the worthlessness of Confederate money. He wrote about hiring an enslaved person to cook food and carry it for the company, the shooting of an enslaved person "trying to get to the enemy and render them assistance" near Vermillion, and catching " three negros, two men and a girl near our camp" attempting to return to Simsport.[84] A strong theme in his letters from 1863 is his fear for the people of Louisiana and the safety of Confederate soldiers, a fear often heightened after he wrote letters on behalf of illiterate comrades or during long lulls between engagements with the enemy.

The regional commitment, steely faith in the Confederacy, and displays of patriotism were mirrored by environmental factors determined by the Red River, a waterway that abided by its own rules. Its capricious behavior resulted in a different, less devastated experience of the Civil War than in other parts of the Confederacy. This was most akin to the experience in southwest Georgia, where the environment similarly buffered and sustained plantation slavery until the last years of the war; the Red River insulated northwest Louisiana from invasion until 1864. The river cushioned white residents from extreme hardship and ravishment, supported an ecosystem in which these profit-focused and market-driven slaveholders diversified the labor of enslaved people into other industries, and provided a significant nexus for the CSA's Department of the Trans-Mississippi West. The Red River created a hard-to-access locality that protected the region physically and ideologically while also establishing it as an indispensable overland connector, used by the CSA and southern slaveholders who refugeed their enslaved property to Texas.[85]

Though the Red River had been altered and somewhat contained by Henry Shreve's engineering work and later teams of the Army Corps, it was not wholly controlled. As chapter 4 will detail, this played an enormous role in the timing and outcome of the Red River campaign. In 1862, the Mississippi and Red Rivers underwent one of the most significant floods in the region.[86] This effectively sealed off the region, rendering it impenetrable to an amphibious invasion by Union forces, but it also inundated croplands with high water. Planter Charles Mathews wrote an anxious letter to his overseer in July 1862 with instructions regarding the "necessity of putting the levee in good fix before we have high water." Certain the river "will come down with a rush," protecting the fields and his home was paramount. He ordered "as many hands as can work at it and do it quickly" to throw up a levee by the house and to make a cross levee.[87]

Elizabeth Scofield vividly recounted the surging water and the unexpectedly quick onset of the flooding. Six days prior, her fields had looked very fine, and she had felt secure with a good food storehouse. Then the cold water from the upper river "came with a rushing, roaring noise that was terrific it was 22 miles deep under my bedroom." The water stayed for twelve days, and she recalled that the watermarks on the trees along the bayou bank stood fifteen feet high. Scofield remarked that "a large steamer would have gone through" her flooded district quickly.[88] Climate and weather thus played a significant role, broadly speaking, in the civilian and military experience of the war after 1862, and this was especially true in northwest Louisiana.[89]

This relatively unassailable region provided a safe haven for the Confederacy and a continued obstacle to Union military plans. New Orleans came under Union control on April 24, 1862, which effectively bifurcated Louisiana. The Union-occupied southern portion of the state reached as far north as Baton Rouge and westward to Bayou LaFourche and Bayou Teche, while the Confederate state of Louisiana extended to the north.[90] Shreveport was increasingly important to the Confederate state. It became the capital in January 1863 and was appointed headquarters of the Confederate Trans-Mississippi Department under the command of General Edmund Kirby Smith. Governor Thomas Overton Moore, and subsequently Governor Henry Watkins Allen—both Red River slaveholders with midsize to large holdings—served their gubernatorial terms from the city.[91] Impenetrable by Union ironclads coming upriver in 1862 and 1863, the river was navigable upstream from within the Confederate state confines, and the region used this isolation to Confederate advantage. This enabled slaveholders on the Red River to provide Confederate forces with foodstuffs, meat (especially beef), clothing and shoes, supplies, and medicine. Just as they had hired out enslaved labor to augment profits during the antebellum period, these market-focused, profit-driven individuals continued to engage with diverse means of generating income. Although the federal naval blockade of New Orleans made trade difficult, Shreveport readily acquired goods from Texas and Mexico at reasonable prices.[92]

Thousands of longhorn cattle were driven to Shreveport, where they were butchered and shipped downriver in boats revived and repaired for service. In 1862, the Confederate congress exempted cattlemen from military service at a rate of one man per five hundred head of cattle. By 1863, cattle prices had reached twenty-five dollars per head and would soar as high as sixty dollars.[93] A supply depot was built near Alexandria to collate and store various army materials. Surplus guns and those needing repair were stored at the warehouse, along with cloth and blankets. A packinghouse was also erected to process and ship beef and pork to the armies in Virginia and Tennessee. Animals were brought overland for slaughter and pickling; in the first winter of the war, more than thirty thousand beeves were slaughtered and preserved at the plant. Confederate troops destroyed the packinghouse in 1863, when General Banks attempted a Red River raid.[94]

Across the state line from Shreveport, in Texas, a foundry was built to make kettles, pots, and pans. Sabine Parish sent the army large quantities of turpentine from its still, while Minden, located twenty-eight miles east of Shreveport, turned out cordage of all kinds at its ropewalk.[95] Shreveport itself also supported and instituted a manufacturing industry to remedy the dearth of manufactured goods. Two shops made and repaired firearms, and a tannery opened, along with a shoe factory that produced civilian and military footwear in 1861. By the spring of 1864, Shreveport had a thriving war-based industry that effectively provided for most Confederate civilian and military needs, ranging from food to medicine. The city and the region had to be self-sufficient.[96]

As governor, Moore stressed the importance of regional support and CSA reliance on those supplies in a letter to Confederate secretary of war George Randolph requesting authorization to raise companies of rangers and armaments. Frustrated that Louisiana had responded vociferously to the Confederate call but was not being provided with guns, money, or a general "as long ago promised," Moore stated that protection of the lifeline offered by northwest Louisiana was imperative. It was "an interest at stake independent of any consideration of state defense" because the army was "wholly dependent for supplies" on open "communication with Texas." Moore underscored that dependence and doubled down on funding for the Louisiana militia that guarded these provisions, stating that if the federal general Butler blocked passage between New Iberia and Alexandria, "the whole army of Beauregard" would be completely detached from "their supplies of beef."[97] The Confederate army's sustenance depended on northwest

Louisiana, and Governor Moore would have that commitment and regional importance recognized and supported with funds and guns.

The high waters of the Red River and the unpredictable raft quarantined northwest Louisiana, which allowed for advantageous utilization by Governor Allen and General Kirby Smith, cemented Shreveport's importance. Allen established a system of state stores, foundries, and factories, while Smith encouraged manufacturing by establishing government industries around his Shreveport headquarters and in Texas and Arkansas. These factories supplied the army with ten thousand pairs of shoes a month and an equal monthly number of hats and caps.[98] Smith set up the Ordnance Bureau to manufacture ammunition, and these factories produced up to ten thousand rounds per day for small arms and lesser quantities for artillery.[99] This infrastructure depended on and utilized enslaved labor, and regional slaveholders reallocated their enslaved property to support these endeavors. Allen and Smith arranged to ship cotton and sugar collected as Confederate tax-in-kind to Mexico, where it was swapped for shoes, machinery, dry goods, and any necessities that could not be manufactured on Louisiana soil.[100]

Salt was a scarce and coveted item in the Confederacy, and high demand ensured that profits were immediate for those possessing salt licks and desiccating facilities. The large saltworks near Natchitoches, which had been in operation for decades, became highly important, and existing saltworks in Bienville, Bossier, and Winn Parishes increased production. When salt from the middle southern states, the main origin point before the war, was cut off by the federal blockade, the Natchitoches saltworks became the production hub. In 1863, the Confederate government contracted to take all produced salt at ten dollars per bushel, although many competitors sold salt at twelve to fifteen dollars per bushel. As the Union army advanced farther into the state and left the sugar country abandoned, the great sugar kettles, "together with the negroes belonging to the plantations," were taken to work at Drake's saltworks and other saltworks in north Louisiana.[101]

John Coleman's father, Robert, remarked on the "great cry for salt" in a letter detailing his foray into that enterprise. He had made forty-six bushels of salt in a week and wrote that he, his wife, and sister-in-law were making salt alongside nine or ten other families. Robert said that salt was selling at forty Confederate dollars a bushel and he was confident he could make "salt enough in one week" to make a full load for trade in Texas. On the return from Texas, he could take the flour—obtained by "swapping it [salt] for flour a few miles out . . . pound for pound"—and exchange it for sugar.[102] D. Y. Milling, a soldier from Bossier Parish, wrote to his brother about the advantages of selling salt. Laid up in a convalescent camp in Little Rock, Milling told his brother that salt used by the army was going for thirty to forty dollars a barrel and was coming from Bossier. He advised his brother to either make salt for the government—using their enslaved people to increase production—or to secure a government salt contract. If the latter case worked out, Milling desired to help his brother with this salt production, asking "to attend to the hands or in some part of the work."[103] Zack Howell wrote to his wife, Isabella, about engaging their overseer and enslaved people in making salt.[104] Henry Winbourne Drake fled his Tensas Parish plantation with his family and enslaved people to refugee in Bienville Parish for the last two years of the war. He also seized the opportunity presented by the increased salt demand and hired out all his enslaved males to the saltworks at Lake Bistineau. After the seizure of the Avery Island salt mines in southern Louisiana, these saltworks became the largest and most important in northwest Louisiana.[105]

While the production of clothing, shoes, foodstuffs, salt, and beef were vital contributions to the Confederacy, the region's manufacture of medicines and distillation of spirits for medicinal use was unquestionably significant. Governor Allen erected state laboratories to manufacture turpentine, castor oil, bicarbonate of soda, and medicinal alcohol. At Mount Lebanon Female College, a hundred newly purchased acres in Bienville Parish were cultivated and produced turpentine, whiskey, castor oil, and a "good grade of opium made from native wild poppies" for anesthetic and pain management. Quinine and additional medicinal drugs were brought in from Mexico, and Keatchie Female College served as a depot for some of these medical supplies.[106]

Bartholomew Egan, a Bienville planter and doctor, was appointed surgeon general of Louisiana in February 1863 and later was tasked to "superintend the preparation of indigenous medicines." Egan was dedicated to establishing efficiency and managing Shreveport's medical department, laboratory, and state hospital. Once again, enslaved people were central to the fruition of these plans and the production of medicines. In a letter to General Manning from Mount Lebanon, Egan stated that he had set out to make Louisiana's medical department efficient and respectable, to supply the state troops "amply with all medical agents," to impress on the state surgeon the need for attention to hygiene, and to "observe the strictest economy consistent with these objects." He was delighted by the realization of these aims, even with the unexpected project of improving the hospital at Shreveport. Egan heaped praise on the "benevolent ladies" of Shreveport for their assistance in "the treatment and cure of so large" a number of ill and wounded soldiers.[107]

Allen's deep concern about the lack of medicine for civilians and soldiers led to the passage of Legislative Act 70 on February 11, 1864, which allowed him to appoint Egan as superintendent. The act established a state laboratory at Mount Lebanon Female College staffed by twenty-nine enslaved men impressed from local plantations, alongside a chemist, distiller, several machinists, and skilled workers. The enslaved men constituted the laboratory's main workforce. The laboratory and surrounding environs grew medicinal herbs and opium poppies and produced turpentine, alcohol (including pure whiskey), castor oil, and morphine, though they were unable to create a substitute for much-needed quinine.[108]

The army also purchased and contracted medicines and medicinal alcohol from other regional druggists. Governor Allen authorized J. P. Breda of Natchitoches to "convert into brandy for hospital use all liquors which may be furnished to you for that purpose." Breda was to confine these operations strictly to supplying the state, and if he needed the "assistance of persons in military service," this would be arranged.[109] William Ball, the superintendent of the state dispensary at Shreveport, wrote to Breda in 1865 to request his "early attention" to delivering "any more brandy" that might be ready for use. Another letter, discussing invoicing, indicated that Breda typically sent distilled medicinal spirits to the army. The dispensary would send him "90 galls of alcohol at $30 per gallon," and he would turn it into brandy at "$35 and then add expenses paid."[110]

From Shreveport, Allen instructed Egan to use the DeSoto-based laboratory to prepare medicines to be "sent to different parts of the state and dispensed as the law requires." He empowered Egan to "purchase and put up such machines as you may think proper" to meet the needs of the army and civilians for medicines, and to secure apparatuses for distilling. He also requested that Egan immediately advertise for "indigenous barks, roots, herb, etc." A few months later, Allen endorsed Egan's request to purchase from anyone who possessed them stills to distill medicine.[111] Egan wrote to General Edmund Kirby Smith in December 1864, with notable pleasure, about his ability to overcome the difficulty of "procuring machinery and labor" despite the "scarcity and cost of materials." The state laboratory not only was functional and producing the necessary medicines but also held the promise of realizing "the benevolent purposes of the governor and legislature." Throughout its tenure, the state laboratory received letters from army headquarters at Shreveport requesting deliveries of the "excellent whiskey" prepared by Egan at Mount Lebanon.[112]

Production of medicines and the running of the state laboratory depended heavily on enslaved people's labor. Egan wrote to Governor Allen in August 1864, concerned about the diminishment of his enslaved workforce by impressment. Allen's response mollified those fears and underscored the significance of the laboratory's production to the war effort. Allen noted that impressment was "a measure which I am averse to except in cases of extreme, urgent, and palpable necessity," but maintaining a steady flow of medicines and medicinal supplies fell into this self-imposed catchment. An October 22, 1864, receipt from headquarters listed fifteen enslaved people sent to work for Egan with instructions to "return them as furnished from those to be impressed." A few weeks later, Governor Allen wrote to Brigadier General Braxton Bragg to follow up and secure the exemption from impressment of the enslaved people working at the laboratory.[113]

As Allen's letter to Breda indicates, individuals who produced items for wartime use could request assistance from enlisted white southerners. Breda wanted one of his sons to help distill medicines as part of his Confederate service, and he wrote a series of letters to Allen for this approval. In one letter, a slightly exasperated Allen denied Breda the use of "effective men from active service" to work as his assistants because they were needed on the fighting lines and cited similar requests that had been denied to "coroners, justices, mayors, police jurymen and other officers." While medicines were essential, the "requirement of the service" for distillation was not proportionate to justify "depriving the CSA of any soldiers."[114]

Allen's cautious application of impressment in the final stretch of the war bookends the more rampant use of impressed enslaved labor to build defensive works throughout the state or to manufacture munitions, and as cooks, teamsters, hospital attendants, and body servants.[115] Like their slaveholding counterparts in isolated southwest Georgia, midsize to large slaveholders in the region permitted impressment of the enslaved at Shreveport headquarters.[116] Many slaveholder letters simply document such impressment through a compensation deal for a deceased enslaved person. Whereas civilian aid pleas were laced with emotion and implored the Confederate state for protection, the documents regarding enslaved people kept with antebellum precedent and were detached and factual. When the Confederate government authorized impressment, it agreed to compensate slaveholders thirty dollars a month, or the value of the enslaved individual in the event of their death. This monetary compensation and guarantee induced slaveholders to grant their enslaved peoples' labor to the Confederacy.

William Benson of DeSoto received a receipt for the impressment of his "negro boy Ellick aged 23 years black color 5ft 7inches high" for sixty days under "call of H. Allen for work on fortifications." DeSoto planter William George Hale's conscripted enslaved labored on public defenses for General Edmund Kirby Smith in 1863.[117] Likewise, N. A. Birge, a captain and assistant quartermaster who had sent his enslaved property to Texas, received a receipt for the hire of "one negro boy in Genl hospital at port monroe, LA as cook" for twenty days for $13.45. Twelve of his enslaved—who were all given number designations instead of names—were also transported from Tallulah in Madison Parish across the river to Vicksburg for impressment duties.[118] Four of William Hutchinson's impressed enslaved worked on the public defenses. Two of these enslaved men—Wash, age twenty-three and valued at $3,000 and Jury, age twenty-two and valued at $1,500—died at "the hospital of the engineers department" at Shreveport. Their death receipts record that Hutchinson was "paid hire till date of death." In addition to his impressed enslaved property, Hutchinson paid the CSA $500 in February 1864 "to have said Hutchinson detailed to oversee his own enslaved population for twelve months."[119]

Impressed enslaved men labored to build Fort DeRussy, located on a bend in the Red River a few miles north of Marksville, Louisiana.[120] Construction of the fort and its river defenses began in late 1862, when the state militia decided to protect the Red River from Union gunboats and transports moving down the Mississippi River from Vicksburg. Five north Louisiana parishes and one Texas county gathered funds ranging from $4,500 to $25,000 for the defensive work, and slaveholders from the Red River region sent countless enslaved men to build this vital defense. Sixty-nine enslaved men died building the fort. Isaac Greg and Daniel Bogan—two men enslaved by Henry Marshall—and Bill Flemming—enslaved by Alfred Flournoy Jr.— were among the dead.[121] For Red River slaveholders, protection of their fertile land and the institution of slavery remained of paramount concern, and they offered their enslaved property to aid the Confederate cause and protect the region, even when they personally incurred considerable financial loss.

Regional slaveholders were alert to the changing political and economic landscape that followed the Kansas-Nebraska Act, the *Dred Scott* decision, and the splitting of the Democratic Party. Convinced that the federal government wanted to limit the expansion of slavery, but more importantly that their right to hold human property was in peril, regional slaveholders across the spectrum committed to secession. Secession and the Confederate government's manifesto aligned perfectly with the ideology and identity of these white southerners, who thrived economically in a world constructed and enforced by racial domination. Fighting to protect the institution of slavery, white slaveholders were enthusiastic volunteers for the Confederate army, and they were further buoyed by the dedication of white women to the Confederate cause. These slaveholding women supported the war effort completely, and they confidently took on plantation management and further control of enslaved people.

Cotton cultivation in the region continued throughout the Civil War, but regional slaveholders remained attuned to the needs and requirements of the marketplace, and as profit-seeking capitalists, they diversified the industries and skills to which enslaved people's labor was allocated. Enslaved people worked cotton fields and expanded cultivation of foodstuffs, but they also were weaving cloth to then sew into Confederate uniforms, making salt, and making medicines and medical supplies, and they were impressed to build Confederate forts. The enslaved people who had made the Red River region incredibly wealthy were now forced to use their bodies and their labor to create goods and crops that supported the Confederacy. Market-focused slaveholders used enslaved people to leverage the environmental protection afforded by the Red River, allowing an escape from the devastation and deprivation that affected other portions of the South and creating a wartime economy that made northwest Louisiana the capital of the Trans-Mississippi West. Though they were cushioned during the first few years of war, fighting would eventually arrive in the Red River valley, and to the astonishment of vitriolic slaveholders, enslaved Blacks would seize opportunities for freedom and self-assertion.

Caspiana plantation big house. William Hutchinson, an early settler
and successful regional planter, owned Caspiana, which is located in Caddo Parish.
It is a traditional "Carolina I" architectural style home. The home was relocated
from the plantation holding and is one of seven buildings at
LSU Shreveport's Pioneer Heritage Center.

The Red River at Grand Ecore.

Dense cotton fields fan out from the Red River in Colfax.

COLFAX RIOT

On this site occurred the Colfax Riot in which three white men and 150 negroes were slain. This event on April 13, 1873 marked the end of carpetbag misrule in the South.

Colfax Massacre state historical marker. Positioned so that it faced the curve at the midpoint of Main Street, the sign stood in front of the courthouse until it was finally removed in May 2021.

The whites-only cemetery in Colfax contains a looming obelisk
memorializing the Colfax vigilantes.

The Colfax vigilante obelisk.

A state sign about the founding of Grant Parish and Colfax, located in Colfax. It is situated at the other end of town from the courthouse but still on Main Street.

"HEAD HEART AND SOUL OF THE CONFEDERACY"

Cotton, the Red River Campaign, and Confederate Surrender

Throughout the Civil War, the Red River region remained market focused. The impassable Red created new boundaries and expectations for enslaved labor, while slaveholder control evolved to accommodate new pressures and needs exerted by the war. Slaveholders' capitalist mindset and economic connections diversified and extended their reach into far-ranging industries. These new avenues of enterprise relied on enslaved labor and the aptitude of enslaved Blacks for reskilling and retraining in time-sensitive conditions. While enslaved people labored across new industries and in the region's cotton fields, slaveholders continued a steady trade in Black bodies, planned for ambitious cotton crops, and sold cotton on the open market. The popularity of refugeeing enslaved people in Texas indicates the continued significance of plantation slavery to Red River slaveholders from an economic, social, and personal identity standpoint.

Abraham Lincoln issued the Emancipation Proclamation on January 1, 1863, which declared enslaved persons within the Confederacy free. The proclamation did not apply to enslaved people in the border states or in portions of the South under federal military control, such as federally occupied Louisiana. The presidential edict decreed immediate freedom for Blacks and did not mention any compensation for slaveholders. Regional white attitudes hardened with unprecedented intensity immediately following the proclamation. The same enthusiasm that had been evidenced during the volunteering excitement at the start of the war now found renewed outlet, channeling long-standing hatred of Lincoln and the federal government into violence against Blacks.

For southerners broadly, and especially for Red River slaveholders, the reasons for secession and the ensuing war remained unchanged, but Lincoln had delineated a clear change in Union motivation and desired outcome. With the federal army's primary goal now explicitly the abolishment of slavery, regional slaveholders, like their slaveholding brethren across the South, withheld from the enslaved news of emancipation. They lashed out at African Americans who attempted to join the federal army or who seized freedom and demonstrated more personal autonomy. This calcification found further outlet and evolution during the Red River campaign and subsequent Confederate defeat.

In the months following the proclamation, federal forces pushed farther into the Confederacy, reaching areas heretofore impacted lightly by Union proximity. The Red River region felt the close presence of federal troops keenly, and an already strong Confederate nationalism intensified, with regional industry and geographic affordances harnessed to further support the war effort. The bountiful late 1863–1864 crop was a bequest of the fine weather, and tens of thousands of bales sat on the banks of the Red, awaiting shipment southward. Additional cotton reserves were still growing, which added further incentive for the capture of Shreveport by the U.S. Army.[1]

The acquisition of cotton was thus a prime motivating factor for the Red River campaign, a major federal campaign to capture Shreveport that took place from early March through late May 1864.[2] In the aftermath of the campaign—in which Confederate forces lost control of Alexandria but prevailed at Mansfield and forced a Union retreat at Pleasant Hill—regional whites remained committed to the Confederate cause, but the steadfast certainty around winning the war diminished. Nonetheless, strong adherence to the Confederate ideology and enduring patriotism lasted long after the war's end and played a significant role in shaping the tenor of postwar racial relations.

The Red River ensured that slavery continued in this region with less upheaval and incursions from the dislocation of the Civil War. Few parts of the South remained as isolated, and these environmental factors afforded slaveholders the ability to command the labor and bodies of enslaved people far longer than was possible elsewhere. In stark contrast to other committed plantation regions, slaveholders along the Red River maintained the hallmark authority and control of racial bondage, forcing enslaved people into fieldwork, impressment, or work in wartime industries. The river allowed continued cultivation of cotton and foodstuffs, with the power structure of enslaved labor reconfigured to support the multiple avenues to profitability available to regional slaveholders. Cotton cultivation continued apace throughout the war, and profit from this cotton was used to purchase supplies from Mexico and Texas for military consumption.

The federal blockade of southern imports and exports began in the summer of 1861, affected all southern ports, and tightened trade.[3] Thereafter, with most southern cotton embargoed, northern Louisiana's cotton took on increased significance. The Confederacy pledged it as security for European loans, and cotton's gold value of more than $8 million represented real assets as Confederate money depreciated.[4] General Edmund Kirby Smith's headquarters in Shreveport included a cotton bureau that reported the purchase of more than eighty thousand cotton bales in Louisiana, with the lion's share from Red River plantations. In 1863, 28,505 bales had been purchased at Shreveport, with 10,602 of those shipped to Texas to procure supplies from Mexico, and more than 12,556 bales stored near Natchitoches.[5] The cotton bureau wanted to keep Confederate government cotton from U.S. government reach, so it instituted a caravan system that traversed northern Louisiana to haul cotton into Texas.[6]

The embargo presented certain difficulties, but white civilians and the Confederate army strove to protect cotton fields. Alfred Flournoy wrote to his son Alfred Jr. about the paucity of money, which echoed sentiments found in D. Y. Milling's letters and underscored the importance of income from cotton grown by the enslaved. Indeed, as Flourney remarked, "everything depends on cotton."[7] The lack of disposable funds, coupled with poor access to credit and the difficulty of selling cotton, intensified white civilian frustrations. Flournoy expressed his exasperation with this conundrum: "Cotton now cannot be sold at any price. All the necessaries of life are scarce and high and cannot be purchased except with money." Nancy Willard espoused similar feelings, writing, "monney is scarce and every thing sells hie," and Letitia Sibley wrote, "Everything is heigh as ever. We cant get a thing."[8] Programs instituted in 1863 by Governor Allen and General Kirby Smith offered greater opportunity to sell cotton and a modicum of pecuniary relief. It also provided a platform—utilized following the Red River campaign—for regional whites to request assistance and provisions from the Confederacy.

Red River slaveholders resolved to prevent their cotton falling into federal hands. If they were unable to sell the cotton to the Confederacy, they preferred direct sales at a depreciated rate, or to burn their cotton. In 1863, William Hutchinson received word from his factor that some of Hutchinson's store of cotton had sold low because "it was the best I could do."[9] William Benson's overseer received a letter from his factors at Mansfield that stated, "In case the necessities of war should compel the destruction of cotton, then as a matter of course, the sale will be thereby cancelled."[10] Nancy Willard indicated that burning cotton to prevent federal seizure was the preferred method in Bossier Parish. Willard, steadfastly optimistic for southern victory, wrote in mid-1862 that planters who had sent their cotton crops to warehouses had "given order to have it burnt if the Yankees should come up here."[11] These choices for cotton disposal reflected the region's enmity toward the U.S. government, and the deep regional attachment to the Confederacy.

Throughout the war, slaveholders on the Red River maintained their market-focused mindset and continued to conceptualize of enslaved people as repositories of wealth, investments, and moveable assets. The passion for purchasing enslaved people did not readily abate. A friend wrote to William Benson that a fellow planter decided to buy "three or four negroes" during the first year of the war because he "had some money and invested it in that way."[12] Zack Howell continued as a local slave trader through the first year of the war, and he kept watch on saleable human chattel while serving in the army. Like other market-oriented, profit-minded slaveholders, Howell saw Confederate economic fluctuations as incentivizing investment in enslaved people. They believed that enslaved property would hold its worth and indeed be valued higher when the Confederacy inevitably won the war. When Confederate currency depreciated or was not accepted, slaveholders frequently chose to transfer Confederate paper money into enslaved people.[13] Eager to profit from the instability swirling around bondage in Unionist Kentucky, Howell effused to his wife, "I have heard of a likely negro woman 21 years old + 3 children appraised at $600." Though it would "take gold to get them," he continued, purchasers could easily procure "a likely negro fellow a cooper at $500."[14]

Most slaveholders, however, sought to refugee their enslaved property while removing themselves from Union proximity. In early 1862, Charles Mathews wrote to urge his son-in-law to protect his chattel investments. Mathews stated that Chase "had better . . . determine what you will do with your negroes if the enemy enters this section of the country."[15] Northwest Louisiana represented one of the safest bastions of enslaved labor in the Confederacy, and its relatively isolated geography, coupled with political security, made it a logical locale to sequester enslaved people. Once U.S. forces occupied southern Louisiana, planters fled to the Red River or Texas, where they refugeed enslaved people. DeSoto Parish was a favorite refugee location for Bayou Teche planters, and numerous others continued to use the well-worn path to Texas.[16] The combination of clustered settlement zones and expanses of land in eastern Texas—specifically in the Gulf Coast region and areas stemming off the Brazos, Sabine, and Trinity Rivers—provided a hospitable landscape for plantation slavery to continue undisturbed.

Most slaveholders sheltering their property in Texas came from Louisiana, followed closely by Arkansas and Missouri.[17] Texas geography ensured that while enslaved Blacks were undoubtedly aware of and recognized the revolutionary impact of Union proximity, as well as of a federal victory, few were able to escape while being transported to Texas soil or while federal troops were garrisoned at Galveston.[18] British observer A. J. Fremantle, writing from Texas in 1863, noted that "the road today was alive with negroes" who were quickly "being 'run' into Texas out of Banks' way" by their owners.[19] In the aftermath of Sherman's march on Savannah, David Pierson wrote to his father that "parties are hurrying off their negroes to west Texas," and sometimes were selling them there. He thought these actions prudent and would do the same "if I had such property." Elizabeth Scofield and her family became caretakers of Oakland plantation when the owner, Mrs. Tanner, and her family refugeed with their enslaved Blacks to Texas. Scofield remarked that a "large number of Louisianans owning a great many slaves ran as refugees to Texas." In a December 1864 letter, Robert Sibley told his son that more neighborhood slaveholders had moved to Texas and noted the commonness of this move.[20]

Joseph Texada was captain with the Eighth Louisiana Cavalry and wrote a series of letters discussing the relocation of his enslaved people following the Battle of Mansfield on April 8, 1864. Joseph instructed his wife, Margaret, to get "your wagons in reddiness and if need be buy one," since he was unsure how long their plantation would remain out of enemy lines. Although the plantation had "but little left," it was imperative to "remove all our negroes and valuables if the enemy should again occupy our parish." Writing from camp in the aftermath of the 1864 Red River campaign, Texada acknowledged the tenuous position he and his fellow cotton planters occupied. Texada, like other slaveholders, knew that his enslaved property constituted most of his wealth and that relocation away from Union forces increased the likelihood of maintaining his property. A few months later, Joseph wrote to Margaret that her "plan of getting our negroes out of the Enemy's reach I think is the best under the circumstances," and he empowered his father or brother "make the bargain."[21]

Issues of racial identity and Confederate loyalty fueled a broad regional dislike for the 1862 Conscription Act, which rankled regional whites for its implications around loyalty, honor, and white identity. Conscription affronted many southerners because it "seemed insulting to force men into service," and this slight to personal honor also could hinder procurement of a substitute. Stemming from the citizen-soldier tradition, many Louisianans, like their southern and northern contemporaries, viewed forced service as lowering the soldier's value to a degraded position.[22] Regional slaveholders agreed with the impressment of some of their enslaved to support the Confederacy, but most whites were rankled when the Confederacy passed a conscription act to raise troops. This national conscription act—the first of its kind in North American history—was passed in April 1862 in response to a widespread drop in volunteering and the expiration of many one-year service contracts. Two subsequent alterations were designed to mitigate social tensions and boost reenlistment numbers, though these intentions were not realized. The Confederacy needed more men, and it required their service for more than one year, so terms of enlistment were extended for the duration of the war and were applicable to drafted white men between eighteen and thirty-five.

The first exemption included in the Conscription Act was that draftees could avoid service through the hire of substitutes. These substitutes could not be from the pool of eligible draftees, so most were foreign nationals. The cost of securing substitutes was unregulated, and since conscripts negotiated their own contracts, the price of a substitute quickly became astronomical.[23] Jas Milling was searching for a substitute for his brother but wrote to inform him that he had had no luck. Finding a substitute on "reasonable terms" was hard, and he even "doubted the propriety" of utilizing substitutes.[24]

Finding individuals willing to take on a term of service was exceedingly difficult, though not impossible. Tom Fullilove, son of Jas G. Fullilove, sent a substitute in his place for the first half of the war. Tom paid his substitute $1,000 and gave him the "best gun he could find" and the best horse he owned. Francis Lawrence served as a substitute for William Hutchinson.[25]

Though substitutes were expensive and difficult to locate, Alfred Flournoy Jr. wrote to his wife from camp in Texas that it was "in force right in this place."[26] William Tamplin wrote to his sister that although he had volunteered, he considered himself a "three years soldier," since the law "takes all from 18teen to 35 years." He was dismayed by the draft, stating outright, "I am willing to serve my country without being forced in to it." He hoped that conscription would not hamper his chances of moving from infantry to a spy cavalry company and fretted about the long absence from his sister.[27]

Forced conscription struck a sour chord with Red River whites, both slaveholding and nonslaveholding, even while the army ranks were regularly filled with able-bodied Louisianans. But small to midsize slaveholders were further upset by the act's second exemption for overseers on larger plantations. This exemption, added in October 1862, has received the most attention from historians. The provision acknowledged the South's requirement for overseers, because it was a country built on the plantation complex and powered by enslaved labor. Slaveholders, white women on the home front, and enlisted men worried that without overseers, enslaved people would run amok, revolt, abuse privileges, escape to Union lines, and fail to cultivate crops. Thus, the Confederacy allowed plantations with twenty or more slaves to maintain an exempt-from-conscription overseer to balance the competing requirements of the army and the need to maintain control of enslaved labor.[28] The exemption applied only to plantations without nondraftable white men on the premises; a planter older than draft age or a member of another exempt group could not get a further exemption as overseer for a son or kinsman. People in certain vital occupations, like teaching, pharmacy, ministry, salt making, and manufacturing of army supplies also were exempted. D. Y. Milling urged his brother to produce salt and to manufacture supplies for the Confederacy to ensure exemption.[29] The slave codes in several southern states also required a white presence on each plantation. In these states, the addition of the overseer law resolved tensions around Confederate federal laws usurping states' rights by stating that the national conscription did not apply to individuals in states already exempted by state law.[30]

The issue, however, was that the overseer exemption mainly benefited large planters while small slaveholders, yeomen, and poor whites fought. In Louisiana, 90 percent of slaveholders owned fewer than twenty slaves, and northwest Louisiana was predominately small and midsize holdings. The "twenty Negro" proviso caused intense discord throughout the South, compounded by uneven enforcement of the act. It was the abuse of the law, and not the law itself, that irked white southerners, making the exemption an easy target for war-weary soldiers and families.[31] John Harris's letter to his wife, Becky, reflects the general sentiments. He was dissatisfied with the exemption because "men who before the war commenced employed the poor man to attend his negroes and never himself went to the fields" were now "the best of overseers, can have more work done and keep the poor negro in better subjugation than the poor man." Harris felt that the rich "ought to face the canon [*sic*]" or, when the Confederacy gained independence, risk forfeiture of their property to those who had fought and served. The disappointment with widespread national service was plain, particularly in Harris's nod to the other occupations exempted from battlefield duty: "Some who would have been ashamed to be caught with an awl and last in hand have turned out to be good shoe makers."[32]

It should be noted that Louisiana did not operate as a monolith, and levels of devotion and disaffection varied throughout the war, with sentiments affected and loyalties colored in areas falling under federal control or in proximity to the federal army.[33] There were small numbers of Unionists in northwest Louisiana, but most left for New Orleans during the war. Certainly, some poor, nonslaveholding whites held Unionist leanings or preferred neutrality in the conflict, but the historical record is silent on their sentiments and thoughts on conscription. The most famous regional Unionist was the prosperous slaveholder James Madison Wells, who would become lieutenant governor of Louisiana in 1864 and governor in 1865. Jayhawkers (pro-Union guerillas) and draft dodgers existed at the region's fringes but were not pervasive. The majority of whites in northwestern Louisiana remained overwhelmingly pro-Confederate and earnestly committed to the war.

Historical memory and the presence of items in archival collections result from conscious choices made by dominant racial and social groups in constructing the historical narrative. This is significant when assessing what the archives reveal about Confederate loyalty, service, and nationalism. White supremacy and the Lost Cause narrative shaped southern historical memory. This crafted collected memory centered on the noble and justified Confederate cause in a war fought for states' rights and not slavery, and fought by the bravest soldiers in history, who were only defeated because of the U.S. government's superior resources. Fabricating collective historical memory also necessitates mythmaking and the omission of facts.

As Adam Domby notes, this rampant narrative fraud and fabrication formed the foundation of the Lost Cause narrative that perpetuated racism and strengthened racist power structures across the South. Fitzhugh Brundage adds that former slaveholding white women positioned themselves as creators and stewards of historical memory and memorialization. Their zeal and determination shaped postwar narratives and established monuments that expunged sectional flash points and rendered all southerners Confederate supporters.[34] Thus, the remaining written regional record highlights only a long-established commitment to the Confederacy and the distress surrounding the Conscription Act. Missing are any records of how conscripted men felt, their experience in the CSA, or how their families felt about their service, as well as any records of dissent by Unionists or yeomen, or societal reaction to conscripted servicemen.

— — —

The Emancipation Proclamation signaled slavery's move from a central issue to the key issue to be decided on the battlefield. Although it was of limited practical effect in areas under Union occupation, the proclamation defined the war's struggle in racialized terms and struck at slavery in places still under Confederate control, like the Red River region. In light of this proclamation, Lincoln believed that the Civil War would accomplish two critical things: the restoration of the Union and the ending of slavery. The words, the intended trajectory, and the intentions of the proclamation became "*things* and powerful things too." Blacks were addressed directly by the document and were welcomed to enlist in the Union army. Moreover, it positioned the Union army as the agent of emancipation and the standard-bearer of the Union's goals and of abolition, substantiating all southern fears and making negotiation moot.[35] Many southerners echoed Jefferson Davis's angry expostulation that the Emancipation Proclamation vindicated the act of secession, a feeling that deepened as formerly enslaved people left for Union lines.[36] The experience of the war and the tumultuous upheaval of emancipation redefined nationalism and citizenship, cementing the narrative of a unified South under attack as foundational to white southern nationalism.[37]

The battle lines at home and on the battlefield were more starkly delineated, and Red River regional sentiment toward Blacks hardened further. The Emancipation Proclamation fractured slaveholders' static conceptualization of their relationship with Blacks across the South. This identity break was seismic in the Red River region and colored the contours of race relations throughout Reconstruction. The detached regional demeanor was heavily laced with an outward vitriol and a palpable disgust for both the concept and presence of newly emancipated Blacks. Where ownership was now curtailed, white supremacy and vigilante violence stepped in, recasting racial domination and extending the ideology of mastery to institutionalize power, privilege, and citizenship as tangible and accessible only to whites.

In Confederate Louisiana, the emancipation announcement held different significance than in portions under federal occupation. Available letters document slaveholders' anger at the proclamation but omit mention of relaying its contents to enslaved people. Enslaved Blacks nearer to Union lines or in large towns may have known about it, but available evidence shows that slaveholders throughout the Red River region withheld this information.[38] These enslavers firmly believed in the sanctity of property rights and used the Red River's geographic protection to control the enslaved population.

New Orleans, under Union control since April 24, 1862, was the capital of occupied Louisiana, which extended northward to Baton Rouge.[39] It was here that the fabric of plantation slavery began to strain and fray. Under Lincoln's pro-Unionist plan, Louisiana became the first southern state to undergo Reconstruction, in the summer of 1863. In tandem with the Emancipation Proclamation, this further embittered Confederate Louisianans' sentiments toward Lincoln, the Union, and Blacks.[40]

With the Union army now focused on the end of slavery, Red River Confederates recommitted to the protection of the institution. The "long continuance of this savage war" sickened John Sibley, and assaults on the cornerstone of the Confederacy amplified the bloodletting on the battlefield.[41] Commitment to the cause remained strong—both in words and in physical defense of the region. One slaveholder declared that "to conquer the Confederacy, or subdue the spirit of the southern people, is as impossible as to jump from New Orleans to the moon."[42] The redoubled efforts of regional slaveholders—assisted by the river itself—to stave off any military campaign in 1863, alongside the building of fortifications at Fort DeRussy and the refugeeing of enslaved, bolstered an untouchable mindset.

It was fortuitous for regional slaveholders that the river had seques-
tered and created a safe bastion that preserved antebellum white power
structures and modes of operation.[43] The available historical record indicates that enslaved labor demands were altered to include other industries
alongside cotton cultivation; enslavers distributed enslaved labor however
they saw fit in response to market demands and profitability. As the gap between the battlefront and the cotton field narrowed, slaveholders were outraged and incensed by the events of late 1863 and throughout the 1864 Red
River campaign. However, the most prevalent manifestation of regional anger was the increased slaveholder animosity toward the Union and Lincoln.
Letters from late spring 1863 onward are laden with vehement hatred of the
Union, of Union soldiers and their destructive methods, and of Lincoln and
his policies.

Gustave Lauve, a Shreveport slaveholder, received a letter from his brother
that chronicled events around their Baton Rouge holding and served as a
bellwether of the collective fears held by slaveholders. Oscar wrote, "The
negroes have all left their owners in this parish. Some planters have not even
one servant left." The privileges heretofore commanded by slaveholders
were dislodged as "our wives and daughters have to take the pot and tubs"
while any men in the parish enter the fields "with the plough and hoe." On
their father's holding "eighty five negroes" had left "but about twenty have
returned." Lauve's letter showcased the social and economic upheaval resulting from the Union's presence and the opportunity to self-emancipate,
which was bravely seized by Black individuals. Enslavers felt and remembered unfolding events through the lens of dislocation and loss of control,
with the layered economic implication of Blacks taking their freedom hitting planters most acutely.

William Sharp vividly remembered the arrival of Union troops and how
"the fiendish, vilainous soldiers" surged into "this beautiful valley" until it
was "overflown by them" and their "thieving hands and torches." The soldiers "drove the unprotected women and children from their native and
luxurious houses," which forced these white women to take shelter beyond
the confines and comforts of their plantations.[44] Governor Thomas Moore
received from a neighbor refugeeing his enslaved people in Texas a letter
that detailed the self-emancipation of several of those Black people. It was
believed that the "2 yellow small negro men" named Nelson and Daniel were
"making their way to Louisiana to try and get to the Yankees." This neigh-

bor wrote of numerous other slaveholders experiencing the same situation: Black people who had taken their freedom and were seeking the security afforded by Union camps. Moore's correspondent requested any information about the two Black men who had claimed their freedom and closed the letter with statements of Confederate patriotism.[45]

Union presence was acute for slaveholders near Alexandria where, John Ransdell wrote, the "advance of the Yankees alone turned the Negroes crazy. They became utterly demoralized at once and everything like subordination and restraint was at an end." Ransdell, a planter at Elmwood plantation, wrote to his neighbor, Governor Moore, about the situation at Elmwood and at Moore's plantation, Emfield. Ransdell's first letter described the upheaval brought by the enemy's approach. Though Moore might have heard of the Union arrival, "it is impossible for language to tell what we had to endure of mental inquietude as well as dread. I tell you nothing but the literal truth."[46] The Union advance upended the expected subordination of Ransdell's enslaved people and the concurrent requirement for total docility. Black people who followed suit and seized freedom throughout the region flew in the face of accepted Black behavior. Like many others of his class, Ransdell's unease only increased as Blacks asserted themselves, disobeyed plantation strictures, self-emancipated, and donned Union blue to fight for freedom.

William Chase, who resided at Coco Bend and Chaseland during the war, wrote to his mother-in-law that by October 1864 more than twenty enslaved people from these plantations had taken their freedom. Of the remainder, "twenty-four men left[.] of these fourteen are over fifty years of age and are not efficient."[47] At Chase's plantations and at Elmwood, Blacks who followed the wave of federal troops also claimed or redistributed other property. Chase lost most of his mules, Ransdell lost all "mules and horses, of any value, wagons, cards, bridles, saddles," while Blacks redistributed beeves, sheep, and hogs at Emfield. Ransdell also wrote of widespread damage and altered circumstances, with "fences torn down and burnt-houses and provender destroyed, cattle turned into the fields, and the negroes on many plantations driven off in a body." At the neighboring Norwood, Smith, and Cannon plantations, Blacks had seized the opportunity to leave and brought "everything else worth taking off" when they departed. Ransdell angrily and incredulously reported to Moore that "the furniture was taken out of your dwelling house and distributed among the negroes," with some of the furniture "taken to the negroes' cabins." Ransdell demanded that enslaved people return the furnishings to the main house. However, the bounds of his control were diminished, as demonstrated by enslaved people's bold actions. Ransdell wrote that a Union "train of negroes" had set up an encampment on Emfield's lawns. Enslaved Blacks on Moore's holding had shown these Black Union soldiers "where every thing was, and then they soon made way with it."[48] The accustomed power dynamic flipped, as some enslaved people "forcibly" put a Confederate soldier in the stocks overnight while Black federal troops asserted control.

Perhaps the most charged section of the letter centered on Ransdell's disgust at enslaved Blacks' defiant expressions against their oppression and their assertions of self. As detailed, they had directed federal troops to valuables and had removed furniture, placing it in their own cabins. It was these enslaved people's vivid demonstration of contempt and anger at being held in bondage that enraged Ransdell. Like other enslaved people in southern regions with Union troops nearby, enslaved people on Moore's plantation radically asserted themselves, making manifest the private emotional turmoil and psychological trauma of enslavement through physical damage to slaveholder property. At Elmfield, Blacks claimed symbols of elite white power and southern society—framed portraits of the white mistresses—for a palpable display of slavery's toll: "Your wife's and Mrs. H's likenessess [sic] were torn out of the frames and taken." Finding these actions unconscionable, Ransdell reacted viscerally, proclaiming that these Black individuals deserved "to be half starved and to be worked nearly to death for the way they've acted."[49]

This animosity was coupled with a heightened fear of federal invasion and widespread panic about Blacks abandoning and looting plantations. Polly Mason, enslaved north of Alexandria, recalled that the closer the Yankees crept to her parish, the more Black men were taken by the men in blue "so that they could make use of them in the army."[50] In her Civil War reminiscences, Margaret Texada recalled her retrieval of a male slave "of mine forced from home by the Feds" during the 1864 occupation of Alexandria.[51] Ransdell and other slaveholders refused to believe that Blacks had seized freedom of their own volition precisely because the slaveholding narrative did not include a category for enslaved people wanting to escape. It was inconceivable to white enslavers in Red River, as it was throughout the South, that Blacks took their freedom voluntarily.

Ransdell wrote that Union soldiers told Blacks "everything was theirs and that they were free to do as they pleased." Now that "the devil was let loose," Ransdell and his fellow slaveholders stayed at home despite not knowing "one half of what was going on." Slaveholders barricaded themselves in their homes while Blacks grabbed the opportunity to leave. Ransdell tabulated the remaining property, leveraging an antebellum conflation that encompassed animals and chattel. He told Moore that "thirty five left home" from Emfield, in Rapides Parish, while "twelve mules and four horses and four negroes" had run off Elmwood. By early June, Ransdell was certain that those Blacks were "in the lines of the enemy," and still denying the voluntary, bold actions of these formerly enslaved people, he declared them unable to return "even if they want to." There were twenty-seven missing enslaved people from Emfield—with twenty-two of those having been field laborers and thus representing a deeply felt economic and financial loss—and eleven individuals gone from Mooreland.[52]

William Sharp sold his Keachie plantation before the war and relocated to Natchitoches in 1862. In a postwar letter, he recalled that when he moved, he "brought with me thirty slaves twenty eight fine horses and mules four fine new iron axle wagons a carriage and buggy." When the war ended, each enslaved person had departed and all that remained were "five head horses three wagons . . . fine lot of hogs."[53] As signified by Emfield, the impact of Black self-emancipation remained greater in the southern portion of the Red River region, but it was present across and impacted the entire region.

On the plantations, reality set in for slaveholders when they were unable to cultivate and bring cotton crops to market without enslaved labor. Preoccupation with labor capacity and reclaiming property permeated Ransdell's bitter letters. Ransdell aimed to re-enslave the Black individuals who had taken their freedom, but they had filtered into Union contraband camps and he returned with "no hopes to get any of our negroes."[54] Invading federals did not hurt Moore's crops, but significant damage had been sustained "from want of work," which made controlling labor activity Ransdell's top priority. Comfortably asserting his mastery once again, Ransdell wrote that it had taken time and force to get the plantations "to work right—negroes hated awfully to go to work again." He had shot several of them and reckoned "more will have to be." After whipping most of the remaining enslaved people, Ransdell authorized the overseers on his property and on Moore's to "chastise" enslaved persons when they "showed fight." When the enslaved man Nathan did just that, the overseer "knocked him down—whipped him pretty severely and put him in the stocks." Ransdell was pleased by this reassertion of racial domination and wrote that Nathan had "pretty well cooled down" and was back to work. The ideological upheaval ushered in by the Emancipation Proclamation and the close proximity of the federal forces further hardened whites' hatred and distrust of Blacks. Ransdell was convinced by the "recent trying scenes" that "no dependence is to be placed on the negro—and that they are the greatest hypocrites and liars that god ever made."[55]

Dependence on the power structure of slavery and visceral reactions to alterations in the Black presence "created an intense ideological and social clash" that resisted compromise with the North and incited slaveholders on the Red River to starkly declare their dislike for and disgust with Blacks.[56] To maintain their identity, the region's slaveholders drew more strongly upon the foundational ideology of mastery and racial control, interwoven with a robust Confederate nationalism. These elements hardened and became brutally resolute as the Civil War gave way to Reconstruction. Ransdell summarized this when he stated that Blacks would get what they deserved, since "my feelings, too, have entirely changed towards the negro."[57]

This hardening in sentiment was visible on the battlefield. Confederate troops broadly abhorred the notion and the reality of fighting Black soldiers. Through the arming of Black men, the Union army both recognized their manhood and ensured the freedom of the enlisted soldier and their families.[58] However, many northerners and federal troops shared the position of Charles Boothby, a U.S. Army captain stationed in New Orleans. Following the Emancipation Proclamation, Boothby wrote to his father that "negro soldiers are a perfect humbug . . . a white soldier never will salute a colored officer."[59]

By the summer of 1863, Black troops had engaged in several major battles, notably at Fort Wagner in South Carolina and at Milliken's Bend in Madison Parish, Louisiana. Confederate soldiers responded with acts of unusual cruelty targeted at Black troops, such as massacring more than three hundred Black soldiers at Fort Pillow, Tennessee, in April 1864. Robert Tyson, a Union soldier, detailed Confederate violence against Black troops during the Red River campaign. He noted in his diary that hundreds of contrabands—a military term used to describe enslaved people who crossed to Union lines—were loaded onto boats at Alexandria.[60] His June 5, 1864, entry recounts the Confederate capture of Major Pollock of the Fifth Engineers and the shooting of the Black troops of that company. Pollock's command of a company of Black soldiers—"suppressing the fact of their being colored"—was the reason Confederates shot him. Captured Black soldiers "were shot in cold blood by the enemy," while Black soldiers captured without a uniform "were sold back from us into slavery."[61]

For Confederate soldiers from northwest Louisiana who were also slaveholders, fighting formerly enslaved men was abhorrent, inglorious, and vulgar. Joseph Texada expressed his disgust at potentially fighting with "contrabands when Yankees are in abundance elsewhere." As a Confederate soldier who was also a slaveholder, there was no "glory in thrashing out negro troops but on the contrary a good deal of disgrace in being defeated by them."[62] Nancy Willard wrote of a "verry bold" enslaved man who joined a group of other enslaved men keen to raise a company and fight for the Union. Aware of unfolding political events and the Emancipation Proclamation, this Black man had boldly told his owner "the North was fight for the Negroes now," which made him "as free as his master." His assertion of an independent viewpoint, command of his own body, and a personal choice to fight for his freedom struck at the core of slaveholding beliefs. This Black man, and others who joined the Union and exercised agency, highlighted the transformation in Black identity ushered in by the Emancipation Proclamation and the proximity of federal troops. To avoid re-enslavement and violent retribution for his radical statements and bold actions, this Black man chose to end his life in a final act of independence after being caught by the Bossier slave patrols. Willard coldly reported that he "hung him self" before the patrollers returned.[63]

Willard chronicled the bald-faced cruelty of slaveholders in another letter that detailed the punishment for an enslaved person who attacked an overseer. The enslaved person had cut the overseer seven times and so received "one hundred lashes for every cut and fifty for the balance of his misconduct." This punishment also served as an example to the "great many Negroes in the woods" who had become fugitives and believed "old Lincoln is a fighting for them." The positioning of slavery at the forefront of Union goals altered the war's tenor and was a deeply felt affront to Confederates. Lincoln and federal troops might be fighting to end slavery, but Willard observed "they will see to their sorrow how their freedom will stand if the yankees gains the day."[64]

The Red River campaign of 1864 brought the battlefield into the region and the war to the doorsteps of these committed and tenacious slaveholders. During the campaign, which stretched from early March to late May 1864, food supplies dwindled and large quantities of cotton were burned or seized by the U.S. Navy. This infiltration by federal forces for a lengthy military campaign that extended across the entirety of the region extinguished the last vestige of the slaveholder's antebellum world.[65] Cotton planters saw all prospects for moneymaking dashed and adopted a pessimistic view. Joseph Texada remarked, "Should the war stop tomorrow with the loss of my cotton and negroes the debts becoming due i should be in a very critical situation."[66] Texada was not alone, for his losses reflected the widespread experience among Louisiana slaveholders, who faced slave flight and financial setbacks as the Union army advanced.

Northwest Louisiana's fealty to the Confederacy was steadfast, but financial, labor, and food concerns intensified throughout 1864. While the region was not subjected to continued military engagements, persistent military traffic, or the deprivations experienced by other southern areas, civilians requested and required government aid for a modicum of relief. Major losses on the battlefield combined with difficulties surrounding cotton export meant that the 1864 campaigns put Confederate faith and stamina to the test and required the Confederate government to administer civilian aid to staunch patriots.[67] As in many other parts of the Confederacy, Governor Allen received imploring letters seeking food and assistance, including help in retrieving enslaved people.[68]

Following the Red River campaign, an overwhelming number of requests to ease the shortage of provisions poured into Governor Allen from across the region, the majority from Rapides. Allen authorized distributions of corn to state agents. He wrote to John Calvert Wise, quartermaster general at Shreveport, to send and distribute 4,100 bushels of corn to "destitute families of Red River, having been despoiled by the enemy."[69] C. E. Hosea of Rapides wrote to Allen about "the great need of bred and meat . . . neither article can be obtained for no price" and requested these foodstuffs for individuals in Rapides "west of the Red River and south of Alexandria."[70] Even after the war, Allen received letters about "suffering for want of bread" and the lack of corn for purchase in Rapides. Citing wartime dedication and families who "lost every male member . . . in the war," J. H. Sullivan and Lewis Texada petitioned for corn to be sent to Cotile landing and "sold out to the needy at cost." Sullivan and Texada outlined logistical arrangements, noting there was a warehouse at the landing and "the entire neighborhood would assist." They underscored that the need for a "few thousand bushells" was "almost absolutely necessary," so much so that money "can be had for it."[71]

Individual slaveholders wrote to Wise for state aid. One Alexandria-area slaveholder, Robert Hyman, wrote to reclaim eight of his slaves from Confederate service. Following the Union invasion, he had just "20 left out of 120 upwards have lost just about 100 negroes." The Union army had burned his gristmill, "cotton house with said cotton," overseer's house, blacksmith shop, hospital, and most of the enslaved community's cabins. His property was "a wide waste" and he had sent most of the contents of his home to Alexandria for safekeeping, only to lose these items to Union fire. Additionally, Hyman lost a tremendous volume of corn, twenty-three horses, 112 cattle, twelve sheep, 130 hogs, and fifteen miles of fencing. He wrote to Wise seeking the return of his impressed enslaved people to rebuild his burned buildings, install new fences, and begin to replant his burned corn and cotton. Another Alexandria slaveholder wrote to Wise to propose a trade of his cotton profit for bacon to feed his enslaved people. With his "negroes about starving" and cotton requiring cultivation, he offered "15 or 20 bales in marketable condition" in exchange for bacon.[72]

Following the Red River campaign, George Guess wrote from Alexandria to a friend in Texas, declaring that Texans knew nothing of "the sufferings produced" by the war. Guess said that every "vestige of food" in the parish was destroyed and "nearly every town and every house burned," leaving white women and children to live in the woods. Whites who had been "in easy circumstances" were now "living on blackberries," and he pleaded that while the Yankees were kept from Texas, Texans would "help, help."[73] Henry Marshall headed an authorized committee of the executive office of the Trans-Mississippi Department that visited slaveholders "whose houses have been invaded and desolated by the recent incursions of the enemy." Marshall was charged with "ascertaining . . . their more pressing wants" while also looking ahead to the next crop by "learning the wishes of planters as to the cultivation of their growing crops." After surveying the planters' needs, the extent of property destruction, and the removal of laborers, Marshall and his committee constructed a plan for Governor Allen with "such measures as you deem practicable and judicious."[74] Although the dislocations of war did not diminish regional commitment to the Confederacy's ideology or faith in southern military triumph, Red River citizens were cash-strapped, and they appealed to the Confederate state government for civilian aid. Regional whites had consistently demonstrated support and thus expected that the Confederate government would provide aid.

The Red River would prove a deciding factor in the outcome of the federals' Red River campaign. The river's mercurial nature continued to plague the U.S. Army, and this reduced the magnitude of the wartime devastation experienced by the region's white inhabitants. The region did experience shortages and deprivation, but it was significantly less than in other sections of the South. Political factors, the desire for cheap cotton, and the need to infiltrate this geographically segregated area galvanized the Union campaign. Possession of the region would trigger readmission into the Union of Texas, Confederate Louisiana, and Arkansas, with important electoral votes for the November 1864 election.[75] Shreveport's strategic location, position on high ground, and significance as the Confederate capital and headquarters of the Trans-Mississippi Department secured its position as a valuable city to capture—after Richmond, Atlanta, and Mobile.[76] Shreveport's fledgling river line and naval force, and the small-scale military industry in north Louisiana, added to the military significance of the Red River capital.

Northwest Louisiana's bountiful cotton crops and related storehouses were all federal strategic goals for the Red River campaign. One Vermont soldier highlighted that those involved in the engagement questioned the integrity of the motives. He was unsure "whether the interest of the government and the advancement of our arms was the main object" or if the "pecuniary motives" of military leaders desiring to "conduct a vast scheme of cotton stealing" propelled events. He recalled that "some said the motive . . . was to occupy Texas and that the objective point was Galveston," and that troops were well prepared to seize the cotton along the Red. The expedition brought "extensive wagon trains, bagging, rope and other facilities for transportation" of the large amounts of cotton.[77]

The swollen Red River, which had kept federal forces away in 1863, now yielded an abundant crop. Tens of thousands of cotton bales had already been harvested by the spring of 1864, and these bales were sitting on the banks of the river and in storehouses, awaiting shipment. John Coleman wrote to his wife, instructing her to move all the cotton at their plantation and his mother's. He warned that the quantity of cotton "will attract attention" and "the authorities are burning all that is in danger." This white gold added to the region's allure and tainted federal involvement. It is estimated that U.S. troops confiscated more than three thousand bales of cotton in and around Alexandria.[78]

The Red River campaign was a two-pronged land-and-river-based engagement, aimed at Shreveport, that began with an air of federal confidence on March 10, 1864. Red River water levels, bad weather, and adverse environmental conditions played a significant role in the timing, planning, and outcome of the campaign for both U.S. and Confederate troops.[79] Described as "a compromise between earth and water," the Red plagued federal troops throughout the engagement and caused an incredible amount of Confederate marching, sometimes up to three hundred miles round-trip. The river also determined the speed and type of federal gunboats brought upriver.[80]

U.S. Army and naval forces made slow progress up the Red, garnering victories at the enslaved-built Fort DeRussy, followed by Henderson's Hill and Alexandria, which Admiral David Dixon Porter claimed on March 12.[81] General Banks did not arrive in Alexandria until March 25, eight days behind schedule, in the company of cotton speculators and treasury agents armed with permits authorizing them to seize and transport cotton through enemy lines. Porter, however, had already confiscated the cotton and branded it with "CSA-USN."[82] After arrival at Grand Ecore, eight miles north of Natchitoches, all assurance of federal campaign victory disappeared in the face of careless leadership and the mercurial Red. Indeed, if rivers could choose sides, the Red River flowed in a decidedly Confederate direction, and it continued to protect slaveholders on the upper Red from federal forces. Though Porter had managed to take his lightest gunboats over the falls at Alexandria, the levels of the Red subsequently dropped, and they remained low for the rest of the campaign. This low water essentially trapped Union tinclads, thwarted their progress toward Shreveport, and stranded Porter's fleet during the Union retreat.[83] Possession of Alexandria did not remain sweet for Porter, as his tinclad *Eastport,* which possessed a wrought iron prow useful for pulling out snags and obstructions in the river, was frequently grounded during this campaign phase.

The campaign involved at least thirty days of hard marching for most soldiers.[84] The two largest land battles were the Battle of Mansfield, a Confederate victory, on April 8, and the Battle of Pleasant Hill, officially a federal tactical victory, on April 9. A week before Pleasant Hill, New York infantryman Charles Dwight confidently noted that Confederates had "retreated before us for 200 miles." While Confederate soldiers were approaching

Pleasant Hill and "will probably give us battle," Dwight reckoned that Union troops would reach Shreveport within the week.[85] At Mansfield, Confederate general Taylor sustained approximately one thousand casualties while Banks lost 2,800 men. Joseph Texada wrote that the Confederates "whipped the enemy in two pitched battled and routed them," forcing a federal retreat. Taylor's men took " a great many prisoners who have been sent to Texas . . . for safekeeping." Texada told his wife the casualties included "many of our friends and acquaintances."[86]

Nathaniel Allen, a commanding Texas infantryman, wrote that General Taylor ordered him to take charge of the federal train heading to Mansfield. He went toward Mansfield with "182 wagons and ambulances, 2 pieces of artillery, and a number of mules and horses." The command "kept on driving the enemy" until nightfall to hinder their progress toward the battlegrounds. As they marched, Allen and his company saw "dead and wounded all about the road" and took grisly comfort in the knowledge that "the enemy suffered tripple" casualties at Mansfield, with Confederates "still holding the battleground."[87]

J. D. Garland wrote to his parents in the aftermath of the battle to inform them of his survival. He outlined the contours of the battle, detailing the artillery and preparations of the Confederates, the causalities, and medical ministrations for the wounded. He burst with pride over the tenacity and bravery of southern soldiers; they fought "like tigers" in one of "the bloodiest fight that was ever fought in the Mississippi valley." The following afternoon, both sides were engaged in battle at Pleasant Hill, which ended in a bloody draw. Garland wrote that the battle took place "over a space of two or three miles," and he was certain Union casualties were "greater killed than it was the first day."[88]

However, General Taylor's right flank became disoriented and wheeled to the left too soon, which prompted two other Confederate units to charge headlong into a company of well-rested veteran federal soldiers. This meant the Confederates were driven successfully from the field and their casualty numbers soared. However, Banks's hasty withdrawal of federal troops downriver to Grand Ecore rendered Pleasant Hill a tactical federal victory but a strategic Confederate victory. Thus, Red River planter John Moncure told his wife that for his regiment the battle was "short but terrific. We obtained a victory . . . the enemy then commenced a retriet," with constant pursuit "by our cavalry." Moncure wrote that Confederate soldiers seized hundreds of wagons and ambulances alongside artillery and ammunition, and captured "2 & 3 thousand prisoners besides and 2000 killed and wounded."[89]

Banks's decision to abandon the capture of Shreveport began a month-long retreat punctuated by Confederate skirmishes and goading. During federal admiral Porter's subsequent retreat downriver, the Red River's level at Alexandria fell to just three feet at the falls and trapped the fleet.[90] The *Eastport* ran aground below Grand Ecore ferry on one of six pre-positioned Confederate torpedoes. The U.S. Navy spent six days moving the *Eastport* just enough to allow the remaining flotilla to pass. Some vessels stayed with the *Eastport* to retrieve men and supplies before it was blown up on April 25 by federal forces.

Confederate troops maximized the tactical effect of the shallow Red River to pin down Union troops and inflict military and civilian casualties. A devastating incident occurred as Porter's remaining fleet struggled downriver on April 26. Confederates fired on the *Cricket,* hitting it thirty-eight times and killing half the crew. One twelve-pound shell punctured the boiler of *Champion No. 3,* a civilian charter packed with approximately 175 Black contraband refugees from Red River plantations farther upriver. These Black individuals had just boarded before the boats left Grand Ecore, eager to begin their lives as freedpeople. The punctured boiler enveloped the *Champion* in a cloud of boiling steam, water, and smoke, and "over a hundred crew and contrabands were instantly scalded to death." Another eighty-seven Black people were so severely burned that they died shortly thereafter; only three people were believed to have survived.[91] The sight of African Americans scalded to death on a Red River steamer underscored the poverty of the Union campaign.

Confederate forces kept on federal heels until the campaign finished on May 19. Charles Boothby wrote to his brother that "rebel batteries planted on the banks of the Red River" severed communication between Banks and New Orleans, while John Carson, a cavalryman in the Texas Partisan Rangers, wrote that his regiment "moved over on Red River to annoy the enemy transport" during the retreat and fired into a federal transport on the river until it surrendered on May 2.[92] Regional whites considered the campaign a Confederate success, a view aligned with final campaign tabulations of an overall Confederate victory, with ranging opinions about the victory's extent. Henry Marston received a letter from Shreveport headquarters proudly stating, "Thanks to our gallant little army headquarters, trans mississippi department was not reached." Instead, a "boastful foe retraces his steps demoralized and defeated."[93]

Confederate victory came at a price. As Marston observed, Confederates held the upper Red River with the loss of "the best blood of the land." The river, the region, and Confederate forces had repulsed U.S. troops and successfully prevented the capture, dismemberment, and occupation of the Trans-Mississippi. In his 1865 annual address, Governor Allen cited the formidable military strength of regional troops, who were "victorious in an eminent degree" and whose numbers had recently been amplified by "four companies of mounted men." Those recruits joined six existing companies that "shared in the hard fought battles of Mansfield and Pleasant Hill."[94] This strong regional defense allowed the Confederate government to maintain its integrity and legacy long past surrender. As successive Union triumphs replaced southern victories through the summer and fall of 1864, this Confederate stronghold encapsulated a sustained morale boost for an increasingly beleaguered Confederacy.

Robert E. Lee's surrender in Virginia on April 9, 1865, ended the military aspects of the long and bloody civil war. The news threw much of the white South into despair and depression and shattered the resolve of soldiers and citizens throughout Louisiana. However, General Edmund Kirby Smith, the commander of the Trans-Mississippi forces, would not concede. He issued a proclamation on April 21 urging troops to continue fighting and on April 26 held a five-hour rally in Shreveport with Governor Allen to rouse regional spirits and patriotism. Their speeches focused thematically on the cause not being lost, arguing that northern Louisiana was the last stronghold of the Confederacy and that the fight must continue. At the end of April, a friend wrote to Shreveport-based Mrs. Morris that "the terms of genl lees surrender, it appears, cover the whole army of northern virginia and not those men only, under his immediate command on the day of surrender," which felled in one swoop the "head heart and soul of the confederacy." Though the "bravest Army the world has ever saw" would fight no more, Morris's friend underscored that "in nenety day the confederacy will be without an army east of the Miss river."[95]

That only the Confederate forces east of the Mississippi would be silenced by the Appomattox surrender provided a glimmer of hope that pulsed steadily in northern Louisiana. Unfortunately, Lee's surrender signaled the futility of continued war, even to committed individuals in the Red River region. Smith and Allen's push for extended support failed to stir many supporters. The lack of pay and the rise in pro-Union jayhawking in the aftermath of the surrender led many soldiers to view continued fighting as futile.[96]

Undaunted, General Smith refused to surrender the Trans-Mississippi forces and organized plans to help Jefferson Davis—a fugitive after Richmond's fall—escape to the Trans-Mississippi instead of to Cuba.[97] In a long May 1865 letter to his father, David Pierson discussed Davis's flight "to this dept with all the specie he could get" and an onslaught of "bad news" "that the confederacy is fast collapsing." A stalwart soldier, Pierson did not believe reports that Smith would accept the terms of surrender but instead believed that the general would delay as much as possible "so as to hear from the President" on his arrival. Lee's surrender was a great blow to Pierson—he baldly wrote that "my last hope died within me when Genl Lee surrendered"—but believed that "this dept might hold out for a year longer by falling back into Texas." As if he was unsure of that statement as soon as it was committed to paper, his next line detailed the pitiful soldier morale: they were "disheartened, disquieted, and determined not to sacrifice their lives to gratify anyboddys ambition."[98]

The fast-paced collapse of the Confederacy and its uncertain vitality in the weeks after Appomattox stirred a litany of sentiments in northwest Louisiana. While allegiance and commitment to white mastery, the tenets of slavery, and a racially grounded societal structure remained unshaken, it was widely deemed futile to shed further "the best blood of the land."[99] James Calvert Wise felt differently. In a despondent letter written to Thomas Moore in early May, as "clouds thicken around us," Wise expressed frustration with considerations of surrender: "What give up this contest now, my god, what can our people be thinking about. Death in any shape would be a thousand times preferable." Wise felt strongly that if the South gave up it would be disgraced forever. This precipice was one of eternal significance because if "we are united and . . . strike now one an all," the South would achieve an unshakeable, indisputable future of "victory and independence." Utterly deflated, with "no confidence in Smith" and aware of General Taylor's "view to capitulate," Wise could write no more on the matter aside from this stark fact: "The yanks look upon the war as over."[100]

For all his fight, General Edmund Kirby Smith faced the reality of federal victory on May 8, when Union colonel John Sprague arrived carrying an ultimatum to surrender from General Pope. Pope demanded surrender on the same unconditional terms that Lee had accepted at Appomattox.[101] A day later, Kirby Smith rejected the terms. He failed to comprehend that with the Confederate government in flight, most soldiers and citizens no longer had the determination to continue a fight against the victorious U.S. Army. By May 18, Smith relocated the Trans-Mississippi headquarters to Houston, citing the need for a concentrated force in case of attack. General Buckner was left in charge in north Louisiana and surrendered on May 20, but Kirby Smith held out until June 2, when he reluctantly surrendered at Galveston.[102] Smith and Allen fled to Mexico, where Allen lived the remainder of his life.

Confederate leaders in the Red River region remained committed to the Confederacy nearly two months after Appomattox, and the region's Confederate loyalty would not cease with General Kirby Smith's reluctant surrender. Red River slaveholders had stood at the vanguard of the secession movement and would not cast aside allegiance to—and indeed, practical implementation of—the ideal and ideology of the Confederacy. Mary Rives's diary entries contain a mix of defiance and dejection that encapsulates regional sentiment at war's end. The Union was still a "cruel, heartless" enemy, and their ascendancy would shatter the "peace we have been enjoying all the while, comparative peace." Everything was a "mockery" and cloaked in "a funeral aspect" as she contemplated the extent of devastation on southern land and people from the "destroyer." She could not fathom a full surrender of "our rights, our homes, our country, our liberty" and declared that while some might live "with the enemy, all will not."[103]

Defeated militarily but not conquered or shaken in their belief in racial control and domination, white men and women in the Red River region emerged from the Civil War firmly committed to the continuation of race-based white supremacy. Their relentless reactions—violent, pragmatic, brutal, racialized, power-based—would all be in response to the utterly foreign ground of Reconstruction and the free status and newly bestowed constitutional rights of African Americans.

– 5 –

"OUR NEGROES ARE GETTING TOO INDEPENDENT TO WORK"

Labor Violence During Reconstruction

Shreveport politician John Moncure wrote a bitter letter home in 1870. A former slaveholder serving in Louisiana's state government, Moncure found an altered political landscape with Black delegates, some of whom were formerly enslaved, composing a portion of the state's representatives. Such equality between former slaves and slaveholders defied logic, morality, and justice for many white Louisianans, and for southerners more broadly. The Thirteenth and Fourteenth Amendments emancipated and bestowed citizenship rights upon all enslaved people. Black men were also granted citizenship privileges and voting rights that allowed them to participate in the body politic and to run for government office. Though Louisiana state conventions had included Black elected representatives since the 1867–1868 session, Moncure continued to find Black political access repulsive and recoiled from the physical proximity of elected Black officials in the state's House of Representatives. As he observed, contact "hourly almost with aspiring, ambitious and disgusting negroes of every shad of color" was anything but enviable, particularly given his view that Black politicians were "crammed to overflowing with manifest consciousness of their importance." Reconstruction era Louisiana, under federal military rule from 1867, found Moncure and his white brethren sharing political, social, and economic space with individuals he denigratingly called "these animals in human shape."[1]

Whites railed against Black emancipation and the concomitant freedoms of movement, labor agency, family creation, public rights, and political involvement. The vitriol of the Red River region's whites reflected a profound disquiet at the tumultuous changes to labor relations imposed by the victorious Union, and the seemingly irreversible transformation in racial relations. The humiliation of sharing political and economic freedoms with people recently held as property was immeasurable, and northwest Louisiana responded to this sting with acts of individual and collective violence throughout Reconstruction. The acrimonious regional response to Black political engagement and labor agency underscored white commitment to an oppressive racial hierarchy, responsive and adaptable to these altered circumstances, that also maintained the centrality of control to white identity. These legacies of slavery were deeply embedded in the ideological, economic, political, cultural, and labor identities that informed and shaped the region's options and prospects for Black freedom during Reconstruction and beyond. The violent tenor of labor relations and politics and the contested nature of freedom reinforced regional whites' tendency to equate Blackness with slavery and both upheld and reinforced embedded conceptions of the perpetuity of racism in all interactions with freedpeople.[2]

Regional veterans and white civilians overwhelmingly incorporated Confederate nationalism and the ethos of invincibility into a pliable white supremacist framework that drew upon mastery and violence as defining features of manhood, privilege, and citizenship. This culture of invincibility informed how regional whites, disconcerted by surrender yet staunchly committed to a racially bifurcated society, refocused their dedication to white supremacy to control freedpeople.[3] Henry Adams, a prominent Caddo Parish Black Republican, evoked the Bible in 1877 when he starkly observed the need for a place to live without violence and white supremacy: "God says . . . that he has a place and land for all his people, and our race had better go to it."[4]

The violent trajectory that had elicited Adams's comments began immediately after the war and steadily accelerated and intensified throughout the 1870s. Red River whites could not revoke emancipation, but they succeeded in making the pathways out of slavery extraordinarily narrow and proscriptive.[5] Set against an ever-changing political landscape, the contest over the form and nature of free labor and Black political involvement created an arena primed for explosive violence.

As Reconstruction progressed, episodes of brazen vigilante violence thrust northwest Louisiana into the national spotlight and rendered it nearly impossible for regional Blacks to exercise freedom or self-determination in the political, economic, social, employment, or personal aspects of their lives. While pockets of the South and the New Orleans area witnessed

Blacks exercising freedoms, enjoying more autonomy, and holding government positions, this corner of Louisiana continually leveraged violence and
white supremacist rhetoric and ideology to subjugate and stymie Black freedom. Political triggers eclipsed labor issues as the flash point for violent oc-
currences. Freedpeople were routinely subjected to violence, intimidation,
threats, harassment, and financial destitution as punishment for making
choices about their labor, negotiating labor terms, deciding to keep women
and children out of the labor force, or traveling of their own volition. Labor-
fueled violence remained a steady current flowing through the din of more
general Reconstruction era violence.

The cessation of fighting did not signal the end of wartime or military
occupation in the South. This transitory period of southern occupation
netted some fundamental changes to U.S. laws and rights but also fortified
white southerners' violent insurgency. Policies emanating from Washington
confirmed the centrality of politics to the conflict and the resulting need to
use the umbrella of war powers to create a protected, liminal state in which
government powers, new rights, and the reestablishment of local southern
governments could proceed. This extension of wartime into a period of occupation in the South meant that surrender at Appomattox was a turning
point in the war but not the conflict's terminus.[6]

The U.S. Army presence in northwest Louisiana rankled whites. It contributed to their violent response to changing social and political access
while it also validated for them the necessity of enforced racial hierarchy
and identities. Believing themselves the victims in a dishonorable national
reunification that promised rights to freedpeople, Red River whites evidenced the paucity of southern compliance through their redoubled fealty
to white supremacy. Indeed, regional whites cleaved to racial supremacy
as the core pillar of their identity, and their postwar negotiations and actions were focused on protecting this embedded ideology from dismantling by franchised African Americans, radical and white Republicans, and
carpetbaggers.[7]

Reconstruction, particularly in the areas of labor control and crop cultivation, was focused on a readmission policy. While federal commanders,
politicians, and policymakers focused on crafting laws and the machinery
of postsurrender occupation, regional whites displayed the opacity of their
contrition. Former Red River slaveholders concentrated on the immediate
and pressing concern of locking in the labor of newly freed Blacks to culti-

vate the cotton crop. Regional whites remained market-oriented and profit-driven capitalists, with the crux of postwar letters centered on maximizing profits and securing Black labor at the lowest price. Their focus on profits, increasing labor productivity, and ensuring cotton cultivation remained.[8]

Southern landowners were required to pledge an oath of loyalty to the Union and to agree to labor management overseen by the Freedmen's Bureau and operating under approved contracts before having all property (apart from the formerly enslaved) restored. Refusal—or failure to apply for individual pardons, in the case of high-ranking Confederate officials and landowners worth more than $20,000—meant the loss of land, labor, livelihood, and voting rights.[9] Former Confederates strongly opposed this northern exercise of victory. Resistance to pledging the oath emerged, which extended to begrudging utilization of approved labor contracts and continued control of the movements and labor of freedpeople. Former slaveholders' identity had been forged in ownership and control of land and labor. Emancipation stripped former slaveholders of the power structure and identity bestowed by slaveholding and denied them monetary compensation for their liberated property. This lack of compensation stuck in their collective southern craw, coloring the meaning of emancipation and affecting the response of Red River planters to political and social Reconstruction. However, because former enslavers retained their land—which obligated Blacks to work for their former owners—they used economic coercion and intimidation frequently and with alacrity as powerful weapons to embed the plantation system within the framework of Reconstruction race relations.[10]

Refusal to take the oath of loyalty was the clearest, most direct response to unification. Henry Allen, the former governor of Confederate Louisiana, followed many former slaveholders and left the state following Appomattox. A letter to close friend and Red River planter Lewis Texada illustrates Allen's unbroken commitment to Confederate ideals and his opposition to the new order. Like General Edmund Kirby Smith, who fled to Mexico and then Cuba, and Thomas Moore, the former Louisiana governor who moved to Crockett, Texas, Allen retreated to Mexico.[11] Allen, who remained fiercely connected with Louisiana until his death in April 1866, was not alone in his preference for exile rather than submission to federal rule. Tom Fullilove wrote to his wife, Lizzie, who was in Alabama at war's end, about plans for them, his father, Jas, and his younger brother Jimmy to move to Liverpool, England, for at least a year. He ordered her not to return to northwest Louisiana, as he and his father would gin two hundred bales of cotton and then fetch her. The Fulliloves did not go to Liverpool, but three years later Tom and his uncle William investigated conditions and the fortunes of relocated southerners in Honduras. Although they did not emigrate, longtime regional families like the Fulliloves found the notion of relocation outside the United States preferable to taking an oath and pledging loyalty.[12]

Writing in January 1866 from Mexico City, Allen responded to Texada's imploring and maneuvering to reenter Louisiana politics. While Allen did not "intend to become a Mexican citizen" and was grateful to "the good people of Rapides for their complimentary vote" in the 1866 election, he vowed to wait patiently in exile until "the proper time comes" for a homecoming less tinged with dishonor and obligatory contrition.[13] In another letter, Allen acknowledged his persona non grata status with northern leaders and the difficulty his friends would face in "raising one dollar for me in the states." The overall lack of money in the South, the personal and familial devastation faced by southerners, and the hamstrung circumstances of "those who would ... give" scuppered any plans to return. Evoking the language of home front letters, Allen wrote of his contentment with "labor[ing] twelve hours every day" and satisfaction with writing about the condition of the South for his newspaper, despite the hard work of editing a paper without the means to hire an assistant. When Allen died in Mexico in 1866, correspondence between Thomas Moore and Bartholomew Egan not only mourned the loss of his "earnest patriotic spirit" but also blamed his "untimely fate" on the oppressive North, which was also "killing [Jefferson] Davis by degrees."[14]

Egan, who stayed in northwest Louisiana, wrote to Moore in Texas about "the patriotic duty of every son of the south to cling to his home." He could not picture Mexico as a "suitable refuge" for southerners because it would require trading a virtuous southern citizenry for "half savage Nomades." The soil and the climate were favorable, but he felt that the "healing influences of time" and "resources, ... if undisturbed in their development," would restore former slaveholders to prosperity and spheres of social and political influence. Egan's confidence in the "ultimate triumph of Johnson's policy" foreshadowed the control bestowed upon regional whites after they took the oath, and their expansive social, economic, and political remit during Reconstruction.[15]

Caddo planter Henry Hyams wrote to Moore from New Orleans about Moore's pardon. Hyams had met with Governor Wells—the Rapides Parish Unionist who became governor after Michael Hahn and who won the special election of 1865 against Allen. Wells had enthused about Moore's "unbending integrity and honourable conduct." In the presence of "a dozen gentlemen," he wrote to President Johnson requesting Moore's return to Louisiana and complete restoration of his political and civil rights. Hyams, prescient in his view that Johnson's policies in concert with Wells's sympathies with the political old guard would ensure ex-Confederates' reinstatement to political office, wrote that he had recently taken the oath "in good faith" and had reopened his law office. He urged Moore to take the oath once pardoned, because Wells's and Johnson's "instincts if not of the State's rights . . . are yet for justice to the south," and they would prove themselves "true to their instincts."[16]

Many former slaveholders and Confederate veterans delayed oath-taking or remained tight-lipped regarding their stance on the oath. Henry Marshall's son-in-law, S. C. Furman, had been lieutenant in the Pelican Rifles, a CSA unit from DeSoto Parish, before he funded and led his own cavalry company—Furman's Rangers. Furman served alongside his brothers-in-law in fiercely committed Louisiana companies, and there are no records or correspondence from the war's end until June 18, 1867, when he signed the oath of allegiance. Likewise, Moore took the oath on January 15, 1867, but does not reference it in his correspondence.[17]

The dearth of recorded oaths of allegiance among private papers indicates that silent resistance and evasion, rather than accommodation, was the pervasive regional attitude. For these individuals, allegiance was not derived from contrition. Their allegiance was being forced, and they capitulated solely because signed oaths were required to draft labor contracts. Moreover, economic necessity, made acute by the lack of financial remuneration for their formerly enslaved property, pushed whites like William Thatcher of Caddo to swear allegiance in 1868, well after the close of Presidential Reconstruction, when the federal government focused on reconciliation policies and laws to stabilize Black labor.[18]

Conversely, financial pressure pushed many of the region's landholders to take the oath sooner than desired. It was impossible to legally bind labor contracts with one's former slaves without swearing the oath, so numerous capitalist-oriented landowners took the oath to ensure their 1865 crop cultivation. Prominent Red River landowner William Hutchinson does not mention his early oath-taking, but on July 11, 1865, he drew up forty-four labor contracts that the newly formed Freedmen's Bureau approved.[19] Labor securitization and control remained paramount, and signing the oath, refusing to sign, and delaying the process all were methods ex-Confederates utilized to display their feelings about reunification.

Red River landowners rushed to secure Black bodies to labor in their fields, often competing with fellow whites for the first time to ensure that enough hands were engaged for the upcoming year. Notably, since former slaveholders retained the acute market-oriented and profit-oriented drive so significant to antebellum regional growth, they struggled to balance having enough freedpeople cultivating cotton with contracting at the lowest possible pay rate. Irritated by and abhorring free Black labor, ex-slaveholders attempted to work immigrant groups at the pace they had utilized during slavery. These experiments proved unsuccessful and underscored for white landowners the suitability of Blacks for hard labor. For instance, Thomas Powell hired "2 irish men one woman just from the old country," and lamented to his cousin that he had "to work with them or be about them" for any work to be done. A frustrated Powell found himself doing the plowing, something he had not done "all day before this year." He found these Irish workers "green as can be" and so unsuited to the work that he planned to "get hands to work my land" because he had "no confidence in white labor . . . negro labor is the cheapest we can get."[20] The continued use of the word *hands* as descriptive nomenclature for Black laborers engaged slaveholding terminology in a free context and reinforced the white landholders' conception that Blacks were optimally suited for the physically demanding nature and rigorous pace of plantation work. In the ex-enslavers' minds' eye, Blackness remained conflated with gang labor, and African Americans were indispensable to this labor.[21]

General Order No. 3, issued on June 19, 1865, affirmed the Emancipation Proclamation and granted freedom to enslaved people in Texas. Numerous slaveholders, including those from the Red River region, had refugeed their enslaved property in Texas during the Civil War, and River landowners now were intensely irritated because this delayed enforcement of emancipation arrived as preparations commenced for the 1865 cotton harvest.[22] Regional planters' opposition to emancipation was deeply personal, and while they were not alone in attempts to mute or conceal the end of slavery, the geography of northern Louisiana helped planters stymie freedom's announcement. Along the Red River, whites scrambled to locate sufficient numbers of laborers to maintain staple crop production. Although in the summer of 1865 attempts were made to revive crop production nearly from scratch in other areas of the South, the Red River region's cotton and staple crops planted in 1864 indisputably needed harvesting. New parameters regarding Black labor made it crucial to contract enough freedpeople to guarantee cultivation. Still steeped in the logic of slavery, wherein the guaranteed core labor supply was occasionally reinforced with hired hands, ex-slaveholders now quickly learned that free labor presented significant challenges to the established plantation system.

Changes in labor availability created an impediment to cotton cultivation, which relied heavily on gang labor or tenants to meet market demand.[23] While low production, scarcity of credit, and political factors were reflected in declining farm values, the region's agricultural economic foundation— cotton production by Black laborers on mostly medium-size plantations— changed only slightly. Even as the plantation system endured in the short term, labor relations were altered. Among the most significant changes were that Black workers were now begrudgingly contracted and earning wages and that larger regional holdings began to decline due to laborer demands, crop woes, and financial pressures.[24]

William Hutchinson corresponded with a friend residing in England who was familiar with the Red River area. Hutchinson's letter must have detailed concerns about cotton prices, market demand, and crop quality, as the response laments the "mist fortune of our friends on red river" who were compelled to take "the low prices" for their cotton along with the "very gloomy" accounts of the crop. The financial misfortunes resulting from flooding and crop disease led some planters like Hutchinson to rent out their plantations to remain market-focused and profit-oriented. Concerns around finances, profitability, and productivity of land and laborers were discussed in correspondence throughout Reconstruction.[25]

Like their counterparts in equally isolated southwest Georgia, regional planters realized that while they remained largely in control, Black laborers were essential for cultivating crops and escaping financial ruin.[26] Planters and managers concentrated on maintaining production despite the transformed labor system. The drive for profit propelled whites to zealously secure freedpeople for fieldwork. In November 1865, Coco Bend's overseer wrote to owner Penelope Mathews with concerns about the plantation's labor force. Although no contracts had been made in the neighborhood for the ensuing year, he was "anxious . . . to hasten so desirable" a result. He had traveled to Alexandria, where he arranged for an agent from the Freedmen's Bureau to come to the plantation and advise the freedpeople "on the necessity of making contracts." He would not wait until year's end to get Coco Bend's laborers and vowed to "push the matter in such a shape as to accomplish shortly the object."[27] Henry Marston had similar concerns about engaging enough laborers early in the year. He noted in a January 1866 diary entry that despite "a considerable number of my negros employed," he was unsure whether his "efforts to obtain them will prove fruitless."[28] In June 1865, Mary Rives had her overseer secure laborers eighteen days after she heard "the negroes are free." Her overseer drew up the "'contract' with the negroes," described as "willing to stay and work a little and be fed, clothed, and doctored." Her October 1865 diary entry, however, impugned freedpeople's work ethic. She wrote that her horses were not cared for as before and that "corn is pulled and left on the ground for four or five days." She even accused a freedman of stealing her "fine mare." Rives left her Mansfield-area plantation on November 1, 1865, because "I could not stay with negroes."[29]

The intense competition for "enviable contracts," as Coco Bend's overseer dubbed them, frightened these planters. Interplanter competition was a new dynamic among white landowners and caused both considerable vexation and newfound tension among whites. Planters had no experience with internal rivalry for the best and hardiest laborers; previously, if a slaveholder of any size required extra brawn, they hired hands, leveraged other enslaved people to purchase more human property, or forcefully bred the next generation of laborers. Free labor introduced competition for strong, diligent, and experienced Black individuals. Regional landowners did not relish the position of fellow planter Hickman, whose Black laborers had left his plantation in Alexandria for other opportunities. Above all, planters wanted to retain "capable and efficient" formerly enslaved people on their plantations without losing any "valuable ones" to other landowners.[30] From Texas, former Louisiana governor Thomas Moore discussed the issue of contract competition in a letter to James Calvert Wise. Moore wrote that freedpeople were "absorbed by contracts of different sorts" and sometimes released and rehired on different contracts with new terms. The varied price points of the contracts were an issue because the Freedmen's Bureau would not approve lowball contracts but landowners wanted competitive contracts

that secured laborers at the lowest possible price.[31] Forced to vie for workers, former slaveholders were now in direct competition with one another to
secure "a sufficiency of labor for their plantations." They placed such importance on labor procurement and crop cultivation that "many are hiring who
are not able to buy food for their white families," according to one planter.[32]

This alarming new trend was compounded by labor shortages and fluctuations in the labor market, particularly during the January hiring season. Worse still, from the landowners' perspective, contracted freedpeople
sometimes left one estate for another in pursuit of better wages, working
conditions, or accommodation. This phenomenon was recorded in depth
by Coco Bend's overseer, Phil Key, who described how "nearly all the force"
was "persuaded off by the young white 'Robertsons'" to work the plantation
they were renting nearby. Key was sure that "the negroes . . . as well as their
employers" assumed that he, as overseer, would be "broken up by their departure." However, as he assured Penelope Mathews—while also reassuring
himself—he had "gotten rid of such worthless trash." Key proclaimed that
poaching on Coco Bend let him replenish ranks with "35 hands and they are
all good hands." Thomas Powell was similarly sure that many of his white
neighbors would "induce hands" from his plantation and noted with disappointment that "if we had labor enough this would not be the case." For
Powell, Key, and their fellow landowners, "good hands" by definition meant
freedpeople who had signed contracts "for the wages," who remained stationary and nonpolitical, who did not test the boundaries of their newly bestowed emancipation, and who did not expect "favors & priveleges from 'old
massa' plantation."[33] By contrast, freedpeople who left former enslavers, as
happened to Henry Marston, William Sharp, Penelope Mathews, Thomas
Moore, and countless others, were the epitome of "incarnate devils."[34]

The unpredictable nature of the Red River further compounded fiscal
and labor woes. Just as the river had shaped and protected the region before
and during the Civil War, so too did it play a pivotal role in postwar livelihoods. Indomitable and untamed, the river overflowed and flooded in 1866
and 1867, ruining both years' crops. A plague of armyworm and boll weevil
followed swiftly behind the flooding, and landholders' letters reflect deep
despair. William Sharp wrote that the "terrible overflow" of the Red destroyed everything, including "the last vegetable in our garden." The overflow in 1867 took away all "but our land."[35] Henry Marston recorded that
the river was very high on April 22, 1866, and continued to swell steadily

through May 20. His 1867 diary echoed the complete devastation of Sharp's letter. In June 1867, he wrote that the flooding was "disasterous indeed," with all of the plantations "more or less underwater."[36] The floodwaters had been accompanied by hailstorms, windstorms, and cold that "infected and retarded the growth of the cotton" and all other crops. The superfluity of water on Coco Bend—as on neighboring holdings—meant the June 1866 receding of the Red provided "no drainage to this plantation excepting in failing to allow the ditches to convey the rainwater."[37] The Red River dashed expectations of comfortable financial returns from the cotton plantings in 1865, 1866, and 1867.

Crop disease followed swiftly behind the rushing water. Autumn brought destruction of the crop by armyworm during the 1866 and 1867 picking season; the estimated 1867 losses were $5 million.[38] James Calvert Wise wrote to Thomas Moore in Texas of the grim situation in Rapides Parish. His descriptions of the terrible situation and prospects prompted Moore to bemoan the parish's predicament. Moore declared they were a "doomed people," before listing the litany of devastation on his Texas plantation, 150 miles west of Shreveport.[39] Bartholomew Egan wrote to Moore about the "terrible overflow" in Alexandria that left "not a stalk of corn or cotton not even a blade of grass" in its wake. In a letter to his cousin—a vocal white supremacist herself—Moore enumerated the crop tribulations facing former slaveholders and placed the onus for these woes squarely on freedpeople. The detrimental impact, Moore wrote, of "fire, sword, flood & caterpillars & taxation," alongside "negro supremacy," to the health and productivity of "this the finest country on earth" were critical factors in the widespread white mobilization to resist taxation, Black autonomy, and Black citizenship.[40]

Crop concerns and flooding vied for prominence in overseer Key's letters from Coco Bend. In April 1866, he wrote to discuss securing laborers and to update on the plantation's health. The water had "gone off with the fall of the river," but the plantation's drains had utterly failed to "convey the rain water from the land as the backwater was meant to do." After incessant rain followed by two weeks of "hail storms, wind storms, and cold," Key admitted that the result "infected and retarded the growth of the cotton, as indeed . . . all other crops." Putting a gloss on the dreary report, he wrote that Coco Bend's crop "looks as well upon the whole as any in the neighborhood" and estimated 150 acres of "very boom cotton" for the yield. Over the subsequent weeks, Key veered from optimistic—in May he wrote of "a large crop, as much to the hand as was usually cultivated by slave labor"—to despondent when the river flooded again in late June. His letter in late September noted the low morale among local plantation holders following the disastrous year.[41]

Flooding also meant an increased reliance on the Freedmen's Bureau by both the Black and the white communities, who faced hunger on inundated holdings. Bossier planters were badly affected and spent most of 1867 attempting to raise funds from cash-strapped landowners to fix and build levees on the Caddo side of the Red River. However, with most of the planters' money put toward raising the crop, cash- and credit-strapped planters had neither money nor credit left to pay freedmen or to procure food for them. Bureau officials nonetheless stepped in to maintain operations. They requested rations and supplies for Caddo and Bossier so landowners could pay, feed, and retain Black laborers.[42] The 1867 crop failure coincided with the onset of a yellow fever epidemic, rendering tens of thousands of freedpeople homeless and without food or clothing. The absence of money, the presence of disease, and the lack of foodstuffs meant federal aid from the bureau was the only solution to an emerging humanitarian crisis, and the only means to preserve the plantation system. In January 1868, the War Department authorized the Freedmen's Bureau to issue supplies to planters and to take a first lien on all crops and equipment used to produce crops.[43]

Whites like Henry Marston and Coco Bend's overseer, Phil Key, took matters into their own hands to guarantee a constant supply of workers. From the start of the contract season they kept on hand the cash required to cement the year's wages and rental prices. This made it possible to pay half of the total accrued wages every four months—a standard practice in the region—with the silver lining of needing less free cash than what "pay proper would amount to" for the entire agricultural year. Key detailed to Mrs. Mathews that to keep cotton cultivation running smoothly, $1,000 was needed "to pay the hands one half of their wages for the four months."[44] Mr. Taylor wrote despondently to Mrs. Buard in Natchitoches about the falling price of cotton and the need to keep Blacks cultivating the crop. He was concerned she might be forced to repay the entirety of a large debt and hoped for a renewal or, at best, "half the debt and interest." Paying off debt required cotton, which required freedpeople toiling in the fields. Taylor had sent three Black laborers, with the promise of sending more laborers despite the cost. Panic about cost needed shunting to the side, Taylor acknowledged, because the region had "at this moment a <u>mania</u> for the negro" and the penalty for looking "too <u>close</u> or to what you give to get the laborers" was failure to obtain the necessary labor for cotton cultivation.[45]

In the immediate postwar period, waged gang work emerged as the first compromise in the free labor system. It predated the 1880s transition to sharecropping, and waged work permitted the maintenance of the familiar plantation modes of production. Free Black laborers worked white-owned fields in large gangs, much as they had under slavery, extending the established economic system of white control and Black dependence.[46] Former slaveholders continued to prize the closed structure of gang work and attempted to replicate it by incentivizing outputs with cash wages or a share of the crop. Waged labor remained sharply distinct from slave labor systems because postbellum gang laborers worked specified hours, completed tasks detailed in a contract, and were nearly always under overseer supervision. This was a significant break with slavery, yet very different from the relative autonomy of sharecropping and tenancy.[47]

Under waged labor, males were divided into three classes with pay that ranged from six to ten dollars per month; three classes of female laborers garnered between five and eight dollars per month. This sliding wage scale held to antebellum precedent, in which the enslaved had been classified by age and fitness into first-, second-, and third-class hands. Wages and the determination of an individual's labor remained tainted with slavery's brush. The same pay bias existed for boys and girls under fourteen, with boys receiving three dollars and girls two dollars monthly, roughly equating to full-hand and half-hand status in antebellum parlance. Skilled workers, including engineers, foremen, and mechanics, were entitled to receive at least five additional dollars per month above the first-class rate.[48]

The strong southern emphasis on contracted labor allowed whites to chronicle the job requirements and set rigid boundaries for freedpeople's permissible actions.[49] Contract parameters, work hours, and privileges varied greatly throughout the region. The forty-four contracted freedpeople on William Hutchinson's Caspiana holding, for instance, were allowed all Saturday "at their sole disposal," in addition to the "privelige of cutting cord wood on that day." Hutchinson agreed to provide mule teams to haul the cordwood to the Red River, where the proceeds from the sold wood would belong to the freedpeople.[50] On Hubbard Bosley's Bossier holding,

he furnished farming utensils, horses and mules, and feed but expected
Black laborers to "furnish their own provision." His 1867 contract agreed
to give the freedpeople "on[e] half of the crop cultivated" from the second
portion as payment. Bosley's requirements relied on patterns held during
slavery, continuing labor conditions that denied Black autonomy and self-
determination. He required that freedpeople care for his horses, toil from
"daybrake til darke, and abide by the plantation bell" and remain in their
cabins during work hours only if ill, and keep up maintenance on the plantation's fences and gates.[51]

Similar work hours were kept at Coco Bend, where laborers "work from
daylight to dark, and from Mon morn til Saturday at noon," and in general,
living conditions, leisure time, and clothing distribution remained strictly
regulated, which perpetuated circumstances exceedingly close to enslavement. At Coco Bend, two suits of clothes and two pairs of shoes were given
yearly—echoing antebellum practices—but no portion of the crop was bestowed on laborers. Instead, Blacks were allowed to "have the half of each
Saturday & a garden or corn patch" if desired. Key also requested funds to
purchase winter clothes for laborers to "prevent them not working" because
of inappropriate attire.[52]

At these three holdings, half of wages were paid every four months. The
overseer at the Tauzin family's Natchitoches plantation scrupulously noted
how many days a month each person worked, from the day the contract
started until he had it approved by the bureau, and withheld wages accord-
ingly.[53] At Raceland, another Mathews family holding, Jas Sibley managed
the labor and paid "$10 to $15 for men and from $6 to $10 for women," with
food provided but no clothing. Unlike at Coco Bend, hands were paid "half
at the end of every month and the balance at the end of the year," echoing the
Tauzin plantation practice. Sibley did not feel that his practices hindered
production; he had managed to pay 1865 rates throughout 1866 and hoped to
continue for the following year. He noted that very few "were willing to sign
the contract," but "I have more hands and they are working better than at any
time during last year." Though 1867 contracts had not been signed, he was
not concerned with maintaining the necessary labor force for Raceland.[54]

These new labor strategies dovetailed with bureau rules, but slavery's
regulatory culture was transposed to these plantation practices and ensured
that landowners continued to leverage personal power, authority, and strictures over African Americans. Particularly jarring to landowners was the

decision by some Black women to absent themselves from field labor, placing their welfare or importance of the familial unit above that of the labor
contract. These personal and individual assertions of autonomy did not cor-
relate with familiar plantation methods, and whites throughout the South
were baffled that Black women exercised individual choice when it came to
how and where they would labor.[55]

Henry Hyams contracted freedman Antony Babcock to work his Natchitoches plantation "for his food and clothing" until the "people return from
Texas." If Babcock worked to Hyams's satisfaction during that period and
"gathered the corn and fodder," he was then allowed to "work out and make
money for himself."[56] Key, Coco Bend's prolific letter-writing overseer, noted
that not all of the expected Black laborers arrived from Texas in November
1865 and that "some valuable ones remained behind, especially my driver
and cooper." Ever alert to the monetary equivalence of labor, Key watched
the erstwhile freedpeople arrive back in Rapides Parish. Of those who had
returned to the plantation, he was delighted that "all the slaves on Cocobend" had been making barrels and cultivating cotton, with enough "slaves
on the plantation to make at least six or seven hundred" bales.[57] Key's
frequent reference to freedpeople as "slaves"—a practice that extended
throughout the postbellum period for many whites—illustrates that the
tangible and ideological bequest of plantation society remained resolute
and that the living legacy of enslavement actively defined and restricted the
parameters of Black freedom.[58]

Overseers and landowners withheld wages to combat the flight problem,
as whites concluded that freedpeople were less inclined to break contracts
or relocate if their wages were only disbursed every four months or at the
end of the agricultural year. By design, these tactics ensured that plantation
production advanced without a large initial outlay, and in fact freedpeople
often found that whites failed to pay their full wages. The containment of
freedpeople's movements was an important component of regional emancipation management. Planters attempted to control the physical movement
of freedpeople on and off the plantation. They also regulated Black relocation from Texas, where many Red River slaveholders had refugeed their enslaved property during the Civil War.

To further tighten the narrow pathway out of slavery, whites utilized
careful wording to revive antebellum rules while maintaining a patina of
complying with the legality of free labor.[59] White southerners mobilized

to form county patrols and home guards that echoed and engaged antebel-lum practices to hinder movement.[60] The Louisiana Black Codes, passed by James Madison Wells days before Christmas 1865, worked in tandem with vagrancy and apprentice laws to regiment and curb the boundaries of Black freedom.[61] The Black Codes continued the confines of antebellum bond-age and sharply truncated the mobility and bargaining possible for Black workers while granting whites power and control over freedpeople's lives and labor.[62] The codes failed to ameliorate the postwar issue of labor flu-idity fully; however, they were former slaveholders' "boldest and most sys-tematic attempt . . . to rectify the 'problem of labor.'"[63] Bossier Parish, for instance, permitted the arrest and forced labor of all Blacks not engaged in some occupation. When rural freedpeople relocated to Shreveport in large numbers in 1866, the Freedmen's Bureau aided in enforcing vagrancy laws and arrested the unemployed. The bureau forced freedpeople to sign plan-tation contracts—as was also done for those who held out on signing yearly contracts—or required them to labor for the state.[64]

Some freedpeople tried to ascertain and test the boundaries of their freedom. Formerly enslaved Henry Adams was keenly aware of white dis-pleasure with any amount of Black freedom but traveled to Shreveport with-out a pass in September 1865. He recalled that he did not travel without ha-rassment. Six miles south of Keachie, four whites "asked me who I belonged to. I told him no one," which elicited a violent retort as "him and two others struck me . . . told me they were going to kill me." Unable to fathom Black independence and wholly blindsided by Blacks' seizing the opportunity to determine their own movements, these white vigilantes manhandled Adams as if he were a fugitive slave. Yet Adams continued his journey, reporting, "I seen twelve colored men and women, beat, shot and hung between there and Shreveport."[65] His experience was replicated many times over, and freed-people did not always walk away alive.

Regional white landholders and the Freedmen's Bureau shared concerns that Black migration and mobility meant idleness and vagrancy.[66] Fixated on making free wage labor successful, the bureau frequently played into the majority white opinion, often forsaking Blacks completely and establishing strict policies and patrols.[67] A core element of the bureau's remit was the completion and approval of contracts binding freedmen to plantation labor. This objective was particularly challenging to bureau personnel in Caddo and Bossier Parishes, who contended with disputed labor contracts alongside racial violence, homicides, and Red River flooding. Planters came to favor bureau involvement in contracts because of a stipulation that allowed docking the wages of workers who refused work or left employment without proper authorization.[68] However, regional whites were less pleased with the Shreveport bureau chief's involvement in matters that curbed personal control over Black laborers. Per landowners' desires to limit Black movement, Red River steamboat captains refused freedpeople passage on their ships. When regional bureau commander Martin Flood investigated a January 1867 incident of denied passage to a Black family, he learned that riverboats along the Red commonly refused freedmen passage to prevent a regional labor shortage.[69]

A secured contract did not imply that freedpeople were protected from abuse and mistreatment. Similarly to the situation in southwest Georgia, Louisiana's freedpeople found that assigned contracts still left them at the mercy of landholders and subject to the use, abuse, and punishment they had experienced while enslaved.[70] Although contracts included nonviolence clauses, whippings were commonplace regionwide. Henry Adams told of his sister being beaten one day by her former mistress and then "whipped . . . nearly to death" the following day by the ex-master. After this incident, Adams and a group of freedpeople left for Shreveport. They were accosted by forty armed white men who shot at them and took Adams's horse, along with "all of our clothing and bed-clothing and money." Adams recalled that while robbing and shooting at the freedpeople, the white assailants declared "they were going to kill every n—— they found leaving their masters."[71] Unwilling to surrender the violent personal power slavery granted to slaveholders, these unwavering Confederates attempted to reinstate the whip; when that failed, as Adams's testimony reveals, they turned to pistols and vigilantism to reinforce white supremacy. This incident underscores the enduring construct of regional white sentiments that only intensified as Reconstruction continued.

The number of homicides and the extent to which violence permeated everyday Black life is both shocking and deeply significant. Caddo Parish was the most violent parish in Reconstruction Louisiana, and despite its relatively sparse population, the parish saw fully 16 percent of Louisiana's homicides during Reconstruction. The Red River region was also the most concentrated zone of violence statewide, with 45 percent of all homicides; 85 percent of these homicide victims were Black, and whites were the perpetrators of at least 84 percent of those Black homicides.[72] To Adams's knowledge, "over two thousand colored people [were] killed trying to get away" from plantations between Shreveport and Logansport, a fifty-mile distance from the top of Caddo Parish to the bottom of DeSoto Parish.[73] Emancipation opened the door to legal bodily autonomy, but many Blacks who exercised these freedoms became the victims of grievous violence.

Regular assaults on freedpeople were one way in which regional whites sought to restore the antebellum world, and here vigilante violence united white men of all classes. Whites who had not been slaveholders found an affirming kinship within the boundaries of white supremacy, which leveraged the rubric of racial, social, and political domination created by violence to bind regional white identity tightly.[74] The dislike of and vitriol directed against Blacks were lodged so deeply into the regional composition that no real provocation was needed to incite violence; many murdered freedpeople were purely in the wrong place at the wrong time. Defeat in the Civil War and the unwelcomed transformations of Reconstruction solidified the visceral regional requirement for white supremacy as the lifeblood and cornerstone of white regional identity. Northern-driven reunification efforts, in tandem with Black emancipation, served as motivation to disempower Red River Blacks politically and economically and to strengthen the omnipresence of white vigilante violence.[75] In this transformation, the regular use of race-based violence to enforce the power structure of the region moved from the long-standing, controlled arena of the plantation to the shared public spaces of riverbanks, town streets, and regional roads.

This public, pervasive, and prevalent use of violence was not alien to the regional culture or political economy. White vigilantism drew directly upon the dehumanized brutality of enslavement along the Red River. It re-dressed it in visible, unapologetic, viscerally violent garb that empowered whites to kill African Americans with alacrity and with impunity. It transplanted ownership as a means to control, subjugate, and subdue formerly enslaved people.[76] Unmasked violence was used to control the labor of freedpeople, as a deterrent for Black voting, to curtail Black demonstrations of citizenship and agency, and to exercise and enforce white superiority. Henry Adams recalled that Black lives "ain't no more than a chicken's" in northwest Louisiana, and the escalating, high-profile displays of white supremacist violence in the region would have long-lasting effects on the entire nation.[77]

Bloodshed was often a calculated response to political involvement, but it frequently was economically or socially driven. Both political and labor-motivated violence were meted out spuriously and without pretext, but the former often eclipsed the latter in government records, newspaper coverage, and testimonials. However, in the testimony of African Americans we not only unearth the incredible regularity of labor-related and socially sparked incidents but also glimpse the personal, private pain resulting from systemic violence. The majority of Black regional testimonies were given by friends and family members on behalf of murdered loved ones; brave survivors hoping for justice gave other accounts. These testimonies were compiled in an 1876 congressional report, *Use of the Army in Certain of the Southern States,* ordered by President Grant, which investigated the rise in vigilante-led southern violence. Presented to Congress in 1877, this marked the first time Red River Blacks entered the historical record in their own voice. Significantly, Blacks made this mass entrance into the formal historical record to detail, in raw and vivid testimony, the violence they and their loved ones had endured. Previously rendered voiceless as commodified enslaved people and now grappling with freedom entirely defined by endemic white supremacy and persistent acts of brutality, it is especially poignant that regional freedpeople appear in hundreds of pages of records to provide evidence of overwhelming violence and a narrative of the constricted parameters of emancipation.[78]

Henry Adams's testimony is the longest inclusive narrative by a single regional freedperson. He was both a personal witness to these campaigns of terror and a spokesperson for the regional Black community. In example after example, he enumerated the myriad ways in which Red River whites constricted the passageways out of slavery. Crop control, debt, and Blacks' failure to submit to white dominance were all prime catalysts for violence, but white rage did not require a trigger. Whites killed, beat, and whipped freedpeople purely out of disdain for their humanity and existence. Adams had seen a dead "colored man hanging to a limb about six miles from Shreveport," a "colored man's head laying side of the road" on his way to Summer Grove in Caddo Parish, and Black men's heads left on stakes along the western road from Shreveport as potent reminders of white vitriol and power. He described how whites employed the whip "as they did before freedom," often riding through cotton fields with bullwhips in their hands and lining freedpeople along the river before whipping them. Well into the 1870s, Adams witnessed Red River freedpeople whipped in fields and on steamboats and ferryboats, and the seizure of their crops.[79]

Freedpeople faced brutality for every conceivable reason. The Fullilove family made violence a family affair. Thomas Fullilove habitually terrorized the freedpeople who lived and worked on his land. Almost certainly formerly enslaved familial property, these freedpeople reminded Fullilove daily of his loss of property, pride, and identity. In 1872, he beat Georgian Poke over the head, and Fullilove's overseer assaulted Aaron Walker on Fullilove's land.[80] Thomas's brother James beat John William in 1873, and James's son James Hill Fullilove whipped Mary Johnson "nearly to death" on his father's plantation in 1872. James Hill's brother severely whipped Fairy White, who worked on his plantation in 1874, while in 1868 an unnamed Fullilove killed Elie Hawkins while bringing the freedman to jail for an unrecorded offense.[81] The Fullilove family's regular use of physical harm encapsulated the regional reliance on aggressive brutality to constrain the permitted bounds of freedom and assert white domination.

Freedpeople were victims of intensely venomous and predatory attacks. Violence was a blunt but overt and expedient method for reasserting control. Robert Parks was beaten over the head with a gun for being in a grocery store; Samuel Smith was beaten, whipped, and "blooded like a hog" for attending church without white permission; Eliza Sanders was badly whipped by her white employer for not working "to suit him"; Patsey McCrady was accused of pulling a watermelon and thus was badly whipped; George Vinson was killed for attending the Methodist church in Keachie.

Ardinire Taylor was cut badly with a knife when she would not agree to sleep with the white landowner, and Mrs. Beckey Robson was whipped and beaten over the head with a gun when she walked two miles to rescue her son. Robson and Taylor were not the only freedwomen to face invasive attacks on their families and their physical and emotional being. Miss Catherine was badly whipped by a white man traveling to Shreveport who demanded she make him dinner without any compensation.

Joe Caslie was accused of stealing meat and thereafter was run off his property and separated from his sole means of economic independence: the crop growing on his small holding; Henry Simon was beaten and whipped and accused of stealing three dollars, which he had to pay his white employer; Hawood Tansey was severely beaten after refusing to throw corn in the crib as directed by a white man; James Molitneri was beaten for not starting work as soon as he was commanded; Dock Puese was killed, tied like a hog and burned, because he had been sick and was thus unable to work; Miss Williams was killed by a white woman because she would not call her "mistress."[82] Name after name, infraction after perceived infraction, Black men and women were cut down, run off, harassed, beaten, robbed, or murdered. African Americans ventured to grasp small measures of freedom but were met routinely with violence and brutality, exemplifying the adaptive nature of white mastery and its resolute denial of Black freedom.

The Red River was frequently used as a watery tomb and a torture site for freedpeople. Adams testified that in 1866 alone he had seen ten to fifteen freedpeople floating in the river. They had been killed in various ways: "some hung by the neck; sides of old logs; some with ropes round his necks. Some was shot and some throats were cut." On plantations from Shreveport to Alexandria, Adams saw gratuitous acts of racial torture as freedpeople were tied around their hands or necks, pushed into the river, and sometimes repeatedly hauled back to shore. Steamboats heading to Shreveport commonly knocked Blacks overboard, whipped and beat them, or ran them off the boat midriver after they had paid their fares.[83]

Following the 1868 Shady Grove Massacre, two separate bands of white vigilantes murdered Blacks in the Red. One group of seventy-five whites from Shreveport took nine Blacks to the banks of the river, told them to swim for their lives, and then shot them all as they rose to the surface. Another thirty freedpeople were taken from Shreveport, marched to the river, tied together with ropes, and shot in the back; their swollen bodies formed a raft that drifted downriver, slowly consumed by alligators.[84] Bureau agent Fulmor wrote in October 1868 of a freedman's body found "floating in Red River" and so "badly decomposed that it could not be examined."[85]

Incidents were also triggered around crop claiming, crop seizure, and labor disputes. White landowners habitually withheld or stole wages, ran Blacks off the land, and seized crops from Black laborers. Freedpeople up and down the Red told Henry Adams that "the whites take all we make and if we say anything about our rights they beat us."[86] Daniel Robinson made a contract to work thirty acres near Shreveport belonging to Colonel Stephen Jones. Robinson produced four bales of cotton, three hundred bushels of corn, and five hundred bushels of sweet potatoes but was refused payment. When Robinson approached his landlord about Jones's use of tools that belonged to Robinson, the freedman was threatened by Jones's son, which prompted Robinson to seek employment on a nearby plantation. He left all of his belongings "locked up in my house" on the Jones holding, only to discover that Jones "broke into my house," stole personal items, and claimed his tools. Robinson was afraid to enter his own home during the day for fear of being shot and was only able to secure personal items under the cover of darkness. Henry Turner was run off his own land—a parcel of eighty acres that he had farmed for two years and had purchased in specie—by a white neighbor determined to have the land. Turner testified that the white man admitted "he had no claim or title" to the land but that "he would have it, and if I did not let him have it quietly, I would be killed before the trouble was over." Fearing for his life, Turner vacated his land.[87]

The testimony gathered by military personnel from DeSoto Parish noted daily complaints from freedpeople "of being maltreated, threatened, and driven terror-struck from their homes and crops." Paltry numbers of incidents elicited investigation by local law authorities, while freedpeople were "systematically plundered of their crops and driven away from their homes." W. B. Phillips testified in 1868 that throughout Rapides, the "spirit of emancipation" was not "fully acquiesced in," with parish planters speaking of "the collared man as still their property and said they would use their guns to prohibit parties from giving them any instructions." Personal violence and death threats occurred at such a high rate that, as Major Lewis Merrill of the Seventh Cavalry wrote from Shreveport, "It is not an exaggeration to say that the entire black population of this section is absolutely terror-struck." Those that did remain in their homes and continued to work the land did so with nearly constant "apprehension of the visits of and violence . . . of White Leaguers," while W. Mudgett wrote that the pervasive disregard for Black life and property, bureau agents, and Republicans in Caddo meant that he and others found themselves "openly threatened on the streets."[88]

Seizing tools and crops, denying pay, and physically assaulting and torturing Black people underscores the central white perception that Blacks were laboring bodies without the right to property or worthy of pay, and that violence and the threat of violence would be employed to assert white dominance over the African American community. Elias Cornel beat a freedman "nearly to death" on his Bossier Parish holding after the freedman completed agreed-upon work and Cornel refused to pay. In four separate instances in 1874, white men or groups of armed whites "shot badly," "beat nearly to death," "beat and whipped," or "whipped" four freedmen on Dr. Allances's DeSoto Parish holding before stealing their crops.[89] Miles Richards's cotton was stolen from him when he brought it to be ginned; Henry Boswell worked shares for John Vance, who sold Boswell's fourteen bales of cotton and kept the money. George Underwood, Benjamin Harris, and Isiah Fuller made a contract to work and produce a crop on Mr. Mc-Moring's place. One July day, while they worked in the field, McMoring and another white man forced them to leave the place by coming after them with guns and sticks—despite protestations from the three men about leaving their homes and the crop without any compensation. The three men were due $180 from McMoring and were not compensated by the terms of their contract. They noted that they had "worked for them as though we were slaves, and then treated like dogs all the time."[90]

Adams was literate and thus uniquely positioned to judge the plight of freedpeople like Underwood, Harris, and Fuller. He audited contract papers, cotton receipts, and accounts to assist the Black community. In 1869 he discovered that thirty-five freedpeople had been cheated out of $1,790. Those freedpeople, who went to the law to press their claims, "got killed and some got good whippings." In subsequent years, Adams and other former soldiers looked over contracts and found that contracted freedpeople were cheated out of "two-thirds of their just and right of what they had made." None of the accounts settled up. Blacks who confronted their white employers about these obvious discrepancies were whipped, sent to jail, or had their cotton and corn seized.

Shreveport stores commonly gave incorrect change to Black customers. Since the majority of Blacks were illiterate and "could not count [their] money," local storeowners and landowners routinely failed to give a freedperson "half of [their] money back" when they were paying or changing money. Whites commonly told freedpeople that their cotton weighed less than the scale measurement while charging Blacks high prices for necessities.[91] Plentiful statements from nonliterate freedpeople enumerate being cheated or finding themselves short of money after making payments, revealing the deceitful steps local whites took to seize any modicum of Black ownership or property and reduce Blacks to witless, naive ciphers lacking autonomy.

Black children were also placed in slavery-like peonage to work off debts that whites claimed the children's families owed. Adams recalled that ten families in Caddo Parish had their children seized, and two children in DeSoto Parish were taken, one for $50 and one for nothing.[92] Aping the mores of an antebellum slave auction, the $50 ransom devalued Black life and rendered Black people into property again. It revealed the startlingly similar ways in which postbellum landlords continued to separate families and exert pressures in ways not dissimilar to methods employed under slavery.

Eighteen-year-old Zion Buggers was stolen from his parents, tied to a mule, and taken toward Texas. His parents, Friday and Ussless, testified that Zion chewed through the ropes that bound him and returned home. Sam Thomplin had lived and worked on John Long's plantation. When Thomplin refused to work on the plantation another year, Long claimed an outstanding debt of $50 before proceeding to take Thomplin's milk cow, a bale of cotton weighing 450 pounds, fifty bushels of corn, a double-barreled shotgun, and a singletree as payment. However, the debt collection didn't stop, and when Thomplin moved to Shreveport, Long followed him and engaged a constable to take Thomplin's fifteen-year-old daughter for the sum of $50.

Parental testimony revealed that Black Bayou on the outskirts of Monroe, more than one hundred miles east of Shreveport, was a favored destination to re-enslave children. Ten children from Caddo were taken in 1873. The children were held in Monroe for debts of various sums and their white captors threatened the parents with death if rescue was attempted. One family noted in 1874 that their children had been taken in 1868 and were still in captivity, but no law would "make them give us our children." This practice continued unabated, with kidnapping, seizure, and assignment of monetary value to Black children.[93]

Throughout the Red River region, there were an overwhelming number of instances of Black people being brutalized, terrorized, and threatened in connection with cultivation, repossession of cotton, mobility, bodily autonomy, and labor autonomy. It caused familial separations, property loss, injury, and death among Black Louisianans, who faced an atmosphere of fear and political intimidation that only narrowed the border between slavery and freedom.[94] The framework of racial domination, with its sanctioned use of violence to subjugate Blacks, bequeathed an enduring legacy to northwest Louisiana that extended slaveholding privileges and mindset into the postemancipation period.[95] Ultimately, the demolition of the power structure of slavery—an edifice upon which southern whites had secured their identity, measured their self-worth, and laid down their lives—did not destroy white commitment to racial enmity or enforcement of racial hierarchy. As chapter 6 will illustrate, Black people in the Red River region were also subjected to extreme violence for their participation in the body politic and for exercising the rights of citizenship and voting.

– 6 –

"THE NEGRO QUESTION AS SETTLED IN LOUISIANA FOREVER"

Political Violence and the Colfax Massacre

In 1875 it was estimated that 3,500 people in Louisiana had been killed in politically inspired violent attacks since 1865; 1,880 of these deaths had resulted from efforts to prevent freedmen from voting.[1] In the Red River region, violence and politics maintained a contorted symbiotic relationship that was sustained throughout Reconstruction and into the twentieth century. Violence constituted a recognizable trait of regional white identity and was frequently used to underscore the unshakeable race-based power structure that determined every aspect of regional life and the rigid definition of eligibility for the body politic. Politically motivated vigilante actions gained further traction as whites leveraged this terrorism as a potent tool of political intimidation and restriction. Delegitimization of Republican control of the South, Black citizenship, and Black voting sat alongside protection of southern womanhood as decisive rhetoric for white violence and paramilitary action.[2]

For the majority of regional whites, and especially for former slaveholders, the policies proposed by Radical Republicans—which included the Civil Rights Act of 1866 and the rewriting of state constitutions, including Louisiana's—was proof positive of political calamity that required correction through their forceful control. An 1866 letter to John Moncure—a Shreveport senator, the most influential Democrat in the lower house, and a former Confederate soldier—described the Civil Rights Act as "bare faced a piece of impudence and audacity." Moncure's correspondent believed that victorious northerners and misguided Republicans were not governing using the "principle of justice and equity" but instead were deploying a "ruthless and desecrating hand upon the rights of the state's [*sic*]" that resulted in no "order, cohesion, or equilibrium" in a "union [that] shall never be what it has been." One year later, the same person wrote to Moncure that "the tyrannical course of the Radicals" was the clearest argument for reasserting southern rights.[3] Red River region whites took control and worked to reestablish prewar political rights through a sustained campaign of violence and vigilante activity that successfully smothered African Americans' political participation, engagement, campaigning, and officeholding. Well before the close of Reconstruction, northwest Louisiana had segregated political access. Violence enabled and maintained a world in which the region's whites considered Black lives valueless in every area of civil, economic, and political life where Blacks were attempting to establish a presence.

Nothing incited regional whites to violence with such force and with such determination to rewrite laws as freedmen's enfranchisement and Black political engagement. Black political involvement, participation, organizing, and access to the franchise catalyzed the large-scale, extremely vicious, and charged acts of violent aggression in Reconstruction era northwest Louisiana. Indeed, the fact that Black communities engaged with the body politic and eagerly educated themselves politically enraged local whites of all classes, who systematically clipped Republican Party grassroots organization from its inception. While coalition building across racial lines, grassroots activism and campaigning, and Union Leagues took hold in other southern regions and states with majority African American populations—such as the Alabama Black Belt; Natchez, Mississippi; southwest Georgia; or York County, South Carolina—active or sustained grassroots organizing remained fledgling in the Red River region during Reconstruction.[4] Regional Black political organizing was severed and truncated almost from the start, and it never flourished here as it did in other rural southern areas.

Politically driven violence was sustained along the Red River, and testimonies from African Americans stress both the constant violent acts and the ingrained feeling that violence might befall them without incitement. Their testimony comprises nearly three-quarters of the recorded instances and testimony in the 550 pages of *Use of the Army in Certain of the Southern States*, which chronicles race-based violence—particularly politically motivated incidents—in the region. Black voices state unflinchingly that violence and the threat of it were omnipresent and that political interest, involvement, and exercise triggered retribution and terror. While economic and socially driven violence fomented an atmosphere of fear and claimed hundreds of Black lives, political violence and vote restricting assaults were pervasive and were the primary triggers for brazen vigilante activities. Restricting Black access to both the ballot box and the political arena remained crucial for white southern control. This galvanized and unified regional whites across a spectrum of class and social backgrounds, including disparate political backgrounds. Regional whites and local leaders rallied support through ideological messaging and rhetoric that promoted the shared goal of restricting and excluding Blacks from politics. Whites in the Red River region were particularly intent on complete curtailment of any exercise of political rights, including election campaigning, Black candidates, and ballot casting.

This reflexive recourse to violence reinforced and mirrored well-established regional ideologies and a familiar white southern imperative to utilize violence that naturalized terror and brutality inflicted on African Americans. The legacy of slaveholding connected with and adapted mastery—the control of Black bodies and the exertion of violence to maintain racial subjugation—as a mindset, behavior, and structural concept, with tangible and impactful outcomes for the region's political landscape during Reconstruction. The normalizing of brutality echoed long-standing racist beliefs that African Americans could only be controlled through violence, in conjunction with misrepresentations about Blacks' imperviousness to pain. It rendered violence a sharply effective, accessible tool in the southern Democratic political arsenal.

Along the Red River, these tools were indispensable in exacting the outcomes that regional whites wanted in various situations. Racial supremacy deftly unified regional whites because it rested on a foundation of words, actions, rhetoric, and ideologies with a deep history. The region's white leaders calibrated both long-standing white supremacist rhetoric and the significance of mastery to personal and collective white identity, all anchored in the rigid racial rubric of enslavement, to respond fulsomely to political, economic, and social changes. Violence permeated the political landscape, just as it had seeped into every facet of enslaved Black life, and its overt presence served as a constant reminder of the durability of white supremacy.[5]

The Red River region's whites embraced political violence to actively shape Blacks' access to and engagement in postwar governing and citizenship. They leveraged mastery and violence as incisive frameworks and tools to respond to a plethora of political and social circumstances, with outcomes that instilled fear and stifled Black political strides.[6] Racially motivated violence and vigilantism in the Red River region was exceptional not because it occurred—though it happened with a frequency and reliability that was hard to rival—but because it consistently exacted what regional whites sought: the suppression of Black political activity, grassroots and community building, and political coalition building. The fluidity of southern politics and coalition building present in other parts of Louisiana and the South was notably absent in this region.[7]

Black political participation and voting rights flew in the face of deeply rooted white conceptions of what masculinity and citizenship meant. The idea that former property zealously flocked to election campaigns, valued staying politically informed and knowledgeable, and diligently turned out for elections was anathema. Bartholomew Egan described the postemancipation political climate as "dark and gloomy," and his letters, like those of most former slaveholders grappling with an undesired new political reality, seethed with resentment and hostility.[8] Regional whites staunchly believed that Black freedom was hacking away at long-standing concepts of white male identity—specifically notions of masculinity—and eligibility for citizenship, and by extension, diminishment of white maleness lowered the sanctity of white womanhood. Thus, reassertion and reclamation of white dominance and control were of paramount importance to save the South and the nation from destruction. This belief that white masculinity, citizenship, and privilege were aggressively curtailed and impinged by Black political involvement fueled violence and vigilantism in the Red River region.

Politically motivated violence hemmed in the rights and privileges of freedpeople not just in northwest Louisiana; court cases that arose from regional racial massacres triggered Supreme Court rulings that deprived African Americans nationwide of their Fourteenth and Fifteenth Amendment rights. The Supreme Court interpreted the Fourteenth narrowly and to the benefit of corporate rights instead of Blacks in the important 1873 *Slaughterhouse* ruling. This ruling focused on the distinction between civil and "social" rights. It leveraged the amendment to overturn efforts to ban racial discrimination by private businesses and to strike down state regulations on working conditions. Likewise, the Supreme Court ruled in *Ex Parte Yarborough* (1884) that the Fifteenth Amendment did not enfranchise individuals but merely barred racial discrimination in voting qualifications. The legislation resulting from these rulings took little account of African Americans and the consequences wrought on their constitutionally guaranteed rights.[9] The particularly brutal, visceral, and commodified tenor of racial regional dynamics directly shaped prospects for freedom, citizenship, and political participation during Reconstruction while simultaneously impinging on rights and shaping the boundaries of freedom beyond northwest Louisiana.

Regional whites viewed violence as a pragmatic and practical response to Reconstruction policies. D. Jewett, the U.S. commissioner for Louisiana, described the region as, "with few exceptions," comprising "rebels and traitors at heart." Likewise, a returning Unionist said, "They may, by mouth, profess union sentiments, but their hearts are filled with hatred." Events of the late 1860s and 1870s proved that "democracy in the South, in the mouths of southern men, means treason and rebellion." Jewett—resigned to witnessing crimes he was unable to punish or prevent—understood intrinsically that racial violence would not cease until "the heavy hand of the nation" was brought upon the Red River region.[10]

However, the heavy hand of the nation would not come to bear on northwest Louisiana. The brazen, public nature of regional violence shocked the nation, but continued offenses against regional Blacks were ultimately overlooked, if not condoned. No substantive action was taken to alter or halt the bloody trajectory of the region, unlike in the Carolinas, where the federal government did try to intervene to stem racially motivated violence.[11] Indeed, the visceral actions at Colfax and Coushatta captured attention and precipitated court cases that had widespread implications for Black civil and political liberties. The headline-grabbing incidents of endemic violence along the Red River commanded national attention. They influenced federal legislation, but the federal government did little in actual practice to renounce the actions of white supremacists along the Red as state and national legislative rulings sliced away African Americans' access to civil and political rights.

— — —

Henry Marshall's daughter Fanny wrote to her sister in 1868 about the efficacy of violence in determining election outcomes. She expressed frustration with neighboring parishes' lack of power and forceful response following the passage of Louisiana's new constitution. Fanny noted with pleasure the successful inducement of freedpeople to vote Democrat, since "a good many negroes were turned off from their former employment for voting the radical ticket." She despaired that passage of Louisiana's constitution left the state "governed by negroes and those who are no better," and she endorsed intimidation as beneficial, plainly stating, "If the other parishes had acted as well as Caddo and DeSoto the constitution could not have passed."[12] In her opinion, aggression netted desirable results, and the levels of violence and tactics used in Caddo and DeSoto Parishes were pitched appropriately to stifle Black participation. She wished that similar methods had been used statewide to prohibit the rewriting of Louisiana's constitution.

Similarly, James Calvert Wise told regional whites that he considered "the negro question as settled in Louisiana forever if the white men will only follow up their late success." Wise felt the methods utilized by regional whites were proving effective but required continued follow-through and assertive action to snuff out Black autonomy and political engagement. He advised deliberate and absolute control of freedpeople to enable whites to "control the negro element to suit themselves." The reversal of total white domination of all aspects of society and all interracial interactions uprooted ingrained expectations and underscored for whites what they believed was at stake in Black enfranchisement. Regional whites heartily agreed with William Randolph, who wrote to Wise, "I would I had a hundred thousand I would freely give it to put down negro equality. Negro Supremacy."[13] Like Randolph, Wise, and Marshall, regional whites engaged in violence and politics as two halves of a whole, especially when radical rule dissipated and federal authorities retreated from Reconstruction.

While Stephen Cuny described the elected officials as "nearly all radical real blue bellies," Mrs. Butler, cousin of former governor Thomas Moore, outlined a clear plan for how white supremacy could halt "the destruction of this the finest country on earth," which was "now under negro supremacy." Her tactic involved violence and coercion, clearly delineated in slaveholders' language. She proposed all new legislation declared "unconstitutional, null & void," and personally engaged in activity to force "all my freedmen" to vote Democratic. She wrote that "it is the determination of all true men in the state ... to see that Louisiana has ... release[d] herself from the clutches of the worst men that ever disgraced the face of this earth." She sent Black laborers contracted on her land to Alexandria one July to attend the Democratic barbeque because she was "determined to fight the devil with fire, & if we can't burn him, to scorch him well . . . nothing shall be left undone that can be for our success in Novr."[14]

Women, particularly former mistresses, were just as effusive and strident as men about restoring white control, and vocal with their participation in and endorsement of white supremacist violence. Coercion was also employed to vote for the Democratic ticket in nearby regions with vastly different predilections than the Red River region. For example, in Alabama's Black Belt, force, intimidation, and threats were often used to strong-arm Democratic votes. In Natchez, where the sizeable Black population gained and maintained access to the formal political sphere and became a grassroots democracy that afforded Black political participation, coercion featured in election cycles.[15]

Upheaval following the 1868 election provided impetus for whites statewide to use their Confederate army experience to form armed vigilante units to stymie Black political involvement, affiliation, and voting. Louisiana was one of three southern states where the Black population surpassed the white. The potential number of Republican votes this populace represented prompted a leveraging of collective military experience for swift and precise organization to suppress Black access to political information, the ballot box, and voter enrollment. The paramilitary organizing of ex-Confederates was particularly successful and effectively deployed in Louisiana's urban and rural regions. In stark contrast, Black U.S. Army service did not provide a platform to secure political inclusion, participation, or citizenship. This military knowledge carried negative implications in northwest Louisiana, which, taken together, also sets this region apart from other portions of the South, where Black military service was integral to establishing Black freedom and political identity.[16] In street battles in New Orleans, countless assaults in northwest Louisiana, and the Colfax and Coushatta massacres, regional paramilitary groups engaged military tactics to assemble, strike quickly, and disband before the state militia or federal troops organized in response.[17] Notably, the strictures imposed by the law were little felt or respected in the Red River region; whites from across the class spectrum directed their vehemence pointedly at freedpeople—as laborers, as citizens, and as voters—and at white Republicans.

Endemic violence throughout the Red River region meant vigilantes did not shroud their enterprise behind costumes or nighttime. The weak grip of federal troops and legal enforcement meant they acted openly and without risk of arrest. Paramilitary groups like the Knights of the White Camelia and the White League were prevalent alongside countless informal vigilante bands that congregated frequently and struck with impunity regionwide. Vigilantism and paramilitary action coalesced around leadership and participation from Confederate veterans—many of whom were well-known local leaders and former slaveholders, vocal about their Confederate service and respected within the white community—to consistently target local gatherings and rallies connected with elections. Vigilantes reinforced the efficacy and popularity of politically derived terror with targeted, individualized incidents stemming from political participation and allegiance.[18]

Regional whites overwhelmingly approved of violent actions and measures to reassert white power. Like Sargent W. Metly, most Democrats felt justified in killing "pretty fast" any freedperson who exercised their political rights. They believed these checks were essential to prohibiting Black access to "the full rights of a white man" and harnessed white vigilantism to protect entrenched racial hierarchies.[19] Theoretically, in the postbellum world, the unwavering racial binaries were replaced with access to opportunity and advancement. Vigilantism provided a common medium for white males, irrespective of class, to unify behind a pivotal, central, and shared element of regional identity. In 1874, the *Shreveport Times* published "The White League," a bold resolution from the Mooringsport taxpayers' association, "in the spirit of self-defense and protection of themselves and property," to ignore party line or political distinctions excepting "distinctions of virtue and intelligence against crime and ignorance." A further resolution urged collective coalescing "of the white people under the party organization known as the White League" and attributed all Reconstruction problems—and apportioned blame for them—to *"white carpet-baggers"* manipulating freedpeople. The paper urged local whites to *"strike this evil"* even if that required *"desperate measures."* Another *Shreveport Times* article asserted that Democrats were undefeatable by "political scoundrels," while preservation of "society and of civil liberty" hinged on unified white action. Red River whites galvanized around white supremacy and the use of vigilantism as the guiding forces for regional salvation and evolution of the core tenants of white identity: mastery over Blacks, control of Black labor and mobility, and total political and racial supremacy.[20]

Louisiana's political situation was a source of ire and despair for ex-slaveholders and substantiated a coherent rationale for why violence was imperative to white control. Whites like stalwart ex-Confederate captain D. E. Hayes blamed Black enfranchisement under a radical Republican Congress for the state's failure to be readmitted to the Union in 1866.[21] New leadership, laws, and freedpeople's political inclusion prompted white fear and anger for Louisiana's political future. To their mind, provisions for Black male citizenship and voting rights and for equal schools and services for freedpeople produced a deplorable political situation in Louisiana. Thomas Powell laid bare his utter distaste for Black political involvement, writing that freedmen would habitually "concentrate so that they can [have] a voice in the government."[22] James Calvert Wise received a letter that echoed the prevalent fear of concentrated Black political power, writing that a district "may be carried by the "nigers" for they have from 50 to 60 majority in the registration."[23]

Freedpeople's dense voting power fueled white ire, and high levels of Black political participation further catalyzed subsequent violent episodes. While the majority of Republicans and northerners did not ascribe to an agenda of complete equality and racial integration, they understood the significance of maintaining freedpeople's political allegiance. The vast turnout and mobilization of Black voters appealed to Republicans but conjured nightmares for Democrats, who retaliated with collective violence. Black enfranchisement sparked a "war of color" in the Red River region that permeated every aspect of Black life and shrank the hold that freedpeople had on freedom.[24] The high-profile battles of this war had far-reaching implications that continue to reverberate nationwide.

In large groups and individually, white men across the region seriously heeded the call of the *Shreveport Times* and exercised their "manly qualities" to intimidate Blacks and ensure that "everyone will know what we want." Intimidation emanated firmly from regional political leadership. The mayor of Alexandria—where the Ku Klux Klan destroyed the Republican newspaper's offices—appointed fifty men as special police during the 1868 municipal election and confiscated Republicans' firearms. Democrats were kept armed, donned red ribbons to denote authority, and followed orders to intimidate Republicans.[25] Corruption and electoral fraud compounded matters. Although there were fewer than two hundred legal voters in Alexandria, between four hundred and five hundred votes were cast. Black witnesses recounted that white men living twenty and thirty miles from Alexandria voted in the election, and predictably enough, they voted Democrat.[26] Targeted political violence in northwest Louisiana made a definitive public display of white power while thwarting attempts at Black mobilization and election participation.[27]

The Red River region was so hostile to Republicans by the late 1860s that W. Mudgett, a Union man, noted that he could not remain in Shreveport unless "protected by militia, or some other force"—a statement corroborated by the area's military commander, General Flood. Both stated that armed men patrolled Shreveport's streets, threatening violence to radicals and any man who voted for Ulysses Grant.[28] Indeed, instances of terrorism and frequency of assaults increased notably in conjunction with the 1868 presidential election cycle, in which Grant was the Republican candidate. Blacks who attended a Republican meeting in Mansfield were fined twenty-five cents for every hour they attended. Marshall Twitchell, a prominent white Republican in Coushatta who lost family members in the Coushatta Massacre, wrote that no Republican could make a speech or act openly about the party in DeSoto Parish "except at extreme risk of his life."[29] Shreveport freedman Solomon Thomas testified that "republicans, white or colored, cannot live in Caddo Parish without the risk of being killed at any minute, day or night." He recalled an attempt to kill him: after searching for the hidden Thomas with "a squad of white men" for several hours to no avail, Thomas's would-be assailant declared to a gathered crowd that whenever they encountered a "radical n—— that would not 'give in'" they should shoot him down. City leaders present heartily seconded this order. Thomas also recalled that all Caddo Parish Blacks were forced to vote for the Democratic ticket, and the polls were "surrounded with armed white men; bands of them went to every colored man's house." The only Black man who voted Republican in the 1868 presidential election, Thomas recounted, was twenty-three-year-old James Watson, who was subsequently shot three times by his former enslaver's son. Freedmen were also frequently subjected to severe whipping and otherwise brutalized during elections.[30]

In DeSoto Parish, vigilantes made death threats against anyone who voted for Grant in 1868. W. Phillips testified that there was no "fairness and but little freedom" during the election cycle for freedpeople, who were "constrained through fear" against voting or forced to vote "contrary to their judgment." The practice of forced voting was substantiated in the statements of Henry Parker, Joe Lewis, and William Lewis, all of Caddo Parish.

These three freedmen were ambushed during the 1868 state and parish elections by seven heavily armed white men and ordered to vote the Democratic ticket at the polls "or they would kill us." When the freedmen objected to forced voting, the white posse retorted, "You shall vote the democratic ticket to-day, or die," before dragging the freedmen under duress to and from the polls. Two weeks later, the posse returned to the freedmen's abode before sunrise and commenced shooting.[31]

Political affiliation provided a perfect flashpoint for vigilantism. Being known as a Republican freedman was reason enough to fear for one's life. Freedman Moses Lawhorn was dragged from his home and murdered; his head was chopped off "to make sure he was dead." The provocation for his death was that he was a Republican. Another freedman, L. James, earnestly wanted the Grant administration to intercede so that Blacks who voted Republican as he did would not "be murdered for being loyal to the Government."[32] Eli Allen of Coushatta was hauled from his home and killed for his Republican sentiments. Allen's body was found with arms and legs broken, his torso riddled with bullets, and his head disfigured by fire. Taylor, a freedman with a political position in DeSoto Parish, was beaten to death with clubs in Shreveport. Fletcher Legardy, secretary of a Caddo Republican club, testified that Blacks had been "intimidated in every possible way" to prevent political participation. Violent measures adopted by Caddo whites included but were not limited to murder by shooting, hanging, and burning; "wound[ing] with shot, knives, bludgeons and whips"; and driving Blacks out by intimidation. Following the 1874 congressional election, Legardy estimated that four hundred freedpeople had been discharged from jobs because of Republican affiliation.[33]

Through murder and mutilation, hanging or decapitation, regional whites strove to erase Black personhood and reassert white authority over independent Black bodies while severing the Black political head from the laboring Black body. In Caddo Parish, described by U.S. soldiers as a "bloody parish" with a "history of blood and crime," murder was commonplace, irrespective of the presence of U.S. troops. During the 1868 presidential election, Solomon Thomas saw four Black men and a boy captured by armed whites who cut holes in each of the captives' hands before they "ran rope through their hand [and] tied them together." The men were marched to the Red River, "and there they shot them and shoved them face forward," where they were still bobbing in the river's drift a month later.[34] Another instance saw thirty freedmen taken from Shreveport, marched to the banks of the Red, tied together with ropes, and shot in the back. This raft of dead bodies, strung together, drifted down the river until alligators consumed the freedmen's bodies and gave them "a burial denied by men." These Black men were killed for political affiliation, as were the seven men chained together to an abandoned building that was then set alight. One testimony figured that 242 Blacks had been murdered in Caddo and Bossier Parishes between September 1 and November 3, 1868, for political leanings alone. In the 1868 presidential election, a mere ten votes in northwest Louisiana were cast for Republican candidate Grant.[35] The "spirit of the emancipation proclamation" had not and would not infiltrate the powers that controlled the Red River region.

While Black Republicans bore the brunt of vigilante violence, white Republicans also feared violence and ostracism because of their political leaning. White Republicans—the sparse numbers of regional Unionists, native-born scalawags, and northern carpetbaggers who relocated to the South postwar—were recipients of ire and hatred across the region.[36] Each group of "southern radicals" meted out varying measures of hatred at different moments, and members of each group were opportunistic when it came to political advancement and personal gain. Louisiana politics during this era saw an incredible amount of allegiance shifting, but northern Louisiana was exemplary in the ironic, complete position reversals on the part of leading white Republicans and Democrats, particularly after the Colfax Massacre. However, the region's white Republicans often held high-ranking political positions and were concentrated in Natchitoches Parish, the Republican Party toehold.

Among the southern-born constituency, Republicans in northwest Louisiana tended to be from wealthy and well-established planter families, prominent members of society before the war, and motivated less by racial egalitarianism than by desire for political control. This differs from other portions of the South, including North Carolina's Piedmont and eastern Tennessee. Northern-born Republicans tended to arrive in the region because of military deployment or with the Freedmen's Bureau. Political affiliation was often a family affair, with an entire side of a family adhering to the Republican Party, in stark contrast to the same family's vehemently Democratic factions.

J. Ernest Breda was a regional scalawag who had been a loyal, serving Confederate. In 1868, he was a known member of the Knights of the White Camelia, who inducted every white man to that group parish-wide.[37] He and his brother, Philippe, had provided the Confederate army with medicines throughout the war. It is unclear what precipitated his decision to switch sides, but at some point before the 1872 presidential election, the brothers and their immediate family became Republicans. Ernest and Philippe both held political positions, faced death threats and periods of exile from their homes, and testified in various trials and cases about political violence and intimidation in the region.

Significantly, and in stark contrast to the Black experience, the Bredas returned to the region in 1880, unmolested, and remained pillars of the community; their sisters and wives were unharmed, though socially ostracized and terrified, despite the Breda brothers' Republicanism. Elcey Breda wrote an anxious and frightened letter to Ernest days before the Colfax Massacre in April 1873. Her husband's political allegiance placed her in a precarious position that threatened their status and safety. She urged him to "give up all these political ideas" and "leave the radicals" because his politics had made vicious enemies and all Democratic friends had abandoned him. She recognized that being a Republican placed Ernest on constant guard and in fear for his life. A public move away from the Republicans would ensure the safety of Breda and his nuclear family and rebuild severed bonds with Democratic family members with prominent positions in Natchitoches.[38]

James Cosgrove, a staunch white supremacist and unwavering Democrat who helmed numerous newspapers, including the Natchitoches *People's Vindicator,* denied that Republicans were ostracized but wrote that "we cannot be expected to associate with a set of blackguards, liars, and thieves, as the southern radicals are."[39] Ernest Breda was fortunate that his family pedigree and landholding status provided an element of protection against the ire that his political standing drew from regional whites. The Red River region's Black Republicans, however, were not extended similar buffers. A *Use of the Army* summary of Caddo Parish's sentiments toward Republicans declared, "The Union men of this parish have suffered fearfully at the hands of their political opponents. They have been hung, drowned, stabbed, and shot without cause and without mercy."[40] Their political allegiance and engagement would provide the catalyst for myriad killings, coercions, and acts of violence throughout Reconstruction.

— — —

Freedpeople maintained a steely determination to vote. They voted Republican with a tenacity that further galvanized white supremacists. Each election cycle used violence to reduce, stultify, and discourage Black participation in the franchise. This fomented an atmosphere of terror that consistently correlated Black political participation with physical harm and the possibility of death. Politically fueled violence targeted Black men and their families, with violent acts extending into the private space of the home and permeating communities.[41] Black citizenship and political engagement in northwest Louisiana were imbued with racist terror from emancipation's declaration. Freedpeople's testimony of racial violence underscores in raw, unflinching terms how violence, violent threats, and politics were so embedded and symbiotic that they could not be divided; political meetings and the newspaper coverage of elections, candidates, and outcomes all deployed aggressive, white supremacist language.[42]

Blacks of the region were physically inhibited from fully experiencing citizenship and were continually excluded from involvement in the body politic. This forced depoliticization quashed freedpeople's political voice and any grassroots mobilization while simultaneously keeping political inclusion and officeholding out of reach. Whites kept Blacks from the polls by force but also destroyed Republican tickets and tampered with the returns.[43] Coercion and compulsion were driven by access—both physical and ideological—to the ballot box. Henry Adams recalled that armed white men stood around the ballot box in Caddo Parish, intimidating Black voters during the 1874 congressional election. Threats included being run off their homes, being forced to abandon crops, and death. Adams witnessed 125 Blacks being turned off the plantations where they labored after voting Republican.[44] Warning blasts from cannon and shotguns thrice greeted Black voters in Mansfield on election morning. One testimonial described the changed layout of the sheriff's office, where the election was held. Instead of each man voting "through the window," the voting was moved upstairs and "Henry Huson, one of the white-leaguers, stood at the bottom of the steps." Republicans were harangued as they ascended the stairs, and one elderly freedman was beaten.[45] In 1875, freedman William Harper estimated that since 1868 more than three hundred freedpeople had been killed and 250 injured in Caddo Parish because of their politics. He noted that "these outrages and murders" were so frequent and "from long custom" that they drew little public notice and made an accurate tabulation of crimes and victims impossible.[46]

A week before the 1868 election, Joseph Texada, ex-Confederate soldier, former slaveholder, and prominent member of regional society, shot a Black man six times. A warrant was issued, but the sheriff reported that Texada was absent from his residence or surroundings. There was no explicit provocation for the shooting apart from the looming election. Witnesses were notified but never came forward. A few days later, Joseph Texada strode into the sheriff's Alexandria office and delivered himself. He was promptly released because the lack of witnesses precluded any action. Freedmen were suitably terrified and did not press charges, while fellow whites deemed Texada's behavior appropriate to control, contain, and quell Black political access.[47]

The Texada incident neatly encapsulates the adaptation of a distorted power structure that allowed regional whites to act with impunity. This commitment to white supremacy evolved from and was fortified by the shared belief that whites needed to protect themselves from unreasonable and unfair northern punishment and to contain Black political, social, and economic autonomy.[48] Strengthened by a framework alight with terror, it unified regional whites through a tangible platform and powerful rhetoric that tapped into entrenched racial hierarchies to reinstate white control, suppress Black activity and political engagement, and regain the political helm.

The horrific, gruesome terror inflicted upon Blacks in northwest Louisiana fills hundreds of pages of *Use of the Army,* leaving the historical record brimming with evidence that terrorism was the language of the region's white supremacists. Incidents of terror built upon the bedrock of the long, customary tradition of white-on-Black violence; the added variables now were systematic election intimidation and pervasive terrorism that corresponded with political participation. Violent terror was charged with meaning and drove the large public massacres at Colfax and Coushatta, which defined the outcome of political rule in Louisiana for the remainder of the nineteenth century and beyond.[49]

To control Black voting and political organizing, parish whites seized freedpeople's firearms, limited the possibilities for Republican club meetings, continually threatened employees if they voted of their own volition, and maintained a steady occurrence of violent and public murders. Many whites forced freedpeople to attend Democratic gatherings, like the one Mrs. Butler made Blacks laboring on her land attend in Alexandria, and threatened Black tenants economically. One freedman equated some whites' saccharine hospitality with the "way you treat a dog kindly if you want that dog to come home with you."[50]

Black Republican W. Mudgett, whose life had been threatened repeatedly and who survived a night raid, wrote to Governor Warmouth imploring him to send "at least two mounted regiments" to Caddo Parish in 1868. He wrote of a complete lack of "safety for life and property" for anyone who disagreed "politically with the democracy of Caddo." A "strong militia force," he continued, was needed to combat the pervasive paramilitary forces entrenched parish-wide. Breda similarly implored the Freedmen's Bureau to station troops near polling stations, to no avail. J. Johnson, a Republican from Mansfield, also demanded troops so that Republicans could vote. He wrote that White Leagues controlled the voting and the only salve would be "a stationary militia . . . let us have a standing troop" to enforce civil rights. Johnson, unable to register to vote, had received death threats and had stayed at home only one night after returning from the New Orleans convention. Boldly, he continued, "Please have this published in the papers, for we are republicans here, and republicans indeed . . . we want troops here . . . we intend to make our nominations in full; we don't intend on being deprived in our nomination if there is any chance."[51] Anti-Republican sentiment forced freedman Sinclair Potter from Shreveport. He recalled that no Republican meetings were held in Shreveport for a month before the 1868 election and estimated that twelve Black acquaintances had left Shreveport because of political intimidation and oppression.[52]

The Freedmen's Bureau was rendered impotent in the Red River region because of a paltry physical military presence in tandem with the futility of enforcing civil rights in a locale captured by white supremacy. In polarized, charged regions like this, where incidents of racial violence occurred with regularity, the military component of the Freedmen's Bureau was particularly crucial to freedpeople to access citizenship, voting, and civil rights, yet reliance on arms to enforce civil rights took the bite out of such constitutionally granted rights, particularly when troop numbers diminished. Black expectations that the bureau would provide the steel behind their access to the body politic—not to mention protecting their welfare and safety while advocating against Black abuse—frequently met with disappointment. Regional Black Republicans often requested troops during the elections, despite lowered expectations that they would arrive, because armed federal soldiers were the visible manifestation of African Americans' right to vote.[53]

As the levels of consistent terror and violence increased and fomented an atmosphere of complete fear throughout northwest Louisiana, the Freedmen's Bureau was further stymied. James Madison Cutts, commander of Shreveport's military district, recognized that paramilitarism wrought chaos and bloodshed. He wrote to a colleague that the region could not be maintained, nor security enforced, without "continued military occupation" and an increased military force.[54] In his dispatch about the 1868 Shady Grove Massacre, T. Fulmor of the Caddo and Bossier Freedmen's Bureau described his inability to lead an investigation. Any effort the bureau might have made was curtailed by the fact that the agents "would share the same fate of some of the missing freedmen." A reliable source had informed Fulmor "that I would have been killed on the night of Oct 1 had it not been for the intercession of some prudent and substantial men."[55]

The "intensely bitter" feeling toward Republicans, plus the hobbled state of the bureau, significantly impacted regional Blacks and effectively paralyzed the Republican Party in Caddo, Bossier, and DeSoto Parishes. General Hatch, head of the bureau in Louisiana, calculated 297 politically related deaths during September and October 1868, though other reports put the number between five hundred and a thousand.[56] This violence persisted throughout the 1872 and 1874 election cycles.[57] As figureheads of the government, bureau agents were targeted, and thus fearing for their own lives, agents were less inclined to investigate atrocities or protect freedpeople. It became customary that freedpeople who were registered to vote were barred from doing so and that votes counted from northwest Louisiana—especially Caddo, Bossier, and DeSoto Parishes—rarely incorporated or accurately reflected freedpeople's ballots. In some elections, no Republican ballots were counted from DeSoto, Bossier, or Bienville Parishes.[58] There were more peaceful elections in Natchitoches Parish, with some traction for the Republican Party, and Black voters voted unmolested with a modicum of success. However, the White League, the Knights of the White Camelia, and vigilante groups thrived in Natchitoches and often crossed parish lines for vigilante activity throughout the Reconstruction period. The exceedingly pro-Democratic and white supremacist Natchitoches newspapers, along with the *Shreveport Times,* were helmed by White League spokesmen.

Circumstances in nearby Alabama and Natchez, Mississippi, provide a counterpoint to the rampant levels of relentless violence in northwest Louisiana. Both areas had significant Black populations, strong Democratic bases, and political violence, but political engagement and community organizing unfolded in ways that allowed freedpeople opportunities and platforms for political and social engagement. In Natchez, radical grassroots political structures took hold and incorporated laboring freedpeople into the political arena. In this blended rural and urban area, some freedpeople cultivated patronage relationships with white landholders, while regional Democrats used patronage appeals that put substantial welfare elements into employment contracts. Crucially, unlike in the Red River region, there was an embedded, active church community and schools that could further leverage labor communities to build a regional political community with the tools to refashion the social order. The passage of the state's radical constitution created a space for freedpeople to govern their communities at a granular local level, which led to new interpersonal relationships across the color line. Natchez freedpeople harnessed the local infrastructure and societal elements instituted during enslavement, and economic projects launched at a state level, to define a political identity. In Alabama's Black Belt, freedpeople were able to deter violence and used collective resistance that was born of close work communities created through the plantation regime.

Interestingly, while racism and violence, particularly individual violence, were features of postwar life, whites could be flexible when circumstances demanded it. As Reconstruction progressed, Black majorities pushed white terrorists into relative inactivity; thus, excepting contentious election times, freedpeople took advantage of a lapse in racially motivated activity. Furthermore, a Democrat initiative to eliminate freedpeople from the political community backfired, which allowed Alabama's competitive biracial Reconstruction order to continue, with particular strength in the Black Belt.[59]

Beginning in 1868, however, a series of attacks on freedpeople commanded attention and gained notoriety in Louisiana, while two massacres, the 1873 Colfax Massacre and the 1874 Coushatta Massacre, trained the national gaze upon this extraordinarily violent region. Louisiana was known as a violent place. It was a locus of the Grant administration's investigation into violence and the difficulty of enforcing the Enforcement Acts. Republicans in Washington recognized Louisiana as exceedingly turbulent and unpredictable, and touchstone events from 1868 focused attention on the Red River region's violence and paramilitary white supremacy. These events gar-

nered more consideration than the continuous threats and instances of violence previously endured and documented by Blacks, in part because of how
this violence unfolded, the quick and assertive dominance by the vigilantes,
and the extent of the casualties. Another was the interconnection among the
violence, critical elections, and the recognition that Republican-led Reconstruction had no traction in northwest Louisiana without military enforcement. The paramilitaries' actions and their ease, familiarity, and comfort
with racialized violence unveiled the distinctive regional tenor of race relations and the capacity of paramilitarism to enforce white supremacy.

Most significantly, the Colfax Massacre starkly demonstrated that white
southerners condoned racial violence and that the U.S. Supreme Court
would not enforce, uphold, or protect African Americans' constitutional
rights. Instead, it provided white supremacists with fodder to systematically strip civil rights from southern Blacks and impose rigid segregation.
The Colfax defendants were released and pardoned after their 1874 Louisiana trial, with the ruling upheld in the 1876 *Cruikshank* Supreme Court case.
Likewise, the Coushatta Massacre perpetrators were never prosecuted.[60]
Hence, the Colfax and Coushatta massacres did not occur in isolation. As
Black and white Louisianans intrinsically understood, the overt paramilitary mission of racial terrorism crippled the Republican Party's electoral
reach while it remained highly effective at responding fulsomely and tacti-
cally to instances of Black access to the body politic and citizenship. Each
violent incident, irrespective of size or number of victims, encompassed a
sustained effort by whites to reassert racial power. These episodes underscore how whites of all classes harnessed the exceptional nature of regional
violence to exact precise outcomes with regard to Black political activity,
political engagement, and expressions of citizenship, suppressing Black civil
and political rights. The efficacy and success of violence as a tool of political
suppression placed the Black experience along Red River in contrast to that
in Alabama, Mississippi, or New Orleans.

The torrent of violence that engulfed northwest Louisiana started with
the Shady Grove Massacre. Alternatively known as the Bossier Massacre,
it began on September 27, 1868, when a white man from Arkansas stopped
in front of freedpeople's homes on Shady Grove plantation. There are a
variety of scattered reports, with much of the information concerning the
massacre coming directly from freedpeople's testimonials about regional
violence. In a harbinger of the later coverage of Colfax, regional office re-

ports laid blame and positioned freedpeople as casualties of their own actions. One Freedmen's Bureau dispatch reported that an intoxicated white man named Gibson "was returning from Shreveport" to Arkansas and "demanded if there were any radical n——s" at Shady Grove. The man noticed an older, reposing freedman and queried his politics. When this question received no response, the Arkansan aimed his rifle and shot at the freedman, missing him twice. Responding to this attack on their physical and political autonomy, the Shady Grove freedmen bravely tackled and chained the Arkansan in their quarters. Believing that this attack should be handled by the civil authorities—demonstrating profound faith in the judicial system and the Freedmen's Bureau—these freedmen held the Arkansan attacker so they could transport him to the parish jail. However, before this happened, other white citizens of Bossier Parish banded together and freed the man.

The Louisiana General Assembly later report on the matter described this as "wholesale murder" begun by an unprovoked white man who freedpeople arrested and attempted to "deliver . . . to civil authorities" before other whites rescued him. He then "brought back with him an armed crowd of one hundred white men who commenced an indiscriminate slaughter." The Freedmen's Bureau record is conflicted, at certain points portraying the attacked Black men as aggressors and their actions as the cause of a situation triggered by a white man's violent display of racial dominance and demand for Black deference. Fulmor initially stated that "a large body" of freedmen congregated and pursued Gibson, overtaking him at "Dr Vance's plantation with the intention of making him prisoner." Then, Fulmor wrote, another group of freedmen "forceably took Gibson" back to Shady Grove, "put a chain around his neck and tied him to a tree." It was these "outrages that had been committed on Gibson" that catalyzed his rescue by local whites. Local whites became terribly alarmed and freedpeople fled terrorized, so Fulmor headed to Shady Grove from Shreveport, reinforced by a detachment of the Twentieth Infantry. While difficulties abounded in procuring militia to ensure Blacks could vote, it proved easier to find troops to support white citizens.

Escaping Shady Grove, Gibson recrossed the state line, gathered a posse of between seventy-five and one hundred men carrying all manner of firearms, and returned the following morning. They opened fire upon arrival, indiscriminately shooting freedpeople. Fulmor recalled they "had killed thirteen men and one woman when I left and probably eight or ten afterwards" before continuing the shooting spree up the road at Gum Springs, killing another seven individuals. Freedman Henry Taylor testified that the vigilantes killed eight men and two women, who were pleading for their husbands' lives, immediately followed by seven more men at the springs. One of the men at the springs was severely wounded; the vigilantes doubled back to shoot him and his wife. At Gum Springs, a freedman was ordered to doff his hat, a request that again underscored the importance of Black's deference and immediate obedience to the vigilantes. The Black man refused to acquiesce to the demand, so they "put a chain around his neck, cut his throat, and hung him up." Lynched and displayed, he remained hanging for three days.[61]

As testimonies detailed throughout have indicated, many Black bodies were mutilated, strung up, or displayed as warnings, or discarded in the Red River by vigilantes and paramilitary aggressors. During the melee at Gum Springs, some freedpeople who had escaped from Shady Grove returned and commenced making coffins for their murdered friends and family. While the coffins were being built, the vigilantes returned and shot these carpenters. It is significant that amid a massacre, mourning their recently murdered kin and eventually becoming victims themselves, these carpenters prepared coffins and planned burials. Although they were living in a region beset by violent white supremacy, these brave individuals consciously demonstrated that Black communities prioritized burial practices to honor and preserve the dead.[62]

Eighteen Black men and three women were killed in Shady Grove that day, and numerous others were taken by the vigilantes and brought to Benton, Louisiana. The vigilantes traveled toward Arkansas, continuing the violence, while a separate group of seventy-five Shreveport citizens, "armed and nearly all mounted," descended on Shady Grove. U.S. Marshal Keeting left the Twentieth Infantry troops at the ferry near Shady Grove before proceeding to Benton with Captain Nutt, the leader of the Shreveport armed posse. Another hundred armed white men were assembled at Benton, but Keeting reported "no colored men in the vicinity," and none were found for five miles around.

By the following morning, an additional two hundred armed, intoxicated white men had descended on Bossier and "talked about killing the colored people that had left the plantations," plus any freedpeople hiding out or on the run. Keeting told Nutt that if the vigilantes dispersed, he would take a group of mounted U.S. troops into the swamps to "counsel the colored men to return to their plantations." Bossier's white men—leading planters and members of the community, according to Taylor's testimony—had collectively determined to hunt and kill freedpeople; the marshal left the scene, allowing them to continue their "negro hunt." For over a week, armed whites, including those who returned from Arkansas to kill five freedpeople, swept through the parish, killing with impunity, with 162 Black people estimated dead.

Issac Young testified that Dr. Whitfield Vance gathered nineteen white men to his plantation in broad daylight on September 30, 1864, and rounded up seven Black men from the plantation. They killed four at Gum Springs, a few miles above Vance's plantation, and two in nearby Benton. On the plantation, they shot Henry Chambers three times at the gate. On the night of October 2, Fred Kinney, a freedman, came to Issac and relayed that Vance and his posse had killed fellow freedman Bob on the road for being a radical. Vance thrust a large bowie knife into Bob's back and into his heart. Vance and his posse then made "the colored men kneel down about the deceased and look him in the eyes" before forcing Kinney and other Blacks to drag Bob to the roadside. As the group continued to Benton, they came across two freedwomen on horseback, who were ordered off their horses and hanged by their lariat ropes on a nearby tree. Once the women were dead, the captured Black men were made to cut them down and leave them by the roadside, as they had been forced to do with Bob.[63]

On October 7, fifty Bossier planters, "well armed and mounted," held a meeting and then divided into squads that killed Blacks on different plantations around Shady Grove. Henry Taylor testified that twenty men were killed that night. Some men were mowed down as they picked cotton, while terrified women and children fled. As Taylor and his wife left the plantation, he saw "twenty-five white men . . . with guns in their hands, and heard them say they intended to kill every man, woman, and child on the Dixon plantation . . . near Carolina Bluff." A firm Shady Grove Massacre body count was never attempted, but estimated deaths from September 27 and October 7, 1868, are between one hundred and three hundred freedpeople.[64]

For those freedpeople who fled Bossier Parish plantations, the period following Shady Grove was tense and tenuous. Henry Boswell came across four dead bodies with their hands and feet bound and throats cut from ear to ear. Freedmen George Nicholson, Charles Wormley, and Elijah hid for three weeks in holes they had dug. Other refugees recalled that laborers were gathered up on plantations and made to stand in rows, where names were called off indiscriminately from a death list. They were then marched to Gum Springs and shot. Henry Ellison recalled two Black men burying a family of six in a cotton sack after their bodies had floated down the Red River. He also came across two beheaded freedmen on the road at Mooringsport.

The violence in Bossier spilled over into Caddo Parish. A bulletin about the violence in October 1868 asserted that "twenty five or thirty dead bodies of colored people have floated down the river, past Shreveport, in the space of one month." The bulletin also called attention to the inaction of author-ities in the October 14, 1868, murder of Robert Gray by a white vigilante. Gray, the elected justice of the peace of Ward 1, had been hiding out in Shreveport since his election, after whites "commenced a persecution of the colored men." Republicans, Black and white, now lived in Caddo Par-ish "only at the risk of their lives." Dr. Moore advised white Shreveporters that "whenever they met a radical n— that would not give in, to shoot him down." On October 12, this advice was eagerly taken when three white resi-dents murdered five freedmen.[65]

As the 1869 Joint Committee of the General Assembly of Louisiana report noted, the string of violent incidents before the 1868 presidential election "fully established the supremacy of the white race" in the region. This solid grip on power was reflected in the voting returns for Caddo and Bossier Parishes. Caddo Parish had three thousand registered Republicans but returned only one vote, while Bossier Parish netted one Republican vote from a registration of two thousand voters.[66] The groundwork was firmly es-tablished for the complete usurpation of democratic institutions and Black enfranchisement in northwest Louisiana.

Between Shady Grove and the Colfax Massacre, three national events further heightened White League behavior and racial enmity. First, the Grant administration passed three Enforcement Acts, in 1870 and 1871, in response to ongoing, widespread southern violence. These acts were in-tended to provide a framework for federal prosecution of people who used violence to bar citizens from exercising their Fourteenth and Fifteenth Amendment rights. The first act focused on elections and forbade voter dis-crimination on the basis of race. It allowed the president to appoint election supervisors. The second act combatted the high rates of racial violence in cities like New Orleans by strengthening enforcement powers. The third act, passed in April 1871, was known as the Ku Klux Klan Act and stemmed from the continued terrorist violence that permeated the South. It aimed to protect freedmen's voting rights, reassert federal law, and prevent criminal activity that would violate civil rights. Theoretically, this meant that attempts by private citizens to thwart Black participation in politics could be prosecuted in federal rather than partisan state courts.[67]

The Enforcement Acts outraged southern whites and further fueled hatred of a Republican-led federal government, vitriol toward freedmen's citizenship and enfranchisement, and disgust at the frequency of federal intervention. The Ku Klux Klan Act should have signaled a sea change in the management of white violence toward freedpeople—particularly politically motivated episodes—but these acts produced little change in the Red River region or in the South writ large. Aside from commissioning an in-depth investigation of southern violence that included the realized violence in northwest Louisiana as captured in *Use of the Army,* the Grant administration distanced itself from action on the policies and issues of Reconstruction. White Leaguers and paramilitaries were frequently pardoned, and military intervention was painfully slow, if present at all, during racially driven conflicts.

In addition to those political developments, the disappointing 1872 cotton crop struck everyone in the Red River region hard. The poor crop returns resulted from a maelstrom of disasters: a cold, wet winter along with a drought, a hurricane, and intense heat. The Panic of 1873 and the depression that followed wreaked havoc on the region's financial health. Credit dried up after a spring and summer of bad weather and caterpillars. The Panic of 1873 was not just the death knell for the prosperity of regional farmers; it also played a critical role in the demonization of Republicans and carpetbagger politicians that suppressed southern Republicanism while changing the playbook utilized by northern Republicans.

Following swiftly on the heels of the Panic was a yellow fever epidemic that destroyed regional populations, particularly affecting small towns in Caddo Parish. The epidemic began in mid-August, and outbreaks had been reported all over the region by the end of September. A correspondent for the *Picayune* wrote that Coushatta was "entirely deserted" as healthy residents fled for the "pine hill places" to wait out the disease. The Red River raft was blamed for the quick spread of disease. Henry Hall, a Caddo Parish judge, lost his entire family to yellow fever. In a retrospective diary entry on the epidemic, he wrote that he heard of cases regularly during August, but on September 1, thirty townspeople were buried. After sporadic visits to town, he avoided journeying from his neighborhood, though he and his wife attended a wedding and visited with neighbors despite casualties. Contagion increased in mid-September, with more than twenty people buried on September 12. Despite reports of more dead the following day, Hall wrote, "We are spared through another day without sickness." Then his family fell ill at month's end, and by October 5, he was without a wife or children.[68] This familial and community destruction played out throughout the region, heightening tensions and paranoia within an already charged interracial dynamic that further frayed the taut sentiments regarding Black political access, citizenship, and civil rights. Additional kindling had been added to a stoked fire, necessitating only a tiny spark to subsume the entire region in a legacy of violent vigilantism and asserted white supremacy.

— — —

Nowhere was the poverty of Reconstruction and the unencumbered, entrenched, and racially driven power of vigilantism displayed more clearly than in the Colfax Massacre. Grant Parish, established in 1869 by the Republican-led Louisiana legislature, was carved from Calhoun family plantation land by William Calhoun—a Republican, former Unionist, and state representative. Three large plantations covered seven hundred acres that curved along seven miles of rich Red River frontage. Calhoun entered the senate through a combination of his economic clout and support from the freedmen who labored on his land. The manifestation of a Calhoun-sponsored bill, Grant Parish was named in honor of President Grant, and the parish seat, Colfax, was named for Vice President Schuyler Colfax. Similarly, Red River Parish, where Coushatta is located, was carved from portions of Natchitoches, DeSoto, Caddo, and Bossier Parishes to create a Republican bastion. Demographics were key for these newly formed parishes; both were carefully demarcated, majority African American, and formed on or included the holdings of powerful white Republicans.[69]

Calhoun had two Republican allies in the parish: William Phillips, an ex-Confederate Alabamian, and Delos White, a former Union soldier, a Freedmen's Bureau agent from New York, and a one-term sheriff of Grant Parish. These three men—like prominent Republican Marshall Harvey Twitchell in Red River Parish—found their lives in constant jeopardy because of their politics and their personal lives. Calhoun and Phillips maintained long-term relationships with Black women and acknowledged their children from those unions. On September 25, 1871, White and Phillips woke at night to find the house they shared on fire. When they rushed outside, White was shot and killed instantly while Phillips feigned death amid the raging fire. The vigilantes who had started the fire affixed one of Phillips's 1868 campaign speeches to a burning stake before riding off. Phillips fled to New Orleans and obtained warrants for the arrests of parish sheriff Alfred Shelby, deputy sheriff Christopher Columbus Nash, and four other men. Though they were arrested and brought to New Orleans, the men were eventually released.[70]

Colfax became infamous for the unrestrained racial carnage of the Colfax Massacre, the single bloodiest incident of Reconstruction. Whites in Colfax and across the region held the authority of state and federal government in contempt, assured in the knowledge that the law could be overcome by violence. The lack of criminal ramifications for the Colfax perpetrators and the complete failure of state and federal courts to substantiate and protect Black enfranchisement, Black citizenship, and Black safety further empowered white supremacists to act with impunity.[71]

As was true of other infamous episodes of paramilitary violence, political factors were significant in the genesis of the Colfax Massacre.[72] William Pitt Kellogg was the Republican nominee in the 1872 state elections against a mixed ticket of Liberal Republicans and Democrat reformers known as the Fusionists, who nominated John McEnery. Henry Clay Warmoth, the former governor against whom the state legislature had brought impeachment proceedings following the 1872 presidential election, supported McEnery. The Republican ticket encapsulated a central problem for Republicanism in the Reconstruction South because it relied on the loyal support of African American voters and a small number of white carpetbaggers. Many Louisiana moderates reacted in opposition to a perceived Republican overreach. The significance of Black voters supporting Republican candidates in parishes outside the Red River region increased tensions and further roused White Leaguers' need to control the allocation of Black votes through violence. Tapping into a tradition of deep distrust for unpopular government rule, Democrats deployed violence against Republicans as part of a concerted, invested effort to regain the political helm. Democrats leveraged the negative perception of the 1872 Republican state tickets as justification for heightened instances of violence, widespread vigilantism, and paramilitary force to secure complete white political dominance at the local, state, and national levels.[73]

The 1872 state election was so laced with fraud that the victor was never firmly determined. The election was highly dishonest, partially because Warmoth, though suspended as governor on impeachment charges, wielded tremendous power over local registrars, which provided opportunities for Fusionists to manipulate votes at the parish level. Additionally, the state-wide returning board was bitterly divided. When the board met to certify the ballot, it was split. Each side declared itself the legal returning board and the other fraudulent; both claimed victory and swore in their chosen officials. The situation of rival governments also meant that two separate sets of appointed local officials jockeyed for permanence and validity, creating a flashpoint in an already tense Colfax.[74] This political situation would gain renewed firepower after Colfax, when at the behest of the Democratic Party the White League organized the 1874 paramilitary street battle that became known as the Battle of Liberty Place. One of five street battles that occurred between 1866 and 1877 in New Orleans, this incident saw the White League control New Orleans for three days before federal troops regained control and reinstated Kellogg to the governorship.[75]

William Ward, a freedman whose attempted candidacy for a parish seat on the state legislature was publicly supported by William Calhoun, headed Colfax's fledgling Black militia and sought Kellogg's support for the installation of a white sheriff, Daniel Shaw, and a Black judge, R. C. Registrar. Fusionists promoted James Hadnot, a man particularly opposed to Black emancipation, as their representative, alongside former deputy Nash as sheriff and Alphonse Cazabat as judge. These bifurcated representatives tensely skirted the issue of political validity for six weeks. The McErney appointees had the support of Grant Parish whites. However, the tiny, primarily Black town of Colfax backed the Kellogg representatives and began to form and train a militia, escalating tensions further.[76] The cataclysmic eruption of racial tension at Colfax decisively and irrevocably solidified the centrality of white supremacy in northwest Louisiana. One regional white summarized the vigilante takeover as the end of "the cruelty and domination of the 'Yankee negro rule'" achieved through "the people" rebelling "in sections and in bands."[77]

In early March, Kellogg certified the Republican officeholders, but McEnery also swore in his officials and set up government in a rival legislature a few blocks from the statehouse. Both sides believed their government to be valid, and metropolitan police massed against the organized McEnery posse in a tense New Orleans. In Colfax, the opposing factions jostled for ownership of the courthouse, and nineteen whites under Hadnot's leadership made a show of strength on April 1, riding at a charge through town with brandished rifles. Violence commenced on April 5 with the point-blank shooting of freedman Jesse McKinney on his property by a group of white men, illustrative of the growing number of regional vigilantes—many of them ex-Confederate soldiers—who heeded Nash's call to descend on Colfax. When McKinney died eight hours later, his wife departed with his body and their children for Mirabeau plantation, on Calhoun's land, to seek safety and a coffin. Her instinctive departure from the isolated countryside to Colfax town boundaries mirrored the movement of numerous freedpeople who established camps in the town, seeking strength in numbers and the protection of William Ward's militia.

Both sides skirmished—with no fatalities—following McKinney's death, as armed white vigilante units converged on Colfax. Ward wrote detailed letters to Kellogg requesting assistance, which Calhoun attempted to bring to New Orleans, but he was seized near Alexandria by armed vigilantes and returned by force to Colfax. Kellogg vacillated before dispatching two militia officers to investigate on April 10. Events, however, were already in motion. More than 250 whites were encamped within the pecan trees that constituted Colfax's perimeter, while several hundred Black men, women, and children were on the other side of the trees, within the small town's limits.

On Easter Sunday, April 13, 1873, at noon, Christopher Columbus Nash led the massed vigilantes across the Red River and up the main road to the courthouse, where they assembled in military formation. Since McKinney's death, freedpeople had erected earthen breastworks around the courthouse grounds. Bearing a white flag, Nash rode out to the freedmen's earthworks and briefly met with Levi Allen, who had replaced Ward as commander. Nash demanded that the freedpeople surrender, give up the courthouse, and put down their weapons. Allen refused. Nash gave the freedmen thirty minutes to move freedwomen and children from the courthouse vicinity before firing commenced.

It is unclear which side fired first, but the fighting was hot and persisted for hours as both sides remained firm. The freedmen sustained many casualties, contrasted with no white deaths. Heavy, continuous fire from the paramilitaries as the afternoon progressed rendered the freedmen's breastworks untenable. Forced from those defenses, some Blacks were killed as they attempted to run to the river, while others hid in the woods. A contingent of approximately sixty-five men retreated to the courthouse, where materials were stockpiled and they felt a strong position could be held. Meanwhile, the paramilitaries selected a Black prisoner named Pinckney Chambers to walk—unarmed—under fire to the courthouse. Chambers walked with a long fishing pole tied with oil-doused rags lit ablaze. With the supremacists' guns fixed on his back, Chambers walked to the courthouse, lifted the pole, and set the shingles alight. Inside, freedmen tried unsuccessfully to knock the burning shingles off the roof while the paramilitaries maintained firing. Freedmen were burning alive inside the courthouse.

Blacks and whites later recollected the next moments differently. In the white version, the burning freedmen waved a makeshift white flag that lured James Hadnot and his men to the courthouse door, where they were promptly shot. An article written years later to refute misstatements maintained that the freedmen kept up a "regular fusillade on the burning spot," and when they indicated a desire to surrender, "the negroes committed one of the most dastardly acts of treachery ever perpetrated by fiends in human shape." In this account, Hadnot, "desirous of allowing the negroes to escape," approached with his men to discuss terms of surrender and was fired on from inside the building.

The *Natchitoches Times's* coverage of the massacre, on April 26, stated that after the courthouse was alight and freedmen's attempts to extinguish the fire failed, "the negroes hung out a white flag in token of surrender." Hadnot and another white man "immediately advanced" to the courthouse door but "were shot down, and the negroes rushed out in a body." Whites were incensed and "fired into the mass as they came out, and following them up, killed them wherever they could find them . . . no quarter was given." Freedmen might have fired as this parlay supposedly began, which provided white justification for further slaughter.

In the Black version, the men still alive in the courthouse were stacking their firearms, and Hadnot was shot by an overexcited member of his own posse. All versions of the events agree that after Hadnot's shooting—after which he was injured but alive—whites shot the freedmen "down like dogs, and those that escaped the first fire were ridden down in the open field . . . and shot without mercy."[78]

Some Blacks were killed in close combat. Many were shot in the head or neck; one man's face was "completely flattened by blows from a broken stock of a double-barreled gun." Almost all "had from three to a dozen wounds," and many "had their brains literally blown out." After the four o'clock cessation of firing, between twenty-eight and forty-eight freedmen were rounded up and held under a pecan tree. Around ten that evening, following dinner and celebratory liquor, the vigilantes decided to execute the wounded and prisoners. One man stated that he had ridden four hundred miles "to kill n——s" and was not ready to stop.

They shot the wounded before rounding up the remaining prisoners. Luke Hadnot, son of James Hadnot, called out five names, closely lined up the men, and killed all five using two bullets. Other paramilitaries selected specific victims to execute. Recalling the commodified, propertied antebellum language, many whites referred to their prisoners as "beeves" or cattle, and they belittled the anguish of freedwomen who witnessed the killings. One member of the posse began a cleanup operation of wounded prisoners. In this manner, most of the prisoners were executed, with many disposed of in the river.[79]

The *Natchitoches Times* printed an eyewitness account in its April 26 issue. One of their journalists was aboard the steamboat *Southwestern*, which had landed about a mile below Colfax. There, "a young fellow armed to the teeth and very much excited" boarded and requested the captain land at Colfax to evacuate the injured James Hadnot, who later died, and two other wounded white men to Alexandria. The journalist and most of the passengers alighted at Colfax to see the "battleground," their morbid curiosity piqued after the armed white man, referred to as "our young friend," promised that if "we wanted to see dead n——s, here was a chance, for there were a hundred or so scattered over the village." As they reached the top of the landing they "began to stumble upon them . . . lying on their faces . . . riddled with bullets." The curious passengers came across bodies every few steps; many were sick from the "horrible smell of burning human flesh" emanating from the courthouse blaze and were informed that "eighteen of the misguided darkies" lying near the landing represented just one-fourth of the number killed.

According to the article, a "storm had been gathering." A few days before the massacre, the "negroes got too numerous for the whites and they were compelled to seek refuge in the surrounding country." Meanwhile, freedpeople "plundered the town and threw up rude fortifications" while grand-standing about how they would drive all whites from the parish. Whites had organized themselves, "reinforced from the adjoining parish," and on Easter Sunday, with Colfax's sheriff leading, they approached Colfax under a flag of truce, beseeching surrender. It was only because "the negroes refused to come to terms" that "whites charged the breastworks" and fighting commenced. Particular emphasis was given to the narrative—repeated ad nauseam in future articles—that freedpeople inside the courthouse waved a white flag only to fire upon the white men when they reached the courthouse. This report estimated between sixty and one hundred freedmen dead but remarked, "People were so excited over the events of the day that nothing very accurate could be gathered from any of them."[80] Most reports—in newspapers, correspondence, and personal recollections—incorrectly stated that Hadnot, Sidney Harris, and Stephen Parish died immediately after being shot at the courthouse door. In reality, they were transported on the *Southwestern* to Alexandria, where they later died of their wounds, but this misstatement provided further justification for the unbridled slaughter of freedmen.[81]

Daybreak displayed terrible carnage, and the bodies, some still smoldering and many unrecognizable, told a harrowing story. The shallow breastworks around the courthouse were filled with the early victims, and numerous bodies fanned out from the courthouse, bottlenecked at the door. The courthouse continued to smolder and held the charred remains of still more freedmen. Additional corpses were scattered across town and the watery tomb of the Red River. Whites carried out a perfunctory body count while also terrorizing Blacks who attempted to count, locate, collect, and bury the dead. The exact number of African American dead is unknown, but the accepted victim count ranges from 70 to 165.[82]

Some Red River whites celebrated the violence but remained concerned about securing their labor force. Many were infuriated by the seizure and arrest of some white perpetrators to stand trial in New Orleans, and the arrival of federal troops was deemed an encouragement to freedpeople to continue to test the permanence of their political rights, to the detriment of the fields. In the aftermath of the massacre, Henry Hyams Sr., who had purchased a pistol and ammunition and sent them to his son on April 4, wrote to nervously inquire after Henry Jr. in light of "this unfortunate business." While he was confident that a "judicial investigation" would "fully and fairly elecit the truth," his attention turned to labor enforcement on their plantations; he hoped "your people" were untouched and unaffected by the catastrophe and were "honestly and quietly at their work."[83]

While Hyams preferred to envisage freedpeople's quiet loyalty in the face of extraordinary violence, Charles Boothby, a former U.S. Army captain serving as superintendent of education for New Orleans, wrote about "political troubles in the country." He acknowledged that the guiding purpose of the violence was to "intimidate the colored men" so they would not register and vote. Northern reporting echoed concerns about voting turnout and participation while condemning the magnitude of the slaughter, often drawing parallels with the Fort Pillow Massacre.[84] Though northern papers acknowledged the grotesque, widespread usage, and ferocity of the violence, reports attributed these actions to the state's violent propensities. Boothby was not sympathetic with or compassionate toward the freedmen, noting, "In all the 'reprisings' of the negroes, . . . no one is killed but the negro." He felt that Black actions cultivated a feeling of bitterness toward the Republicans and that African Americans used "the claim that they are deprived" of their elected officers as "their excuse for all there rebellion." Boothby did not confine his distaste to Louisiana's freedpeople but broadly extended to Blacks the blame for a violent South. His letter assured his family that the "old rebel element" was taking control of this growing problem and had plans to "obtain control of the state governments."[85]

Contrary to Boothby's belief, three whites were killed during the Colfax Massacre: James Hadnot, Stephen Parish, and Sidney Harris. The Alexandria-based *Louisiana Democrat* eulogized James Hadnot, writing that he "lost his life at the hands of a mob" and died as a result of wounds "received while in the interest of peace and order, endeavoring to hold a parley with the rioters under a flag of truce."[86] Years later, Hadnot's son John was remembered as "an active participant in the Colfax Riot" and as "one of the prisoners taken to New Orleans and tried for the part he took in maintaining white supremacy in the parish." He had been a magistrate and "evinced extra good judgment in his administration of the law." As was true of other white participants, John Hadnot maintained prominence within the community in the years after the massacre.[87]

For the majority of whites in the region, Nash and his fellow vigilantes were heroes who deftly deployed violence to reassert control to ensure that the region was under white Democratic leadership and that white supremacy was reaffirmed. As the leader of the vigilantes, no one became more esteemed in the community than Christopher Columbus Nash. The region's whites lauded Nash for what they deemed his measured treatment and dealings with freedpeople before the April 13 massacre. A glowing article in Shreveport's aptly named *Caucasian* described Nash in superhero terms, noting that he had rescued white women from the clutches of political, nonsubmissive freedmen.[88] An ex-Confederate soldier with a "splendid war record seeing long and hard service," Nash was memorialized by Milton Dunn, a member of the Colfax posse, for raising a "force of white men" when the "war of Reconstruction in Grant Parish took place." Nash gallantly led the defense at Colfax after the freedmen "took possession . . . and drove the white people out," commanding "his posse" during the "three and a half hours of fighting" when "185 white men defeated 800 negroes, killing 168 of them." Hero terminology ascribed to the violence—a "gallant act"—was underscored by the instantaneous "restoration of peace" in the parish.[89] Nash epitomized the visible, brazen, proud, and unwavering composition of Red River white supremacy. His commitment to Confederate ideals and his stalwart assault on the courthouse ensured that he evaded arrest for his Colfax involvement, further elevating his status.

John William recollected the dark period before the Colfax Massacre, asserting, "daylight never did break until the great day of Colfax known as the Colfax Riot."[90] The region's whites consistently recast the Colfax Massacre as a reassertion of white political, economic, and social control, a further entrenchment of white power, and an act of racial justice. Paramilitaries maintained that the provocations for violence were numerous and amplified by freedmen asserting their political rights and organizing in a militia. This was ample validation for harnessing vituperative violence to hem in the boundaries of freedom throughout the Red River region.[91] This backdrop also provided a platform for a gendered reinscription of Colfax that extolled the white paramilitaries for preserving the sanctity of white womanhood. This narrative coexisted alongside a robust commitment to the Confederate legacy and allowed regional whites, particularly women, to play a leading role in the commemoration and memorialization of Reconstruction violence and white supremacy.

Kate Grant, from a well-established parish family, wrote a melodramatic and formulaic nineteenth-century romance novel called *From Blue to Gray, or The Battle of Colfax,* proclaimed on the dedication page as "a woman's tribute of admiration to the heroes of Grant, Louisiana and her sister parishes, who fought so valiantly side by side with Sheriff C. C. Nash." The preamble told readers of "the pure patriotic spirit with which the Sheriff and his Posse were imbued" and strove in "my descriptions of the various outrages upon the people of Grant, to adhere solely to the truth." She lists established parish families who witnessed the massacre and who would vouch for and "corroborate the charges made by me against the Republican mob concentrated by fraud and violence" at Colfax. Even more telling is the novel's postscript endorsement signed by Christopher Columbus Nash, the president of the police jury, along with nineteen other leading parish men.

The novel is a stereotypical nineteenth-century romance novel. Alongside a saccharine and breathless love triangle involving a beautiful belle, a handsome carpetbagger, and an honorable southern gentleman runs a parallel story of animal-like freedpeople, bloodthirsty and desperate to kill their former owners and incited by conniving Republicans to frenzied mob action. Grant casts the story in stark terms to show how terrible and ominous radical rule was in Colfax and in northwest Louisiana writ large, in contrast to the "prosperity, peace and plenty" that "crown Democratic Rule in Grant" following the massacre. *From Blue to Gray* is as much a tribute piece to white supremacy as an overt display of regional female loyalty to the Colfax vigilantes. Grant credits them with saving white womanhood, restoring order in the parish, and reinstating political control. The vigilantes who carried out the paramilitary actions of the Colfax Massacre are Kate Grant's heroes, wholly responsible for the "present blessings" parish residents now enjoyed.[92]

The Colfax Massacre marked the apex of years of persistent tension and violence that fueled an onslaught of political takeovers and paramilitary incidents throughout Louisiana. Ten thousand white men statewide formally joined paramilitary companies such as the White Leagues while Fusionist leaders bypassed any pretense of legality and pushed Republicans from office.[93] News of the massacre traveled quickly, but action was laconic, and there was a delay in bringing a handful of Colfax perpetrators to stand trial. The two militiamen sent by Governor Kellogg on April 12 did not arrive in Colfax until April 15, too late to quell the violence. Theodore DeKlyne, the head of that mission, wrote a report that became a critical document and particularly benefited the white supremacists in the state trial. DeKlyne later returned to Colfax with military escorts to make arrests.

President Grant likewise delayed the federal response to dispatch troops. Although a military unit of ninety-eight men was mobilized on April 17, they could not find transportation for two days. White supremacist forces within New Orleans warned boat captains of personal and political repercussions for bringing troops to Colfax, which accounted for the delay and the exorbitant price for their eventual transport.[94] The blue-clad Nineteenth Infantry received a frosty reception in Grant Parish, and the inflamed public opinion in the region redoubled the feeling of insecurity and isolation in hostile territory that overtook federal troops, who withdrew thirty miles to the relative safety of Pineville.

A grand jury was appointed for the Colfax case in late April, which enraged whites. The *Natchitoches Times* wrote that U.S. District Attorney Beckwith had been instructed to "spare no pains or expense" in arresting those involved and making a "thorough investigation of the affair in Grant Parish." The secretary of war was also called upon to "render all military aid necessary to enforce the process."[95] On the ground, the investigation was commanded by U.S. Marshal Samuel Packard and conducted by Inspector DeKlyne and the Nineteenth Infantry. Violence and brazen paramilitary activity remained at a steady hum and prompted President Grant to declare portions of Louisiana in a state of insurrection on May 22. This triggered the martial law provisions of the Enforcement Acts that suspended habeas corpus for the suspects of the Colfax Massacre as the case moved from a local grand jury case to a federal investigation.

J. Ernest Breda, whose wife had beseeched him against Republicanism, was the parish district attorney. He also served as prosecutor on the case and began indictments in early July "against about 140 of the Colfax murders." Court was adjourned until July 24, but no sooner had R. C. Register, the parish judge, opened the court than seventy armed men "openly + violently threatened to break up the court" and forced its closure. The posse included many of the Colfax indicted and Judge Register was shot. Breda wrote to U.S. Attorney General George Williams about the regional mood and inclination toward additional aggression. Breda had fled Colfax to save his life, "for I knew + can establish the fact that it would have been taken + I felt no disposition to offer myself as a sacrifice when the other officers, those of the U.S. want to take no steps to assist or protect the courts." Indeed, he noted that whites had determined "that if they are to be prosecuted for killing negroes on April 13th" that there was little to lose if they killed "a few more negroes + radicals."[96]

Breda wrote to Packard two weeks later about the dangerous situation in Colfax and the need to employ military aid to investigate, since "the courts are threatened and we will be murdered if any attempt is made . . . to arrest any man connected in these Colfax troubles." He was frustrated by the presence of federal soldiers in Pineville, thirty miles away, "while we were exposing our lives in holding court." If action was intended against the Colfax perpetrators, Breda asked, then "why on earth put so much delay in it," especially because the prosecution "cannot give our lives for we would not be noticed any more than the unfortunate murdered of April 13th." More dead bodies would not reset the scales of justice. Breda continued by telling the U.S. marshal that he had petitioned Grant, "urging action" and requesting active protection from troops "who will not remain idle in Pineville or elsewhere, when danger of murder + bloodshed is threatening in all directions, but there."[97] He made the same statement to the U.S. attorney general, requesting that the government put teeth into prosecuting the Colfax vigilantes. Breda saw "no necessity for U.S. officers" in Louisiana if "they are here to no purpose," and he remained flummoxed that "80 or 100 of our citizens are unmercifully murdered and we cannot even have the matter properly investigated," and that there was no chance of "protection against a repetition of similar outrages."[98]

The Red River inserted itself into the trial proceedings when the *Ozark*, the decommissioned yet reliable Civil War monitor from the Red River campaign, transported the Colfax perpetrators to New Orleans. Despite ninety-seven names listed on the federal indictment, *United States v. Columbus Nash et al.*, only seven individuals were successfully arrested and brought to trial. On December 4, 1873, those seven suspects were remanded into federal custody, with two additional suspects located and arrested in 1874. Nash, whose name stood in the case heading and signified all the Colfax vigilantes, notably eluded arrest.

While in New Orleans, the defendants were supported by "the ladies . . . [who] supplied them with all their needs." These ladies would appear daily in the courtroom bearing flowers that they placed on the defense table and cheering supportively in response to the defense attorney's motions. Within the Red River region, the community organized galas and benefits to raise funds and donated extensively through parish subscription funds for prisoners' relief. The defense lawyers also worked pro bono.[99] The Colfax vigilantes had the full support of whites in both the Red River region and the state.

U.S. attorney James Beckwith presented an indictment with thirty-two criminal counts. He had limited funds to investigate and provide security for the 140 prosecution witnesses, most of whom were freedpeople. The testimony of the wounded, survivors, and bereaved family members did not carry the same gravitas for the jurors. Beckwith's charges addressed fundamental questions: What and whom did the Constitution protect? Which privileges and immunities were guaranteed? Which branches of the government bore the responsibility for protecting them? Beckwith built his argument around the federal government's obligation to be the guardian of constitutional rights. In essence, the trial vetted the constitutionality of the Enforcement Acts and provided an opportunity to rebalance the power between the federal government and southern state governments.

Catastrophically, Beckwith did not stress the racial motivation behind the massacre and did not identify specific charges tied to racial animus as the motivation for the massacre. The case went before the Supreme Court because of this failure to establish and demonstrate the organized and explicit white supremacist link between McKinney's murder on April 6 and the massacre on April 13, 1873. Two circuit trials were held in 1874, after the first ended in a mistrial in March 1874. Supreme Court justice Stephen Bradley presided over the second circuit trial—*U.S. v. Cruikshank et al.* The circuit ruling in *Cruikshank* was immensely significant and more impactful and precedent-setting than the subsequent 1876 Supreme Court ruling that arose from the case's progression to the nation's highest court.[100]

The second trial's defense team requested that the presiding judge dismiss all the charges on the grounds that the Enforcement Acts had been rendered void by the *Slaughterhouse* ruling and that Justice Bradley, on his annual circuit of the lower courts, should preside over the trial. The *Slaughterhouse* case, in which Bradley had offered a dissenting opinion, was a Fourteenth Amendment ruling that afforded federal action and protection a very narrow scope, particularly on civil rights, which remained overwhelmingly a state matter. It applied the Fourteenth Amendment universally and determined that there were two citizenship classes, national and state. The power of the state to regulate matters within its borders could not be impeded by federal legislation. In an ironic twist of fate, the *Slaughterhouse* decision was handed down the day after the Colfax Massacre.[101]

Cruikshank went to trial on June 7, with Justice Bradley present, and the jury delivered a not guilty verdict on June 10. Three of the defendants—William Cruikshank, J. P. Hadnot, and Bill Irwin—were convicted of conspiracy to violate their Black victims' civil rights. This conviction was the reason the case entered the Supreme Court. Bradley, as circuit court judge, overturned these convictions, voided Beckwith's indictment, and in his June 27 opinion declared critical sections of the Enforcement Acts unconstitutional. Bradley's circuit court ruling effectively suspended federal law enforcement throughout Louisiana and the South. It allowed white supremacists to use violence against Blacks—armed or not—in politically motivated contexts without interference from federal law enforcement or enactment of federal legal protections.

Bradley's circuit ruling in *Cruikshank* was a complicated ruling with a complex legacy. It forms the backbone of a series of Reconstruction era court rulings that extended until *Ex Parte Yarbrough* in 1884. When *Cruikshank* is viewed as the cornerstone of Bradley's voting rights theory and his seminal jurisprudence on state action doctrine, the different categories of rights distinguished in nineteenth-century interpretations of the Constitution, and the concept of state neglect, move into focus. This highlights the complexity of a ruling that left white supremacists, vigilantes, and paramilitaries unpunished—emboldening politically motivated racial violence throughout the South and leaving Blacks with no course for redress—while also writing into law a robust blueprint for how federal indictments on racial violence should be brought and adjudicated.

The federal elections jurisprudence ruling in *Cruikshank* drew upon state action doctrine, heavily informed by the concept of state neglect.[102] In the nineteenth century, Americans understood rights to be of two types: natural rights, which predate the Constitution but are declared by the Constitution, or rights that are created, given, or granted by the Constitution. State action doctrines were tied to congressional enforcement of natural rights and were contingent on state denials of rights. State neglect derived from this understanding of natural rights because it gave the federal government power to punish and enforce in instances of state action denial. A private assault is one for which remedies are normally available—state power and legal reach cover punishment for these types of assault—and for which state action would occur; if remedies and redress are not ordinarily available, this gives the color of law or custom and falls into the category of state neglect. Thus, punishment had to be contingent on the failure to provide remedies to punish a private individual whose assault has, in the language of the enforcement provision of the Civil Rights Act of 1866, "gained the color of law . . . or custom."[103]

The central thrust of *Cruikshank* drew from state action doctrine and the Fifteenth Amendment exemption, which provided a strong framework for direct federal prosecution in race-based interferences and violence in voting, irrespective of state behavior. Thus, the federal government could intervene to punish private instances of racially based voting interference regardless of state behavior. Because Beckwith did not indicate that a racial motive triggered the violence, the decision declared that the massacre had not been proven to be racially motivated, despite overwhelming evidence and testimony, and thus "the power of congress . . . does not extend to the passage of laws for the suppression of ordinary crime within the states." The Fifteenth Amendment created a new right within the prohibitory language of its clauses, which extended the right to exemption from racial interference in voting. The federal government could intervene and prosecute when racially based motivations impacted Black voting. State action doctrine encompassed punishment of "ordinary crimes"; lacking an identified racial animus for the Colfax Massacre, the Enforcement Acts held no judicial firepower and showed federal reluctance to put teeth into enforcing the citizenship rights of Black Americans, and a lack of legal protections to enable equal access to the ballot.[104] Beckwith had not irrefutably proven that the arc of events leading to the slaughter on April 13 had been racially driven. Justice Bradley thus ruled that the state action doctrine did not apply, and the Colfax perpetrators walked free.[105]

Rights distinction was significant to Bradley and determined whether the court would hold that the federal government could protect those rights. In his rulings, the language of the Constitution and the rights at issue were paramount. Bradley interpreted state action through a clear-cut distinction wherein the law protected Blacks from unpunished racial violence in instances of contracts, property, and voting but decidedly did not cover integrated schools or public accommodations, which Bradley saw as social rights. The *Cruikshank* circuit ruling also blocked efforts by centrist Republicans, who saw political and racial violence as tied to state neglect, to include political violence against white Republicans within the equal protection clause. By narrowing the equal protection clause to race, Bradley indicated that state action applied only to the Fourteenth Amendment and filtered political violence out of the concept of state neglect.

Cruikshank hollowed out the privileges and immunities clause of the Fourteenth Amendment, and the Supreme Court cited the circuit ruling instead of its own decision until 1907. It racialized the equal protection clause, in a blow to white southern Republicans, placed political violence out of reach of the Fourteenth Amendment, and made explicit evidence and indication of racial motivation as the cause of violence the threshold for any indictment. Rights created by the Fifteenth Amendment gave the federal government the power to adjudicate and punish racially motivated voting interference.

The evidence threshold for punishing white supremacist violence not only meant no convictions for Colfax defendants; subsequent cases of vigilante violence had to prove that violence was motivated by race rather than politics. Bradley's ruling, while nuanced and part of a more comprehensive series of voting rights jurisprudence, used Beckwith's failure to baldly portray the political drivers of Colfax as a long-standing matter of race in order to drop all charges against the Colfax perpetrators. *Cruikshank* dismissed the prosecution case against the Colfax vigilantes and signaled to White Leagues and paramilitaries that killing freedpeople with impunity was permissible unless it was abundantly clear that the violence was racially motivated.[106]

The freed defendants were feted for the entire journey back to Colfax. Music and cannon fire salutes followed as they moved up the Red River, once again onboard the *Ozark*. The men were celebrated as heroes and valiant warriors in the fight against the crushing rule of Radical Republicanism. An enormous outdoor barbeque was held in their honor in Colfax on July 25, 1874. The pro-white, pro-Democrat paper *the Caucasian* called it the "mass meeting" for organizing "the White Man's Party for the Fall meeting." The *Louisiana Democrat,* an Alexandria-based publication, marked the defendants' return and the court ruling as the moment when "our rights, so long crushed by Federal bayonets . . . have finally been accorded us by the highest judicial tribunal in the land."[107]

Emboldened in the aftermath of the ruling, white supremacists and vigilantes operated without fear of reprisal and killed with absolution. A few short weeks later, paramilitary violence erupted in Coushatta, another Republican pocket fifty miles north of Colfax, continuing and strengthening the power of politically fueled racial violence.

– 7 –

"INTO THE HANDS OF THE VERY MEN THAT HELD US SLAVES"

The Coushatta Massacre and White Supremacy

Three days after the Colfax Massacre, Marshall Harvey Twitchell received an anonymous death threat. The letter arrived at his plantation, Starlight, and bluntly stated, "Next week your town is to be overrun and all your n— officers and sum of your white men are to be killed." The author had been "in the file at Colfax" along with "a lawyer from your town . . . and one of your deputy sheriffs," and with their blood up but not satiated, "the matter was all fixed." The vigilantes would gather from Grant Parish and Pleasant Hill, near Shreveport, and also would include Twitchell's own neighbors. Canny to the local shifts in allegiance and support within Coushatta, the writer noted, "You have men among you who pass for friends but who are enemies."[1]

In this instance, the threat was an empty one, but Twitchell and his allies regularly received them in the months leading up to and following the Coushatta Massacre, another incident of politically motivated violence, which occurred fifty miles upriver from Colfax. Like Colfax, the Coushatta Massacre was an extremely violent incident of racial aggression, with widespread participation from local white supremacists, that demonstrated the pervasiveness of political catalysts for regional vigilantism and white supremacist violence in northwest Louisiana. In a continuation of the intertwined timing of events in Colfax and Coushatta, the final ruling in *U.S. v. Cruikshank* was handed down five weeks before the threat to Twitchell's life.

There were differences, however, in the victims and the legal outcomes of the Coushatta Massacre. The legal remedy sought after the Coushatta Massacre demonstrated the impact of the *Cruikshank* circuit court ruling in curtailing the successful adjudication of racial and political violence. Bradley's ruling narrowed the Fifteenth Amendment exemption and stated that a racial motive—not a political motive—must be given in indictments for federal intervention and enforcement. It truncated legal redress even as it empowered racially motivated paramilitary violence and vigilantism.

Twitchell was a Vermont-born Republican senator who had lived in northern Louisiana since the end of the Civil War, first as a Freedmen's Bureau agent and then as a landowner and politician. A former federal army officer, Twitchell was a notorious carpetbagger who shepherded a bill through the state senate to create Red River Parish in 1870 and registered most of the parish's Black voters. From its inception, the parish was majority Republican, with Twitchell and his business and political partner, Edward Dewees, serving as the parish party leaders. Many of Twitchell's family members also relocated from Vermont to Coushatta, and his brother and brother-in-law held Republican offices.

The northern takeover of the parish's political leadership, and their party allegiance, infuriated southern-born, former slaveholding whites. Twitchell had enjoyed a great deal of economic and political success until the 1870s, including backing from Coushatta's businesses and leading men, until 1872, when that faction split briefly into two camps—one pro-Twitchell and the other pro–White League—before unifying behind the White League in 1874.

While Twitchell was a state senator in 1873, his brother, Homer, was Red River Parish's tax collector, which was a precarious office to hold. When Republicans ascended to the state government in 1868, a sizeable preexisting debt was exacerbated by additional spending by Governors Kellogg and Warmoth. In addition, land taxes, which were assessed and collected locally, were soaring. In May 1873, shortly after the Colfax Massacre, leading Coushatta Democrats—all White League members—held a "mass meeting" helmed by Thomas Abney, a prominent Coushatta merchant and leader of the White League, that petitioned Homer Twitchell to delay tax collection.[2] Likewise, in bordering DeSoto Parish, tax collector Robert Dewees, brother to Edward, was sent a stark warning. He received a grisly death threat from "Ten DeSoto Tax Payers" to "leave Mansfield inside of 48 hours, or suit the penalty, which shall be **death** and your **body burned.**" These ten taxpayers would not "**stand** such insolence" from their carpetbagger tax collector, and the letter closed with a chilling postscript filled with vehement hatred: "Hell is gaping for you and unless you heed what we had said; she will soon close her everlasting jaws upon your stinking smoking carcass."[3] Dewees fled Mansfield for Coushatta and the relative protection afforded by Marshall Twitchell.

THE COUSHATTA MASSACRE AND WHITE SUPREMACY   209

Alongside tensions heightened by tax collection and land assessment, Red River Parish sentiment flashed around Black political affiliation, involvement, and exercise of political power, and white Republicans holding office. In the summer of 1874, George King—Twitchell's brother-in-law and chief constable, parish juror, and later mayor of Coushatta—and Henry Scott, Twitchell's friend, received a written warning about having "too much to say to negroes." Three local white men had determined that these interactions "must be stopped" to let the "negroes vote as they please" without Republican involvement.[4] Far from wanting freedpeople to vote of their own volition, of course, these White Leaguers wanted less interaction between Republican officeholders and Black voters so that that they could forcefully redirect Black political activity toward the Democratic Party. Parish whites were particularly rankled by the prominence of northerners within local political and business spheres. Twitchell's formidable landholdings, combined with his friends and family holding multiple political offices, intensified politically motivated violence parish-wide. However, the Coushatta Massacre was set apart from Colfax in that in this case the violence was directed toward white Republicans alongside Black Republicans.

Race-based violence remained pervasive and prevalent throughout the Red River region as the tensions in Coushatta increased. Among the daily instances of violence were pointed threats against Twitchell and his associates, which led directly to the massacre. As neighboring states began to shed Republican dominance at the state government level and a unified, non-localized White League strategy emerged, local newspapers throughout the Red River region published manifestos. Generally, the local White League leadership was the same as the Democratic leadership, mutually reinforcing the use of violence and control to reassert political dominance and recast racial mastery.[5] These manifestos reflected the evolution and recalibration of ingrained white attitudes and identity within the regional fabric, which now aligned in perfect synchrony with a hard-line white supremacist ethos gathering momentum throughout the South.

The Democratic Party was swiftly gaining traction and it used violence—the most potent and effective tool in its arsenal—to secure long-lasting results. Twitchell wrote that "Democrats seemed discouraged and inactive" until fresh orders from White League leadership in Shreveport arrived in late July 1874, resulting in a surge of activity that left Republicans "perfectly paralized . . . by the outrages daily taking place around them," and threats came daily "to the radical headquarters of north Louisiana at Coushatta."[6] By August, there was no corner of Louisiana without an active White League.

The White Leagues were intent on usurping Governor Kellogg and placing John McEnery in his stead. To accomplish this, the league added bulldozing to its tactical arsenal. Bulldozing presented two options to Republican officials—resignation or the lynch mob—and the practice was instantaneously adopted statewide, causing swift Republican collapse. At mass meetings held every two to three weeks throughout the summer, the White League recruited heavily, marched and drilled, and visited with most of the parish's white families, whipping up enthusiasm and vigor for political violence and public ousting.[7] The key White Leaguers in Coushatta were Thomas Abney, who owned one of the two large mercantile stores, and David Pierson, an incredibly prominent member of the Democratic Party. James Cosgrove, the staunchly white supremacist editor of the Natchitoches *People's Vindicator,* and Alfred Leonard, the equally emphatic and vituperative editor of the *Shreveport Times,* kept the ideological framework of race-based politics at the forefront of their articles and pushed the rhetoric of violence as a means to recalibrate and dominate the political, social, and economic landscape.

Writing to Twitchell on July 30, 1874, Frank Edgerton, the white Republican sheriff of Red River Parish, described the heightened—almost frenzied—atmosphere at these local Democratic rallies. His letters foreshadowed the violence of the Coushatta Massacre weeks later, where he and seven other white officeholders and eight Black officeholders would be killed. In the first letter, Edgerton noted that a political speech by Pierson declared white Republicans were "staking our all," and then threatened freedpeople if they supported, voted for, or attempted to "sustain any radical in office it will cost you your lives." Pierson was heartily cheered by the crowd for these remarks. Edgerton wrote of his plans to gather a local militia "of black men, number about 50, and put them under an oath so strong," but he would begin with "what white men we have," which totaled "12 or 15 which is sufficient." The militia would only be used "if strictly necessary to maintain peace and order." Edgerton closed the letter by discussing the risk to Twitchell's life. Local vigilantes believed he had gone in search of federal troops for protection and Edgerton warned that it was his "firm belief" that Twitchell could live in Coushatta only "on horseback in the woods if you do not get them."[8]

A second, more frantic letter proclaimed that the feeling in Coushatta was focused on "extermination of the carpetbagger/scalawag element. Nothing more or less." Pierson and Abney had returned from Natchitoches "red hot and on the warpath," where they had held a meeting a previous day. Edgerton wrote that Pierson "was very bitter and his sentiments fully endorsed by the committee . . . Expression is too strong for us to doubt their meeting any longer." Edgerton stated plainly that he hoped to stave off Republican resignations for a while longer and "if necessary make them commit murder before they make my man resign." He stressed the need for intervention from Governor Kellogg to defuse the mounting tension and provide protection for white and Black Republicans in Coushatta, as the situation was "on the verge of civil war, an accident, a drunken man or a crazy fanatic is liable to start it at any moment." Without troops from the federal or state governments, he estimated that they might be able to delay a crisis for around two weeks. He closed his letter with an ominous postscript: "Bear in mind a conflict here is inevitable. Pierson in his speech to the Negroes tells them if they vote radical ticket it will cost them their lives."[9]

Twitchell wrote to Edgerton that he had conferred with Kellogg, but until "some overt act" had occurred, a marshal and troops would not be sent to Coushatta. He recommended that if Edgerton was certain violence would be used to force his resignation as sheriff, "then to save your life, resign."[10] Things had further deteriorated when parish attorney William Howell wrote to Twitchell two weeks later that Coushatta was "on the very verge of Civil War" because the "White Leaguers demands are many and out of all reason." A steady stream of "strange ruffians" congregated in town, boastful about killing Republicans, and Howell was certain they could only stave off violence if troops were sent, although those same troops might ignite violence. Interestingly, Howell noted that while the Republican Party could not safely organize due to threats, the White League was adamant that federal troops were in place to hold elections, which likely derived from their knowledge that troops would not be sent. He warned, firmly, that Twitchell and Dewees could not live in Coushatta or run for office "without soldiers."[11]

Tensions increased steadily during August, until they reached a tipping point on the evening of August 25. Ten miles from Coushatta, at a small enclave named Brownsville, two Black farmers, Daniel Wynn and Thomas Floyd, had a verbal altercation with two whites. Thomas Floyd's wife, Mathilda, testified that white men came to their home, called to Floyd, and fired into the home. She was ordered to make a light, and when she was slow to find kindling, one of the vigilantes punched her in the face. Floyd reacted quickly, defending his wife's mistreatment in the face of the mob's fury, eliciting vulgarities from one man, who recognized Mathilda and the Floyds' daughter, Roselia. Floyd was ordered to dress and then was pushed out of the house and marched into the field. Mathilda attempted to follow but was thrust back inside. A few moments later she "heard the report of 5 guns & heard some of the men say shoot him in the head." Following that statement, Roselia remembered hearing "God damn him shoot his brains out." The coroner's report noted that Floyd's head was "shot through . . . with a load of buck shot . . . blowing out the entire brains."[12] Frightened and bereft, the women did not stay the night in their home but sought shelter in the woods.

While Thomas was marched to his death, a few of the vigilantes peeled off and headed down the road to Daniel Wynn's residence. Both Mathilda and Roselia heard the report of guns and Roselia recalled hearing someone yell "Hallo help help." Wynn's wife, Francis, recalled that white men approached their home and shot through the front door. Wynn returned fire and a member of the posse was wounded. Panicked, Wynn hid under the bed and then up to the top of the house, escaping out of the chimney. Once outside, the vigilantes fired "a good many shots," and although he was struck in the left arm, Wynn made his escape. However, he died of his wounds on August 30.[13]

A few days later, the final escalation preceding the Coushatta Massacre occurred in the center of town. Thomas Abney threw a party to mark the opening of his new Front Street store on Thursday, August 27, despite the fact that he was in Shreveport on business. Around dusk, a white teenager reported to the packed soiree that armed Blacks were marching to Brownsville. Thomas Paxton and other White League executives discussed the matter with Republican officials in attendance while Edgerton and Robert Dewees set off to Brownsville. The party and revelry continued and Edgerton and Dewees returned from a quiet Brownsville, now fully aware that the report had been a ploy. Marshall Twitchell later testified that this ruse had provided opportunity for "pre arranged couriers" riding to the surrounding parishes "with tales of murder and outrage" to gather vigilantes.

Edgerton and Dewees conferred with Homer Twitchell and sent word out to local freedmen to converge on Homer's home; they intended to fight if attacked by the White League. Abney's dance concluded around ten p.m. and coincided with Homer and his companions realizing they had boxed themselves in an untenable position. If they were attacked and overpowered, they would be slaughtered, but if they fought, their action would be branded a rebellion. Homer told the freedmen to head home quietly, but two mounted White Leaguers stumbled upon a pair of Black men in the dark. Instinctively, the whites fired a shot, rode back to town, reported to the rest of the group, and then returned. They confronted Twitchell in his yard and a concealed freedman, Paul Williams, rose up from the bushes and unloaded both his shotguns at the vigilantes.[14] The powder keg had been lit.

Early the next morning, vigilantes from a fifty-mile radius converged on Coushatta, and they continued arriving through Saturday. It is estimated that between several hundred and more than a thousand white supremacists descended on the small town, intent on rooting out Republicans. On Friday afternoon, White League leadership jumped into action, arresting Homer Twitchell, Henry Scott, and Clark Holland. Another posse arrested Frank Edgerton, Gilbert Cone, Robert Dewees, and William Howell and concurrently rounded up twenty prominent Black Republicans. All twenty-seven men spent the night in the basement of Abney's store. The white Republicans' wives gathered and spent the night at Starlight plantation, the Twitchell residence, and wrote worried letters to their spouses; the surviving responses are full of gallows optimism. There is no record of how the Black Republican wives passed the night.

Abney returned from Shreveport on Friday, and on Saturday a pretense of a trial was conducted on the store's main floor. Each man was hauled up from the basement and cross-examined as a bloodthirsty, restless mob prowled outside the store. The trial concluded in the late afternoon, and the White Leaguers presented the white Republicans with a resignation document to sign, demanding their relinquishment of office and departure from the state. A companion document was also drafted by the White League that depicted the Republican officials as bad men, guilty of "inculcating vicious ideas into the minds of the colored people of Red River."[15] Though it was officially announced the following day, the white Republicans' resignations were public knowledge in Coushatta within an hour, and the documents signed under duress formed the last official statements of Dewees, Edgerton, Holland, Howell, and Twitchell.

Saturday evening saw the white prisoners preparing for the relocation journey out of the state via Shreveport. They were staying on the second floor of the Coushatta Hotel, where Abney had relocated them to keep them safe from the restless mob. The white Republican prisoners were acutely aware that as long as they were in Coushatta, their lives were in danger. The mob needed satiating, which prompted the combined decision of the white prisoners to agree to leave Coushatta the next day instead of remaining at Abney's store. Henry Scott, who might have received special treatment from Abney owing to being a fellow master mason, had not been forced to sign the resignation document and was given safe passage out of the state as a nonprisoner.

Abney selected twenty-five men to escort the five prisoners out of Coushatta on August 30. In a last-minute addition, the mob forced Monroe Willis, Marshall Twitchell's brother-in-law, to rejoin the prisoner ranks. Thus, the six white Republicans proceeded out of town and made it thirty miles before forty to fifty dust-covered, inflamed men swooped in on the line of prisoners.[16] These vigilantes ordered the escorts away from the prisoners—a directive swiftly followed, giving the white Republicans no chance of escape. Dewees was killed in a hail of bullets as he tried to mount his horse; Homer Twitchell shouted for a gun to protect himself before a bullet shattered his face; Edgerton flung himself onto his horse and "made considerable distance before he was finally shot from his horse." Holland, Willis, and Howell surrendered. They were moved to a store nearby and the vigilantes spent several hours debating their fate. They ultimately formed a firing squad and executed Howell and Willis but amused themselves by offering Holland the chance to make a run for it. He refused. The six bodies were buried in two graves two miles apart. Marshall Twitchell, who learned of the massacre by telegram in New Orleans, later wrote that the bodies of the murdered men "were robbed even of their clothes, were mutilated in the most barbarous and inhumane manner," and the graves were unmarked and undisclosed for weeks, to hide all evidence.[17]

A Republican Black man not associated with the murdered officeholders or the captive Black officeholders was brutally killed on that same Sunday. Community leader Levi Allen lived south of Coushatta. During the election cycle two years earlier, a white man had attempted to trample Allen in the street, but Allen fought back. A few hours after the Coushatta Massacre, Allen was seized by vigilantes and brought to the woods, where his arms and legs were broken and he was tortured to death over an open fire.[18] Meanwhile, the Black parish officeholders were transported back to Coushatta jail and another vigilante trial began, lasting for three days. On Wednesday evening, Louis Johnson and Paul Williams were hanged. The other eighteen men were released.

Life became increasingly difficult for Republicans in the Red River region in the aftermath of the Coushatta Massacre, which further emboldened White League activity locally. The steady regularity of violence, motivated by Black political involvement and election participation, picked up further momentum and acceptance as the rest of the state put into action the methods used with such success at Colfax and Coushatta. The Coushatta Massacre coincided with the upsurge in campaigning for the 1874 election, where the Democratic Party garnered election results at the state level that would translate into a Democratic takeover in the 1876 presidential election. Democrats throughout Louisiana and the South used vigilantism, paramilitary action, and pervasive White League activity to make manifest a South that was "redeemed" from carpetbagger rule and Black political engagement and officeholding, and where Blacks were denied their civil rights. The Coushatta Massacre demonstrated that regional whites were unafraid to use violence as a powerful political determiner to force the abdication of Republican Party rule in Louisiana.

On September 14, mere weeks after the Coushatta Massacre, several thousand White Leaguers gathered at the foot of Canal Street in New Orleans. They had organized into twenty-six infantry companies with two improvised artillery batteries and had been drilling in the streets during the evenings. Intent on gaining military weaponry to defeat the Louisiana state militia and oust Republican leaders from office, the White League opted for a coup d'état. The fighting lasted only sixty minutes, but by the following morning the paramilitaries had stockpiled munitions, the Louisiana state militia had ceased to exist, and Governor Kellogg had lost "the moral authority" and obedience of his troops. Known as the Battle of Liberty Place, the clash brought white Louisianans a complete, though temporary, political unanimity.[19] Colfax had illuminated paramilitary violence as an efficacious method to capture and control local political power and destroy the Republican Party, while Coushatta had frightened white Republicans and emboldened the paramilitary action in New Orleans.

Marshall Twitchell attempted to bring the Coushatta perpetrators to trial, even after he endured a failed assassination attempt in 1876 and complications from the wounds he sustained led to the amputation of both arms. His close political partner, Edward Dewees, and a brother-in-law, George

King, were also assassinated; King was killed during the attempt on Twitch-ell's life. The Coushatta Massacre and Twitchell's assassination attempt were examined as part of a wider U.S. House of Representatives commit-tee investigation centered on corruption in the New Orleans customhouse. Over two days in the Coushatta courthouse, thirty-four witnesses were questioned, including six who previously had been arrested but not charged for participating in the massacre. While no one recognized Twitchell's as-sassin, who had donned very distinctive green-lensed goggles, they seized the opportunity to tarnish Twitchell's record and reputation as a parish of-ficeholder. When the interrogation finished, the committee concluded that Twitchell's assassination attempt was not politically motivated. They also declined to press charges on behalf of any of the Coushatta Massacre vic-tims, which ensured that the massacre was never prosecuted. The case, *U.S. v. Abney,* was never formally dismissed or brought to trial.[20]

— — —

When the Colfax perpetrators returned to Colfax from New Orleans amid fireworks and celebration, it signaled the ascension of white supremacy and the solidification of southern politics along a white-versus-Black axis. The *Cruikshank* ruling transferred jurisdiction over civil rights violations and political rights to state governments unless a racial motivation, not a politi-cal motive, was clearly presented and evidenced. In Louisiana, where white home rule was ascendant, this decision had serious repercussions. Paramil-itary political terrorism reigned practically unchecked and vigilantes could wage war against Black civil rights without risk of any legal repercussion. In the short term, the ruling bestowed blanket validation on racial incidents already committed and underscored the effectiveness of violence as a tool of political control. *Cruikshank* enumerated the broad parameters within which vigilante violence and paramilitary action were condoned and per-mitted, while it oversimplified the factors that fueled racial and political violence in northwest Louisiana. White supremacists took the blueprint for prosecution given in the ruling—a threshold that established that mo-tivation had to be race-based and not political—as carte blanche to wield racial violence as a sanctioned tool of white supremacy across the South. *Cruikshank* left African Americans without legal recourse and protection from white supremacist and vigilante violence.

The Colfax Massacre and the *Cruikshank* decision represented the high water mark of Red River white supremacy, empowering the region's whites to use race-based violence as an effective method to suppress Black political activity and engagement, stifle Republican reach, and reassert white political, economic, and social control. It dealt a devastating blow to African American enfranchisement and political participation and left the administrative power over core civil liberties to the discretion of the states, with no legal redress at the federal level. This local, state, and national acquittal affirmed home rule, and white vigilantes did not tarry.[21] Following the *Cruikshank* decision, paramilitaries and white landowners exerted still more pressure on Black participation in the Republican Party and limited, through terror and economic pressure, Black–white coalition building.

Although it would be twenty years before the Supreme Court sanctioned racial segregation in the case of Louisiana native Homer Plessy, the language and identity of race politics had crystalized. Throughout the Red River region and across Louisiana, Black access to the ballot box was further constricted as the Grant administration drastically disengaged from its campaign against vigilante violence. The administration pulled back from applying the Enforcement Acts, including the Ku Klux Klan Act, in any meaningful way in Louisiana, as well as in states like South Carolina, which had significant levels of vigilantism and Klan activity. At every level of government and for the vast majority of citizens, attention turned starkly away from racialized violence. Grant noted that "Republicans in Louisiana were always in trouble and always wanting the U.S. to send troops," while a general weariness pervaded federal interactions with state government issues.[22]

The question of establishment of African Americans as full-fledged members of American society through the protection and promotion of their political, social, ideological, economic, and emotional welfare receded almost entirely from public view. Black political participation continued in the cane parishes and parishes along the Mississippi River. However, African American polling and political participation eased perceptibly in places where white majorities secured and held political power, particularly after the end of the military occupation of Louisiana. In northwest Louisiana, the steady crescendo of violence offered an incredibly efficient, effective, and defining tool of political power that also extended the results of politically motivated violence far beyond the region. It had become the hymn sheet sung by paramilitaries and White Leagues throughout the South, and it delivered consistent results that reshaped politics, reasserted white control at every level of daily life, and pushed Blacks—and their dreams of widening the pathway out of slavery and embracing citizenship—to the periphery.[23] In the Red River region, white supremacy had won the battle and the war.

The Louisiana state government directly cited the *Cruikshank* ruling in 1879 when the Bourbon Democrats, reactionary conservatives (also known as Redeemers) who opposed political and social equality for nonwhites and desired stringent social controls to guarantee a subservient labor force, harnessed the changed political mood to heavily curtail Black enfranchisement. The ruling's statement that "the Constitution of the United States has not conferred the right of suffrage upon anyone" provided the fuel legislators needed to craft the 1879 Louisiana constitution and reverse the radical thrust of the 1868 version. The new state constitution set the political tenor of Louisiana for the next twenty years, as white Democrats restricted the rights and liberties of freedmen, relocated the capital to Baton Rouge, and authorized five state supreme court justices with twenty-year terms to exercise supervisory authority over the lower courts.[24]

The *Cruikshank* ruling played a critical role in legitimizing politically motivated intimidation of and violence against Blacks in Louisiana during the 1876 state and national elections. White Leagues dominated state politics, adeptly closed voting registration to freedmen, and intimidated the large numbers of freedpeople who were determined to vote. This intimidation practice was known as "bulldozing" and was particularly rampant during the 1876 election. Democrats attempted to recast their platform as focused on administrative and political reform; they claimed to welcome Black voters but instead actually forced Blacks to cast Democratic ballots. For the 1876 election, Democrats carefully ensured that all violence occurred before the election so that incidents would not jeopardize the validity of the poll results, because events would not be correlated directly with curbing Black access to the franchise based on race. Voter intimidation aimed at white and Black Republicans increased across Louisiana following the Colfax and Coushatta massacres. This was particularly acute in majority Black parishes and required intervention from the returning board to determine the outcome of votes statewide.

The 1876 election was one of the most closely monitored in Louisiana's history, and it was incredibly corrupt. The Department of Justice sent 840 federal marshals to New Orleans, setting up six at each polling station, and

2,800 temporary marshals served in country parishes. When the votes were counted, the Democrats easily carried northwestern parishes like DeSoto. The statewide vote leaned heavily toward Democrat Francis Nicholls and against Stephen Packard for Louisiana governor, and for Samuel Tilden over Rutherford Hayes for U.S. president. Once again, this fraught election begot a contested result, with both parties swearing in their candidate as Louisiana governor on January 8, 1877. When Tilden fell one vote short of a majority in the Electoral College, Louisiana's Republican-helmed returning board snapped into action. South Carolina and Florida had similar returns, and as in Louisiana, those returning boards invalidated and discarded votes for Tilden through fraud, intimidation, and violence.

The Louisiana returning board, helmed by Red River Republican James Madison Wells, discarded votes from white and Black voters not only in the cane parishes, which had a strong Republican showing, but also in numerous other parishes to ensure a Hayes win. While reallocating votes in the presidential contest, the board also fixed the returns in several local elections to place particular individuals, like Red River white Republican J. Ernest Breda, in office. In 1878, the House established the Potter Committee to investigate fraud in the 1876 election. Led by Democrats, the Potter Committee unearthed fraud, bribery, and corruption on the part of both parties in Louisiana. Republicans, desperate for state and federal positions, fixed their hopes on Hayes, who instead gave patronage roles to Democrats. Democrats had waged a bulldozing campaign in Black majority parishes, and telegrams showed that Tilden had tried to buy the election by bribing Republican officials.

The Compromise of 1877 elevated Rutherford Hayes to the presidency and definitively terminated the Reconstruction period in the South. In exchange for the Louisiana, South Carolina, and Florida electoral votes, Republican participants in the Hayes-Tilden compromise promised to recognize Democratic control of the southern state legislatures and to avoid intervening in local affairs. White Louisianans and their southern compatriots rejoiced and declared the South "redeemed." Republican rule was overthrown, the revolutionary politics of emancipation arrested, and white supremacy violently reasserted. The return of the Democratic regime would have a profound influence on the lives of Blacks for generations.[25]

Hayes's presidential ascendancy made former slaveholder and sugar planter Francis Nicholls, now the Democratic governor-elect, the Redeemer governor of Louisiana. Nicholls was sworn into office on April 24, 1877, as Louisiana was concurrently demilitarized. For Louisiana Blacks, and particularly those in northwest Louisiana, the formal end of Reconstruction and the withdrawal of troops meant that freedpeople "lost all hopes." As Henry Adams bitterly observed, "the very men that held us slaves" now governed Louisiana.[26]

While the Hayes-Tilden compromise brought Reconstruction to a formal close, the *Cruikshank* ruling that stemmed from the Colfax Massacre served as Reconstruction's curtain call in the Red River region. In the massacre's aftermath, racial tensions and unabated violence rendered it impossible for regional Blacks to experience any of freedom's privileges. To be seen as more than laboring bodies, to engage in and experience a measure of their freedom, and to escape violence, Blacks throughout the Red River region partook in a collective migration to Kansas, known as the Exoduster movement, from 1879 through the 1880s.

Henry Adams was the movement's backbone in northwest Louisiana. He formed a committee to gather information on freedpeople's treatment, which morphed into the Colonization Council after the Colfax Massacre. This council originally proposed that Blacks emigrate to Liberia, an idea that would gain traction and regional participation through the first decades of the twentieth century. The council focused efforts on a four-pronged plan to improve the conditions of Blacks, and after the Compromise of 1877, it also included an appeal to the president and Congress for a Black-only territory within the United States. Adams's leadership played a significant role in encouraging the Exoduster migration among Louisiana freedpeople.[27]

Adams organized the Colonization Council for the Shreveport area and the tristate region of Louisiana, Texas, and Arkansas in 1876. They petitioned President Grant for a territory "where they could live" and even evinced willingness to emigrate to Liberia. Adams and other politicized Blacks rode across several northern Louisiana parishes, reactivating local Republican clubs despite tremendous white opposition. They encountered Blacks demoralized by the persecution they faced and the lack of justice in Louisiana. Indeed, "in 1876, the rural people were more eager to leave the South than were Adams and his men." Traveling across northern Louisiana in 1877, Adams delivered public speeches advocating emigration. The Colonization Council's petition included the signatures of ninety-eight thousand men, women, and children eager to go to Liberia or another territory of the

United States. Most of these individuals lived in Louisiana; a September 1877 meeting in Shreveport produced a petition with three thousand names attached, though the delegates claimed to represent the wishes of twenty-nine thousand souls.[28] The formerly enslaved of the Red River region had been pushed to the breaking point, and thousands fled the region throughout the 1880s. More than five thousand African Americans ultimately left northern Louisiana for Kansas. Henry Adams, sadly, disappeared from the historical record in 1884 after violent threats to his life caused him to flee Shreveport for New Orleans in 1878. It is unknown whether he emigrated to Liberia with the waves of Blacks who settled there throughout the later 1880s as part of the colonization movement.[29]

— — —

In the decades after Colfax, numerous newspaper articles detailed and chronicled the day. A substantial number were written in the 1920s, when interest was galvanized by monument installation. A 1921 article by the editor of the *Colfax Chronicle* refuted misstatements from an 1882 article by the *New Orleans Mascot,* opining that the earlier article had done "such an injustice to a majority of the whites" that the *Chronicle* published the article side by side with the corrections. The article focused on refuting "the manner in which the negroes were killed." Unsurprisingly, the *Chronicle*'s editor placed the aggression firmly with the freedpeople. They had assembled in Colfax on April 1 "to the number of two hundred or more" and were "nearly all armed and exhibited their weapons with such freedom and made such open threats of violence" around the possibility of white Democrats holding a meeting to discuss parish government that "it was deemed best not to assemble." As more and more freedpeople gathered in Colfax, there were "terrible threats" from freedpeople, who were behaving in such an "insolent and violent manner that the whites became terrorized and fled from their homes under the cover of night." With white homes vacated, the *Chronicle* claimed, freedpeople "broke them open and took possession rifling the stores and residences of everything in them" and the article cataloged the litany of freedpeople's crimes before the Massacre to include "robbery, rape, and murder." Whites of Grant Parish were "terror stricken" and spread the alarm into adjoining parishes, where the "call of the citizens" was answered by sending "about two hundred men to their assistance." Particular atten-

tion was given to fleshing out the "most dastardly acts of treachery ever perpetrated by fiends in human shape": the narrative about freedpeople in the
courthouse raising a white flag and then shooting whites once they reached
the courthouse door.[30]

A history of Grant Parish published in 1969 describes this incident similarly. It focuses on descriptions of freedpeople as a "mob of armed negroes"
who "forced out the white office holders and installed new ones" as they "in-
sultingly refused" the daily proposals from white leaders for peace.[31] Kate
Grant's unpublished novel *From Blue to Gray* incorporated all of these touch
points too, and lavishly detailed how the region's whites were terrorized,
vandalized, and lived in fear of freedpeople incited to violence and egged on
by "political hornets" from the North.[32]

Milton Dunn was heavily involved in conversations and remembrance
activities throughout the 1920s. His responses to articles on facts of the
massacre, and to letters to him from people organizing or inquiring about
Colfax, are scattered throughout the clippings about the massacre kept by
Natchitoches resident and owner of Melrose plantation, Cammie Henry. In
1920, Dunn received a letter from the Grant Parish Police Jury requesting
more information "concerning Sidney Harris—where he came from, who
his people were, the manner in which he was killed"—because they had allocated funds to mark his grave and Dunn was the acknowledged local authority.[33] A few months later, Dunn received a note from a former Colfax resident, Rita Leochard Breath, who had relocated with her family from Colfax
to Bay Saint Louis, Mississippi, and had a small cannon that held great significance to Colfax whites. The cannon had built up its own mystique and
lore in the aftermath of the massacre, although it doesn't play a significant
role in any accounts given immediately after the events. In a previous note,
Dunn had requested the cannon's return on behalf of the Colfax veterans, for
commemorative events in 1921. Breath had written back promptly but was
disheartened to report that she could not immediately return the cannon
as it was in transit to her new farmstead. She noted that her two daughters
were "very much attached to this relic—but I will talk the matter over with
them and see if they will not consent to give it to the son of their dear father's friend." After stating that she would send the cannon to Colfax, Breath
openly professed her convictions, pride, and gratitude for the paramilitary
actions of the Colfax Massacre. She wrote, "There is no southern woman
who appreciates more than I do what our gallant boys done to save us in reconstruction days—my dear old uncle, now passed away, Col. Chas Shoulder

of Keachie LA, kept us entranced many times with his tales of the conflict and instilled in my heart an undying love and affection for the brave men in grey of whom so pitifully few are left."[34]

It is magnificently ironic that three prisoners at Louisiana State Penitentiary (Angola) undertook the first in-depth, non-white-biased investigative research into the Colfax Massacre and the political events that catalyzed the violence. Their article, "Tragedy at Colfax," appeared in the November/December 1989 issue of *the prison's magazine, the Angolite*. It is a fascinating article that digs into the political climate, scours the press coverage of the massacre, and interviews African Americans from Colfax. It begins by citing the fact that the Colfax paramilitary actions were used as validation for a 1910 local court case.

Mary Jane Jones, an African American woman who lived in Colfax, was convicted of arson for burning down a cabin. In closing arguments given in the new Colfax courthouse, which had been built on the footprint of the former edifice, the prosecutor evoked the massacre as the reason that "every drop of my white man's blood did boil in me, and the white man's blood of other white men in the courthouse in the parish of Grant," when Jones's white lawyer had accused the prosecutor of losing his self-control. The defense likely raised questions about the police handling of the investigation, because the prosecutor lost control over the "slanderous . . . language against the officers of Grant Parish and against white men."

Jones was convicted and given a five-year sentence at Angola but won on appeal in *State v. Jones*. In vacating her sentence, the Louisiana Supreme Court cited the massacre and the continued social and racial tensions. They did not want this ruling to ignite another racially motived massacre. However, the associate justice saluted the triumph and effectiveness of white supremacist violence, writing, "These white jurymen are at the same time called upon to bear in mind that in 1873 [37 years previous] nothing but the quickness of action of the white men of the country around Colfax saved the white people of Colfax from massacre by the negroes."[35] In this telling, white supremacy and vigilante violence had secured Colfax from the perceived threat of freedpeople during Reconstruction, and continued white domination did not require the court system or enacted laws to continue to preserve and perpetuate regional white power and safety.

Veterans groups made concerted local efforts from 1910 to the 1920s to collect material and organize gatherings to honor the "Colfax veterans." On April 13, 1914, at a meeting held at the courthouse, the "survivors of the men

who participated in the Colfax Riot" held a reunion that enjoyed community participation. At the event, a motion was passed to form a "permanent
organization of the Colfax Veterans," with Milton Dunn elected secretary.[36]
To mark the massacre's fiftieth anniversary, the *Shreveport Times* ran a
piece entitled "Grant Parish Thrills with History of Strong Men in Fight for
Right." It is a familiar rehashing of the unfolding of events but is notable
for emphasizing that the violence at Colfax was part of a sustained plan to
"put a sudden and complete finish" to racial equality, voting rights, and access to the franchise. The article focused on the far-reaching impact and
implications of the two court cases that stemmed from the massacre. The
Colfax community was lauded for supplying assistance, aid, and legal counsel for the white paramilitaries transported to New Orleans as prisoners.
The decision by the U.S. Supreme Court, on appeal, to free the prisoners and
clear their names "gave freedoms to all the white people in the south. It extracted the teeth and the fangs of the monster, Reconstruction" and made
the massacre "the most important event in the history of this country after
Appomattox."[37]

On April 13, 1921—the forty-eighth anniversary of the massacre—the
white townspeople of Colfax unveiled a monument erected in the Colfax
Cemetery in memory of "the heroes" James Hadnot, Stephen Parish, and
Sidney Harris, and "to the memory of the white victims of the memorable
riot of 1873." The three men were honored for spilling "their life's blood in a
battle in Colfax in order that white supremacy might reign supreme."[38] The
monument still commands pride of place in the whites-only Colfax Cemetery. There are no racially integrated burial grounds in Grant Parish.[39]

More than forty veterans attended the event. The commemoration committee, which wanted all surviving participants to attend, organized special
hotel accommodation and a banquet for the veterans. Mary Hadnot—James
Hadnot's daughter—and Sidney Harris's wife, who had interred her husband's ashes under the monument, conducted the ceremony. The commemoration ceremony included the monument's unveiling, addresses from the
two women and local dignitaries, and a procession to the pecan tree in front
of the Cameron House, locally dubbed the "Riot Tree." A dedication service
marked the tree as a "monument commemorative of the battle of '73."[40]

Cammie Henry remained firmly on the side of the paramilitary, and her
personal scrapbooks contain revealing commentary. She annotated a Colfax Riot tree photo with the following horrified statement: "And to think the

Mayor of Colfax allowed this sacred tree to be cut for firewood for darkies! What a crime." Her marginalia alongside the April 1921 *Colfax Chronicle* article reads, "Colfax Riot indeed! Why not Colfax Martyrs?"[41] Clearly, the effects of the action taken by Nash and his paramilitary forces went far beyond the recalibration and rewriting of laws on the local, state, and national levels. Vigilante violence not only wrenched from the Red River region's Blacks access to the polls, an electoral voice, and presence in the body politic, and severely hemmed in the contours of freedom more generally, but also inculcated in the regional white consciousness a hero worship and reverence for the paramilitary activities.

In the lead-up to the Colfax monument's unveiling, various articles appeared glorifying the actions of Easter Sunday 1873. People were urged to attend the ceremony to remember "the heroes who fought these battles" during the "dark days . . . that hung over our beloved Louisiana like a death pall." Attendance at the monument unveiling would acknowledge that the "blood of our heroes becomes sacred" and encourage the community to "emulate your heroes. A land without memories and traditions of patriots is a land without Liberty."[42]

The Colfax Massacre—alongside the continual episodes of political, economic, and socially fueled violence—was consistently remembered, memorialized, and enshrined as a powerful episode of white reassertion and reclamation that realigned and corrected the evils of Reconstruction. Colfax served as an enduring reminder of the power of white supremacy and the ability of white power to define the course of political, economic, and social events. It demonstrated viscerally and visibly that violent white supremacy could constrain and diminish the freedom of regional African Americans in multiple ways. Southerners adeptly used historical legacies and ideology—including racial slavery and postwar atrocities such as Colfax—to reinforce rhetoric and institutionalize frameworks of white monopolized political, economic, and military power.[43] Those key messages are reflected in how northwest Louisiana still remembers the Colfax Massacre.

In contrast, the dearth of memorials or commemorational activity for the Coushatta Massacre, along with its lesser prominence in historical discourse, might stem from the victims being both white northern transplants and Black Republicans. The absence of prosecution for the murders could factor into the overlooking of Coushatta's significance in examinations of politically motivated violence.[44] In Colfax, the massacre is known, referred to, and remembered by regional whites to this day as a riot. The region continues to project an unapologetic stance concerning all racially motivated Reconstruction violence, and indeed, remains proud of the legacy of enslavement and unshakeable Confederate loyalty. These elements of the regional white identity are not challenged within a localized context but are accepted as unabashed features of local ideology and history that require neither apology nor investigation.

EPILOGUE

When one enters present-day Colfax from the riverside, the large court-house is around the curve on Main Street and set back from the river. Until May 15, 2021, a state historical marker sat in the courthouse's foreground, positioned outward but in the midpoint of the road, unmissable upon entering or exiting the tiny town. The sign read, "Colfax Riot. On this site occurred the Colfax Riot, in which three white men and 150 negroes were slain. This event on April 13, 1873 marked the end of carpetbag misrule in the South."[1] Those two short sentences succinctly defined the regional and state perception. In this definition, the massacre was an event that was necessary to bring about the end of northern, Republican directorship of southern politics, and it provided a toehold for regional whites to wrest back control and influence. Semantics matter, and the usage, evocation, and insistence that this was a riot actively places the onus for the massacre onto African Americans.

Across the street from the courthouse and the library—the actual ground on which the violence unfolded as paramilitary forces approached from the riverbank—is the Colfax Baptist Church. In the church graveyard stands a memorial obelisk to the three whites killed during the Colfax Massacre. It towers above all the other gravestones, dominating the area and demanding attention. Written across the face proudly directed at the river reads the inscription: "Erected to the memory of the heroes, Stephen Decatur Parish, James West Hadnot, Sidney Harris, who fell in the Colfax Riot fighting for white supremacy. April 13, 1873." Etched in marble to commemorate these vigilantes is the undeniable purpose of the massacre: to protect, promote, and ensure white supremacy. Here is the irrefutable and baldly proclaimed reason for the massacre and the affirmation of the end result.

Then, as now, the region does not shroud its white identity, firmly grounded in racial supremacy, from view, preferring instead to display this unreconstructed ideology. The commemorative tableaux of the region cen-

ter racial violence as a unifying force deployed by regional white supremacists and vigilantes that advanced white interests and protected political
control. The region's purposefully exclusionary commemorative culture—
with no room for Black memorialization or commemoration in public
spaces—draws on the long history of the Lost Cause narrative, which presents white racial privilege as the inescapable outcome of history.[2]

No one became more esteemed in the community following the massacre and subsequent court cases than Christopher Columbus Nash. He
served as sheriff before being appointed in 1877 as Grant Parish tax collector
by Governor Nicholls. Nash's political future brightened alongside his economic prospects after his marriage to the daughter of a prominent Natchitoches planter and establishment of a commercial firm. In June 1888, Nash
was chosen as president of the Grant Parish Police Jury and elected mayor
of Colfax. As sheriff in 1873, the ex-Confederate soldier with a "splendid war
record seeing long and hard service" led whites in the Colfax Massacre and
was lauded by regional whites for his measured treatment and dealings with
freedpeople. Milton Dunn, a young Colfax Massacre participant who dedicated his life to memorializing and writing about the heroism of the raised
"force of white men" when the "war of Reconstruction in Grant Parish took
place," frequently remembered and eulogized Nash. Dunn wrote that Nash
commanded "his posse" during the "three and a half hours of fighting," when
"185 white men defeated 800 negroes, killing 168 of them." Like local novel-
ist and ardent supporter of paramilitary violence Kate Grant, Dunn wrote
about Nash in glowing, heroic terms and stressed how after the massacre—
described as a "gallant act"—there was a "restoration of peace" in the parish,
and Nash continued to lead "a quiet and peaceful life."[3]

How northwest Louisiana remembered and commemorated the Civil
War, Confederate loyalty, and Reconstruction era vigilante violence has an
immense bearing on a continuing discussion about memorialization. Devoid of the canonical backstory that places events within their historical
framework and context, current discussions of Civil War memory and Reconstruction memorialization are often approached in medias res. Placing
events, ideologies, political progressions, and racial injustices within the
necessary dynamic historical context vividly demonstrates that history—
and our modern ideology and political climate—does not occur in a vacuum,
and it presents us collectively and individually with accurate and effective
tools to deconstruct and focus the national narrative. The language that has

enveloped current discussions reverts to the pre–Civil War dichotomy of North versus South, with rigid, preordained racial binaries and inflamed rhetoric. An open and frank discussion, led by academics, public historians, and community leaders, is desperately required to move our national discourse into a place of understanding, acknowledgment of the legacies of slavery and racial hierarchies, and forward progress. This book supports that process by showing the palpable connections between nineteenth-century northwest Louisiana and the present day.

White terrorism and vigilantism crafted a Civil War memory and peppered the physical landscape with Confederate monuments that entwine race, citizenship, political involvement, and equality before the law. The brazen erection of monuments like the Colfax Massacre obelisk defined the Red River landscape as one where violence, and the wielding of it, remained central to defining both regional and southern memory making. These monuments controlled the landscape and the method of remembering on a local and national scale and contributed to an enduring refashioning of historical events.

Just as Reconstruction era tropes defined Lost Cause rhetoric and actions as necessary to protect white womanhood and to manage Black political and social access, present-day white Americans use the Lost Cause narrative and symbolism as a uniting code against perceived outsiders.[4] The exclusionary public culture of memorialization that became de rigueur in the South was particularly proscriptive in the Red River region. Here, Black Americans did not establish public memorials, partake in parades or picnics to mark significant days, or enjoy any of the Progressive Era pushes for public commemoration. Whites had the latitude and authority to determine how the past was remembered and passed down, from the monuments to the school curriculums to the inculcation of racial privilege as inevitable and proper.[5] This has played a significant role in the dispensing of justice and the opportunities for equitable judicial recourse. There is a notably high sentencing and incarceration rate for Blacks in the Red River region, with particularly disjointed sentencing practices routinely used. Caddo Parish has made headlines for the enforcement of manipulative practices against Blacks as well as for overt racism demonstrated by senior district attorneys and judges.[6]

As Blacks left the Red River region, and as those who remained were shoved to the margins of society, the individuals who partook in the Colfax

Massacre and other vigilante violence continued to hold positions of power and visibility. Nash was not the massacre's only beneficiary. Governor Nicholls appointed John Hadnot—son of James Hadnot, one of the white casualties of the massacre—to the police jury, and Albert Leonard, the former editor of the *Shreveport Times,* was made Louisiana's attorney general. Most of the vigilante participants in Colfax and the countless other violent acts of white supremacy throughout Reconstruction were considered upstanding members of society. As such, they not only embodied and perpetuated the regional white identity but also propagated Lost Cause memorialization and usage of white violence to confine the parameters of freedpeople's freedom. Colfax remained at the forefront of the memories of townspeople and whites across the region and reminded them of the shackles they had thrown off.[7] It became the undeniable and unshakeable proof that violence was effective, definitive, and unquestioned as a tool of political and racial power, which also constructed a limited postemancipation identity for African Americans.

That steadfast commitment to systemic white supremacy and the deployment of vigilantism and paramilitary activity to control the boundaries and actualization of African American freedom follows a sustained arc of continued mastery and a race-based regional power structure and identity. This unwavering reliance on violence to redefine the contours of African American citizenship, political access, and economic and social freedom re-dressed slaveholding mastery as violent white supremacy. This regional celebration of vigilante violence, including unswerving memorialization of the Colfax Massacre as the triumphant pinnacle of white supremacy, essential to reclaiming white political control, has continued to inform race relations, social and economic conditions for the region's Blacks, political allegiance and attitudes, and voting patterns. The centrality of violence to regional white identity and racial dynamics from the antebellum period through to Reconstruction has ensured that the Red River region remains unreconstructed.

NOTES

INTRODUCTION

1. United States War Department, *Use of the Army,* 409.

2. Vandal, "Bloody Caddo," 374, 376.

3. Fields, "Ideology and Race in American History."

4. Seminal works on whiteness studies discuss particularly how ethnic groups became accepted as white in America and how the social construct of "white" has changed drastically over time. See Roediger, *Working Toward Whiteness*; Painter, *History of White People;* Morrison "Playing in the Dark." See also Kendi, *Stamped from the Beginning.*

5. See Roediger, *Working Toward Whiteness;* Hale, *Making Whiteness;* Painter, *History of White People;* Kendi, *Stamped from the Beginning.*

6. Fields, "Ideology and Race in American History," 144, 152–155; Jones-Rogers, *They Were Her Property,* 1–5, 15–17; Holt, "Marking."

7. For regulatory use of violence in central Texas, see Carrigan, *Making of a Lynching Culture,* 2–3, 10, 13, 30.

8. Critical race theory's concept of intersectionality has bearing here, especially since these constructed social parameters disadvantaged all African Americans and relegated white women to a figurehead position, which was leveraged when protecting the virtue of collective white womanhood and southern honor but without giving women any voice or expression of citizenship separate from that of their male kin. Critical race theory has been used as a lens across a variety of disciplines, such as sociology and political economy, to examine the legacy of slavery, including racial inequality in healthcare. See Acharya et al., "Political Legacy of American Slavery," *Deep Roots;* Reece, "Whitewashing Slavery," "Color Crit."

9. The literature on violence and white supremacist ideology in the South is voluminous. Some key texts include Tolnay and Beck, *Festival of Violence;* Carrigan, *Making of a Lynching Culture;* Pfeifer, *Rough Justice;* Waldrep, *Roots of Disorder;* Brundage, *Lynching in the South* and *Southern Past;* Zuczek, *State of Rebellion;* Baker, *This Mob Will Surely Take My Life;* Fitzgerald, *Reconstruction in Alabama* and *Splendid Failure* and "Extralegal Violence and the Planter Class"; Emberton, *Beyond Redemption;* Feimster, *Southern Horrors;* Parsons, *Ku-Klux;* Ward, *Hanging Bridge;* Glymph, *Out of the House of Bondage;* Rosen, *Terror in the Heart of Freedom;* Trelease, *White Terror;* Rable, *But There Was No Peace;* Vandal, *Rethinking Southern Violence;* Chalmers, *Hooded Americanism.*

10. "Testimony of Henry Adams Regarding the Negro Exodus," in Aptheker, *Documentary History,* 715.

11. This book builds on the work of O'Donovan, *Becoming Free in the Cotton South;* Glymph,

Out of the House of Bondage; Roark, *Masters Without Slaves;* and Kaye, "Second Slavery." Kaye's comprehensive synthesis advocates a reexamination of antebellum southern history to draw out that slaveholders were at the vanguard of American international development and slavery was essential to market growth.

12. The literature on nineteenth-century politically motivated violence and its impact on southern and national racial relations is fruitful and deeply provocative with regard to continued legacies. This work is in dialogue with Parsons, *Ku-Klux;* Fitzgerald, *Reconstruction in Alabama;* Williams, *They Left Great Marks on Me;* Behrend, *Reconstructing Democracy;* Nystrom, *New Orleans After the Civil War.*

13. The most recent additions to the literature deal with the exploitative and capitalistic aspects of slavery and the world of cotton. They include Johnson, *River of Dark Dreams;* Baptist, *The Half Has Never Been Told;* Beckert, *Empire of Cotton;* Rothman, *Flush Times.* For discussion of the similarities between plantation and the carceral state, see chapter 8 in Johnson, *River of Dark Dreams;* Baptist, *The Half Has Never Been Told.* See also Young, "Ideology and Death"; Genovese, *Roll, Jordan, Roll;* Genovese and Fox-Genovese, *Fatal Self-Deception.*

14. This definition is similar to that given in Clegg, "Capitalism and Slavery," 282, 285.

15. Two instructive articles that parse the differences and similarities in the new capitalism scholarship, and situate those arguments within the existing historiography, are Clegg, "Capitalism and Slavery" and Nelson, "Who Put Their Capitalism in My Slavery?." Both assist in seeing where this work aligns with recent scholarship and where it diverges.

16. Nelson, "Who Put Their Capitalism in My Slavery?," 295.

17. My thinking on this is informed by Robert Brenner's conception of capitalism, as elegantly summarized in Clegg, "Capitalism and Slavery," 284–285.

18. On paternalism, see Genovese, *The World the Slaveholders Made,* chapters 1–2, and *Roll, Jordan, Roll;* Fox-Genovese, *Within the Plantation Household,* 53, 55. For a detailed discussion of interpretations of slavery, capitalism, Marxist analysis, and the definition problem, see Huston, "Slavery, Capitalism."

19. Kaye, "Second Slavery," 633.

20. Beckert, *Empire of Cotton,* 205; Rothman, *Flush Times,* 6; Gray, *History of Agriculture,* 691. A bale of cotton weighs five hundred pounds.

21. Beckert, "Cotton and the U.S. South," 40–41, *Empire of Cotton,* 206. The 1860 value is $5.7 billion in 2015 terms, using the Consumer Price Index. See "Seven Ways to Compute the Relative Value of a U.S. Dollar Amount—1790 to Present," *Measuring Worth,* https://www.measuringworth.com/uscompare.

22. There is a fantastic body of scholarship that explores the intersections, layers, and complexities of Native and Black history—most especially when triangulated with the political, economic, military, and societal demands and domination of whites—throughout American history. One of these works is Miles, *Ties That Bind,* which reinscribes the Native story into the narrative about both southern history and the history of the Civil War and Reconstruction, rendering it a more inclusive and far-reaching story. See also Roberts, "A Different Forty Acres"; *I've Been Here All the While.*

23. For a nuanced overview of the complexities and factions within the abolitionist and antislavery movements and how they changed throughout the colonial and antebellum periods, see Kendi, *Stamped from the Beginning.*

24. Hartman, *Scenes of Subjection*. For an erudite explanation of the drawbacks and omitted nuances of the Works Progress Administration interviews, see the introduction to Glymph, *Out of the House of Bondage,* footnotes 38–39. On the importance of who is writing the story, who determines what gets omitted from the historical narrative, and what Black survivors felt comfortable telling, see Jones-Rodgers, *They Were Her Property;* Berry, *Price for Their Pound of Flesh;* Glymph, *Out of the House of Bondage;* Rosen, *Terror in the Heart of Freedom;* Williams, *They Left Great Marks on Me;* Hunter, *Bound in Wedlock;* Miles, *Ties That Bind;* Xendi, *Stamped from the Beginning.*

25. LSU Libraries' Louisiana and Lower Mississippi Valley Collection, in Baton Rouge, contains the ledgers of only two regional plantations—Pre Aux Cleres and Willow Point. The ledgers span a few years but are not continuous. George Marshall's daybook provides limited additional information.

26. Jones-Rodgers, *They Were Her Property,* 22, 27–29, 31, 47, 64, 79, 86. See also Censer, *North Carolina Planters,* 137.

27. Gutman, *The Black Family in Slavery and Freedom,* 185; Berry, *Price for Their Pound of Flesh,* 47,

28. Malone, *Sweet Chariot,* 231.

29. Berry, *Price for Their Pound of Flesh,* 6–7, 61–62, 206–207.

30. Stowe, *Intimacy and Power,* 253.

31. Trouillot, *Silencing the Past,* 48–52.

32. Johnson, "On Agency," 114. Johnson's article asks historians to think about what they mean and what they miss when they ask the now standard questions associated with the agency as a "master trope of the new social history" (113). He critiques the notion that agency needs to be granted retroactively—a critique with which I agree—and cautions us to remember the constraints of the times that impact the actions of historical actors. He calls out the manner in which historians ask whether African Americans are agents of their own destiny, arguing that this replicates the framework and analytical limits, steeped in white supremacist assumptions, that made these questions possible—and that makes it necessary to ask these questions in the first place.

33. Other books that investigate the role of nature in shaping regional settlement include Klingle, *Emerald City;* O'Donovan, *Becoming Free in the Cotton South;* Morris, *The Big Muddy.*

34. For an illuminating discussion of the postwar occupation of the South, see Downs, *After Appomattox.*

35. For an insightful comparison between violence in northwest Louisiana and in South Africa, see Higginson, "Making Sense of 'Senseless Violence.'"

36. Acharya et al., *Deep Roots,* "Political Legacy of American Slavery." On the prevalence and long legacy behind voter restrictions in Louisiana, see Keele et al., "Suppressing Black Votes." See also Ward, *Hanging Bridge.*

1. "THE RED RIVER BOTTOMS ARE NEARLY THE BEST COTTON LANDS IN THE WORLD"

1. D. B. Allen to "Dear Mother," November 13, 1851, D. B. Allen Letter, Mss. 3572, Louisiana and Lower Mississippi Valley Collection, LSU Libraries, Baton Rouge (hereafter LLMVC).

2. "Red River Raft," *De Bow's Review* 19, no. 4 (October 1855): 437, http://name.umdl.umich .edu/acg1336.1-19.004. See also Johnson, *River of Dark Dreams,* 90.

3. Humphries, "Photographic Views of Red River Raft, 1873," 102.

4. "Navigation of Red River," *Caddo Free Press,* March 28, 1839; "Red River Raft."

5. Henry Shreve to "Dear Sir," July 1, 1835, July 6, 1836, J. Fair Hardin Collection, Mss. 1014, LLMVC.

6. Gudmestad, *Steamboats,* 143.

7. "The Splendid Steamer," "Belle of Red River," *Caddo Gazette,* February 11, 1846. Steamboat schedules ran in the *Caddo Gazette* through 1855.

8. "Steamboat Rodolph," *Caddo Gazette,* February 11, 1846. See also *Shreveport Journal, Caddo Gazette, DeSoto Intelligence,* and *South West Shreveport.*

9. Gudmestad, *Steamboats,* 150.

10. Watson, "Slavery and Development," 49.

11. Chaplin, *An Anxious Pursuit,* 278.

12. Schoen, "Burdens and Opportunities," 69; Rockman, "Future of Civil War Era Studies."

13. Ransom and Sutch, "Capitalists Without Capital," 133, 135, 138. A good investigation into some limitations of the established capitalism and slavery arguments can be found in Tomich, *Through the Prism of Slavery,* which examines the nuance and specificity of local slave societies connected to global processes, and how asymmetries inform the capitalist world economy.

14. Kaye, "Second Slavery," 633.

15. *History of the Flournoy Family,* compiled by Meredith Flournoy Ingersoll, Alfred Flournoy Papers, Mss. 628, LLMVC; Jane Fullilove Mason, *Dear Lizzie: Letters of a Confederate Cavalryman,* Fullilove family binders, vol. 1, LSU Shreveport Archives and Special Collections, Noel Memorial Library (hereafter LSUS). On chain migrations of plain folk settlers— nonslaveholding farmers with land, and farmers with up to one hundred acres of land and a few slaves, but with significant familial ties to the planter elite—see Sherrod, *Plain Folk.*

16. Baptist, "Toxic Debt," 4–6. The Bank of the United States was the single biggest national lender.

17. Wright, *Slavery and American Economic Development,* 61; Kaye, "Second Slavery," 631– 632; Baptist, "Toxic Debt," 6. On the considerable role women slaveholders played in the narrative of slavery, as invested members of the slaveholding class and as property owners, see Jones-Rogers, *They Were Her Property.* For an erudite look at the ways in which enslaved people coped with and responded to their monetary value throughout their lives, see Berry, *Price for Their Pound of Flesh.*

18. Miller, *South by Southwest,* 5, 8.

19. Rothman, *Slave Country,* 46. On the continued significance of cotton prices in the Gilded Age, see Baker and Hahn, *Cotton Kings.*

20. Baptist, *Creating an Old South;* Burke, *On Slavery's Border;* Kelley, *Los Brazos de Dios.* For additional investigation on kinship networks and migration, see Billingsley, *Communities of Kinship.*

21. Cashin, *A Family Venture,* 29, 79. Billingsley disagrees with Cashin regarding the splintering of families and the isolated nature of females in the new Southwest. Letters from white slaveholding women in this region indicate a blended experience, with isolation and yearning

for extended family prevalent in the earlier antebellum period but easing in the 1850s and 1860s, either as more family members relocated or as children set up plantation households in the vicinity.

22. Burke, *On Slavery's Border,* 45. See also Berry, *Price for Their Pound of Flesh;* Jennison, *Cultivating Race.*

23. "In Memoriam, Mrs. T. H. Fullilove," Samford C. Fullilove Papers, collection 256, LSUS. Census information compiled from www.ancestry.com.

24. Di Maio, *Gërstacker's Louisiana,* 28; Gudmestad, "Steamboats and the Removal of the Red River Raft," 396.

25. Hodgson, "Forest Park," 31-3.

26. Samuel Whitworth to Isabella Whitworth, March 9, 1855, Samford C. Fullilove Papers, collection 256, LSUS.

27. Samuel Whitworth to Isabella Whitworth, January 15, 1858.

28. Gudmestad, *Steamboats,* 127.

29. Gould, *Fifty Years on the Mississippi,* 210; Gudmestad, *Steamboats,* 130

30. Gudmestad, "Steamboats and the Removal of the Red River Raft," 391.

31. Henry Marshall to Maria Marshall, November 7, November 28, 1836, Marshall–Furman Family Papers, Mss. 2740, 4042, LLMVC.

32. Martel, "Early Days in Northwest Louisiana," 120–121.

33. Belich, *Replenishing the Earth,* 114. See also Paskoff, *Troubled Waters.*

34. Bartholomew Egan to James Egan, January 5, 1850, Egan Family Collection, Mss. 1-G-3, Cammie G. Henry Research Center, Watson Memorial Library, Northwestern State University of Louisiana, Natchitoches (hereafter CGHRC).

35. James Burns Wallace diary, Mss. 3476, LLMVC.

36. Olmsted, *Journey Through Texas,* 43.

37. Moffatt, "Transportation in Arkansas, 1819–1840," 188–189; McNeilly, *Old South Frontier,* 20.

38. Wells, *Civil War, Reconstruction, and Redemption,* 9.

39. Gould, *Fifty Years on the Mississippi,* 235. Steamboats entered the Red River beginning in 1815 but were sporadic until 1824–1825.

40. James S. Laroe diary, Mss. 253, LLMVC. The seven dollar rate is equivalent to $285 in 2024 and five dollars is equivalent to $204.

41. Memoirs of Ellison Moultrie Adger, Mrs. Mary Moultrie Adger family and plantation records, collection 93, LSUS.

42. Rothman, *Flush Times,* 2, 6, 13.

43. Miller, *South by Southwest,* 92, 97; Wright, *Political Economy of the Cotton South,* 16–17, 22.

44. The interrelations between small, midsize, and large slaveholders in this region thus share some similarities with the South Carolina Lowcountry, as demonstrated by Stephanie McCurry. However, since there are scant archival records around Red River yeomen farmers— defined by McCurry as any self-working farmer, a definition I utilize—this is not a like-for-like comparison. Instead, there are strong commonalities because small and midsize planters comported and proved themselves as masters, and their embrace of mastery was recognized and strengthened by large-scale planters. In the Red River region, the master class comprised plant-

ers with myriad holding sizes and estate valuations, with a shared vision of white identity and power. On yeoman farmers in South Carolina, see McCurry, *Masters of Small Worlds.*

45. Oakes, *Ruling Race,* 52.

46. "Eastern Texas—Soda Lake, Port Caddo, Tuscumbia," *Caddo Free Press,* March 28, 1839.

47. Henry Marshall to Maria Marshall, October 18,1833, Josephine C. Means Papers, collection 335A, LSUS.

48. Henry Marshall to Maria Marshall, November 1, 1863, Josephine C. Means Papers, collection 335A, LSUS; Henry Marshall property inventory, July 22, 1864, Josephine C. Means Papers, collection 335, LSUS. In 2023 terms, these figures are approximately $3.4 million, $740,000, $1.09 million, and $744,000.

49. William Hutchinson land grant 1829, William Joseph Hutchinson family and plantation records, collection 75, LSUS.

50. McClellan, *William Joseph Hutchinson and Family of Caspiana Plantation,* 13, 21, 24, 183.

51. Ibid. On the important role of guardian see Billingsley, *Communities of Kinship,* 43.

52. Smallwood, *Saltwater Slavery.* This sensitive and introspective investigation into the process of commodification describes saltwater slavery as the absolute exclusion from any social community for individuals captured and sold into the slave trade. This fracture rendered their social death complete and irreversible. As such, Smallwood challenges the use of "Middle Passage" as a phrase and framework to define this traumatic transitory stage because it fails to capture the lived experiences of enslaved Africans. Berry, *Price for Their Pound of Flesh,* exquisitely reconstitutes the humanity of enslaved people and shows their independent spiritual value. The book introduces the concept of soul value, or "the recognition of the self-actualized values of their souls" (6).

53. For discussion of the rupture rendered by removal and the layered dislocation felt by Cherokees, Afro-Cherokees, and Blacks during the late 1830s–1840s, see Miles, *Ties That Bind,* chapters 8 and 9.

54. Johnson, *Soul by Soul,* 25.

55. Berry, *Price for Their Pound of Flesh,* 8, 11–15, 19, 41, 60.

56. Jones-Rodgers, *They Were Her Property,* xi, xiii, 2–3. Indeed, as Jones-Rodgers explores in depth, enslaved people remembered mistresses as invested in slave management, and some employed more brutal methods of discipline than their husbands (xvi). Censer, *North Carolina Planters,* highlights the preference of those planters to gift their daughters enslaved people, particularly since the enslaved "constituted helpful additions to family income and autonomy" (107).

57. Kilbourne, *Debt, Investment, Slaves,* 41.

58. Baptist, "Toxic Debt," 9; Martin, "Slavery's Invisible Engine," 821.

59. Follett, *Sugar Masters,* 42.

60. Wright, *Slavery and American Economic Development,* 69; Martin, "Slavery's Invisible Engine," 822.

61. Alfred Flournoy to Martha Flournoy, April 23, 1824, Alfred Flournoy Papers, Mss. 628, LLMVC.

62. Martin, "Slavery's Invisible Engine," 818.

63. Wright, *Slavery and American Economic Development,* 70. On the use of the enslaved as security on loans given to family in the eastern and Piedmont regions of North Carolina, see Censer, *North Carolina Planters.*

64. Henry Marshall to Maria Marshall, March 3, 1835, Marshall–Furman Family Papers, Mss. 2740, 4042, LLMVC.

65. Henry Marshall to Maria Marshall, November 8, 1833, Josephine C. Means Papers, collection 335A, LSUS.

66. Wright, *Slavery and American Economic Development,* 69; Jennison, *Cultivating Race,* 5, 25; Martin, "Slavery's Invisible Engine," 818–819; Kilbourne, *Debt, Investment, Slaves,* 39; Deyle, "An 'Abominable' New Trade," 840–841; Marler, *Merchants' Capital,* 91.

67. Baptist, "Toxic Debt," 10, 12.

68. Johnson, *Soul by Soul;* Jones-Rodgers, *They Were Her Property;* Berry, *Price for Their Pound of Flesh.*

69. Martin, "Slavery's Invisible Engine," 829, 840.

70. J. S. Clark to W. J. Hutchinson, May 20, 1859, William Joseph Hutchinson family and plantation records, collection 75, LSUS.

71. Slave sale document, April 23, 1857; shipment of slaves and goods, September 21, 1857; slave sale documents, October 4, 1856, November 5, 1857, Charles L. Mathews and Family Papers, Mss. 910, LLMVC.

72. Rothman, *Slave Country,* 121.

73. Olmsted, *Journey in the Seaboard Slave States,* 628.

74. Kilbourne, *Debt, Investment, Slaves,* 3, 64.

75. Preemption by settlement document, January 26, 1818, George B. Marshall Family Papers, Mss. 969, LLMVC; Dupre, *Transforming the Cotton Frontier,* 116.

76. John Texada land office registry, April 5, 1832, Lewis Texada and Family Papers, Mss. 2985, LLMVC; Rohrbough, *Land Office Business,* 200–202; Johnson, *River of Dark Dreams,* 37.

77. Henry Marshall to Maria Marshall, December 21, 1839, Marshall–Furman Family Papers, Mss. 2740, 4042, LLMVC.

78. John Texada land purchase, original June 8, 1836, and legal copy February 27, 1858, Lewis Texada and Family Papers, Mss. 2985, LLMVC. The archived legal copy is in the Texada Papers.

79. Limerick, *Legacy of Conquest,* 67.

80. Louis Texada notarized land document, January 12, 1852, Lewis Texada and Family Papers, Mss. 2985, LLMVC. The younger Texada's first name is spelled as both Lewis and Louis.

81. Jane Powell letter to "My Dear Aunt," June 1, 1845, Hubbard S. Bosley Papers, Mss. 963, LLMVC.

82. Gould, *Fifty Years on the Mississippi,* 226, 229.

83. Jane Powell letter to "My Dear Aunt," June 1, 1845.

84. Henry Marshall to Maria Marshall, November 1, 1833, Josephine C. Means Papers, collection 335A, LSUS.

85. Henry Marshall to Maria Marshall, November 28, 1836, Marshall–Furman Family Papers, Mss. 2740, 4042, LLMVC; Henry Marshall to Maria Marshall, December 22, 1833, Josephine C. Means Papers, collection 335A, LSUS.

86. Bartholomew Egan to James Egan, January 7–18, 1850, Egan Family Collection, Mss. 1-G-3, CGHRC.

87. Ancestral Homes of DeSoto, Josephine Chatham Means Collection, collection 335, LSUS.

88. Henry Marshall letter to Maria Marshall, December 22, 1833.

89. J. Prestuge to W. Benson, March 25, 1857, Benson Family Papers, Mss. 2424, 2440, LLMVC.

90. Burke, *On Slavery's Border*, 63. For further examples, see Oakes, *Ruling Race;* Baptist, *Creating an Old South;* Campbell, *Empire for Slavery;* Miller, *South by Southwest;* Cashin, *A Family Venture.*

91. Clinton, *Plantation Mistress*, 60, 166–167, 233.

92. Cashin, *A Family Venture*, 45, 65, 94.

93. Jane Powell letter to "My Dear Aunt," June 1, 1845.

94. Hong, "Structural Transformation," 71. On the significance and influence of post offices, see John, *Spreading the News.*

95. *Caddo Gazette*, June 2, 1855; Hodgson, "Forest Park," 36.

96. Henry Marshall to Maria Marshall, December 24, 1841, Marshall–Furman Family Papers, Mss. 2740, 4042, LLMVC.

97. Limerick, *The Legacy of Conquest*, 67.

98. Rothman, *Flush Times*, 97.

99. Jane Powell letter to "My Dear Aunt," June 1, 1845.

100. Silas Flournoy to Elizabeth Flournoy, April 11, 1838, J. Fair Hardin Collection, Mss. 1014, LLMVC.

2. "FARMING HERE IS A SURE ROAD TO A FORTUNE"

1. Follett et al., *Plantation Kingdom*, 2; Barnes et al., *Old South's Modern Worlds*, 4, 12.

2. Schoen, "Burdens and Opportunities," 69, 76–77.

3. Beckert, *Empire of Cotton*, xviii, 30–40, 63, 91–92.

4. "Cotton—Its Improved and True Culture," *American Cotton Planter and Soil of the South* 1, no. 2 (February 1853): 52, S1.A35, LLMVC; *Historical Statistics of the United States, Colonial Times to 1970*, U.S. Department of Commerce, Bureau of the Census, 209.

5. Earle, *Geographical Inquiry*, 234. A staple crop is grown for sustenance. Plantation crops are grown for profit and necessitate the acreage of a plantation, bringing into focus how each crop is produced.

6. *Monopodial* means that the cotton plant grows upward from a single point, with a single trunk or stem with auxiliary branches. Monopodial branches are the vegetative limbs, whereas sympodial branches are the reproductive, fruiting branches.

7. Brown and Ware, *Cotton*, 99–100, 103–104, 106, 115.

8. O'Donovan, *Becoming Free in the Cotton South*, 19; Berlin and Morgan, *Cultivation and Culture*, 20.

9. Kaye, *Joining Places*, 103. On tasking, see Berlin and Morgan, *Cultivation and Culture;* Dusinberre, *Them Dark Days;* Joyner, *Down by the Riverside;* Innes, *Work and Labor in Early America;* Wood, *Women's Work, Men's Work.*

10. Miller, "Plantation Labor Organization," 158. On labor methods used in sugar cultivation in Cuba, see Scott, *Degrees of Freedom.*

11. Northup, *Twelve Years a Slave*, 96–97.

12. Solomon Northup discusses drivers and overseers at the Epps plantation. He was "promoted" to driver during his enslavement and describes how he frequently made it seem as if he was using the whip and driving his fellow enslaved people in the fields when Epps was watching

ity he was whipping the air. Northup, *Twelve Years a Slave,* 132–134.

13. Wright, *Political Economy of the Cotton South,* 55.

14. James M. Chambers, "On the Treatment and Cultivation of Cotton," *American Cotton Planter* 1, no. 7 (July 1853): 201.

15. "Planting and Cultivating Cotton," *American Cotton Planter* 1, no. 8 (August 1853): 234–235. Northup explains the cotton cultivation cycle similarly in chapter 12 of *Twelve Years a Slave.*

16. Sarah Hunter to "My dear husband," January 27, 1847, Robert and Sarah Jane Hunter letters, Mss. 4072, LLMVC.

17. February 22, 1859, entry, Willow Point plantation ledgers, Joseph Toole Robinson Papers, Mss. 1413, LLMVC.

18. John Houston to William Allen, September 3, 1858, William M. Allen correspondence, Mss. 2287, 701, LLMVC.

19. Pirella Powell to "Dear Aunt," June 1, 1845, Hubbard Bosley Papers, Mss. 963, LLMVC; Joseph Olcott to Ann Payne, June 20, 1844, Joseph H. Olcott letter, Mss. 2125, LLMVC.

20. George Mathews to "My Dear Wife," October 9, 1829, September 27, 1831, Mathews–Ventress–Lawrason Family Papers, Mss. 4358, LLMVC.

21. A. Robinson to Charles Mathews, May 22, June 14, 1855, Charles L. Mathews and Family Papers, Mss. 910, LLMVC; Henry Marshall to Maria Marshall, December 3, 1839, Marshall–Furman Family Papers, Mss. 4042, LLMVC.

22. A. I. Robinson to Charles Mathews, October 30, 1856, Mathews–Ventress–Lawrason Family Papers, Mss. 4358, LLMVC.

23. Stoll, *Larding the Lean Earth,* 14, 17.

24. William Sharp to Joseph Pownall, May 8, 1850, William A. Sharp letters, Mss. 4302, LLMVC.

25. Moore, *Emergence of the Cotton Kingdom,* 32–33.

26. R. S. Hardwick, "Hill Side Ditching No. 1," *American Cotton Planter* 1, no. 1 (January 1853), 14–18, and "Hill Side Ditching No. 2," *American Cotton Planter* 1, no. 2 (February 1853), 42–43, S1.A35, LLMVC.

27. Henry Marshall to Maria Marshall, December 3, 1839, Marshall–Furman Family Papers, Mss. 2740, 4042, LLMVC.

28. Libby, *Slavery and Frontier Mississippi,* 40.

29. Sarah Hunter to "My dear husband," January 27, 1847.

30. Smith and Cothren, *Cotton,* 293, 295, 572.

31. 1853–1854 plantation box, Pre Aux Cleres plantation record books, Mss. 684, LLMVC.

32. Jennison, *Cultivating Race,* 243. For further discussion, see O'Donovan, *Becoming Free in the Cotton South;* Libby, *Slavery and Frontier Mississippi;* Berry, *Swing the Sickle;* Reidy, *From Slavery to Agrarian Capitalism;* May 26, 1854 entry, Willow Point plantation ledgers, Joseph Toole Robinson Papers, Mss. 1413, LLMVC.

33. Northup, *Twelve Years a Slave,* 100.

34. Ibid., 98, 101.

35. George Mason Graham to E. A. C. Mason, October 6, 1848, G. Mason Graham letters, Mss. 163, LLMVC; George Mathews to "My dear wife," September 27, 1831, Mathews–Ventress–Lawrason Family Papers, Mss. 4358, LLMVC; Henry Marshall to Maria Marshall, February 18, 1839, December 3, 1839, Marshall–Furman Family Papers, Mss. 4042, LLMVC.

36. On safety-first food production, see Wright, *Political Economy of the Cotton South* and *Slavery and American Economic Development;* Wright and Kunreuther, "Cotton, Corn and Risk," 526-551. On self-sufficiency, see Hillard, *Hog Meat and Hoecake;* Fogel, *Without Consent or Contract,* 132-137; Metzer, "Rational Management," 130-132.

37. "The Cotton Culture," *De Bow's Review* 2, no. 2 (September 1846): 133. See also Gray, *History of Agriculture,* 700; Libby, *Slavery and Frontier Mississippi,* 41. On agricultural implements, see McClelland, *Sowing Modernity;* Moore, *Emergence of the Cotton Kingdom;* Evans, "Plantation Hoe," 71-100.

38. Gray, *History of Agriculture,* 701-702.

39. Moore, *Emergence of the Cotton Kingdom,* 27; Schoen, "Burdens and Opportunities," 74.

40. Gray, *History of Agriculture,* 703-704.

41. Johnson, *River of Dark Dreams,* 152, 154.

42. Moore, "Cotton Breeding in the Old South," 97. For a more recent account, see Olmstead and Rhode, "Biological Innovation."

43. Moore, "Cotton Breeding in the Old South," 95-96.

44. Olmstead and Rhode, "Biological Innovation," 28.

45. Patsey was an enslaved woman on the Epps plantation with Northup and was "chiefly famous" for her picking skill. "Such lightning-like motion was in her fingers as no other fingers ever possessed, and therefore it was, that in cotton picking time, Patsey was queen of the field." Despite her prowess at picking, however, Patsey was whipped "oftener, and suffered more, than any of her companions." Northup, *Twelve Years a Slave,* 110.

46. In *The Half Has Not Been Told,* Baptist holds that the higher picking rates were a result of Blacks training themselves to move their fingers faster in response to torture. While Blacks certainly did train their fingers to move faster and to maintain stamina through incredibly long workdays, stating that quick picking was the only reason for high rates negates the added expectation slaveholders heaped on enslaved laborers to pick extraordinary amounts of cotton because of the heavy investment in seed varietals. It also ignores the fact that enslaved people were subjected to violence and brutality both when the crop was plentiful and when it was stricken. The argument in this book is not as singular as Baptist's; instead, I build off of economic historians' contributions and acknowledge the role that market competition played in increasing slaveholder violence. For a similar standpoint, see Clegg, "Capitalism and Slavery," 289-295.

47. Malone, *Sweet Chariot,* 53.

48. Wright, *Political Economy of the Cotton South,* 87. On slavery's flexibility for diverse labor requirements, see Morris, "Articulation of Two Worlds," 982-1007. On slavery as ideal for the southern approach to staple crops and labor, see Wright, *Slavery and American Economic Development;* Earle, *Geographical Inquiry;* Berlin and Morgan, *Cultivation and Culture;* Fogel and Engerman, *Time on the Cross;* Ransom and Sutch, "Capitalists Without Capital."

49. 1854 plantation journal, February 10 entry, Joseph Toole Robinson Papers, Mss. 1413, LLMVC.

50. 1855, 1856, and 1858 plantation diaries, Henry Marston and Family Papers, Mss. 624, LLMVC; Northup, *Twelve Years a Slave,* 95.

51. 1855 plantation journal, Joseph Toole Robinson Papers, Mss. 1413, LLMVC; Morgan, "Task and Gang Systems," 200.

52. On gang size and efficiency, see Fogel and Engerman, *Time on the Cross;* Fogel, *Without Consent or Contract;* Miller, "Plantation Labor Organization"; Coclanis, "How the Low Country Was Taken to Task"; Follett, *Sugar Masters,* 95–100; Wright, *Political Economy of the Cotton South;* Metzer, "Rational Management."

53. Northup, *Twelve Years a Slave,* 95–96.

54. 1854, 1855, 1856, 1859, and 1860 plantation journals, Joseph Toole Robinson Papers, Mss. 1413, LLMVC; 1852 and 1853 plantation journals, Pre Aux Cleres plantation record books, Mss. 684, LLMVC. In many other parts of the South, gangs were ranked first, second, third, and so on. On differentiation in labor gangs, see Miller, "Plantation Labor Organization"; Moore, *Emergence of the Cotton Kingdom.*

55. 1854–1881 daybook, George B. Marshall Family Papers, Mss. 969, LLMVC.

56. Northup, *Twelve Years a Slave,* 96.

57. 1854 plantation journal, March 26 entry, Joseph Toole Robinson Papers, Mss. 1413, LLMVC.

58. O'Donovan, *Becoming Free in the Cotton South,* 30; Gray, *History of Agriculture,* 701; Johnson, *River of Dark Dreams,* 157. For discussion of innovative changes to the plantation hoe, see Evans, "Plantation Hoe."

59. Gray, *History of Agriculture,* 702.

60. Libby, *Slavery and Frontier Mississippi,* 42.

61. George Mathews to "My Dear Wife," October 7, 1827, Mathews–Ventress–Lawrason Family Papers, Mss. 4358, LLMVC; Walter Moore to Thomas Moore, September 24, November 23, 1830, Ezra Adams Collection, account 314, CGHRC; Northup, *Twelve Years a Slave,* 96, 117.

62. Gray, *History of Agriculture,* 702.

63. 1858 plantation diary, Henry Marston and Family Papers, Mss. 624, LLMVC.

64. Gray, *History of Agriculture,* 703.

65. A. I. Robinson to Charles Mathews, June 14, 1855, Charles L. Mathews and Family Papers, Mss. 910, LLMVC.

66. 1855 plantation journal, Joseph Toole Robinson Papers, Mss. 1413, LLMVC.

67. 1852 plantation journal, Pre Aux Cleres plantation record books, Mss. 684, LLMVC. For insight on relative output, see Fogel and Engerman, *Time on the Cross;* Rosenthal, "From Memory to Mastery," 732–748; Fogel, *Without Consent or Contract;* Morris, "Articulation of Two Worlds"; Wright, "Slavery and the Cotton Boom," 439–451.

68. George Mason Graham to Mrs. E. A. C. Mason, October 6, 1848.

69. Trouillet, *Silencing the Past,* 3, 5, 23, 25.

70. Silas Flournoy to Elizabeth Flournoy, "My dear Elizabeth," April 11, 1838, Alfred Flournoy Papers, Mss. 628, LLMVC.

71. Wright, *Slavery and American Economic Development,* 94. On markets, capital, and expansion, see also Appleby, "Vexed Story," 1–18; Egerton, "Markets Without a Market Revolution," 207–221; Davis, "Looking at Slavery from Broader Perspective," 452–466; Wright, "Slavery and the Cotton Boom"; Ransom and Sutch, "Capitalists Without Capital"; Metzer, "Rational Management"; Miller, *South by Southwest;* Morris, *Becoming Southern;* Jennison, *Cultivating Race;* Dupre, *Transforming the Cotton Frontier;* Reidy, *From Slavery to Agrarian Capitalism;* Rothman, *Slave Country* and *Flush Times.*

72. "Cotton and the Cotton Planters," *De Bow's Review* 3, no. 1 (January 1847): 4, http://name.umdl.umich.edu/acg1336.1-03.001.

73. Berry, *Price for Their Pound of Flesh,* 6–7, 46; Jones-Rodgers, *They Were Her Property,* 23–24. This internal value and quality is what Berry has termed "soul value." The soul value is important to reintegrate into discussions of enslaved life, since it was stripped away and ignored by slaveholders, who failed to recognize the humanity of enslaved African Americans.

74. Berry, *Price for Their Pound of Flesh,* 11–13.

75. Ibid., 13, 15, 21, 32. Jones-Rogers, *They Were Her Property,* notes that enslaved men in their most productive years might have a higher price but that over the long term, enslaved women were more valuable "because of the children they would potentially produce" (21).

76. Deyle, *Carry Me Back,* 4, 44; Johnson, *Soul by Soul,* 6. On the experiences, especially the psychological trauma, of enslaved Blacks in slave auctions and the internal slave marketplace, see Berry, *Price for Their Pound of Flesh;* Jones-Rodgers, *They Were Her Property.*

77. Deyle, *Carry Me Back,* 5–7, 57; Deyle, "An 'Abominable' New Trade," 836, 839; Pritchett and Freudenberger, "A Peculiar Sample," 110.

78. Malone, *Sweet Chariot,* 29; Deyle, *Carry Me Back,* 4, "An 'Abominable' New Trade," 834–835.

79. Gudmestad, *Troublesome Commerce,* 8, 20, 97.

80. Pargas, "In the Fields of a 'Strange Land,'" 563–564.

81. Johnson, *Soul by Soul,* 12, 49.

82. Tadman, "Hidden History," 12. For enslaved people, the slave market was a "mobile, spatially unbounded economic network" and it encompassed urban, rural, physical, built, and outdoor spaces. Jones-Rodgers, *They Were Her Property,* 82–83.

83. Deyle, *Carry Me Back,* 106; Tadman, "Hidden History," 12, 14, 16.

84. Finley, "Considering the Slave Trade as a Family Business"; Jones-Rodgers, *They Were Her Property,* 130.

85. Johnson, *Soul by Soul,* 79.

86. April 18, 1859, entry, Zack Howell pocket diary for 1859, Samford C. Fullilove Papers, collection 256, LSUS; Gudmestad, *A Troublesome Commerce,* 4–5, 67. The Blacks sold to Golfraith would be valued at $753,000 in 2015 terms.

87. November 8, 1859, March 8, April 10, 1860, entries, Zack Howell pocket diary for 1859.

88. August 22, September 26, 1860, entries, Zack Howell pocket diary for 1859.

89. September 28, 1860, entry, and undated entry, Zack Howell pocket diary for 1859; Jones-Rodgers, *They Were Her Property,* 134, 151.

90. McClellan, *William Joseph Hutchinson and Family of Caspiana Plantation,* 24–25. The Hutchinsons' Caddo holdings were Rocky Mount, Caspiana, and Magnolia plantations.

91. Slave receipts, May 5, 1843, March 2, 1847, April 26, 1849, Hubbard S. Bosley Papers, Mss. 963, LLMVC.

92. Slave receipts, May 3, 1852, January 24, March 8, 1853, January 28, 1854, Hubbard S. Bosley Papers, Mss. 963, LLMVC.

93. Tomich, *Through the Prism of Slavery,* 3.

94. Berlin and Morgan, *Cultivation and Culture,* 5; Miller, "Plantation Labor Organization," 158.

95. Pollard, "Aging and Slavery," 228; Northup, *Twelve Years a Slave,* 109; White, *Ar'n't I*

a Woman?, 53. See also Malone, "Searching for the Family and Household Structure of Rural Louisiana, 1810–1864," 357–379; Fogel, *Without Consent or Contract*, 55.

96. Memoirs of Ellison Moultrie Adger, Mrs. Mary Moultrie Adger family and plantation records, collection 93, LSUS.

97. 1859 and 1860 plantation journals, Joseph Toole Robinson Papers, Mss. 1413, LLMVC; Berry, *Price for Their Pound of Flesh*, 131–132.

98. On disability and its effect on enslaved African Americans, see Boster, *African American Slavery and Disability*.

99. Forret, "Deaf & Dumb, Blind, Insane, or Idiotic," 507, 512–513, 515, 519–522.

100. Cholera epidemics were prevalent throughout the 1830s and 1840s, and the South was particularly impacted in 1833. See Steckel, "Slave Mortality," 86–113. Major yellow fever epidemics occurred in New Orleans and Louisiana in 1833 and 1853.

101. On the impact of malaria and yellow fever, see Savitt and Young, *Disease and Distinctiveness;* Savitt, *Medicine and Slavery;* Stowe, *Doctoring the South;* Carrigan, "Privilege, Prejudice, and the Strangers' Disease," 568–578; Merrens and Terry, "Dying in Paradise," 533–550.

102. William Waglaz to Hubbard Bosley, June 10, 1854, Hubbard S. Bosley Papers, Mss. 963, LLMVC. On "seasoning," see Fett, *Working Cures*.

103. Stowe, *Doctoring the South*, 5; Kiple and King, *Another Dimension to the Black Diaspora*, 50. On malaria and other diseases affecting fertility, see Morgan, *Laboring Women*, 111.

104. George Mason Graham to Mrs. E. A. C. Mason, February 8, 1849, G. Mason Graham letters, Mss. 163, LLMVC; Mary Wells Sibley to Mrs. Thomas Henry Morris, May 31, 1855, Morris–Sibley Family Papers, Mss. 562, LLMVC.

105. Stowe, *Doctoring the South*, 117.

106. There is a vast body of literature on sexuality and sexual coercion during enslavement. Some titles to consider include White, *Ar'n't I A Woman?;* Morgan, *Laboring Women;* Berry, *Price for Their Pound of Flesh;* Berry, *Swing the Sickle;* Berry and Harris, *Sexuality and Slavery;* Jones, *Labor of Love;* Malone, *Sweet Chariot;* Stevenson, *Life in Black and White;* Hunter, *Bound in Wedlock;* Glymph, *Out of the House of Bondage;* Sommerville, *Rape and Race;* Block, *Rape and Sexual Power;* Hodes, *White Women, Black Men;* Baptist, "'Cuffy,' 'Fancy Maids,' and 'One-Eyed Men'"; Johnson, *River of Dark Dreams*.

107. Berry, *Swing the Sickle*, 79; Morgan, *Laboring Women*, chapter 4; Berry, *Price for Their Pound of Flesh*, 11–13, 20–27, 31–34. See also Stevenson, "What's Love Got to Do with It?," Jones-Rodgers, "Rethinking Sexual Violence"; Doddington, "Manhood, Sex, and Power."

108. Hunter, *Bound in Wedlock*, 7, 15–16, 26, 31, 45.

109. Ibid., 65–83; Forret, *Slave Against Slave*, 238, 252, 261–263, 268, 344, 378; Morris, "Within the Slave Cabin," 268–272; Rothman, *Impossible Witness*, 12.

110. 1856 and 1859 plantation journals, Joseph Toole Robinson Papers, Mss. 1413, LLMVC.

111. Steckel, "Fluctuations in a Dreadful Childhood"; Forret, *Slave Against Slave*, 369. See also Steckel, "Birth Weights and Infant Mortality."

112. Savitt, "Black Health on the Plantation," 342; Hillard, *Hog Meat and Hoecake*, 58.

113. "Black Code," section 87, in *Statutes of the State of Louisiana*, 67; Vandal, "Regulating Louisiana's Rural Areas," 71.

114. Kiple and King, *Another Dimension to the Black Diaspora*, 82; 1854 plantation journal, Joseph Toole Robinson Papers, Mss. 1413, LLMVC.

115. Hillard, *Hog Meat and Hoecake,* 153, 162.

116. Savitt, "Black Health on the Plantation," 342; Kiple and King, *Another Dimension to the Black Diaspora,* 88–100.

117. Northup, *Twelve Years a Slave,* 99; 1856 plantation journal, Joseph Toole Robinson Papers, Mss. 1413, LLMVC.

118. Hillard, *Hog Meat and Hoecake,* 104.

119. Kiple and King, *Another Dimension to the Black Diaspora,* 77, 97, 98, 100; Steckel, "Slave Mortality," "A Dreadful Childhood," and "A Peculiar Population," 721–741.

120. Fogel and Engerman, *Time on the Cross,* 39; Steckel, "Women, Work, and Health," 55–56. For discussion of fecundity as a component of articulation, see Morris, "Articulation of Two Worlds."

121. White, *Ar'n't I a Woman?,* 75, 79. For pregnancy and neonatal work patterns and infant mortality rates, see Steckel, "A Dreadful Childhood."

122. Johnson, "Work, Culture, and the Slave Community," 349; Polly Mason oral interview, Mss. 4700.0041, LLMVC; King, *Stolen Childhood,* 21, 24–25.

123. Johnson, "Work, Culture, and the Slave Community," 339.

124. 1854 plantation journal, Joseph Toole Robinson Papers, Mss. 1413, LLMVC.

125. Reidy, "Obligation and Right," 142, 149.

126. Henry Marshall to Maria Marshall, February 18, 1839, Marshall–Furman Family Papers, Mss. 2740, 4042, LLMVC; September 28, November 16, 1856, entries, Henry Marston 1856 diary, Henry Marston and Family Papers, Mss. 624, LLMVC; 1854 plantation journal, Joseph Toole Robinson Papers, Mss. 1413, LLMVC.

127. Smith, *Mastered by the Clock,* 5, 112, 117, 118.

128. Smith, *Listening to Nineteenth-Century America,* 6, 13, 37–38.

129. Berlin et al., *Remembering Slavery,* 84–86; Northup, *Twelve Years a Slave,* 99.

130. McDonald, *Economy and Material Culture of Slaves,* 129–131; Vlach, *Back of the Big House,* 22, 153, 158.

131. Vlach, *Back of the Big House,* 12, 156.

132. 1854 plantation journal, Joseph Toole Robinson Papers, Mss. 1413, LLMVC.

133. Northup, *Twelve Years a Slave,* 99.

134. 1854, 1855, 1856, 1859, and 1860 plantation journals, Joseph Toole Robinson Papers, Mss. 1413, LLMVC; 1852 and 1853 plantation journals, Pre Aux Cleres plantation record books, Mss. 684, LLMVC; September 17, 1856, entry, Henry Marston 1856 diary, Henry Marston and Family Papers, Mss. 624, LLMVC.

135. 1854, 1855, 1856, 1859, and 1860 plantation journals, Joseph Toole Robinson Papers, Mss. 1413, LLMVC. On knowledge of irrigation brought from Africa, see Smallwood, *Saltwater Slavery;* Joyner, *Down by the Riverside;* Carney, *Black Rice.*

136. Beveridge and McLaughlin, *Papers of Frederick Law Olmsted,* 216. On enslaved communities in other plantation regions, see Kaye, *Joining Places.*

137. Gutman, *The Black Family in Slavery and Freedom,* 186; Kolchin, *American Slavery,* 45.

138. This was common practice across the South, and many children were not listed separately from their mothers, or with a different name, until the age of ten. See Johnson, *Soul by Soul;* Berry, *Price for Their Pound of Flesh;* Jones-Rodgers, *They Were Her Property;* Deyle, *Carry Me Back.*

139. Northup, *Twelve Years a Slave,* 72; Gutman, *The Black Family in Slavery and Freedom,* 253.

140. 1854–1881 daybook, George B. Marshall Family Papers, Mss. 969, LLMVC; 1854, 1855, 1856, 1859, and 1860 plantation journals, Joseph Toole Robinson Papers, Mss. 1413, LLMVC; Agreement of Partnership Dissolution Between Robert Hutchinson and William Hutchinson, December 2, 1857, William Joseph Hutchinson family and plantation records, collection 75, LSUS; 1852 and 1853 plantation journals, Pre Aux Cleres plantation record books, Mss. 684, LLMVC; Inventory of Property for Colonel Henry Marshall, July 22, 1864, Josephine Chatham Means Collection 335, LSUS.

141. Jefferson called enslaved people "moveables," and Blacks were often described similarly to livestock or furniture. Oakes, *Freedom National,* 8; Rothman, *Beyond Freedom's Reach,* 31.

142. Anonymous letter, Mss. 1008, LLMVC. Emphasis in original.

143. 1854, 1855, 1856, 1859, and 1860 plantation journals, Joseph Toole Robinson Papers, Mss. 1413, LLMVC.

144. On the uncomfortably similar terminology used today for USDA meat grading, see Berry, *Price for Their Pound of Flesh,* 68.

145. Baptist, "'Cuffy,' 'Fancy Maids,' and 'One-Eyed Men'"; Johnson, *Soul by Soul;* Stevenson, *Life in Black and White;* Genovese, *Roll, Jordan, Roll,* 416.

146. Bill of sale by William H. Dameron to Elizabeth P. Haynes, Ewing Family Papers, Mss. 183, LSUS. For a concise handling of the interstate trade in and market for attractive enslaved women, see Baptist, "'Cuffy,' 'Fancy Maids,' and 'One-Eyed Men.'"

147. Eliza Powell will, undated [1860], Hubbard S. Bosley Papers, Mss. 963, LLMVC.

148. Douglass, *Narrative of the Life of Frederick Douglass,* 49.

149. On the flexibility afforded by slave hiring, see Martin, *Divided Mastery;* Barton, "Good Cooks and Washers," 436–460. Alexandria and Shreveport were the only two regional cities, which meant limited urban demand for hired slaves. The enslaved were also hired on smaller plantations during peak season. See Seip, "Slaves and Free Negroes in Alexandria, 1850–1860," 147–165; Foshee, "Slave Hiring in Rural Louisiana," 63–73.

150. Slave hire, March 9, 1851, plantation diary 1851–59, Benjamin Philip Cuny family papers, Mss. 4246, LLMVC.

151. Receipt for R. H. Draughton hire, July 1857, and slave hire bill for J. F. Overton, July 1, 1857, Henry Marston and Family Papers, Mss. 624, LLMVC.

152. Slave hire bill to E. W. Barnes, January 1857, to Clinton and Port Hudson Railroad Co., January 1857, and to R. H. Draughton, January 29, 1857, Henry Marston and Family Papers, Mss. 624, LLMVC.

153. Letter to "My Dear Brother," May 18, 1855, Charles L. Mathews and Family Papers, Mss. 910, LLMVC.

154. P. M. Butler to H. Marshall, May 16, 1844, Marshall–Furman Family Papers, Mss. 4042, 2740, LLMVC.

155. Mary Wells Sibley to Mrs. Thomas Henry Morris, May 31, 1855, Mary Wells Sibley to Mrs. W. F. Murray, May 5, 1856, Morris–Sibley Family Papers, Mss. 562, LLMVC.

156. 1859 plantation journal, Joseph Toole Robinson Papers, Mss. 1413, LLMVC.

157. Glymph, *Out of the House of Bondage,* 5; Jones-Rodgers, *They Were Her Property.*

158. Beveridge and McLaughlin, *Papers of Frederick Law Olmsted,* 217; Franklin, *Militant*

South, 35. See also Wyatt-Brown, *Southern Honor;* Gorn, "Gouge and Bite," 18–43; Carrigan, *Making of a Lynching Culture.*

159. Burnard, *Planters, Merchants, and Slaves,* 6, 35–37, 48, 54, 80. On the complicated relationship among pain, religion, and slavery, see Abruzzo, *Polemical Pain,* 1–2, 5–10, 17, 19, 51–57, 195–200, 210, 230.

160. Burnard, *Planters, Merchants, and Slaves,* 31.

161. For work on violence as a learned behavior in antebellum culture, see Franklin, *Militant South;* Glymph, *Out of the House of Bondage;* Wyatt-Brown, *Southern Honor;* Burnard, *Planters, Merchants, and Slaves;* Jones-Rogers, *They Were Her Property;* Camp, *Closer to Freedom;* Miles, *Ties That Bind;* Carrington, *Making of a Lynching Culture;* Lee et al., "Revisiting the Southern Culture of Violence."

162. For numerous examples, see Glymph, *Out of the House of Bondage;* Jones-Rogers, *They Were Her Property.*

163. Northup, *Twelve Years a Slave,* 152–153; 155.

164. Northup, *Twelve Years a Slave,* 105.

165. Anonymous letter, Mss. 1008, LLMVC. Emphasis in original; Di Maio, *Gërstacker's Louisiana,* 28.

166. Glymph, *Out of the House of Bondage,* 33, 45; Forret, *Slave Against Slave,* 180. On "calm and deliberate" whipping, see Genovese, *Roll, Jordan, Roll,* 64–67.

167. Beveridge and McLaughlin, *Papers of Frederick Law Olmsted,* 219–220.

168. "Black Code," in *Statutes of the State of Louisiana,* 50–83; Forret, *Slave Against Slave,* 183.

169. Northup, *Twelve Years a Slave,* 63–70, 103, 105.

170. Malone, *Sweet Chariot,* 231.

171. Hartman, *Scenes of Subjection,* 140.

172. Forret, *Slave Against Slave,* 42; Fogel and Engerman, *Time on the Cross,* 147.

173. Wright, *Slavery and American Economic Development,* 90.

174. Northup, *Twelve Years a Slave,* 94–97.

175. Mrs. Mary Wells Sibley to Mrs. Thomas Henry Morris, June 23, 1855, Morris–Sibley Family Papers, Mss. 562, LLMVC.

176. Berlin et al., *Remembering Slavery,* 147–149. Terrill's punishment is also chronicled in Malone, *Sweet Chariot,* 222, 250.

177. For more discussion, see Forret, *Slave Against Slave.*

178. Hartman, *Scenes of Subjection,* 66; Berry, *Price for Their Pound of Flesh,* 17.

179. J. P. Flournoy, "Shreveport and Caddo Parish as I Remember it in the Early Sixties," Alfred Flournoy Papers, Mss. 628, LLMVC.

180. Hadden, *Slave Patrols,* 80, 82, 107–109.

181. Delbanco, *War Before the War,* 10, 18–20, 66, 68, 80–81, 84–85, 167–169, 178–180, 208, 260–264. On the infamous three-fifths clause, see page 71.

182. 1852–1853 plantation journal, Pre Aux Cleres plantation record books, Mss. 684, LLMVC.

183. William Powell to "Dear Sir," August 9, 1854, Hubbard S. Bosley Papers, Mss. 963, LLMVC.

184. "Stop the Runaways," *South West Shreveport,* November 22, 1854; "Runaway," "Committed to Jail," *South West Shreveport,* June–August 1854.

185. Mary Wells Sibley to Mrs. Thomas Henry Morris, June 23, 1856, Morris–Sibley Family Papers, Mss. 562, LLMVC.

3. "THEY WILL HAVE YANKEE MASTERS AS WELL AS US"

1. Oakes, *Freedom National,* 2, 3–8, 22.

2. Ibid., 32, 43–44, 57, 73; Barney, *Rebels in the Making,* 2–8; Richardson, *How the South Won the Civil War,* chapter 2.

3. Barney, *Rebels in the Making,* 8–9.

4. Oakes, *Freedom National,* 57; Richardson, *To Make Men Free,* 10–23; Foner, *Free Soil, Free Labor, Free Men,* 40–46, 59.

5. "Dred Scott v. Sandford," *Oyez,* https://www.oyez.org/cases/1850-1900/60us393; *Dred Scott, Plaintiff in Error, v. John F. A. Sandford,* 60 U.S. 393, December 1856, in *Legal Information Institute,* Cornell Law School, https://www.law.cornell.edu/supremecourt/text/60/393; Delbanco, *War Before the War,* 72, 331–334, 346–347.

6. Oakes, *Freedom National,* 22, 43–44; Richardson, *How the South Won the Civil War,* 39–41.

7. Quigley, *Shifting Grounds,* 41–44.

8. Barney, *Rebels in the Making,* 41–42.

9. Ibid., 74–83.

10. Sacher, *Perfect War of Politics,* 222–223. For party vote breakdowns by region for elections from 1834 to 1860, see 182–183.

11. Ibid., 249, 253–254.

12. Barney, *Rebels in the Making,* 108–111.

13. "Your cousin Bosley" to "My dear cousin," August 31, 1858, Hubbard S. Bosley Papers, Mss. 963, LLMVC.

14. Foner, *Fiery Trial,* 143–144. For additional information, see Greer, "Louisiana Politics, 1845–1861," 444–483; McLure, "Election of 1860 in Louisiana," 601–702; Kendall, "Interregnum in Louisiana in 1861," 374–408; Halstead, *Three Against Lincoln.*

15. Sacher, *Perfect War of Politics,* 289.

16. Ibid., 290, 287–292.

17. Draft of secession speech, undated, Thomas O. Moore Papers, Mss. 305, 893, 1094, LLMVC; Roland, "Louisiana and Secession," 392–393.

18. Sacher, *Perfect War of Politics,* 298; Dew, "Who Won the Secession Election in Louisiana?," 19, 21.

19. R. W. Estlin to Colonel Henry Marshall, November 9, 1860, Josephine Chatham Means Collection, collection 335, LSUS; Sacher, *Perfect War of Politics,* 295.

20. Virginia Yenger to "My dear cousin," December 9, 1860, Hubbard S. Bosley Papers, Mss. 963, LLMVC. Quigley, *Shifting Grounds,* points out that the success of secessionists masked the strength and health of southern Unionism and that, particularly for nonslaveholders, northern aggression did not yet warrant political separation (125–126).

21. Roland, "Louisiana and Secession," 395–396; Barney, *Rebels in the Making,* 111.

22. Dew, "Long Lost Returns," 358. Dew collated the official vote returns in one location. He and other historians indicate issues with the vote returns at the time and in the historical record.

23. Dew, "Who Won the Secession Election in Louisiana?," 29; Barney, *Rebels in the Making*, 216–217. For a description of the secession conventions and outcomes in all seceded states, see Barney, *Rebels in the Making*.

24. Dew, "Long Lost Returns," 357–358. Dew states that the fairest test of the returns is based on the totals from the senatorial districts, since they had fewer unopposed candidates.

25. Ibid., 359, 361, 363, 366; Caddo Parish election results, January 7, 1861, Caddo Parish Civil War election records, collection 26, LSUS.

26. Wooster, "Louisiana Secession Convention," 112, 114, 118–119.

27. See Glatthaar, *General Lee's Army*, 17–20, 31, 36.

28. J. E. Wallace by request of Capt. J. M. Williams to Henry Marshall, January 28, 1861, Marshall–Furman Family Papers, Mss. 4042, 2740, LLMVC; Ancestral Homes of DeSoto, Josephine Chatham Means Collection, collection 335, LSUS; *Henry Marshall: Louisiana Pioneer, Planter and Statesman,* compiled by Ella Chandler Edwards, 1967, Henry Marshall Collection, account 1-H-4, CGHRC.

29. Samuel M. Hyams certificate of commission, January 21, May 9, 1861, Chaplin, Breazeale, and Chaplin Papers, Mss. 952, 967, 1028, LLMVC.

30. "Shreveport Greys Were Formed Here," Confederate veterans reunion 1936, Alfred Flournoy Sr. Family Papers, collection 78, LSUS; Glatthaar, *General Lee's Army*, 35–36.

31. L. H. Bowden to Henry Marshall, May 20, 1861, Josephine C. Means Papers, collection 335A, LSUS. Emphasis in original.

32. John Houston to "Friend William," September 29, 1861, William M. Allen correspondence, Mss. 2287, 701, LLMVC. For a complete list of Louisiana's military units, see Booth, "Louisiana Confederate Military Records, Addenda"; for unit lists from Caddo Parish, see McClure and Howe, *History of Shreveport and Shreveport Builders;* for details on Rapides Parish, see Whittington, "History of Rapides Parish," 427–440; regarding mustering units, see Casey, "Confederate Units from North Louisiana," 105–115. On prevalence of elites raising troops, see Barney, *Rebels in the Making,* 274.

33. Alfred Flournoy Sr. to Alfred Flournoy Jr., March 16, 1862, Alfred Flournoy Papers, Mss. 628, LLMVC.

34. Casey, "Confederate Units from North Louisiana," 112; Marion-Landais, "The Alfred Flournoy Jr. Letters to Theodosia, His Wife, 1861," 92–93.

35. History of the LA State Seminary of Learning, Antal Vállas and Family Papers, Mss. 4439, LLMVC.

36. Casey, "Confederate Units from North Louisiana," 106; Alfred Flournoy Sr. to Alfred Flournoy Jr., March 16, 1862.

37. H. G. Hargis to W. B. Benson, May 15, 1861, Benson Family Papers, Mss. 2424, 2440, LLMVC.

38. Manning, *What This Cruel War Was Over,* 31; Delbanco, *War Before the War,* 34; Glatthaar, *General Lee's Army,* 31–35. For a discussion about north Louisiana's early commitment to the war, especially in Bossier Parish, see Peyton, "The Civil War Began and Ended in North Louisiana," 75–77.

39. Alexander Stephens, "Cornerstone Speech," March 21, 1861, *American Battlefield Trust,* https://www.battlefields.org/learn/primary-sources/cornerstone-speech.

40. Casey, "Confederate Units from North Louisiana," 107. *Index of the Official Records of*

the Union and Confederate Armies is a useful resource to trace the route of a particular company. For more details about the Greenwood Guards, the Shreveport Greys, and the Caddo Rifles, see Jones, "Shreveport Goes to War," 391–401.

41. Alfred Flournoy Sr. to Alfred Flournoy Jr., March 16, 1862; "Shreveport Greys Were Formed Here"; Alfred Flournoy Sr. to Alfred Flournoy Jr., March 7, 1861, Alfred Flournoy Jr. correspondence, collection 65, LSUS. For discussion of enlistment and sectional commitment, see Manning, *What This Cruel War Was Over;* Rubin, *Shattered Nation;* McCurry, *Confederate Reckoning;* Quigley, *Shifting Grounds;* Faust, *Creation of Confederate Nationalism.*

42. Letter to "Dear Brack," October 13, 1861, Hubbard S. Bosley Papers, Mss. 963, LLMVC; Rubin, *Shattered Nation,* 12; Barney, *Rebels in the Making,* 145–146.

43. C. B. Johnson to "Dear Wife," April 27, 1862, Hubbard S. Bosley Papers, Mss. 963, LLMVC.

44. David Pierson to "Dear Father," April 21, 1861, David Pierson Letter, Mss. 1612, LLMVC.

45. "Land's End Plantation," undated document; Henry Marshall to Maria Marshall, March 10, 1861, Josephine Chatham Means Collection, collection 335, LSUS.

46. Alfred Flournoy Sr. to Alfred Flournoy Jr., March 16, 1862, August 18, 1861, Alfred Flournoy Jr. correspondence, collection 65, LSUS.

47. Phillips, *Diehard Rebels,* 2–9.

48. John Houston to "Friend William," September 29, 1861; Rubin, *Shattered Nation,* 1.

49. Wells, *Civil War, Reconstruction, and Redemption,* 18; Streater, "'She-Rebels' on the Supply Line," 88–90; Jones-Rodgers, *They Were Her Property,* 156; Barney, *Rebels in the Making,* 147.

50. Quigley, *Shifting Grounds,* 195; Rubin, *Shattered Nation,* 3–4.

51. Letter to "My Darling Brother," April 29, 1861, Hubbard S. Bosley Papers, Mss. 963, LLMVC.

52. Faust, "Altars of Sacrifice," 1209.

53. Faust, *Creation of Confederate Nationalism,* 84; Rubin, *Shattered Nation,* 6–11, 29–30.

54. Phillips, *Diehard Rebels,* 8–9, 18–21.

55. Letter to "My Darling Brother," April 29, 1861.

56. Roberts, "Confederate Belle," 195, 198; Forrester, "Disrupting the Domestic Sphere," 36–54; Glymph, *Out of the House of Bondage,* 113.

57. Miss Sidney Harding diaries, Mss. 721, LLMVC.

58. Theodosia Flournoy to Alfred Flournoy Jr., June 3, July 26, August 4, 1861, Alfred Flournoy Jr. correspondence, collection 65, LSUS; Theodosia Flournoy to Alfred Flournoy Jr., July 22, 1861, Alfred Flournoy Papers, Mss. 628, LLMVC.

59. Annie Jeter Carmouche memoirs, 1858–1870, Annie Jeter Carmouche Papers, Mss. 585, Louisiana Research Collection, Tulane University, New Orleans (hereafter LaRC).

60. Faust, "Altars of Sacrifice"; letter to "My Darling Brother." Emphasis in original.

61. On steadfast patriotism and Confederate nationalist sentiment, see Gallagher, *Confederate War.*

62. Theodosia Flournoy to Alfred Flournoy Jr., June 3, June 17, June 27, July 11, August 21, 1861, Alfred Flournoy Jr. correspondence, collection 65, LSUS.

63. Alfred Flournoy Jr. to Theodosia Flournoy, September 6, 1861, Alfred Flournoy Jr. correspondence, collection 65, LSUS.

64. Elizabeth Ann Scofield letter, December 24, 1865, Mss. 5001, LLMVC.

65. Alfred Flournoy Sr. to Alfred Flournoy Jr., March 16, 1862, Alfred Flournoy Jr. correspondence, collection 65, LSUS; Alfred Flournoy Sr. to Alfred Flournoy Jr., August 18, 1861, Alfred Flournoy Sr. correspondence, collection 78, LSUS.

66. C. Chase to Charles Mathews, October 19, 1863, and C. Chase to Harriet Mathews, October 5, 1864, Mathews–Ventress–Lawrason Family Papers, Mss. 4358, LLMVC.

67. Joseph Texada to Margaret Texada, June 5, 1864, Ker–Texada Papers, Mss. 545, LaRC; Joseph Texada to Margaret Texada, June 24, 1864, Texada Family Papers, Mss. 5119, LLMVC.

68. John Sibley to Nancy Sibley, November 14, December 8, 1862, January 8, 1863, John Coleman Sibley Collection, Mss. 4-D-2, CGHRC.

69. William Henry Chase to Annie Chase, February 10, March 3, 1862, Mathews–Ventress–Lawrason Family Papers, Mss. 4358, LLMVC. McCurry, *Confederate Reckoning*, 204. For Revolutionary analogies in Confederate rhetoric, see Rubin, *Shattered Nation*.

70. Rubin, *Shattered Nation*, 13, 18, 117. The exemption of slavery from nationalistic rhetoric also served to unify white Southerners, especially nonslaveholders and yeomen. See Faust, *Creation of Confederate Nationalism;* Manning, *What This Cruel War Was Over*.

71. Letter to "Dear Brother," January 1, 1863, Hubbard S. Bosley Papers, Mss. 963, LLMVC.

72. Joiner, *Little to Eat,* 154; Cousin Letitia to John Sibley, January 12, 1863, John Coleman Sibley Collection, Mss. 4-D-2, CGHRC; Nancy and Dustin Willard to Micajah and Nancy Wilkinson, January 20, 1862, Micajah Wilkinson Papers, Mss. 707, LLMVC. For discussions of Louisiana women wearing homespun, see Roberts, "Confederate Belle."

73. W. H. Buck to Charles Mathews, October 29, 1861, Charles L. Mathews and Family Papers, Mss. 910, LLMVC.

74. Wells, *Civil War, Reconstruction, and Redemption,* 19; Cashin, "Hungry People in the Wartime South," 162–163; Glatthaar, *General Lee's Army,* 217–218.

75. John C. Sibley Civil War diary, May 18, June 22, 1863, November 1863, September 8, 1864, John Coleman Sibley Collection, Mss. 4-D-2, CGHRC.

76. John Sibley to Lizzie Sibley, August 25, August 27, October 19, December 8, 1862, March 12, 1863, John Coleman Sibley Collection, Mss. 4-D-2, CGHRC.

77. Alonzo Flournoy to Alfred Flournoy Jr., undated letter, J. Fair Hardin Collection, Mss. 1014, LLMVC.

78. Alfred Flournoy Sr. to Alfred Flournoy Jr., June 16, 1861, Alfred Flournoy Sr. correspondence, collection 78, LSUS.

79. John T. Sibley to E. P. Ellis, March 10, 1863, Morris–Sibley Family Papers, Mss. 562, LLMVC. On the "us and them" mentality, hatred for the Union, Southern persistence, and ethos of invincibility, see Phillips, *Diehard Rebels,* especially 3–4, 41, 52–54, 74.

80. Nancy and Dustin Willard to Micajah and Nancy Wilkinson, May 28, 1861, Micajah Wilkinson Papers, Mss. 707, LLMVC.

81. William Tamplin to Betincia Tamplin, May 3, May 7, 1862, February 20, March 29, May 15, 1864, and undated letter, William H. Tamplin Papers, Mss. 3015, LLMVC.

82. John Harris to Rebecca Harris, February 18, 1862, John Harris Civil War letters, collection 209, LSUS.

83. Alfred Flournoy Jr. to Theodosia Flournoy, May 22, July 8, 1861, J. Fair Hardin Collection, Mss. 1014, LLMVC.

84. John C. Sibley Civil War diary, April 16, September 10, October 29, December 30, 1863, November 20, 1864, January 7, 1865, John Coleman Sibley Collection, Mss. 4-D-2, CGHRC.

85. O'Donovan, *Becoming Free in the Cotton South,* examines southwest Georgia from slavery to freedom in an area of the South that also had profit-focused slaveholders, and highlights similar aspects of the regional experience during the Civil War.

86. Gould, *Fifty Years on the Mississippi,* 259.

87. Charles Mathews to J. A. Shultz, July 26, 1862, Charles L. Mathews and Family Papers, Mss. 910, LLMVC.

88. Elizabeth Ann Scofield letter, December 24, 1865.

89. Noe, "Fateful Lightning," 17, 20.

90. Taylor, *Louisiana Reconstructed,* 4–5.

91. Winters, *Civil War in Louisiana;* Gilley, *North Louisiana.*

92. It is unclear from the archives whether the Trans-Mississippi armies and Robert E. Lee's armies in Virginia used all of these goods. My hunch is that mainly Trans-Mississippi forces availed themselves of these goods, while some supplies, such as salted meats, filtered to eastern parts of the army.

93. Drago, *Red River Valley,* 103.

94. Whittington, *Rapides Parish Louisiana, A History,* LLMVC, 147–148.

95. "Shreveport Greys Were Formed Here."

96. Gilley, *North Louisiana,* 166, 180; Winters, *Civil War in Louisiana,* 321; Joiner, *One Damn Blunder,* 17.

97. Thomas O. Moore to George Randolph, July 8, 1862, Thomas O. Moore Papers, Mss. 305, 893, 1094, LLMVC.

98. Ibid., 321. One factory was in Shreveport, four were in Texas towns, and one was in Arkansas.

99. Winters, *Civil War in Louisiana,* 318–319; Gilley, *North Louisiana,* 180.

100. Winters, *Civil War in Louisiana,* 318–319.

101. "Historic Salt Works near Natchitoches," undated clipping, Melrose scrapbooks, box 69, Mss. 15-B-1, CGHRC.

102. R. L. F. Sibley to John Coleman Sibley, September 23, 1864, John Coleman Sibley Collection, Mss. 4-D-2, CGHRC.

103. D. Y. Milling to Jas Milling, January 10, 1863, D. Y. Milling letters, Mss. 3758, LLMVC; Gilley, *North Louisiana,* 180.

104. Zack Howell to Isabella Howell, July 25, 1862, Samford C. Fullilove Papers, collection 256, LSUS.

105. Drake and Drake, "Two Letters of H. Winbourne Drake," 75. On salt in the Confederacy, see Lonn, *Salt as a Factor in the Confederacy.* Salt and salt production also played a significant role in southwest Georgia, an area that was similarly protected by dint of geography. In that instance, slaveholders and white southerners descended on the Florida panhandle and established shanty camps where slaves extracted salt from seawater. See O'Donovan, *Becoming Free in the Cotton South,* 91.

106. Winters, *Civil War in Louisiana,* 318–319; Gilley, *North Louisiana,* 180. Mount Lebanon Female College (now Mount Lebanon University) and Keachi Female College were used as Confederate hospitals after the Battle of Mansfield, as was Henry Marshall's Land's End plantation.

107. Bartholomew Egan to Thomas Manning, December 23, 1863, appointment receipt for B. Egan, February 6, 1863, Egan Family Collection, Mss. 1-G-3, CGHRC.

108. Legan, "Drugs for Louisiana," 193–202; "Shreveport Greys Were Formed Here." A bottle of whiskey could be sold for as much as $150 (more than $3,000 in today's money) in parts of the Confederacy, and its ready availability in the Shreveport area did lead to some alcohol-fueled crime.

109. Henry Allen to J. P. Breda, June 23, 1864, J. P. Breda Family Papers, Mss. 953, 966, 1021, LLMVC.

110. William Ball to J. P. Breda, April 4, April 18, 1865, J. P. Breda Family Papers, Mss. 953, 966, 1021, LLMVC.

111. Henry Allen to Bartholomew Egan, February 24, May 18, 1864, Egan Family Collection, Mss. 1-G-3, CGHRC.

112. Bartholomew Egan to Edmund Kirby Smith, December 12, 1864, note from Shreveport HQ, December 15, 1864, Egan Family Collection, Mss. 1-G-3, CGHRC.

113. Henry Allen to Bartholomew Egan, August 10, 1864, list of slave laborers, October 22, 1864, Henry Allen to Brig. General Bragg, November 7, 1864, Egan Family Collection, Mss. 1-G-3, CGHRC.

114. Henry Allen to J. P. Breda, July 8, July 25, 1864, J. P. Breda Family Papers, Mss. 953, 966, 1021, LLMVC.

115. Litwack, *Been in the Storm So Long,* 37, 41.

116. O'Donovan, *Becoming Free in the Cotton South,* 80–811.

117. William Benson receipt from William Freret, January 21, 1865, Benson Family Papers, Mss. 2424, 2440, LLMVC; receipt for conscription, 1862–1863, William G. Hale Papers, Mss. 2426, LLMVC.

118. Receipt for hire, October 29, 1862, and receipt for transportation, October 30, 1862, N. A. Birge Papers, Mss. 918, 1036, LLMVC. The men were listed as numbers 29, 37, 166, 264, 311, 336, 350, 356, 445, 458, 462, and 543.

119. Receipt from Trans-Mississippi Department for slave Wash, September 10, 1863, for slave Jury, September 19, 1863, death receipt for Jury, February 16, 1864, for Wash, February 16, 1864, pass for boy Henry, September 6, 1863, receipt from Trans-Mississippi Department for slave Charles, March 20, 1864, receipt of payment for overseer by William J. Hutchinson, February 27, 1864, receipt for W. J. Hutchinson claims collection, June 24, 1864, William Joseph Hutchinson family and plantation records, collection 75, LSUS.

120. "Reminiscences of the Civil War and Early Days by Mrs. Thomas Pope Fullilove," Fullilove family binders, binder 1, Fullilove family history, collection 583, LSUS.

121. Mayeaux, *Earthen Walls, Iron Men,* 3–11, 321–323. Among the sixty-nine dead enslaved, the names of four are unknown. Daniel Bogan was killed by wounds received while serving as a bugler with a Confederate artillery unit during an engagement with Union forces.

4. "HEAD HEART AND SOUL OF THE CONFEDERACY"

1. Joiner, *One Damn Blunder,* 3–4.

2. Cotton's critical role is a key feature of the literature on the Red River campaign. See Johnson, *Red River Campaign;* Smith, "For Love of Cotton."

3. Gentry, "White Gold," 229–230; Gilley, *North Louisiana*, 166; Winters, *Civil War in Louisiana*.

4. Gentry, "White Gold," 230; Lebergott, "Through the Blockade," 868.

5. Winters, *Civil War in Louisiana*, 321–322.

6. Gentry, "White Gold," 233.

7. Alfred Flournoy Sr. to Alfred Flournoy Jr., March 16, 1862, Alfred Flournoy Papers, Mss. 628, LLMVC; D. Y. Milling to Jas Milling, January 10, 1863, D. Y. Milling letters, Mss. 3758, LLMVC.

8. Alfred Flournoy Sr. to Alfred Flournoy Jr., March 16, 1862; Nancy and Dustin Willard to Micajah and Nancy Wilkinson, January 20, 1862, Micajah Wilkinson Papers, Mss. 707, LLMVC; Letitia Sibley to John Coleman Sibley, January 12, 1863, John Coleman Sibley Collection, Mss. 4-D-2, CGHRC.

9. J. R. Moore to William Hutchinson, August 8, 1866, William Joseph Hutchinson family and plantation records, collection 75, LSUS.

10. A. J. Rugley & Co. to W. G. Hale, July 8, 1862, Benson Family Papers, Mss. 2424, 2440, LLMVC.

11. Nancy Willard to Micajah and Nancy Wilkinson, May 15, 1862, Micajah Wilkinson Papers, Mss. 707, LLMVC.

12. H. G. Hargis to W. B. Benson, May 15, 1861, Benson Family Papers, Mss. 2424, 2440, LLMVC.

13. Colby, "Negroes Will Bear Fabulous Prices," 440–442, 444–449.

14. Zack Howell to Isabella Whitworth Howell, November 1, 1862, Samford C. Fullilove Papers, collection 256, LSUS. On the purchase of enslaved people during the Civil War, see Glymph, *Out of the House of Bondage;* Colby, "Negroes Will Bear Fabulous Prices."

15. Charles Mathews to W. H. Chase, October 12, 1862, Mathews–Ventress–Lawrason Family Papers, Mss. 4358, LLMVC.

16. Malone, *Sweet Chariot*, 58.

17. Campbell, *Empire for Slavery*, 243. On the eastern seaboard, many slaveholders refugeed their slaves in southwest Georgia.

18. Mears, *And Grace Will Lead Me Home*, 6–7; Sutherland, "Looking for a Home," 344; Moneyhon, *Texas After the Civil War*, 12.

19. Roark, *Masters Without Slaves*, 82. See also Manning, *Troubled Refuge*, 35.

20. David Pierson to William Pierson, January 14, 1864, Kuntz Collection, Mss. 600, LaRC; Elizabeth Ann Scofield letter, December 24, 1865, Mss. 5001, LLMVC; R. L. F. Sibley to John Coleman Sibley, December 11, 1864, John Coleman Sibley Collection, Mss. 4-D-2, CGHRC.

21. Joseph Texada to Margaret Texada, June 24, October 22,1864, Texada Family Papers, Mss. 5119, LLMVC.

22. On the republican origins of the citizen-soldier tradition and the broader conceptions of white and Black citizenship, changed by the Civil War and Union occupation, see Lang, *In the Wake of War*.

23. Sacher, "Very Disagreeable Business," 156–159, "'Twenty-Negro,' or Overseer Law."

24. Rubin, *Shattered Nation*, 47; Jas Milling to D. Y. Milling, January 1, 1863, D. Y. Milling letters, Mss. 3758, LLMVC.

25. Jane Fullilove Mason, "Dear Lizzie, Letters of a Confederate Cavalryman," Fullilove

family binders, binder 1, Fullilove family history, collection 583, LSUS; substitute note, October 1, 1862, William Joseph Hutchinson family and plantation records, collection 75, LSUS.

26. Alfred Flournoy Jr. to Theodosia Flournoy, January 31, 1864, Alfred Flournoy Jr. correspondence, collection 65, LSUS.

27. William Tamplin to Betincia Tamplin, May 3, 1862, William H. Tamplin Papers, Mss. 3015, LLMVC.

28. Sacher, "'Twenty-Negro,' or Overseer Law," 269–273.

29. D. Y. Milling to Jas Milling, January 10, 1863.

30. Sacher, "'Twenty-Negro,' or Overseer Law," 275–276.

31. Foner, *Reconstruction,* 15; Taylor, "Discontent in Confederate Louisiana," 2, 414–415; Sacher, "'Twenty-Negro,' or Overseer Law," 277.

32. John Harris to Becky Harris, February 14, 1863, John A. Harris Civil War letters, collection 209, LSUS.

33. Sacher, "Very Disagreeable Business," 141–169, Sacher, "'Twenty-Negro,' or Overseer Law," 269. See also Sacher, "Our Interest and Destiny Are the Same," 261–286.

34. Domby, *False Cause,* 4–21; Brundage, *Southern Past,* 3–4, 7–8, 10, 22–23, 35.

35. Foner, *Fiery Trial,* 243; Oakes, *Freedom National,* 311, 328. Quote from Boston entrepreneur and Republican activist John Murray Forbes, in Grimsley, *Hard Hand of War,* 123, 133. Emphasis in original.

36. Oakes, *Freedom National,* 346, 391. Emancipated Blacks faced difficulties once they arrived at Union camps, with Black women in military camps subjected to new constraints on selfhood, personal autonomy, and rights. This included determinations around the legitimacy of enslaved marriages and the withholding of benefits. See Lang, *In the Wake of War,* 43–50, 130–137; McCurry, *Women's War,* 91–103; Hunter, *Bound in Wedlock,* 151–152, 168–170, 173, 200; Manning, *Troubled Refuge,* 34.

37. Quigley, *Shifting Grounds,* 213. See also Foner, *Second Founding;* Domby, *False Cause,* 28, 35; Lang, *In the Wake of War.*

38. Throughout the antebellum period and into the Civil War period, enslaved people received information through informal networks of communication. This was likely a way that Red River Blacks gathered information, too, but no archival proof has surfaced of its usage in this region during the antebellum or Civil War periods.

39. Taylor, *Louisiana Reconstructed,* 4–5, 38–40. Occupied Louisiana reached northward to Baton Rouge and extended between Bayou Lafource and Bayou Teche.

40. Escott, *"What Shall We Do with the Negro?,"* 99.

41. John Sibley to E. P. Ellis, March 10, 1863, Morris–Sibley Family Papers, Mss. 562, LLMVC.

42. Letter to "Dear Sir," February 18, 1863, Layssard Family Papers, Mss. 2875, LLMVC.

43. Similar behavior patterns occurred in southwest Georgia. See O'Donovan, *Becoming Free in the Cotton South,* 59–110.

44. Oscare Lauve to Gustave Lauve, June 26, 1863, Gustave Lauve letter, Mss. 893, LLMVC; William Sharp to Joseph Pownall, August 16, 1870, William A. Sharp letters, Mss. 4302, LLMVC.

45. J. R. Mainor to Thomas Overton Moore, July 7, 1864, Thomas O. Moore Papers, Mss. 305, 893, 1094, LLMVC.

46. John Ransdell to Thomas Overton Moore, May 24, 1863, John H. Ransdell Papers, Mss. 959, LLMVC. Emphasis in original. Moore also owned Lodi and Mooreland plantations.

47. William Chase to Harriet Mathews, October 5, 1864, Mathews–Ventress–Lawrason Family Papers, Mss. 4358, LLMVC.

48. John Ransdell to Thomas Overton Moore, May 24, May 26, 1863, John H. Ransdell Papers, Mss. 959, LLMVC; John Ransdell to Thomas Overton Moore, May 31, 1863, Thomas O. Moore Papers, Mss. 305, 893, 1094, LLMVC.

49. John Ransdell to Thomas Overton Moore, May 24, 1863. For accounts of similar behavior and of the enslaved in Georgia claiming items from the big house as Union troops approached, see Young, "Ideology and Death"; Hunter, To 'Joy My Freedom; Rable, Civil Wars.

50. Polly Mason oral interview, Mss. 4700.0041, LLMVC. On Black recruitment and positioning in the U.S. Army, see Lang, In the Wake of War; Hunter, Bound in Wedlock; Oakes, Freedom National.

51. Margaret Texada, "Reminiscences of the Civil War," Texada Family Papers, Mss. 5119, LLMVC.

52. John Ransdell to Thomas Overton Moore, May 24, May 31, June 6, 1863, John H. Ransdell Papers, Mss. 959, LLMVC. A June 12 letter noted that Henry, the blacksmith at Emfield, and Clem from Moorefield had returned, but when they were questioned about the whereabouts of Moore's other enslaved people, they "pretended as if they had not seen any of the rest of your negroes at all." Emphasis in original.

53. William Sharp to Joseph Pownall, August 16, 1870.

54. John Ransdell to Thomas Overton Moore, May 26, May 31, 1863, John H. Ransdell Papers, Mss. 959, LLMVC. In his May 31 letter, Ransdell also relayed news of the camps set up around Simsport. He wrote "there were scattered about more negro "fixings" than you ever saw in your life." Emphasis in original.

55. John Ransdell to Thomas Overton Moore, May 26, June 3, 1863, John H. Ransdell Papers, Mss. 959, LLMVC. Emphasis in original.

56. Jimerson, Private Civil War, 2-3.

57. John Ransdell to Thomas Overton Moore, June 6, 1863, John H. Ransdell Papers, Mss. 959, LLMVC.

58. Foner, Fiery Trial, 249-250; Litwack, Been in the Storm So Long, 52-79; Manning, Troubled Refuge, introduction and chapter 1. Two new titles demonstrate the complications and challenges experienced by Black Union soldiers in garrisons and by Black women within Union lines or connected to Black male soldiers. See Lang, In the Wake of War; Hunter, Bound in Wedlock.

59. Charles Boothby to "Respected Father," January 15, 1863, Charles W. Boothby Papers, Mss. 4847, LLMVC. For discussion of white Northern soldiers' feelings about Black equality and enlistment, see Manning, What This Cruel War Was Over; Lang, In the Wake of War.

60. April 26, April 30, April 31, 1864, entries, Robert A. Tyson diary, Mss. 1693, LLMVC. For discussion of contrabands, see Manning, Troubled Refuge; Gerteis, From Contraband to Freedman; Fabrikant, "Emancipation and the Proclamation," 313-343; Masur, "A Rare Phenomenon of Philological Vegetation," 1050-1084; Voegeli, "A Rejected Alternative," 765-790.

61. June 5, 1864, entry, Robert A. Tyson diary, Mss. 1693, LLMVC. On re-enslavement, see Oakes, Freedom National, 405.

62. Joseph Texada to Margaret Texada, September 5, 1864, Texada Family Papers, Mss. 5119, LLMVC. On honor, see Wyatt-Brown, Southern Honor; Gorn, "Gouge and Bite"; Greenberg, "The Nose, the Lie, and the Duel," 57-74; Clark, "Sacred Rights of the Weak," 463-493.

63. Nancy Willard to Micajah and Mary Wilkinson, May 28, 1861, Micajah Wilkinson Papers, Mss. 707, LLMVC.

64. Nancy Willard to Micajah and Mary Wilkinson, May 15, 1862, Micajah Wilkinson Papers, Mss. 707, LLMVC. See also Phillips, *Diehard Rebels,* 52–54, 60.

65. Forsyth, *Red River Campaign,* 114.

66. Joseph Texada to Margaret Texada, June 24, 1864.

67. Phillips, *Diehard Rebels,* 76.

68. For discussions of Confederate States of America aid requests, see Roark, *Masters Without Slaves;* McCurry, *Confederate Reckoning;* Downs, *Declarations of Dependency.*

69. Henry Allen to J. C. Wise, April 29, 1864, James Calvert Wise Papers, Mss. 3239, LLMVC.

70. C. E. Hosea to Henry Allen, April 10, 1865, James Calvert Wise Papers, Mss. 3239, LLMVC.

71. J. H. Sullivan and Lewis Texada to Henry Allen, January 20, 1865, James Calvert Wise Papers, Mss. 3239, LLMVC.

72. Robert Hyman to James Calvert Wise, May 21, 1864, K. M. Clark to James Calvert Wise, April 17, 1865, James Calvert Wise Papers, Mss. 3239, LLMVC.

73. George Guess to Sarah Cocksell, June 30, 1864, George W. Guess Papers, Mss. 793, LLMVC. Emphasis in original.

74. Executive Office, Shreveport, to Henry Marshall, May 3, 1864, Marshall–Furman Family Papers, Mss. 4042, 2740, LLMVC.

75. Forsyth, *Red River Campaign,* 46; Brooksher, *War Along the Bayous,* 7; Joiner, *One Damn Blunder,* 8.

76. Joiner, *One Damn Blunder,* 3, 15. Grand Ecore, about sixty miles downstream as the crow flies, was the only other high ground.

77. Account of the Red River Expedition, Mss. 3422, LLMVC.

78. John C. Sibley to Elizabeth Sibley, March 18, 1864, John Coleman Sibley Collection, Mss. 4-D-2, CGHRC; Joiner, *One Damn Blunder,* 3–4, 62.

79. Kenneth Noe states that weather had a significant effect (33 to 40 percent) in determining the outcome of the Red River campaign. Noe, "Fateful Lightning."

80. Brooksher, *War Along the Bayous,* 61; Robertson, *Red River Campaign and Its Toll,* 93; Smith, *Tinclads in the Civil War,* 8.

81. For an account from one of the region's soldiers, see John Coleman Sibley diary, March 23, 1864, entry, John Coleman Sibley Collection, Mss. 4-D-2, CGHRC.

82. Forsyth, *Red River Campaign,* 59; Smith, *Tinclads in the Civil War,* 194, 202; Trudeau, "Red River Fiasco." On Alexandria's occupation and destruction of property, see Dollar, "Red River Campaign," 411–432.

83. Smith, *Tinclads in the Civil War,* 192, 203–209; Forsyth, *Red River Campaign,* 4, 83.

84. Account of the Red River Expedition, Mss. 3422, LLMVC.

85. Charles Dwight to James Supman Jr., April 3, 1864, Alfred Lippman collection of Civil War letters, collection 993, LaRC.

86. Joseph Texada to Margaret Texada, April 23, 1864, Texada Family Papers, Mss. 5119, LLMVC.

87. April 8, April 9, 1864, entries, diary of N. S. Allen, Nathaniel Allen Family Papers, collection 144, LSUS.

88. J. D. Garland to "My dear parents," April 12, 1864, J. Fair Hardin Collection, Mss. 1014, LLMVC.

89. John Moncure to "My dear wife," April 12, 1864, J. Fair Hardin Collection, Mss. 1014, LLMVC.

90. Forsyth, *Red River Campaign,* 17. Forsyth maintains that had Taylor been given the forces he requested, he could have made a strong move to prevent the naval fleet's escape in May.

91. Smith, *Tinclads in the Civil War,* 203-208; Trudeau, "Red River Fiasco."

92. Charles Boothby to George Boothby, May 21, 1864, Charles W. Boothby Papers, Mss. 4847, LLMVC; John Carson Civil War diary, John H. Carson Papers, Mss. 1960, LLMVC.

93. Thomas Allan to Henry Marston, April 26, 1864, Henry Marston and Family Papers, Mss. 624, LLMVC. Most historians agree on the potential of the campaign to change the course of the war, but ultimately it only postponed its end.

94. "Annual Message of Governor Henry Watkins Allen, to the Legislature of the State of Louisiana, January 1865," Documenting the American South, https://docsouth.unc.edu/imls /lagov/allen.html.

95. W. F. Murray to Mrs. Thomas Morris, April 30, 1865, Morris–Sibley Family Papers, Mss. 562, LLMVC.

96. Damico, "Confederate Soldiers Take Matters into Their Own Hands," 194–197. See also Winters, *Civil War in Louisiana;* Peyton, "The Civil War Began and Ended in North Louisiana," 75–77.

97. Damico, "Confederate Soldiers Take Matters into Their Own Hands," 196. Davis was captured on May 10, 1865, by Union cavalry in Georgia.

98. David Pierson to William Pierson, May 9, 1865, Kuntz Collection, Mss. 600, LaRC.

99. John T. Sibley to E. P. Ellis, March 10, 1863, Morris–Sibley Family Papers, Mss. 562, LLMVC.

100. James Calvert Wise to Thomas Moore, May 8, 1865, Thomas O. Moore Papers, Mss. 305, 893, 1094, LLMVC.

101. For a nuanced discussion of surrender and its meaning for those who experienced it, see Varon, *Appomattox.*

102. Peyton, "The Civil War Began and Ended in North Louisiana," 76; Damico, "Confederate Soldiers Take Matters into Their Own Hands," 201–204.

103. May 12, 1865, entry, diary of Mary Elizabeth Rives, collection 40, LSUS.

5. "OUR NEGROES ARE GETTING TOO INDEPENDENT TO WORK"

1. John Moncure to "My Dear Wife," January 6, 1870, J. Fair Hardin Collection, Mss. 1040, LLMVC; Manning, *Troubled Refuge,* 13–15; Emberton, *Beyond Redemption,* 18–24; Scott, "Discerning a Dignitary Offense," 520–522, 526, 535–538.

2. Follett, "Legacies of Enslavement," 53–54; Emberton, *Beyond Redemption,* 9; Dailey, *Before Jim Crow,* 13, 15–16.

3. Phillips, "Rebels in War and Peace," 156, 166.

4. Painter, *Exodusters,* 84.

5. On the importance of not confusing emancipation with giving freedom meaning, and not mistaking surrender for the end of racial subjugation, see O'Donovan, *Becoming Free in the*

Cotton South; Hahn, *Nation Under Our Feet;* Fitzgerald, *Urban Emancipation;* Schwalm, *Hard Fight for We;* Manning, *Troubled Refuge;* Downs, *After Appomattox;* Brundage, *Southern Past.*

6. Downs, *After Appomattox,* 2–11; Lang, *In the Wake of War,* 8–10, 42–56, 183; Foner, *Second Founding,* xx–xxvii, 16–20, 50–54; Williard, "Criminal Amnesty and Reconstruction," 109–113, 123–124.

7. Downs, *After Appomattox,* 36; Rubin, *Shattered Nation,* 141–145; Dailey, *Before Jim Crow,* 5–8.

8. Dailey, *Before Jim Crow,* 30–40; Carter, *When the War Was Over,* 3–4, 28; Sibler, *Romance of Reunion.*

9. Foner, *Reconstruction,* 182, 187–195. See also McKitrick, *Andrew Johnson and Reconstruction.* For discussions of ex-planters and the economic loss of enslaved people, see Ransom and Sutch, "Impact of the Civil War"; Roark, *Masters Without Slaves,* especially chapters 4 and 5; Wright and Kunreuther, "Cotton, Corn and Risk"; Fite, "Southern Agriculture Since the Civil War"; Woodman, "Post–Civil War Southern Agriculture and the Law"; Goldin and Lewis, "Economic Cost of the American Civil War."

10. For similar behavior in South Carolina, see Zuczek, *State of Rebellion,* 5, 17, 48–53.

11. On Confederates in exile, see Guterl, *American Mediterranean;* Rubin, *Shattered Nation;* Winters, *Civil War in Louisiana;* Sutherland, "Looking for a Home"; Roark, *Masters Without Slaves,* 124–131.

12. "Dear Lizzie, Letters of a Confederate Cavalryman," Fullilove family binders, binder 1, Fullilove family history, collection 583, LSUS.

13. Henry Allen to Lewis Texada, January 10, 1866, Lewis Texada and Family Papers, Mss. 2985, LLMVC.

14. Henry Allen to "My Dear Texada," Texada Family Papers, Mss. 5119, LLMVC; Henry Allen to "My Dear Davis," October 30, 1865, Henry Watkins Allen letters, M 38, LaRC; Bartholomew Egan to Thomas Moore, June 25, 1866, Thomas O. Moore Papers, Mss. 305, 893, 1094, LLMVC.

15. Bartholomew Egan to Thomas Moore, May 25, 1866, Thomas O. Moore Papers, Mss. 305, 893, 1094, LLMVC. Emphasis in original.

16. Henry Hyams to Thomas Moore, September 10, 1865, Mss. 305, 893, 1094, LLMVC. Emphasis in original.

17. Oath of allegiance, June 18, 1867, Marshall–Furman Family Papers, Mss. 2740, 4042, LLMVC; oath of allegiance, January 15, 1867, Thomas O. Moore Papers, Mss. 305, 893, 1094, LLMVC.

18. Oath of allegiance, October 9, 1868, William Thatcher Papers, Mss. 893, LLMVC. Presidential Reconstruction lasted from 1865 to 1867 and saw the introduction of Black Codes, states enacting harsh apprenticeship laws, and the passage of sweeping vagrancy and labor contract laws. Hallmarks of this period were laws that focused on controlling Black labor and limited their options beyond plantation toil. Radical Reconstruction followed, lasting from 1867 to 1877, and embraced wartime expansion of federal authority. Undergirded by a civic ideology centered on a definition of American citizenship in which citizens enjoyed equal civil and political rights, the Radical Republicans passed the Civil Rights Act of 1866. Throughout Radical Reconstruction, as later chapters will show, traditional assumptions that law enforcement primarily lay with the states remained, but latent federal presence would be triggered by discriminatory state

laws. On oath-taking as an outward expression of both loyalty and patriotism for Blacks but a blurred line between power and allegiance for former Confederates, see Emberton, "Reconstructing Loyalty."

19. Freedmen labor contracts, July 11, 1865, William Hutchinson family and plantation records, Mss. 75, LSUS.

20. Thomas Powell to Mary Bosley, May 6, 1873, Hubbard S. Bosley Papers, Mss. 963, LLMVC.

21. Follett, *Slavery's Ghost,* 75. Desiring the cheapest yet hardest-working laborers, former slaveholders ran through a battery of other groups deemed appropriate. See Follett, *Slavery's Ghost;* Jung, *Coolies and Cane;* Whayne, *Shadows over Sunnyside.*

22. On emancipation in Texas, see Smallwood, *Time of Hope, Time of Despair.* Black communities in Texas have celebrated Juneteeth, sometimes known as Emancipation Day, since June 19, 1865, and they transplanted it to other regions during the Great Migration. The day, which celebrates freedom and the courage exhibited by Blacks in seizing that freedom, was made a federal holiday in the United States in 2021.

23. Ransom and Sutch, "Impact of the Civil War," 14.

24. Highsmith, "Some Aspects of Reconstruction in the Heart of Louisiana," 474–475.

25. J. R. Moore to William Hutchinson, August 8, 1866, M. W. Philips to William Hutchinson, November 12, 1870, William Hutchinson family and plantation records, collection 75, LSUS; William Sprout to Messr. Chaplin & Son, July 21, 1871, Chaplin, Breazeale, and Chaplin Papers, Mss. 952, 967, 1028, LLMVC.

26. O'Donovan, Becoming Free in the Cotton South, 126.

27. Phil Key to Penelope Mathews, November 24, 1865, Mathews–Ventress–Lawrason Family Papers, Mss. 4358, LLMVC.

28. January 23, 1866, entry, 1866 diary, Henry Marston and Family Papers, Mss. 624, LLMVC.

29. June 28, October 9, November 1, 1865, entries, diary of Mary Elizabeth Rives, collection 40, LSUS.

30. Phil Key to Penelope Mathews, November 24, 1865; Taylor, *Louisiana Reconstructed,* 90–91. Alabama passed a law prohibiting the enticement of labor, aimed at precisely this issue. The law was "intended to reduce conflict within the planter class" while preventing Mississippi agents from poaching Alabama Blacks. When this was unsuccessful, Alabama whites turned to the Ku Klux Klan to control plantation organization. See Wiener, *Social Origins of the New South,* 60–61.

31. Thomas Moore to James Calvert Wise, December 31, 1865, James Calvert Wise Papers, Mss. 3239, LLMVC.

32. Phil Key to Penelope Mathews, November 24, 1865, Thomas Moore to James Calvert Wise, December 31, 1865, James Calvert Wise Papers, Mss. 3239, LLMVC.

33. Phil Key to Penelope Mathews, December 31, 1865, Mathews–Ventress–Lawrason Family Papers, Mss. 4358, LLMVC. Emphasis in original. Thomas Powell to "Dear Cousin Mary," February 26, 1873, Hubbard S. Bosley Papers, Mss. 963, LLMVC.

34. William Sharp to Joseph Pownall, August 16, 1870, William A. Sharp letters, Mss. 4302, LLMVC.

35. William Sharp to Joseph Pownall, August 16, 1870. On postwar regional flooding, see

Highsmith, "Some Aspects of Reconstruction in the Heart of Louisiana"; Smith, "Freedmen's Bureau in Shreveport."

36. Henry Marston diary, April 22, May 20, 1866, June 22 (first quote), June 27, 1867 (second quote), entries, Henry Marston and Family Papers, Mss. 624, LLMVC.

37. Phil Key to Penelope Mathews, June 29, 1866, Mathews–Ventress–Lawrason Family Papers, Mss. 4358, LLMVC.

38. Henry Marston diary, September 3, 1867, entry, Henry Marston and Family Papers, Mss. 624, LLMVC; Wayne, *Reshaping of Plantation Society,* 63–65. See also Roark, *Masters Without Slaves;* Smith, "Freedmen's Bureau in Shreveport"; White, *Freedmen's Bureau in Louisiana.*

39. Thomas Moore to James Calvert Wise, May 29, 1866, James Calvert Wise Papers, Mss. 3239, LLMVC.

40. Bartholomew Egan to "My Dear Gov.," June 25, 1866; Thomas Moore to Mrs. P. M. Butler, July 25, 1868, Ezra Adams Collection, account 314, CGHRC.

41. Phil Key to Penelope Mathews, April 7, May 9, June 29, September 23, 1866, Mathews–Ventress–Lawrason Family Papers, Mss. 4358, LLMVC.

42. 1867 parish police minutes, Bossier Parish, reel 50: Bienville and Bossier, WPA Collection, Historical Records Survey Transcriptions of Louisiana Police Jury Records, Mss. 2984, LLMVC; Smith, "Freedmen's Bureau in Shreveport," 438, 446. On issues of planter solvency, see Wayne, *Reshaping of Plantation Society,* 76–88.

43. White, *Freedmen's Bureau in Louisiana,* 124–126. The 1867 epidemic is believed to have begun in Jamaica. Yellow fever epidemics usually commenced in July or August and continued as late as December; see Carrigan, "Impact of Epidemic Yellow Fever." For a twentieth-century parallel, see Woodruff, *American Congo.*

44. Phil Key to Penelope Mathews, January 6, March 14, April 7, 1866, Mathews–Ventress–Lawrason Family Papers, Mss. 4358, LLMVC; Follett, *Slavery's Ghost,* 50–52. See also Carter, *When the War Was Over,* 99–102.

45. I. Taylor to Mrs. Buard, February 27, March 21, 1866, P. E. Cloutier Collection 1-B-1, CGHRC. Emphasis in original.

46. For similar labor circumstances during the earliest days of Reconstruction, see Zuczek, *State of Rebellion;* Fitzgerald, *Reconstruction in Alabama;* O'Donovan, *Becoming Free in the Cotton South.*

47. See Wiener, *Social Origins of the New South,* 35–37; West, "A General Remodeling of Every Thing."

48. White, *Freedmen's Bureau in Louisiana,* 107–108.

49. Fitzgerald, *Splendid Failure,* 30.

50. Freedmen labor contracts, July 11, 1865, William Hutchinson Family and Plantation Records, Mss. 75, LSUS.

51. Freedmen labor contracts, January 1867, Hubbard S. Bosley Papers, Mss. 963, LLMVC.

52. Phil Key to Penelope Mathews, January 6, 1866, Mathews–Ventress–Lawrason Family Papers, Mss. 4358, LLMVC.

53. Payroll of laborers, January 8, 1865, Marcelin Tauzin and Family Papers, Mss. 912, LLMVC.

54. Jas Sibley to "Dear Madam," March 10, 1866, Charles L. Mathews and Family Papers, Mss. 910, LLMVC.

55. There is a rich literature that discusses Black women's embrace of choice with regard

to their labor across the South. Many of these works also discuss the anger and violence with which these acts of personal autonomy and selfhood were met throughout Reconstruction. For some further reading, see Hunter, *Bound in Wedlock* and *To 'Joy My Freedom;* Rosen, *Terror in the Heart of Freedom;* Stanley, *From Bondage to Contract;* O'Donovan, *Becoming Free in the Cotton South;* Carter, *When the War Was Over.*

56. Antony Babcock labor contract, July 26, 1865, Chaplin, Breazeale, and Chaplin Papers, Mss. 952, 967, 1028, LLMVC.

57. Phil Key to Penelope Mathews, November 16, November 24, 1865, Mathews-Ventress-Lawrason Family Papers, Mss. 4358, LLMVC.

58. Follett, *Slavery's Ghost,* 50-52.

59. Wayne, *Reshaping of Plantation Society,* 41; Taylor, *Louisiana Reconstructed,* 93-94, 98-103. See also Roark, *Masters Without Slaves,* chapters 4 and 5.

60. Rable, *But There Was No Peace,* 27.

61. See Cohen, *At Freedom's Edge,* especially chapters 1 and 2; Stanley, *From Bondage to Contract,* 122-133.

62. Illingworth, "Erroneous and Incongruous Notions of Liberty," 40. On the Black Codes, see Foner, *Reconstruction;* Litwack, *Been in the Storm So Long;* Wayne, *Reshaping of Plantation Society;* Wiener, *Social Origins of the New South;* Stanley, *From Bondage to Contract;* Carter, *When the War Was Over.*

63. Rodrigue, *Reconstruction in the Cane Fields,* 67.

64. Englesman, "Freedmen's Bureau in Louisiana," 183, 185.

65. Henry Adams testimony from Senate Report 693, 46th Congress, 2nd session, in Sterling, *The Trouble They Seen:* 7-8. See also Rable, *But There Was No Peace,* 27.

66. Whites conflated Black movement and self-determination with vagrancy, which also became a trigger for violence in other Southern areas. For a close examination of postwar migration to Memphis and correlated violent massacre, with an emphasis on gendered violence, see Rosen, *Terror in the Heart of Freedom.* Additionally, on synergy between Black movement, Black emancipation, and white vigilante violence in New Orleans, see Hogue, *Uncivil War;* Nystrom, *New Orleans After the Civil War.*

67. Englesman, "Freedmen's Bureau in Louisiana," 157-164, 174-191.

68. Gerteis, *From Contraband to Freedman;* Smith, "Freedmen's Bureau in Shreveport," 436, 438; White, *Freedmen's Bureau in Louisiana,* 107; Wiener, *Social Origins of the New South,* 52.

69. Smith, "Freedmen's Bureau in Shreveport," 440. On Red River captains and Black travelers, see Scott, "Discerning a Dignitary Offense," 542-550.

70. O'Donovan, *Becoming Free in the Cotton South,* 227.

71. Henry Adams testimony, from Senate Report 693, 46th Congress, 2nd session, in Sterling, *The Trouble They Seen,* 8. For similar declarations from Franklin Parish, see Pfeifer, "Origins of Postbellum Lynching," 194-195. On Freedmen's Bureau agents agreeing with whipping, see Emberton, *Beyond Redemption,* 6.

72. Vandal, "Bloody Caddo," 374, 376. Vandal uses data sets pulled from cases with clear information, including victim's name, date, place, and type of violence. As such, though many government reports and witnesses list three hundred freedpeople killed in Caddo in 1868, Vandal retained only the 185 cases adhering to his data requirement. For additional discussion, see Vandal, *Rethinking Southern Violence,* chapter 1.

73. Sterling, *The Trouble They Seen,* 7-8. See also Rable, *But There Was No Peace,* 27.

74. Kantrowitz, "One Man's Mob Is Another Man's Militia," 67. The region's few white Republicans offered limited support against the violent onslaught and were themselves intimidated and subjected to violence, most notably at the Coushatta Massacre.

75. Blum, *Reforging the White Republic,* 6. See also Hogue, *Uncivil War.*

76. Burnard, *Planters, Merchants, and Slaves,* 6, 35–37, 48, 54.

77. Sterling, *The Trouble They Seen,* 437. See also Emberton, *Beyond Redemption,* 9, 20, 46, 151–155.

78. For discussion on the power of freedpeople's testimony, see Williams, *They Left Great Marks on Me,* 3–9.

79. United States War Department, *Use of the Army,* 410–415.

80. Ibid., 418. Tabitha and Jas Fullilove's family tree is found in Samford C. Fullilove Papers, collection 256, LSUS.

81. United States War Department, *Use of the Army,* 431.

82. Ibid., 416–445.

83. Ibid., 409–416. For discussion of the emotional and sensory impact of pain, violence, lynching, and brutality, see Scarry, *The Body in Pain;* Wood, *Lynching and Spectacle;* Hartman, *Scenes of Subjection.*

84. Vandal, "Bloody Caddo," footnote 34. Chapter 6 will examine the Shady Grove Massacre in depth.

85. Agent Fulmor to Major Hutchins, October 20, 1868, Bureau of Refugees, Freedmen and Abandoned Lands, film 21, reel 1, collection 77, LSUS.

86. Sterling, *The Trouble They Seen,* 274.

87. United States War Department, *Use of the Army,* 190–191. On sharecroppers' legal status, see Fitzgerald, *Splendid Failure,* 157.

88. United States War Department, *Use of the Army,* 193, 280, 335. On the creation of a voluntary state militia and the decline of military personnel in the Red River region, see Hogue, *Uncivil War,* 68–74.

89. United States War Department, *Use of the Army,* 165.

90. Ibid., 167, 204.

91. Ibid., 409–416; *The Trouble They Seen,* 271–274. For additional examples of discrepancies in pay relative to the amount cropped, see Marcelin Tauzin and Family Papers, Mss. 912, LLMVC.

92. United States War Department, *Use of the Army,* 415.

93. Ibid., 422, 431, 441. For discussion of naming practices, see chapter 2.

94. For countless examples, see United States War Department, *Use of the Army,* 416–427, 441–450.

95. Williams, *They Left Great Marks on Me,* 18.

6. "THE NEGRO QUESTION AS SETTLED IN LOUISIANA FOREVER"

1. Hogue, *Uncivil War,* 2. For close and methodical analysis of homicídes in Reconstruction era Louisiana, see Vandal, *Rethinking Southern Violence,* especially chapter 2.

2. Emberton, *Beyond Redemption,* 155. See also Proctor, "From the cradle to the grave"; Feimster, *Southern Horrors;* Rosen, *Terror in the Heart of Freedom;* Tolnoy and Beck, *Festival*

of Violence; Pfeifer, *Rough Justice;* Carrigan, *Making of a Lynching Culture;* Ash, *Massacre in Memphis;* Hogue, *Uncivil War.*

3. C. J. Voligney to John Moncure, June 5, 1866, July 5, 1867, J. Fair Hardin Collection, Mss. 1014, LLMVC.

4. On coalition building, grassroots activism and campaigning, Union Leagues, and other forms of Black political involvement in other parts of the south, see Dailey, *Before Jim Crow;* Feimster, *Southern Horrors;* Fitzgerald, *Reconstruction in Alabama;* O'Donovan, *Becoming Free in the Cotton South;* Behrend, *Reconstructing Democracy;* Nystrom, *New Orleans After the Civil War.*

5. Emberton, *Beyond Redemption,* 9; Kantrowitz, *Ben Tillman and the Reconstruction of White Supremacy,* 4.

6. Burnard, *Planters, Merchants, and Slaves,* 6, 35–37, 48, 54. See also Rosen, *Terror in the Heart of Freedom;* Carrigan, *Making of a Lynching Culture,* 46–49, 87–88, 93–103. On the significance of violence to shaping citizenship in the South, along with the double-edged legacy of military service for determining Blacks' worthiness for citizenship, see Emberton, *Beyond Redemption;* Lang, *In the Wake of War;* Downs, *After Appomattox.*

7. On coalition building and fluidity in southern politics, see Dailey, *Before Jim Crow.* Dailey's eloquent assertions about cross-racial and party alliances in Virginia, along with the rockier path of racial oppression she outlines, is markedly different from political and racial trajectories in northwest Louisiana.

8. Bartholomew Egan to Thomas Overton Moore, August 17, 1866, Thomas O. Moore Papers, Mss. 305, 893, 1094, LLMVC.

9. Foner, *Second Founding,* 128–150. See also Brandwein, *Rethinking the Judicial Settlement of Reconstruction;* Goldstone, *Inherently Unequal.* The legislative legacies of regional massacres will be discussed in more detail later in this chapter.

10. United States War Department, *Use of the Army,* 382; Fairclough, *Revolution That Failed,* 74.

11. The federal government passed three Enforcement Acts aimed at protecting civil and political rights and mitigating paramilitary violence. President Grant used the third act, known as the Ku Klux Klan Act, in 1871 in South Carolina, to combat racial violence. The literature on this is extensive, including Parsons, *Ku-Klux;* Trelease, *White Terror;* Zuczek, *State of Rebellion;* Baker, *This Mob Will Surely Take My Life;* Brundage, *Under Sentence of Death.*

12. Fanny Marshall to Sarah Marshall, May 5, 1868, Josephine Chatham Means Collection, collection 335, LSUS.

13. James Calvert Wise to "Gentlemen," November 11, 1868, William Randolph to James Calvert Wise, August 1868, James Calvert Wise Papers, Mss. 3239, LLMVC.

14. Stephen Cuny to Benjamin Cuny, October 4, 1868, Cuny (Benjamin Philip) Family Papers, Mss. 4246, LLMVC; Mrs. P. M. Butler to Thomas O. Moore, July 25, 1868, Ezra Adams Collection, account 314, CGHRC. Descriptions of violence and threats of death by fire were popular regionally.

15. Behrend, *Reconstructing Democracy,* 78–109; Fitzgerald, *Reconstruction in Alabama,* 168–174.

16. On the significance of Black military service in establishing a hold on citizenship and political identity in other parts of the South, which contrasts with the Red River region, see Emberton, *Beyond Redemption,* "Only Murder Makes Men," "Reconstructing Loyalty"; Hunter,

Bound in Wedlock; Lang, *In the Wake of War;* Fitzgerald, *Reconstruction in Alabama;* Proctor, "From the cradle to the grave."

17. Hogue, *Uncivil War,* 4, 11–12, 49–52, 125; United States War Department, *Use of the Army,* 383. See also Parsons, "Klan Skepticism and Denial in Reconstruction-Era Public Discourse."

18. Pfeifer, "Origins of Postbellum Lynching," 189–201; Hogue, "The 1873 Battle of Colfax," 6; Parsons, *Ku-Klux,* 1–6.

19. United States War Department, *Use of the Army,* 81. Ward, *Hanging Bridge,* details a similar unification of whites in Shubuta, Mississippi, around the use of racial terrorism and violent white supremacy to suppress Black mobility and political engagement throughout the twentieth century.

20. United States War Department, *Use of the Army,* 375–376. Emphasis in original. For additional pro-white newspaper coverage, see also 194, 385–389.

21. Emberton, *Beyond Redemption,* 155; D. E. Hayes to "Friend Texada," May 21, 1866, Texada Family Papers, Mss. 5119, LLMVC. Louisiana would not be readmitted to the Union until 1868.

22. Thomas Powell to "Dear Cousin Mary," May 6, 1873, Hubbard S. Bosley Papers, Mss. 963, LLMVC. Emphasis in original.

23. B. Haines to James Calvert Wise, September 30, 1871, James Calvert Wise Papers, Mss. 3239, LLMVC. Emphasis in original.

24. Thomas Powell to "Dear Cousin Mary," July 2, 1872, Hubbard S. Bosley Papers, Mss. 963, LLMVC. On collective white-on-Black violence and the Klan, see Parsons, *Ku-Klux,* 1–14, 28–31, 63–68. See also Pfeifer, *Rough Justice;* Baker, *This Mob Will Surely Take My Life;* Carrigan, *Making of a Lynching Culture.*

25. Emberton, *Beyond Redemption,* 173–174; United States War Department, *Use of the Army,* 381. On the performative aspects of the Klan and vigilantes, see Parsons, *Ku-Klux,* "Midnight Rangers."

26. United States War Department, *Use of the Army,* 170, 339.

27. Kantrowitz, "One Man's Mob," 79.

28. United States War Department, *Use of the Army,* 159–160.

29. Ibid., 251, 276.

30. Ibid., 359, 420. *Use of the Army* is bursting with examples of this brutality.

31. Ibid., 335, 360. On hopes of Ulysses S. Grant carrying Louisiana, and Black fidelity to Grant, see Charles Boothby to "My Dear Mother," May 18, 1872, Charles W. Boothby Papers, Mss. 4847, LLMVC.

32. United States War Department, *Use of the Army,* 370.

33. United States War Department, *Use of the Army,* 251, 283, 361. On Eli Allen, who was killed the same day as the Coushatta Massacre, see Tunnell, *Edge of the Sword,* 206.

34. Tunnell, *Edge of the Sword,* 129.

35. United States War Department, *Use of the Army,* 379–380. For details on the bloody tactics and methods that made voting nearly impossible for Republicans, see 380–382. On violence and crime in northwest Louisiana, see Vandal, *Rethinking Southern Violence.* On violence fueled by political engagement, see Rosen, *Terror in the Heart of Freedom;* Rable, *But There Was No Peace,* Williamson, *Rage for Order;* Tunnell, *Crucible of Reconstruction;* Hogue, *Uncivil War;*

Nystrom, *New Orleans After the Civil War;* Ash, *Massacre in Memphis;* Fitzgerald, *Reconstruction in Alabama;* Behrend, *Reconstructing Democracy.*

36. For background on the region's most famous carpetbagger, Marshall Harvey Twitchell, who is discussed in chapter 7, see Tunnell, *Edge of the Sword.*

37. Fairclough, *Revolution that Failed,* 111. On the Knights of the White Camelia, see Webb, "Organization and Activities," 1-5.

38. Elcey Breda to Ernest Breda, April 11, 1873, J. P. Breda Family Papers, Mss. 953, 966, 1021, LLMVC; Fairclough, *Revolution that Failed,* 285. For elegant discussions of challenges faced by Unionists in the postwar South, see Fitzgerald, *Reconstruction in Alabama;* Astor, *Rebels on the Border.*

39. Fairclough, *Revolution that Failed,* 173.

40. United States War Department, *Use of the Army,* 362.

41. On the trauma and suffering in Black testimony, see Williams, "The Wounds That Cried Out." See also Hartman, *Scenes of Subjection.*

42. Rosen, *Terror in the Heart of Freedom,* 4. In addition to Rosen's erudite examination of freedpeople's testimony, see Williams, *They Left Great Marks on Me;* Emberton, *Beyond Redemption;* Proctor, "From the cradle to the grave"; Williams, "Wounds That Cried Out."

43. Williamson, *A Rage for Order,* 153-154; Tunnell, *Crucible of Reconstruction,* 153-154, 175. See also Baker, *This Mob Will Surely Take My Life,* 10-19.

44. United States War Department, *Use of the Army,* 415.

45. Tunnell, *Edge of the Sword,* 226; United States War Department, *Use of the Army,* 366.

46. United States War Department, *Use of the Army,* 361.

47. Ibid., 343-344. See also Vandal, "Policy of Violence."

48. United States War Department, *Use of the Army,* 369. On the shared white commitment to violence, see Pfeifer, *Rough Justice,* 9-14, 22, 50, 66-69; Carrigan, *Making of a Lynching Culture.*

49. Bradley Proctor, "A General State of Terror: A Survey of Klan Violence in the Carolinas During Reconstruction," a presentation at the Organization of American Historians Annual Meeting 2017, New Orleans, Louisiana, April 6-9, 2017. See also Baker, *This Mob Will Surely Take My Life,* 40; Zuczek, *State of Rebellion,* 48, 130; Taylor, *Louisiana Reconstructed,* 158.

50. Fairclough, *Revolution that Failed,* 120.

51. United States War Department, *Use of the Army,* 280, 366-367; Fairclough, *Revolution that Failed,* 242.

52. United States War Department, *Use of the Army,* 359, 380.

53. Downs, *After Appomattox,* 122, 180, 249; United States War Department, *Use of the Army,* 150. On the hindered state and federal powers of the Freedmen's Bureau, see Downs, "Anarchy at the Circumference"; Lang, *In the Wake of War.* On bureau agents' racist views about freedpeople's aptitude for citizenship, see Emberton, *Beyond Redemption.*

54. James Madison Cutts to Thomas Ewing, August 7, 1867, James Madison Cutts letter, Mss. 4856, LLMVC.

55. T. Fulmor to Lieutenant Lee, October 12, 1868, Bureau of Refugees, Freedmen, and Abandoned Lands, collection 77, LSUS.

56. T. Fulmor to Lieutenant Lee, October 12, 1868, T. Fulmor to Major Hutchins, October 20, 1868, Bureau of Refugees, Freedmen, and Abandoned Lands, collection 077, LSUS; Fairclough,

Revolution that Failed, 112. For a study that views the Freedmen's Bureau as more successful and northwest Louisiana as less violent, see de Vries, "Politics of Terror."

57. Both the body count and the atmosphere of fear continued to accrue in the region following the 1868 elections. While other regions of the South experienced a dip in violence (and perhaps a decrease in the threat of violence) for the 1872 election, primary sources and Black testimony about the Red River region underscore that physical violence and the threat of violence continued in the 1872 and 1874 election cycles. See Foner, *Second Founding.*

58. United States War Department, *Use of the Army,* 380. See also Tunnell, *Edge of the Sword,* 226-227; Fairclough, *Revolution that Failed.*

59. Behrend, *Reconstructing Democracy,* 7, 59, 83, 116, 126; Fitzgerald, *Reconstruction in Alabama,* 9, 108, 170, 188, 230, 256.

60. Emberton, *Beyond Redemption,* 174, 191; Tunnell, *Edge of the Sword;* Goldstone, *Inherently Unequal.* Three books detail daily events of the Colfax Massacre: Keith, *Colfax Massacre;* Lane, *The Day Freedom Died;* and Lemann, *Redemption.* Tunnell, *Edge of the Sword,* investigates the Coushatta Massacre in depth.

61. United States War Department, *Use of the Army,* 212-213, 291-293, 379, 389-390, 392; T. Fulmor to Lieutenant Lee, October 12, 1868, Bureau of Refugees, Freedmen, and Abandoned Lands, collection 77, LSUS; "The Massacre in Bossier Parish, September 21, 1868," "Bossier Parish," xv-xvi, 87-93, in Louisiana Report of the Joint Committee of the General Assembly, *Supplemental Report of Joint Committee,* LLMVC. See also Tunnell, *Crucible of Reconstruction,* 155-160; Rable, *But There Was No Peace,* 75-79.

62. For a discussion of other engagement with burial practices by Black communities following violent episodes, see Ward, *Hanging Bridge,* 108-109, 256.

63. Ibid., 389.

64. United States War Department, *Use of the Army,* 293-294, 390-391; "Massacre in Bossier Parish," "Bossier Parish," xv-xvi, 87-93.

65. United States War Department, *Use of the Army,* 205, 213; "The Massacre in Caddo Parish About October 12, 1868," xvi-xvii, in Louisiana Report of the Joint Committee of the General Assembly, *Supplemental Report of Joint Committee,* LLMVC; T. Fulmor to Major Hutchins, October 20, 1868, Bureau of Refugees, Freedmen, and Abandoned Lands, collection 77, LSUS; Dauphine, "Knights of the White Camelia," 183. Ward, *Hanging Bridge,* details similar proclamations from white vigilantes and prominent citizens decades later, and details the limits of the National Association for the Advancement of Colored People's campaign to stem lynching and racial violence in Shubuta, Mississippi.

66. "Massacre in Bossier Parish," "Massacre in Caddo Parish."

67. Foner, *Reconstruction,* 454-459, 528; Rable, *But There Was No Peace,* 102-125; Creswell, "Enforcing the Enforcement Acts"; Taylor, *Louisiana Reconstructed,* 172-180; Nystrom, *New Orleans After the Civil War,* 128-138; Keith, *Colfax Massacre,* 75-77.

68. Bloom, *Mississippi Valley's Great Yellow Fever Epidemic,* 74-76; Keith, *Colfax Massacre,* 79-81; Henry Hall diary, collection 16, LSUS.

69. Sipress, "From the Barrel of a Gun," 305-306; Harrison and McNeely, *Grant Parish, Louisiana;* "Grant Parish," *Louisiana Democrat,* April 14, 1869, 2; Tunnell, *Edge of the Sword,* 140-141; Hogue, *Uncivil War,* 106-108; Keith, *Colfax Massacre,* 55-81.

70. Wikberg et al., "Tragedy at Colfax," 39-40; Keith, *Colfax Massacre,* 54-57, 66-71; Fairclough, *Revolution that Failed,* 239. By 1876, Phillips was a prominent Democrat. On White's

killing, see W. B. Phillips, "Editor Republican," October 5, 1871, p. 1, "Speech," October 8, 1871, p. 1, *New Orleans Semi-Weekly Louisianian*; Keith, *Colfax Massacre*, 71. See also Taylor, *Louisiana Reconstructed;* Hogue, *Uncivil War;* Wikberg et al., "Tragedy at Colfax"; Sipress, "From the Barrel of a Gun."

71. Waldrep, *Roots of Disorder*, 2, 162, 167–169. On "unqualified contempt for authority figures" in Louisiana's Florida parishes, see Hyde, *Pistols and Politics,* 140. See also Tunnell, *Edge of the Sword;* Nystrom, *New Orleans After the Civil War.*

72. My discussion of the Colfax Massacre centers on the long-standing political triggers that incited white violence, concentrating on how Black attempts to seize citizenship and participation in politics fueled endemic racial tensions and ratcheted up acts of violence in the Red River region in the lead-up to Colfax. That the Colfax Massacre was a large-scale assertion of white power and reclaiming of the body politic, particularly following the *Cruikshank* rulings, is also central to my analysis. In contrast, David Ballantyne's recent article, "Remembering the Colfax Massacre," has focused more on white justifications for the violence, particularly the numerous alleged Black-on-white rape narratives and allegations of Black criminality. Keith, *Colfax Massacre,* provides a detailed discussion of the events of the massacre and subsequent legal trials, while Lane, *The Day Freedom Died,* focuses on the courtroom proceedings following the massacre.

73. Nystrom, *New Orleans After the Civil War,* 132, 138, 163; Rable, *But There Was No Peace,* 122–124.

74. Hogue, *Uncivil War,* 91–96; Taylor, *Louisiana Reconstructed,* 241; Tunnell, *Edge of the Sword.*

75. The Battle of Liberty Place occurred on September 14, 1874. The aim was to oust Governor Kellogg and replace him with the Democratic choice, John McEnery. While ultimately unsuccessful, the outcome was the effective end to Reconstruction policies in Louisiana. White Leaguers used the momentum from the Colfax Massacre and the judicial rulings in the circuit ruling that arose from the massacre, *U.S. v. Cruikshank,* to gain further support for paramilitary organization and emboldened paramilitary violence. *Cruikshank* will be discussed in more depth later in this chapter. For a thorough and definitive look at the Battle of Liberty Place as well as the four other New Orleans street battles, see Hogue, *Uncivil War.* See also Nystrom, *New Orleans After the Civil War.*

76. Keith, *Colfax Massacre,* chapter 7; Wikberg et al., "Tragedy at Colfax," 41–43; Hogue, *Uncivil War,* 108–109; "Grant Parish Riot of 1873 Recalled in WPA Inventory," August 30, 1940, Melrose scrapbooks, box 65, account 15-B-1, CGHRC. On Hadnot's selection, see *Louisiana Democrat,* October 2, 1872, p. 2, January 15, 1873, p. 2. Ward was a Democrat in 1876.

77. Undated document, Judge Jones Collection, account 1-G-4, CGHRC.

78. "Facts of the Colfax Riot: Written by the Late Editor of the Chronicle to Refute Misstatements," *Colfax Chronicle,* April 9, 1921, Ella V. Aldrich Schwing Papers, Mss. 3374, LLMVC; "Grant Parish Riot of 1873 Recalled in WPA Inventory," *Colfax Chronicle,* August 30, 1940, Melrose scrapbooks, box 65, account 15-B-1, CGHRC; "The Grant Parish Troubles," *Natchitoches Times,* April 26, 1873, Melrose scrapbooks, box 67, account 15-B-1, CGHRC; Harrison and McNeely, *Grant Parish, Louisiana,* 74–76.

79. Keith, *Colfax Massacre,* chapter 7; Lemann, *Redemption,* 12–29; Wikberg et al., "Tragedy at Colfax," 43–45; "The Louisiana Murders," *Harper's Weekly,* May 10, 1873, Melrose scrapbooks, box 67, account 15-B-1, CGHRC. See also *Louisiana Democrat,* April 9, 1873, 1; "Facts

About Colfax: Statement of Judge W. R. Rutland," *Ouchita Telegraph,* May 31, 1873, 1; "Statement of a Citizen," *Ouchita Telegraph,* April 26, 1873, 4. On James Hadnot's death, see *Louisiana Democrat,* April 15, 1873, 1. For additional details on arson during the massacre, see O. W. Watson, "An Incident of My Boyhood Days," Colfax Riot Collection, Colfax Public Library, Colfax, LA.

80. "The Grant Parish Troubles," *Natchitoches Times,* April 26, 1873, Melrose scrapbooks, box 67, account 15-B-1, CGHRC.

81. E. E. Davis, "Colfax Riot," Ruby and Woodrow Hughes Collection, account 2-E-3, CGHRC.

82. Keith, *Colfax Massacre,* 109; Watson, "An Incident of My Boyhood Days"; "The Louisiana Murders," *Harper's Weekly,* May 10, 1873, Melrose scrapbooks, box 67, account 15-B-1, CGHRC; Davis, "Colfax Riot"; Foner, *Reconstruction,* 437. For lists of victims, see United States War Department, *Use of the Army,* 168, 307, 338, 436–438.

83. Henry Hyams to "My Dear Son," April 4, April 26, 1873, Henry M. Hyams Family Papers, Mss. 1392, 1564, LLMVC. On freedpeople and "incitement," see Wells, *Civil War, Reconstruction, and Redemption,* 72.

84. The Fort Pillow Massacre occurred on April 12, 1864. When the Union garrison at Fort Pillow, Tennessee, surrendered, Confederates killed more than three hundred African American soldiers, whom they refused to acknowledge as prisoners of war.

85. Charles Boothby to "Dear Mother," April 18, 1873, Charles Boothby to "Dear Brother George," September 25, 1874, Charles W. Boothby Papers, Mss. 4847, LLMVC. For contemporary northern coverage of Colfax, see "The Colfax Massacre," *Evening Post,* April 18, 1873, 4; "The Colfax Massacre," *Albany Evening Journal,* April 18, 1873, 3; "The Colfax Massacre," *Evening Post,* April 19, 1873, 2; "The Colfax Massacre," *Massachusetts Spy,* June 2, 1873, 1; "The Louisiana Massacre," *New York Commercial Advertiser,* April 18, 1873, 4; "The War of Races in Louisiana," *New York Herald,* April 18, 1873, 6; "Re-Enactment of the Fort Pillow Massacre," *Indianapolis Sentinel,* April 19, 1873, 1; "The Colfax Massacre," *Boston Daily Advertiser,* April 19, 1873, 1; "Further Details of the Colfax Massacre," *Portland Daily Press,* April 17, 1873, 3.

86. "To the Memory of Jas W. Hadnot," *Louisiana Democrat,* May 7, 1873, Ker–Texada Papers, Mss. 545, LaRC; "Unveiling Program," *Colfax Chronicle,* April 9, 1921, Ella V. Aldrich Schwing Papers, Mss. 3374, LLMVC; "Colfax Riot Monument Unveiled: Fitting Ceremonies," *Colfax Chronicle,* April 16, 1921, Melrose scrapbooks, box 67, account 15-B-1, CGHRC.

87. Obituary for John Hadnot, February 16, 1899, Melrose scrapbooks, box 67, account 15-B-1, CGHRC.

88. "Sheriff Nash," *The Caucasian,* May 16, 1874, 1. On violent defense of white womanhood, see Feimster, *Southern Horrors.*

89. Milton Dunn, "Christopher Columbus Nash: A Tribute," Melrose scrapbooks, box 67, account 15-B-1, CGHRC. On ex-Confederates as participants and leaders in vigilante violence, see Williard, "Executions, Justice, and Reconciliation."

90. John A. Williams, History of Colfax, La., Mss. 4293, LLMVC.

91. Proctor, "From the cradle to the grave," 18.

92. Kate Grant, *From Blue to Gray, or The Battle of Colfax,* undated manuscript, Layssard Family Papers, Mss. 2875, LLMVC.

93. Hogue, *Uncivil War,* 112, 116; Lane, *The Day Freedom Died,* 217.

94. Keith, *Colfax Massacre,* 113.

95. "The Colfax Affair at Washington," *Natchitoches Times,* April 26, 1873, Melrose scrapbooks, box 67, 15-B-1, CGHRC.

96. J. Ernest Breda to George Williams, August 11, 1873, J. Ernest Breda letters, collection M 616, LaRC.

97. J. Ernest Breda to J. Packard, August 11, 1873, J. Ernest Breda letters, collection M 616, LaRC.

98. J. Ernest Breda to George Williams, August 11, 1873.

99. "History, Legend, and Tradition," *Natchitoches Times,* April 1921, Melrose scrapbooks, box 67, account 15-B-1, CGHRC.

100. Keith, *Colfax Massacre,* 107-152; Lane, *The Day Freedom Died,* 154-229; Fairclough, *Revolution that Failed,* 178-179.

101. Goldstone, *Inherently Unequal,* 84-86.

102. State neglect, as conceived by legal historian Pamela Brandwein, "permitted the federal government to punish private individuals whose race-based violence and intimidation went unpublished by states." For definitions, see Brandwein, *Rethinking the Judicial Settlement of Reconstruction,* 11-14.

103. Ibid., 11, 28-35, 53-59, 73-120, 161-164. Brandwein's book contributes significantly to discussions on the complex implications of Reconstruction era rulings; chapters 1, 2, 4, and 6 are especially instructive. See also Foner, *Second Founding,* 138-149.

104. Keith, *Colfax Massacre,* 142-146; Brandwein, *Rethinking the Judicial Settlement of Reconstruction,* 97-100.

105. Keith, *Colfax Massacre,* 107-152; Lane, *The Day Freedom Died,* 154-229.

106. Goldstone, *Inherently Unequal,* 84-86, 91-97; Fairclough, *Revolution that Failed,* 178-179; Tunnell, *Edge of the Sword,* 260; Keith, *Colfax Massacre,* 155-158; Lane, *The Day Freedom Died,* 210-212.

107. Lane, *The Day Freedom Died,* 215; Keith, *Colfax Massacre,* 148; Colfax Riot Collection; Tunnell, *Edge of the Sword,* 260.

7. "INTO THE HANDS OF THE VERY MEN THAT HELD US SLAVES"

1. "A True Friend" to Marshall Harvey Twitchell, April 16, 1873, Marshall Twitchell Papers, Mss. M76, Department of Special Collections, Prescott Memorial Library, Louisiana Tech University, Ruston (hereafter PML).

2. Tunnell, *Edge of the Sword,* 132-141, 175-177.

3. "Ten DeSoto Tax Payers" to Robert Dewees, undated [1874], Marshall Twitchell Papers, Mss. M76, PML. Emphasis in original. On tax associations, see Fairclough, *Revolution that Failed,* 182-189.

4. "Capt. Jacks Haghts" to G. King and Henry Scott, undated [1874], Marshall Twitchell Papers, Mss. M76, PML. Emphasis in original.

5. Hogue, *Uncivil War,* 126.

6. Marshall Harvey Twitchell statement, undated, Ted Tunnell Collection, account 747, CGHRC. On hard-line white supremacist ethos throughout the South, see Trelease, *White Terror;* Chalmers, *Hooded Americanism;* Ayers, *Vengeance and Justice;* Carrigan, *Making of a Lynching Culture.*

7. For meeting reports, see Report on Meetings of the Citizen of Coushatta, August 17, 1874, Resolutions from Meeting of the Citizen of Coushatta, August 17, 1874, Marshall Twitchell Papers, Mss. M76, PML. See also Nystrom, *New Orleans After the Civil War,* 162, 164–166; Lane, *The Day Freedom Died,* 217–218; Snay, "Democracy and Race."

8. Frank Edgerton to Marshall Harvey Twitchell, July 30, 1874, Marshall Harvey Twitchell Papers, Ms. M76, PML. Emphasis in original.

9. Frank Edgerton to Marshall Harvey Twitchell, July 30, 1874. Emphasis in original. On the political situation in New Orleans, see Nystrom, *New Orleans After the Civil War;* Hogue, *Uncivil War;* Taylor, *Louisiana Reconstructed.*

10. Tunnell, *Edge of the Sword,* 196.

11. William Howell to Marshall Harvey Twitchell, August 17, 1874, Marshall Harvey Twitchell Papers, Ms. M76, PML.

12. Testimony of Mathilda Floyd, testimony of Roselia Floyd, inspection of victims' bodies, Marshall Harvey Twitchell Papers, Ms. M76, PML; United States War Department, *Use of the Army,* 251. For more on violence toward women, and their testimonies, see Rosen, *Terror in the Heart of Freedom;* Williams, *They Left Great Marks on Me.*

13. Testimony of Francis Wynn, Marshall Harvey Twitchell Papers, Ms. M76, PML; United States War Department, *Use of the Army,* 251.

14. Tunnell, *Edge of the Sword,* 198–200; Marshall Harvey Twitchell statement, undated.

15. Tunnell, *Edge of the Sword,* 200–203.

16. Ibid., 204–205; United States War Department, *Use of the Army,* 252; Marshall Harvey Twitchell statement, undated. See also Shoalmire, "Carpetbagger Extraordinary," 150–178.

17. Marshall Harvey Twitchell statement, undated; Tunnell, *Edge of the Sword,* 206. These men were buried, which displays a sliver of respect not accorded to Black victims of regional racial violence.

18. Tunnell, *Edge of the Sword,* 207; United States War Department, *Use of the Army,* 252.

19. Hogue, *Uncivil War,* 131–138; Nystrom, *New Orleans After the Civil War,* 176–178; Lane, *The Day Freedom Died,* 220.

20. Marshall Harvey Twitchell statement, undated; Tunnell, *Edge of the Sword,* 253–259.

21. Keith, *Colfax Massacre,* 157; Wikberg et al., "Tragedy at Colfax," 47. See also Lemann, *Redemption;* Lane, *The Day Freedom Died.* On violence in the Red River region during the 1874 election, see Sanson, "White Man's Failure," 39–58, and "Rapides Parish, Louisiana, During the End of Reconstruction," 167–182; Vandal, "Policy of Violence," 159–182.

22. Fairclough, *Revolution that Failed,* 251.

23. Colfax is cited as the blueprint for the violence in Barber County, Alabama, and specifically for the Eufaula coup of 1874, in Cowie, *Freedom's Dominion,* chapter 9.

24. Keith, *Colfax Massacre,* 159; Hogue, *Uncivil War,* 124. See also Taylor, *Louisiana Reconstructed;* Nystrom, *New Orleans After the Civil War;* Tunnell, *Edge of the Sword;* Fairclough, *Revolution that Failed.*

25. Woodward, *Reunion and Reaction;* Perman, *Road to Redemption,* 172–277; Taylor, *Louisiana Reconstructed,* 481–507. See also Follett, "Legacies of Enslavement," 50–84. Fairclough, *Bulldozed and Betrayed,* is the newest scholarship focusing specifically on the 1876 election in Louisiana and the Potter Committee's findings of corruption, including the seedy underside of Louisiana Republican activities.

26. Woodward, *Reunion and Reaction,* 233, 261–267; Taylor, *Louisiana Reconstructed;* Sterling, *The Trouble They Seen,* 479.

27. Caldwell, "Any Place but Here," 52–53; Peoples, "'Kansas Fever' in North Louisiana," 129–130; Fairclough, *Revolution that Failed,* 300–302; "Testimony of Henry Adams Regarding the Negro Exodus," in Aptheker, *Documentary History,* 715.

28. Painter, *Exodusters,* 84–85. See also Follett, "Legacies of Enslavement"; Mitchell, *Righteous Propagation;* Scott, *Degrees of Freedom.* On Liberian emigration, see Barnes, *Journey of Hope.*

29. Peoples, "'Kansas Fever' in North Louisiana," 122. On the Exodusters' struggles, see Painter, *Exodusters,* 202–212, 225–265, and "Millenarian Aspects," 331–338. Following a similar ideological underpinning of Black self-reliance and economic development, northwest Louisiana strongly embraced Garveyism and the Universal Negro Improvement Association movement in the 1910s. For an excellent investigation of Garveyism, see Rolinson, *Grassroots Garveyism.*

30. "Facts of the Colfax Riot: Written by the Late Editor of the Chronicle to Refute Misstatements," *Colfax Chronicle,* April 9, 1921, Ella V. Aldrich Schwing Papers, Mss. 3374, LLMVC.

31. Harrison and McNeely, *Grant Parish, Louisiana,* 74, 76.

32. Kate Grant, *From Blue to Gray, or The Battle of Colfax,* undated manuscript, Layssard Family Papers, Mss. 2875, LLMVC. On white women's involvement in recasting postwar narratives and memorial associations, see Janney, *Remembering the Civil War,* 7, 99, 140, 238, 242; Domby, *False Cause;* Brundage, *Southern Past.*

33. J. H. McNeely to Dr. M. A. Dunn, April 10, 1920, Melrose scrapbooks, box 67, account 15-B-1, CGHRC.

34. Rita Leochard Breath to Milton Dunn, June 11, 1920, Melrose scrapbooks, box 67, account 15-B-1, CGHRC.

35. Wikberg et al., "Tragedy at Colfax," 35.

36. "The Reunion of Colfax Veterans," April 13, 1914, Melrose scrapbooks, box 67, account 15-B-1, CGHRC. On veterans reunions, see Janney, *Remembering the Civil War.*

37. "Grant Parish Thrill with History of Strong Men in Fight for Right," *Shreveport Times,* April 1923, Melrose scrapbooks, box 67, account 15-B-1, CGHRC.

38. "Unveiling Program," *Colfax Chronicle,* April 9, 1921, Ella V. Aldrich Schwing Papers, Mss. 3374, LLMVC; "Colfax Riot Monument Unveiled: Fitting Ceremonies," *Colfax Chronicle,* April 16, 1921, Melrose scrapbooks, box 67, account 15-B-1, CGHRC.

39. Richard Rubin, "The Colfax Riot," *Atlantic Monthly,* July/August 2003: 155–158.

40. "Unveiling Program"; "Unveiling of Colfax Riot Monument," Melrose scrapbooks, box 67, account 15-B-1, CGHRC.

41. Cammie Henry marginalia, "Colfax Riot Monument Unveiled," and Colfax Riot tree, undated photograph, Melrose scrapbooks, box 67, account 15-B-1, CGHRC.

42. "History, Legend, and Tradition," *Natchitoches Times,* April 1921, Melrose scrapbooks, box 67, account 15-B-1, CGHRC.

43. Kantrowitz, *Ben Tillman and the Reconstruction of White Supremacy,* 8. See also Janney, *Remembering the Civil War,* 10, 102, 191.

44. There also are no memorials for or commemorations of the Shady Grove Massacre,

and this might be the first book of historical scholarship to discuss the event (see chapter 6). I learned of Shady Grove from primary source records and Black testimony.

EPILOGUE

1. Two Louisiana State University doctoral candidates chronicled their efforts to remove the sign, which began in 2017. A combination of their efforts, the Louisiana Economic Development initiative, and two citizens with familial connections to the massacre (one's ancestor was a perpetrator and the other is a descendant of Jesse McKinney) resulted in the removal of the sign. According to the candidates' blog post, the Grant Parish Police Jury allowed a presentation on the sign at a board meeting but stonewalled progress when they realized that proposed changes would describe this as a massacre.

There is very light coverage of the sign's removal; the aforementioned blog post is the most granular. See Tom Barber and Jeff Crawford, "Removing the White Supremacy Marker at Colfax, Louisiana: A 2021 Success Story," *Muster,* July 6, 2021, https://www.journalofthe civilwarera.org/2021/07/removing-the-white-supremacy-marker-at-colfax-louisiana-a-2021 -success-story; Dave McNamara, "Colfax Massacre," *Heart of Louisiana,* November 23, 2021, https://heartoflouisiana.com/colfax-massacre; Charles Lane, "Opinion: Not Far from Tulsa, a Quieter but Consequential Correction of the Historical Record," *Washington Post,* June 8, 2021.

2. On memorials, commemoration, women's prominence in memorialization, and veterans associations, see Blight, *Race and Reunion;* Janney, *Remembering the Civil War,* especially chapters 5–8; Domby, *False Cause;* Brundage, *Southern Past;* Brown, *Civil War Monuments.*

3. Milton Dunn, "Christopher Columbus Nash: A Tribute," Melrose scrapbooks, box 67, account 15-B-1, CGHRC.

4. For deeper discussion of the intertwining of monuments and the Lost Cause narrative into a "heritage of hate," see Domby, *False Cause.*

5. See Brundage, *Southern Past;* Fairclough, *Revolution that Failed.*

6. Some recent articles in major newspapers include Campbell Robertson, "The Prosecutor Who Says Louisiana Should 'Kill More People,'" *New York Times,* August 7, 2015; Adam Liptak, "Exclusion of Blacks from Juries Raises Renewed Scrutiny," *New York Times,* August 17, 2015; Zach Beaird, "Dale Cox Brings Bad Press to Caddo," *Shreveport Times,* July 15, 2015; Josie Duffy Rice, "In Louisiana, Harsh Prosecutors Are Moving from Parish to Parish," *The Appeal,* June 29, 2018; Yolanda Young, "America's Death Penalty Capital: Can a Black DA Really Change the System?," *Guardian,* March 13, 2016; Rachel Aviv, "A Death Sentence Overturned in Louisiana," *The New Yorker,* November 23, 2016; Jay Michelson, "The Death Penalty Election: A Louisiana Parish Is Ground Zero for the Capital Punishment Debate," *Daily Beast,* October 26, 2015; Jim Mustian, "Meet the 'Controversial' Louisiana Prosecutor," *Advocate,* June 3, 2017; Radley Balko, "How a Fired Prosecutor Became Louisiana's Most Powerful Law Enforcement Official," *Washington Post,* November 2, 2017; "Outlier Counties: Legacy of Racism Persists in Caddo Parish," *Death Penalty Information Center,* September 23, 2016, https://deathpenaltyinfo.org/outlier-counties-legacy-of-racism-persists-in-caddo-parish-which-had-nations-second-highest-number-of-lynchings.

7. Lane, *The Day Freedom Died,* 256; Lemann, *Redemption,* 24. For more on Albert Leonard, see Vandal, "Albert H. Leonard's Road."

BIBLIOGRAPHY

PRIMARY SOURCES

Manuscript Collections

Cammie G. Henry Research Center, Northwestern State University, Natchitoches
  Ezra Adams Collection
  Lucille Carnahan Collection
  P. E. Cloutier Collection
  Egan Family Collection
  Fortson Family Collection
  Ruby and Woodrow Hughes Collection
  J. M. Jones Civil War diary
  Judge Jones Collection
  Henry Marshall Collection
  Melrose scrapbooks
  Captain M. I. Scovell reminiscences
  John Coleman Sibley Collection
  Ted Tunnell Collection
  James Calvert Wise Papers

Colfax Riot Collection, Colfax Public Library, Colfax, Louisiana

Historic New Orleans Collection, New Orleans
  Cane River Collection
  Maria Louise Deloach sketch
  Duncan Kenner letter
  John J. Moore Papers
  Henry Rust diary
  Henry C. Sampson diary
  Charles F. Sherman Civil War letters
  James E. White letters

Louisiana and Lower Mississippi Valley Collection, Hill Memorial Library, Louisiana State University, Baton Rouge

Account of the Red River Expedition

American Cotton Planter

Henry Anderson letter

The Angolite

Charles B. Allaire letter

D. B. Allen letter

William M. Allen correspondence

Anonymous medical ledger 1854–1919

Anonymous Confederate civilian letters

Anonymous Civil War diary, nos. 3210 and 3328

Anonymous letter 1851

Anonymous Reconstruction letters

Arthur P. Bagby letter

Nathaniel P. Banks letter book

George W. Bennett records

Benson Family Papers

Birge (N. A.) Papers

Charles W. Boothby Papers

Hubbard S. Bosley Papers

David F. Boyd Papers

J. A. Bray Papers

J. P. Breda Family Papers

Henry A. Bullard estate

Annie Jeter Carmouche Papers

John H. Carson papers/diary

A. G. Carter letter

Chaplin, Breazeale, and Chaplin papers

James Madison Cutts letter

Benjamin Philip Cuny Family Papers

John Eaton letter

Charles D. and Emily J. Elliot Papers

Alfred Flournoy Papers

C. C. Gaines and Company Papers

General Order no. 105

Guess (George W.) letters

William George Hale Papers

George Mason Graham letters

John Hammond letter

J. Fair Hardin Collection

Miss Sidney Harding diaries

Home Farm for Freedmen invoice

Robert and Sarah Jane Hunter letters

Henry M. Hyams Papers

John S. Kyser collection

James S. Laroe diary

Gustave Lauve letter

Layssard Family Papers

Louisiana Constitutional Convention document, 1868

Louisiana Militia document

Louisiana Report of the Joint Committee of the General Assembly, 1869 supplement, *Supplemental Report of Joint Committee of the General Assembly of Louisiana on the Conduct of the Late Elections and the Condition of Peace and Good Order in the State*

Polly Madison oral interview

John J. Marshall plantation ledgers

George B. Marshall Family Papers

George B. Marshall Family Papers—daybook

Marshall–Furman Family papers

Henry Marston and Family Papers

Charles L. Mathews and Family Papers

Mathews–Ventress–Lawrason Family Papers

Jeptha McKinney Papers

Anderson McNutt Estate Papers

D. Y. Milling correspondence

Mary W. Milling letter

Thomas O. Moore Papers

Morris-Sibley Family Papers

E. B. Norman and N. Philip collection

Joseph H. Olcott letter

Robert T. Parish diary

Frank P. Peak sketch

David Pierson letter

David D. Porter letter

Pre Aux Cleres plantation record books

John H. Ransdell Papers

Joseph Toole Robinson Papers

Valle J. Rozier scrapbook

Ella V. Aldrich Schwing Papers

Elizabeth Ann Scofield letter
William A. Sharp letters
William T. Sherman letters, in David French Boyd Papers
Moses Smith letter
William H. Tamplin Papers
Marcelin Tauzin and Family Papers
Miles Terrell and Family Papers
Texada Family Papers
Lewis Texada and Family Papers
William Thatcher Papers
Robert A. Tyson diary
Antal Vallas and Family Papers
James Burns Wallace diary
Joseph Watson correspondence
W. A. Webster letter
George W. Whittlesey letters
John A. Williams History of Colfax, Louisiana
Micajah Wilkinson Papers
James Calvert Wise Papers
James Calvert Wise Papers—oversize items
WPA Collection: Historical Records Survey Transcriptions of Louisiana Parish
    Police Jury Minutes for Rapides, Grant, Bossier, Desoto, and Caddo Parishes

Louisiana Research Center, Tulane University, New Orleans
Henry Watkins Allen letters
J. Ernest Breda letters
Anne Jeter Carmouche Papers
Civil War Collection
Ker–Texada Papers
Kuntz Collection
Alfred Lippman collection of Civil War letters

**Marshall Harvey Twitchell Papers, Prescott Memorial Library, Louisiana Tech
University, Rustin**

Noel Memorial Library, Louisiana State University, Shreveport
Mary Moultrie Adger family and plantation records
Nathaniel Allen Family Papers
Emerson Bently diary and notes
Emerson Bently journal
Booher and Martin Family Papers

Bossier Parish land records
Bureau of Refugees, Freedmen and Abandoned Lands, Louisiana Records
Caddo Parish Civil War election records
Ewing Family Papers
Foster Family Papers
Fullilove family binders
Samford C. Fullilove Papers
Alfred Flournoy Jr. correspondence
Alfred Flournoy Sr. Family Papers
John Harris Civil War letters
William Joseph Hutchinson family and plantation records
James Lankford collection
Albert Harris Leonard memoirs
Josephine C. Means Papers
Josephine Chatham Means Collection
Mary Elizabeth Rives (Carter) diary

Contemporaneous Periodicals and Newspapers
American Cotton Planter and Soil of the South
Bossier Banner
Caddo Free Press
Caddo Gazette
Colfax Chronicle
De Bow's Review
Louisiana Democrat
Ouachita Telegraph
People's Vindicator
Planters Intelligence and Rapides Advertiser
Shreveport Semi-Weekly News
South West Shreveport
Southern Cultivator
Southern Planter

Travelers' Accounts, Memoirs, Commentaries, and Published Correspondence
Di Maio, Irene, trans. *Gërstacker's Louisiana: Fiction and Travel Sketches from Ante-*
    bellum Times Through Reconstruction. Baton Rouge: Louisiana State University
    Press, 2006.
Douglass, Frederick. *Narrative of the Life of Frederick Douglass, An American Slave.*
    1845. New York: Barnes and Noble Books, 2003.
Gould, E. W. *Fifty Years on the Mississippi; or Gould's History of River Navigation.*
    Saint Louis: Nixon Jones, 1889.

McClellan, Margaret Hutchinson. *William Joseph Hutchinson and Family of Caspiana Plantation.* Bossier City, LA: Tipton, 1975.

Northup, Solomon. *Twelve Years a Slave.* 1853. Edited by Sue Lyles Eakin. Spring, TX: Eakin Films and Publishing, 2013.

Olmsted, Frederick Law. *The Cotton Kingdom: A Traveller's Observations on Cotton and Slavery in the American Slave States.* New York: Da Capo Press, 1996. (reprint)

———. *A Journey in the Back Country.* 1860. Ithaca, NY: Cornell University Press, 2009.

———. *A Journey in the Seaboard Slave States: With Remarks on Their Economy.* 1856. Cambridge: Cambridge University Press, 2009.

———. *A Journey Through Texas: Or a Saddle-Trip on the Southwestern Frontier.* 1857. Lincoln: Bison Books, 2004.

———. *The Slave States.* 1856. Capricorn Books, 1959.

Sterling, Dorothy, ed. *The Trouble They Seen: Black People Tell the Story of Reconstruction.* Garden City, NY: Doubleday, 1976.

Wells, Carol, ed. *Civil War, Reconstruction, and Redemption on Red River: The Memoirs of Dosia Williams Moore.* Ruston, LA: McGinty, 1990.

Government Documents

Constitution Adopted by the State Constitutional Convention of the State of Louisiana, March 7, 1868. New Orleans, 1868. https://www.loc.gov/item/01018727

The Statutes of the State of Louisiana. Revised and prepared by U. B. Phillips, under the direction of a Joint Committee of the Legislature. New Orleans: E. La Sere, 1855.

United States Department of Commerce, Bureau of the Census. *Historical Statistics of the United States, Colonial Times to 1970. Bicentennial edition.* Washington, DC, 1975.

United States War Department. *Use of the Army in Certain of the Southern States.* 1877. Reprint, New York: Arno Press, 1969.

SECONDARY SOURCES

Abruzzo, Margaret. *Polemical Pain: Slavery, Cruelty, and the Rise of Humanitarianism.* Baltimore: Johns Hopkins University Press, 2011.

Acharya, Avidit, Matthew Blackwell, and Maya Sen. *Deep Roots: How Slavery Still Shapes Southern Politics.* Princeton, NJ: Princeton University Press, 2018.

———. "The Political Legacy of American Slavery." *Journal of Politics* 78, no 3 (July 2016): 621–641.

Anders, Curt. *Disaster in Damp Sand: The Red River Expedition.* Indianapolis: Guild Press of Indiana, 1997.

Anderson, Eric, and Alfred A. Moss Jr., eds. *The Facts of Reconstruction: Essays in Honor of John Hope Franklin.* Baton Rouge: Louisiana State University Press, 1991.

Appleby, Joyce Oldham. "The Vexed Story of Capitalism Told by American Historians." *Journal of the Early Republic* 21, no. 1 (Spring 2001): 1–18.

Aptheker, Herbert, ed. *A Documentary History of the Negro People in the United States.* New York: Citadel, 1951.

Ash, Stephen. *A Massacre in Memphis: The Race Riot that Shook the Nation One Year After the Civil War.* New York: Hill & Wang, 2013.

Astor, Aaron. *Rebels on the Border: Civil War, Emancipation, and the Reconstruction of Kentucky and Missouri.* Baton Rouge: Louisiana State University Press, 2012.

Ayers, Edward L. *The Promise of the New South: Life After Reconstruction.* New York: Oxford University Press, 2007.

Ayers, Thomas. *Dark and Bloody Ground: The Battle of Mansfield and the Forgotten Civil War in Louisiana.* Dallas: Taylor Trade, 2001.

Baker, Bruce E. *This Mob Will Surely Take My Life: Lynchings in the Carolinas, 1871–1947.* London: Continuum Books, 2008.

———. *What Reconstruction Meant: Historical Memory in the American South.* Charlottesville: University of Virginia Press, 2007.

Baker, Bruce E., and Barbara Hahn. *The Cotton Kings: Capitalism and Corruption in Turn-of-the-Century New York and New Orleans.* New York: Oxford University Press, 2015.

Baker, Bruce E., and Brian Kelly, eds. *After Slavery: Race, Labor, and Citizenship in the Reconstruction South.* Gainesville: University Press of Florida, 2013.

Ballantyne, David T. "Remembering the Colfax Massacre: Race, Sex, and the Meanings of Reconstruction Violence." *Journal of Southern History* 87, no. 3 (August 2021): 427–466.

Baptist, Edward E. *Creating an Old South: Middle Florida's Plantation Frontier Before the Civil War.* Chapel Hill: University of North Carolina Press, 2002.

———. "'Cuffy,' 'Fancy Maids,' and 'One-Eyed Men': Rape, Commodification, and the Domestic Slave Trade in the United States." *American Historical Review* 106, no. 5 (December 2001): 1619–1650.

———. *The Half Has Never Been Told: Slavery and the Making of American Capitalism.* New York: Basic Books, 2014.

———. "Toxic Debt, Liar Loans, and Securitized Human Beings: The Panic of 1837 and the Fate of Slavery." *Common-Place* 10, no. 3 (April 2010).

Barnes, Kenneth C. *Journey of Hope: The Back-to-Africa Movement in Arkansas in the Late 1800s.* Chapel Hill: University of North Carolina Press, 2004.

Barnes, L. Diane, Brian Schoen, and Frank Towers, eds. *The Old South's Modern Worlds: Slavery, Region, and Nation in the Age of Progress.* New York: Oxford University Press, 2011.

Barney, William. *Rebels in the Making: The Secession Crisis and the Birth of the Confederacy.* New York: Oxford University Press, 2020.

Barton, Keith C. "'Good Cooks and Washers': Slave Hiring, Domestic Labor, and the Market in Bourbon County, Kentucky." *Journal of American History* 84, no. 2 (September 1997): 436–460.

Beckert, Sven. "Cotton and the U.S. South: A Short History." In *Plantation Kingdom,* ed. Follett, Beckert, Coclanis, and Hahn, 39–60.

———. *Empire of Cotton: A New History of Global Capitalism.* London: Allen Lane, 2014.

Behrend, Justin. *Reconstructing Democracy: Grassroots Black Politics in the Deep South After the Civil War.* Athens: University of Georgia Press, 2015.

Belich, James. *Replenishing the Earth: The Settler Revolution and the Rise of the Anglo-World, 1783–1939.* Oxford: Oxford University Press, 2009.

Bercaw, Nancy. *Gendered Freedoms: Race, Rights, and the Politics of the Household in the Delta.* Gainesville: University Press of Florida, 2003.

Berlin, Ira. *Many Thousands Gone: The First Two Centuries of Slavery in North America.* Cambridge, MA: The Belknap Press of Harvard University Press, 2000.

Berlin, Ira, Marc Favreau, and Steven F. Miller, eds. *Remembering Slavery: African Americans Talk About Their Personal Experiences of Slavery and Emancipation.* New York: New Press, 1998.

Berlin, Ira, Barbara J. Fields, Thavolia Glymph, Joseph P. Reidy, and Leslie S. Rowland, eds. *Freedom: A Documentary History of Emancipation, 1861–1867.* Series 1, vol. 1, *The Destruction of Slavery.* Cambridge: Cambridge University Press, 1985.

Berlin, Ira, Steven F. Miller, Joseph P. Reidy, and Leslie S. Rowland, eds. *Freedom: A Documentary History of Emancipation.* Series 1, vol. 2, *Wartime Genesis of Free Labor.* Cambridge: Cambridge University Press, 1991.

Berlin, Ira, and Philip D. Morgan, eds. *Cultivation and Culture: Labor and the Shaping of Slave Life in the Americas.* Charlottesville: University Press of Virginia, 1993.

Berry, Daina Ramey. *The Price for Their Pound of Flesh: The Value of the Enslaved, from Womb to Grave, in the Building of a Nation.* Boston: Beacon Press, 2017.

———. *"Swing the Sickle for the Harvest Is Ripe": Gender and Slavery in Antebellum Georgia.* Urbana: University of Illinois Press, 2007.

Berry, Daina Ramey, and Leslie Harris, eds. *Sexuality and Slavery: Reclaiming Intimate Histories in the Americas.* Athens: University of Georgia Press, 2018.

Berry, Stephen, ed. *Weirding the War: Stories from the Civil War's Ragged Edges.* Athens: University of Georgia Press, 2011.

Beveridge, Charles E., and Charles Capen McLaughlin, eds. *The Papers of Frederick Law Olmsted. Vol. 2, Slavery and the South, 1852–1857.* Baltimore: Johns Hopkins University Press, 1981.

Billingsley, Carolyn Earle. *Communities of Kinship: Antebellum Families and the Settlement of the Cotton Frontier.* Athens: University of Georgia Press, 2004.

Blail, William. *With Malice Toward Some: Treason and Loyalty in the Civil War Era.* Chapel Hill: University of North Carolina Press, 2014.

Blight, David. *Race and Reunion: The Civil War in American Memory.* Cambridge, MA: Harvard University Press, 2001.

Bloom, Khaled. *The Mississippi Valley's Great Yellow Fever Epidemic of 1878.* Baton Rouge: Louisiana State University Press, 1993.

Blum, Edward J. *Reforging the White Republic: Race and Religion and American Nationalism, 1865–1898.* Baton Rouge: Louisiana State University Press, 2005.

Boster, Dea. *African American Slavery and Disability: Bodies, Property, and Power in the Antebellum South, 1800–1860.* New York: Routledge, 2013.

Booth, A. B. "Louisiana Confederate Military Records, Addenda." *Louisiana Historical Quarterly* 4, no. 3 (July 1921): 379–411.

Brandwein, Pamela. *Rethinking the Judicial Settlement of Reconstruction.* Cambridge: Cambridge University Press, 2011.

Brooksher, William Riley. *War Along the Bayous: The 1864 Red River Campaign in Louisiana.* Washington, DC: Brassey's, 1998.

Brown, Harry Bates, and Jacob Osborn Ware. *Cotton.* New York: McGraw-Hill, 1958.

Brown, Thomas J., ed. *Reconstructions: New Perspectives on the Postbellum United States.* New York: Oxford University Press, 2006.

Brundage, W. Fitzhugh. *The Southern Past: A Clash of Race and Memory.* New York: The Belknap Press of Harvard University Press, 2008.

Budiansky, Stephen. *The Bloody Shirt: Terror After Appomattox.* New York: Viking, 2008.

Buchanan, Thomas. *Black Life on the Mississippi: Slaves, Free Blacks, and the Western Steamboat World.* Chapel Hill: University of North Carolina Press, 2004.

Burton, H. Sophie, and F. Todd Smith. *Colonial Natchitoches: A Creole Community on the Louisiana-Texas Frontier.* College Station: Texas A&M University Press, 2008.

Burnard, Trevor. *Planters, Merchants, and Slaves: Plantation Societies in British America, 1650–1820.* Chicago: University of Chicago Press, 2015.

Bynum, Victoria. *Unruly Women: The Politics of Social and Sexual Control in the Old South.* Chapel Hill: University of North Carolina Press, 1992.

Caldwell, Joe Louis. "Any Place but Here: Kansas Fever in Northeast Louisiana." *North Louisiana Historical Association Journal* 21, no. 2/3 (Spring/Summer 1990): 51–70.

Camp, Stephanie. *Closer to Freedom: Enslaved Women and Everyday Resistance in the Plantation South.* Chapel Hill: University of North Carolina Press, 2004.

Campbell, John. "Work, Pregnancy, and Infant Mortality Among Southern Slaves." *Journal of Interdisciplinary History* 14, no. 4 (Spring 1984): 793–812.

Campbell, Randolph. *An Empire for Slavery: The Peculiar Institution in Texas, 1821–1865*. Baton Rouge: Louisiana State University Press, 1989.

Carney, Judith. *Black Rice: The African Origins of Rice Cultivation in the Americas.* Cambridge, MA: Harvard University Press, 2001.

Carter, Dan T. *When the War Was Over: The Failure of Self-Reconstruction in the South, 1865–1867.* Baton Rouge: Louisiana State University Press, 1985.

Carrigan, Jo Ann. "Impact of Epidemic Yellow Fever on Life in Louisiana." *Louisiana History: The Journal of the Louisiana Historical Association* 4, no. 1 (Winter 1963): 5–34.

———. "Privilege, Prejudice, and the Strangers' Disease in Nineteenth-Century New Orleans." *Journal of Southern History* 36, no. 4 (November 1970): 568–578.

Carringan, William D. *The Making of a Lynching Culture: Violence and Vigilantism in Central Texas, 1836–1916.* Urbana: University of Illinois, 2004.

Casey, Powell A. "Confederate Units from North Louisiana." *North Louisiana Historical Association Journal* 6, no. 2 (Spring 1975): 105–115.

Cashin, Joan. *A Family Venture: Men and Women on the Southern Frontier.* Baltimore: Johns Hopkins University Press, 1991.

———. "Hungry People in the Wartime South: Civilians, Armies, and the Food Supply." In *Weirding the War*, ed. Berry, 160–175.

———, ed. *Our Common Affairs: Texts from Women in the Old South.* Baltimore: Johns Hopkins University Press, 1996.

Censer, Jane Turner. *North Carolina Planters and Their Children, 1800–1860.* Baton Rouge: Louisiana State University Press, 1984.

Chalmers, David J. *Hooded Americanism: The History of the Ku Klux Klan.* Durham, NC: Duke University Press, 1987.

Chaplin, Joyce E. *An Anxious Pursuit: Agricultural Innovation and Modernity in the Lower South, 1730–1815.* Chapel Hill: University of North Carolina Press, 1993.

Cimbala, Paul, and Randall Miller, eds. *The Great Task Remaining Before Us: Reconstruction as America's Continuing Civil War.* New York: Fordham University Press, 2010.

Clark, Elizabeth. "'The Sacred Rights of the Weak': Pain, Sympathy, and the Culture of Individual Rights in Antebellum America." *Journal of American History* 82 (September 1995): 463–493.

Clegg, John. "Capitalism and Slavery." *Critical Historical Studies* (Fall 2015): 281–304.

Clinton, Catherine. *The Plantation Mistress: Woman's World in the Old South.* New York: Pantheon, 1984.

Clinton, Catherine, and Nina Sibler, eds. *Divided Houses: Gender and the Civil War.* New York: Oxford University Press, 1992.

Coclanis, Peter. "How the Low Country Was Taken to Task: Slave-Labor Organization in Coastal South Carolina and Georgia." In *Slavery, Secession, and Southern*

History, ed. Robert Paquette and Louis Ferleger. Charlottesville: University of Virginia Press, 2000.

Cohen, William. *At Freedom's Edge: Black Mobility and the Southern White Quest for Racial Control, 1861–1915.* Baton Rouge: Louisiana State University Press, 1991.

Colby, Robert. "'Negroes Will Bear Fabulous Prices': The Economics of Wartime Slave Commerce and Visions of the Confederate Future." *Journal of the Civil War Era* 10, no. 4 (December 2020): 439–468.

Cooper, William J. *The South and the Politics of Slavery 1828–1856.* Baton Rouge: Louisiana State University Press, 1978.

Cowie, Jefferson. *Freedom's Dominion: A Saga of White Resistance to Federal Power.* New York: Basic Books, 2022.

Creswell, Stephen. "Enforcing the Enforcement Acts: The Department of Justice in Northern Mississippi, 1870–1890." *Journal of Southern History* 53, no. 3 (August 1987): 421–440.

Dailey, Jane. *Before Jim Crow: The Politics of Race in Postemancipation Virginia.* Chapel Hill: University of North Carolina Press, 2000.

Dailey, Jane, Glenda Elizabeth Gilmore, and Bryant Simon, eds. *Jumpin' Jim Crow: Southern Politics from Civil War to Civil Rights.* Princeton, NJ: Princeton University Press, 2000.

Dauphine, James G. "The Knights of the White Camelia and the Election of 1868: Louisiana's White Terrorists; A Benighting Legacy." *Louisiana History* 30, no. 2 (Spring 1989): 173–190.

Davis, David Brion. *Challenging the Boundaries of Slavery.* Cambridge, MA: Harvard University Press, 2003.

——. *Inhuman Bondage: The Rise and Fall of Slavery in the New World.* New York: Oxford University Press, 2006.

——. "Looking at Slavery from Broader Perspectives." *American Historical Review* 105, no. 2 (April 2000): 452–466.

Damico, John Kelly. "Confederate Soldiers Take Matters into Their Own Hands: The End of the Civil War in North Louisiana." *Louisiana History: The Journal of the Louisiana Historical Association* 39, no. 2 (Spring 1998): 189–205.

Daniels, Christian, and Michael Kennedy, eds. *Over the Threshold: Intimate Violence in Early America.* New York: Routledge, 1999.

De Vries, Mark. "The Politics of Terror: Enforcing Reconstruction in Louisiana's Red River Valley." PhD diss., University of Leiden, 2016.

Delbanco, Andrew. *The War Before the War: Fugitive Slaves and the Struggle for America's Soul from the Revolution to the Civil War.* New York: Penguin, 2018.

Dew, Charles B. "The Long Lost Returns: The Candidates and Their Totals in Louisiana's Secession Election." *Louisiana History: The Journal of the Louisiana Historical Association* 10, no. 4 (Autumn 1969): 353–369.

——. "Who Won the Secession Election in Louisiana?" *Journal of Southern History* 36, no. 1 (February 1970): 18–32.

Deyle, Steven. "An 'Abominable' New Trade: The Closing of the African Slave Trade and the Changing Patterns of U.S. Political Power, 1808–60." *William and Mary Quarterly* 66, no. 4 (October 2009): 833–850.

——. *Carry Me Back: The Domestic Slave Trade in American Life*. New York: Oxford University Press, 2005.

Doddington, David. "Manhood, Sex, and Power in Antebellum Slave Communities." In *Sexuality and Slavery*, ed. Berry and Harris, 145–158.

Dollar, Susan E. "The Red River Campaign, Natchitoches Parish, Louisiana: A Case of Equal Opportunity Destruction." *Louisiana History: The Journal of the Louisiana Historical Association* 43, no. 4 (Autumn 2002): 411–432.

Domby, Adam. *The False Cause: Fraud, Fabrication, and White Supremacy in Confederate Memory*. Richmond: University of Virginia Press, 2020.

Downs, Gregory. *After Appomattox: Military Occupation and the Ends of War*. Cambridge, MA, Harvard University Press, 2015.

——. *Declarations of Dependency: The Long Reconstruction of Popular Politics in the South, 1861–1908*. Chapel Hill: University of North Carolina Press, 2011.

Downs, Gregory, and Kate Masur, eds. *The World the Civil War Made*. Chapel Hill: University of North Carolina Press, 2015.

Drago, Harry Sinclair. *Red River Valley: The Mainstream of Frontier History from the Louisiana Bayous to the Texas Panhandle*. New York: Clarkson N. Potter, 1962.

Drake, Brian Allen, ed. *The Blue, the Gray, and the Green: Toward an Environmental History of the Civil War*. Athens: University of Georgia Press, 2015.

Drake, W. Magruder, and H. Winbourne Drake. "Two Letters of H. Winbourne Drake, Civil War Refugee in Northwest Louisiana." *Louisiana History: The Journal of the Louisiana Historical Association* 7, no. 1 (1966): 71–76.

Dupre, Daniel S. *Transforming the Cotton Frontier: Madison County, Alabama, 1800–1840*. Baton Rouge: Louisiana State University Press, 1997.

Dusinberre, William. *Them Dark Days: Slavery in the American Rice Swamps*. New York: Oxford University Press, 1996.

Earle, Carville. *Geographical Inquiry and American Historical Problems*. Stanford, CA: Stanford University Press, 1992.

Egerton, Douglas. "Markets Without a Market Revolution: Southern Planters and Capitalism." *Journal of the Early Republic* 16, no. 2 (Summer 1996): 207–221.

Emberton, Carole. *Beyond Redemption: Race, Violence, and the American South After the Civil War*. Chicago: University of Chicago Press, 2013.

——. "'Only Murder Makes Men': Reconsidering the Black Military Experience." *Journal of the Civil War Era* 2, no. 3 (September 2012): 369–393.

——. "Reconstructing Loyalty: Love, Fear, and Power in the Postwar South." In *The Great Task Remaining Before Us*, ed. Cimbala and Miller, 173–182.

Emberton, Carole, and Bruce Baker, eds. *Remembering Reconstruction: Struggles over the Meaning of America's Most Turbulent Era*. Baton Rouge: Louisiana State University Press, 2017.

Englesman, John. "The Freedmen's Bureau in Louisiana." *Louisiana Historical Quarterly* 32, no. 1 (January 1949): 145–221.

Escott, Paul. *"What Shall We Do with the Negro?": Lincoln, White Racism, and Civil War America*. Charlottesville: University of Virginia Press, 2009.

Evans, Chris. "The Plantation Hoe: The Rise and Fall of an Atlantic Commodity, 1650–1850." *William and Mary Quarterly* 69, no. 1 (January 2012): 71–100.

Fabrikant, Robert. "Emancipation and the Proclamation: Of Contrabands, Congress, and Lincoln." *Howard Law Journal* 49, no. 1 (Winter 2006): 313–343.

Fairclough, Adam. *Bulldozed and Betrayed: Louisiana and the Stolen Elections of 1876*. Baton Rouge: Louisiana State University Press, 2021.

———. *The Revolution that Failed: Reconstruction in Natchitoches*. Gainesville: University Press of Florida, 2018.

Faust, Drew Gilpin. "Altars of Sacrifice: Confederate Women and the Narratives of War." *Journal of American History* 76, no. 4 (March 1990): 1200–1228.

———. "The Civil War Soldier and the Art of Dying." *Journal of Southern History* 67, no 1 (February 2001): 3–38.

———. *The Creation of Confederate Nationalism: Ideology and Identity in the Civil War South*. Baton Rouge: Louisiana State University Press, 1988.

———. "Culture, Conflict, and Community: The Meaning of Power on an Ante-Bellum Plantation." *Journal of Social History* 14, no. 1 (Autumn 1980): 83–97.

Fett, Sharla. *Working Cures: Healing, Health, and Power on Southern Slave Plantations*. Chapel Hill: University of North Carolina Press, 2002.

Fields, Barbara. "Ideology and Race in American History." In *Region, Race, and Reconstruction: Essays in Honor of C. Vann Woodward*, ed. J. Morgan Kousser and James McPherson. New York: Oxford University Press, 1982.

———. "'Origins of the New South' and the Negro Question." *Journal of Southern History* 67, no. 4 (November 2001): 811–826.

———. "Whiteness, Racism, and Identity." *International Labor and Working-Class History* 60 (Fall 2001): 48–56.

Finley, Alexandra. "Considering the Slave Trade as a Family Business." Presentation at the 131st Annual Meeting of American Historical Association, Denver, CO, January 5–8, 2017.

Fite, Gilbert. "Southern Agriculture Since the Civil War: An Overview." *American History* 53, no. 1 (January 1979): 3–21.

Fitzgerald, Michael W. *Reconstruction in Alabama: From Civil War to Redemption in the Cotton South*. Baton Rouge: Louisiana State University Press, 2017.

———. *Splendid Failure: Postwar Reconstruction in the American South*. Chicago: Ivan R. Dee, 2007.

———. *Urban Emancipation: Popular Politics in Reconstruction Mobile, 1860–1890.* Baton Rouge: Louisiana State University Press, 2002.

Fogel, Robert William. *The Slavery Debates: A Retrospective, 1952–1990.* Baton Rouge: Louisiana State University Press, 2003.

———. *Without Consent or Contract: The Rise and Fall of American Slavery.* New York: W. W. Norton, 1989.

Fogel, Robert William, and Stanley L. Engerman. *Time on the Cross: The Economics of American Negro Slavery.* London: Wildwood House, 1974.

Follett, Richard. "Legacies of Enslavement: Plantation Identities and the Problem of Freedom." In *Slavery's Ghost,* ed. Follett, Foner, and Johnson, 50–84.

———. *Sugar Masters: Planters and Slaves in Louisiana's Cane World, 1820–1860.* Baton Rouge: Louisiana State University Press, 2005.

Follett, Richard, Sven Beckert, Peter Coclanis, and Barbara Hahn. *Plantation Kingdom: The American South and Its Global Commodities.* Baltimore: Johns Hopkins University Press, 2016.

Follett, Richard, Eric Foner, and Walter Johnson. *Slavery's Ghost: The Problem of Freedom in the Age of Emancipation.* Baltimore: Johns Hopkins University Press, 2011.

Foner, Eric. *The Fiery Trial: Abraham Lincoln and American Slavery.* New York: Norton, 2010.

———. *Free Soil, Free Labor, Free Men: The Ideology of the Republican Party Before the Civil War.* New York: Oxford University Press, 1970.

———, ed. *Our Lincoln: New Perspectives on Lincoln and His World.* New York: W. W. Norton, 2008.

———. *Reconstruction: America's Unfinished Revolution, 1863–1877.* New York: Harper & Row, 1988.

———. *The Second Founding: How the Civil War and Reconstruction Remade the Constitution.* New York: W. W. Norton, 2019.

Ford, Lacy. "Reconfiguring the Old South: 'Solving' the Problem of Slavery, 1787–1838." *Journal of American History* 95, no. 1 (June 2008): 95–122.

Forrester, Kristen L. "Disrupting the Domestic Sphere: The Civil War and North Louisiana Women, 1861–1865." *North Louisiana Historical Association Journal* 26, no. 1 (Winter 1995): 36–54.

Forret, Jeff. "'Deaf & Dumb, Blind, Insane, or Idiotic': The Census, Slaves, and Disability in the Late Antebellum South." *Journal of Southern History* 82, no 3 (August 2016): 503–548.

———. *Race Relations at the Margins: Slaves and Poor Whites in the Antebellum Southern Countryside.* Baton Rouge: Louisiana State University Press, 2006.

———. *Slave Against Slave: Plantation Violence in the Old South.* Baton Rouge: Louisiana State University Press, 2015.

Forsyth, Michael J. *The Red River Campaign of 1864 and the Loss by the Confederacy of the Civil War.* Jefferson, NC: McFarland and Company, 2002.

Foshee, Andrew W. "Slave Hiring in Rural Louisiana." *Louisiana History: The Journal of the Louisiana Historical Association* 26, no 1 (Winter 1985): 63–73.

Foster, Gaines. *Ghosts of the Confederacy: Defeat, the Lost Cause, and the Emergence of the New South.* New York: Oxford University Press, 1987.

Fox-Genovese, Elizabeth. *Within the Plantation Household: Black and White Women of the Old South.* Chapel Hill: University of North Carolina Press, 1988.

Franklin, John Hope. *The Militant South, 1800–1861.* 1956. Urbana: University of Illinois Press, 2002.

———. *Reconstruction After the Civil War.* 3rd ed. Chicago: University of Chicago Press, 2013.

Gallagher, Gary. *The Confederate War.* Cambridge, MA: Harvard University Press, 1997.

Gaspar, David Barry, and Darlene Clark Hine, eds. *More than Chattel: Black Women and Slavery in the Americas.* Bloomington: Indiana University Press, 1996.

Genovese, Eugene. *The Political Economy of Slavery: Studies in the Economy and Society of the Slave South.* New York: Random House, 1965.

———. *Roll, Jordan, Roll: The World the Slaves Made.* New York: Vintage, 1976.

———. *The World the Slaveholders Made: Two Essays in Interpretation.* New York: Vintage, 1969.

Genovese, Eugene, and Elizabeth Fox-Genovese. *Fatal Self-Deception: Slaveholding Paternalism in the Old South.* New York: Cambridge University Press, 2011.

Gentry, Judith F. "White Gold: The Confederate Government and Cotton in Louisiana." *Louisiana History: The Journal of the Louisiana Historical Association* 33, no 3 (Summer 1992): 229–240.

Gerteis, Louis S. *From Contraband to Freedom: Federal Policy Toward Southern Blacks, 1861–1865.* Westport, CT: Greenwood Press, 1973.

Gilley, B. H., ed. *North Louisiana—Volume One: To 1865. Essays on the Region and Its History.* Ruston, LA: McGinty Trust Fund Publications, 1984.

Glatthaar, Joseph. *General Lee's Army: From Victory to Collapse.* New York: Free Press, 2008.

Glover, Lorri. *Southern Sons: Becoming Men in the New Nation.* Baltimore: Johns Hopkins University Press, 2007.

Glymph, Thavolia. *Out of the House of Bondage: The Transformation of the Plantation Household.* Cambridge: Cambridge University Press, 2008.

Goldin, Claudia, and Frank Lewis. "The Economic Cost of the American Civil War: Estimates and Implications." *Journal of Economic History* 35, no. 2 (June 1975): 299–326.

Goldstone, Lawrence. *Inherently Unequal: The Betrayal of Equal Rights by the Supreme Court, 1865–1903.* New York: Walker & Company, 2011.

Gorn, Elliot J. "'Gouge and Bite, Pull Hair and Scratch': The Social Significance of Fighting in the Southern Backcountry." *American Historical Review* 90 (February 1985): 18–43.

Gray, Lewis Cecil. *History of Agriculture in the Southern United States to 1860*. Clifton, NJ: Augustus Kelley Publishers, 1973.

Greenberg, Kenneth. *Honor & Slavery: Lies, Duels, Noses, Masks, Dressing as a Woman, Fights, Strangers, Death, Humanitarianism, Slave Rebellions, the Pro-Slavery Argument, Baseball, Hunting, and Gambling in the Old South*. Princeton, NJ: Princeton University Press, 1996.

——. "The Nose, the Lie, and the Duel in the Antebellum South." *American Historical Review* 95, no. 1 (February 1990): 57–74.

Greer, James Kimmins. "Louisiana Politics, 1845–1861." *Louisiana Historical Quarterly* 13 (January 1930): 444–483.

Grimsley, Mark. *The Hard Hand of War: Union Military Policy Toward Southern Civilians, 1861–1865*. New York: Cambridge University Press, 1995.

Gudmestad, Robert H. "Steamboats and the Removal of the Red River Raft." *Louisiana History: The Journal of the Louisiana Historical Association* 52, no. 4 (Fall 2011): 389–416.

——. *Steamboats and the Rise of the Cotton Kingdom*. Baton Rouge: Louisiana State University Press, 2011.

——. *A Troublesome Commerce: The Transformation of the Interstate Slave Trade*. Baton Rouge: Louisiana State University Press, 2003.

Guterl, Matthew Pratt. *American Mediterranean: Southern Slaveholders in the Age of Emancipation*. Cambridge, MA: Harvard University Press, 2008.

Gutman, Herbert G. *The Black Family in Slavery and Freedom, 1750–1925*. New York: Vintage, 1976.

——. *Slavery and the Numbers Game: A Critique of Time on the Cross*. Urbana: University of Illinois Press, 1973.

Hadden, Sally E. *Slave Patrols: Law and Violence in Virginia and the Carolinas*. Cambridge, MA: Harvard University Press, 2001.

Hahn, Steven. *A Nation Under Our Feet: Black Political Struggles in the Rural South from Slavery to the Great Migration*. Cambridge, MA: Harvard University Press, 2005.

——. *The Political Worlds of Slavery and Freedom*. Cambridge, MA: Harvard University Press, 2009.

Hale, Grace Elizabeth. *Making Whiteness: The Culture of Segregation in the South, 1890–1940*. New York: Vintage, 1999.

Halstead, Murat. *Three Against Lincoln: Murat Halstead Reports the Caucuses of 1860*. Baton Rouge: Louisiana State University Press, 1960.

Harris, William. *With Charity for All: Lincoln and the Restoration of the Union*. Lexington: University of Kentucky Press, 1997.

Harrison, Mabel Fletcher, and Lavinia McGuire McNeely. *Grant Parish, Louisiana: A History Published to Celebrate Grant Parish Centennial and Louisiana Pecan Festival 1969*. Baton Rouge: Claitor's Publishing Division, 1969.

Hartman, Saidiya. *Scenes of Subjection: Terror, Slavery, and Self-Making in Nineteenth Century America*. New York: Oxford University Press, 1997.

Highsmith, William E. "Some Aspects of Reconstruction in the Heart of Louisiana." *Journal of Southern History* 13, no. 4 (November 1947): 460–491.

Hillard, Sam Bowers. *Hog Meat and Hoecake: Food Supply in the Old South, 1840–1860*. Carbondale: Southern Illinois University Press, 1972.

Heppen, John, and Samuel M. Otterstrom. *Geography, History, and the American Political Economy*. Lanham, MD: Lexington Books, 2009.

Hodgson, Gene. "Forest Park: History of a Plantation Home and the Family that Built It." *North Louisiana Historical Association Journal* 18, no. 1 (Winter 1987): 31–40.

Hogue, James K. "The 1873 Battle of Colfax: Paramilitarism and Counterrevolution in Louisiana." Paper presented at the Southern Historical Association Conference, November 6, 1997.

———. *Uncivil War: Five New Orleans Street Battles and the Rise and Fall of Radical Reconstruction*. Baton Rouge: Louisiana State University Press, 2006.

Holt, Thomas. *"From Slavery to Freedom* and the Conceptualization of African-American History." *Journal of Negro History* 85, no 1/2 (Winter–Spring 2000): 22–26.

———. "Marking: Race, Race-making, and the Writing of History." *American Historical Review* 100, no. 1 (February 1995): 1–20.

Hong, Keumsoo. "The Structural Transformation of the Antebellum Red River Valley Settlement Systems in Louisiana." In *Geography, History, and the American Political Economy*, ed. Heppen and Otterstrom, 65–98.

Hospodor, Gregory S. "'Bound by all the ties of honor': Southern Honor, the Mississippians, and the Mexican War." *Journal of Mississippi History* 62, no. 1 (Spring 1999): 1–29.

Howell, Thomas. "The Colfax Massacre: An Essay Review." *Louisiana History: The Journal of the Louisiana Historical Association* 51, no. 1 (Winter 2010): 69–74.

———. "Finding the Line: The Origin of Grant Parish and the Recent Dispute over Its Boundary." *Louisiana History: The Journal of the Louisiana Historical Association* 51, no. 2 (Spring 2010): 215–230.

Humphries, Hubert. "Photographic Views of Red River Raft, 1873." *Louisiana History: The Journal of the Louisiana Historical Association* 12, no. 2 (Spring 1971): 101–108.

———. "The Red River Raft Briefly Revisited." *North Louisiana Historical Association Journal* 1, no. 1 (Fall 1969): 10–16.

Hunter, Tera. *Bound in Wedlock: Slave and Free Black Marriage in the Nineteenth Century*. Cambridge, MA: Harvard University Press, 2017.

——. To 'Joy My Freedom: Southern Black Women's Lives and Labors After the Civil War. Cambridge, MA: Harvard University Press, 1998.

Huston, James. "Slavery, Capitalism, and the Interpretations of the Antebellum United States: The Problem of Definition." Civil War History 65, no. 2 (June 2019): 119–156.

Illingworth, James. "'Erroneous and Incongruous Notions of Liberty': Urban Unrest and the Origins of Racial Reconstruction in New Orleans, 1865–1868." In After Slavery, ed. Baker and Kelly, 35–57.

Innes, Stephen, ed. Work and Labor in Early America. Chapel Hill: University of North Carolina Press, published for the Institute of Early American History and Culture, 1988.

Janney, Caroline. Remembering the Civil War: Reunion and the Limits of Reconciliation. Chapel Hill: University of North Carolina Press, 2013.

Jennison, Watson W. Cultivating Race: The Expansion of Slavery in Georgia, 1750–1860. Lexington: University Press of Kentucky, 2012.

Jimerson, Randall C. The Private Civil War: Popular Thought During the Sectional Conflict. Baton Rouge: Louisiana State University Press, 1988.

Johnson, Ludwell. Red River Campaign: Politics and Cotton in the Civil War. Kent, OH: Kent State University Press, 1993.

Johnson, Michael P. "Work, Culture, and the Slave Community: Slave Occupations in the Cotton Belt in 1860." Labor History 27, no. 3 (1986): 325–355.

Johnson, Walter. "On Agency." Journal of Social History 37, no. 1, special issue (Autumn 2003): 113–124.

——. River of Dark Dreams: Slavery and Empire in the Cotton Kingdom. Cambridge, MA: Harvard University Press, 2013.

——. Soul by Soul: Life Inside the Antebellum Slave Market. Cambridge, MA: Harvard University Press, 1999.

Joiner, Gary Dillard, ed. Little to Eat and Thin Mud to Drink: Letters, Diaries, and Memoirs from the Red River Campaigns, 1863–1864. Knoxville: University of Tennessee Press, 2007.

——. One Damn Blunder from Beginning to End: The Red River Campaign of 1864. Wilmington, DE: Scholarly Resources, 2003.

——. Through the Howling Wilderness: The 1864 Red River Campaign and Union Failure in the West. Knoxville: University of Tennessee Press, 2006.

Jones-Rogers, Stephanie. They Were Her Property: White Women as Slave Owners in the American South. New Haven, CT: Yale University Press, 2019.

Joyner, Charles. Down by the Riverside: A South Carolina Slave Community. Urbana: University of Illinois Press, 1984.

Kantrowitz, Stephen. Ben Tillman and the Reconstruction of White Supremacy. Chapel Hill: The University of North Carolina Press, 2000.

——. "One Man's Mob Is Another Man's Militia: Violence, Manhood, and Authority in Reconstruction South Carolina." In *Jumpin' Jim Crow*, ed. Dailey, Gilmore, and Simon, 67–87.

Kaye, Anthony. *Joining Places: Slave Neighborhoods in the Old South*. Chapel Hill: University of North Carolina Press, 2007.

——. "The Second Slavery: Modernity in the Nineteenth-Century South and the Atlantic World." *Journal of Southern History* 75, no. 3 (August 2009): 627–650.

Keele, Luke, William Cubbison, and Ismail White. "Suppressing Black Votes: A Historical Case Study of Voting Restrictions in Louisiana." *American Political Science Review* 115, no. 2 (2021): 694–700.

Keith, LeeAnna. *The Colfax Massacre: The Untold Story of Black Power, White Terror, and the Death of Reconstruction*. New York: Oxford University Press, 2008.

Kelley, Sean M. *Los Brazos de Dios: A Plantation Society in the Texas Borderlands, 1821–1865*. Baton Rouge: Louisiana State University Press, 2010.

Kendall, Lane C. "The Interregnum in Louisiana in 1861." *Louisiana Historical Quarterly* 16 (April 1933): 374–408.

Kendi, Ibram X. *Stamped from the Beginning: The Definitive History of Racist Ideas in America*. New York: Bold Type Books, 2016.

Kerby, Robert. *Kirby Smith's Confederacy: The Trans-Mississippi South, 1863–1865*. New York: Columbia University Press, 1972.

Kilbourne, Richard Holcombe Jr. *Debt, Investment, Slaves: Credit Relations in East Feliciana Parish, Louisiana, 1825–1885*. Tuscaloosa: University of Alabama Press, 1995.

Kiple, Kenneth F., and Virginia Himmelsteib King. *Another Dimension to the Black Diaspora: Diet, Disease, and Racism*. Cambridge: Cambridge University Press, 1981.

King, Wilma. *Stolen Childhood: Slave Youth in Nineteenth-Century America*. Bloomington: Indiana University Press, 1995.

Kolchin, Peter. *American Slavery, 1619–1877*. New York: Hill and Wang, 1993.

Lane, Charles. *The Day Freedom Died: The Colfax Massacre, the Supreme Court, and the Betrayal of Reconstruction*. New York: Henry Holt, 2008.

Lang, Andrew. *In the Wake of War: Military Occupation, Emancipation, and Civil War America*. Baton Rouge: Louisiana State University Press, 2021.

——. "Union Demobilization and the Boundaries of War and Peace." *Journal of the Civil War Era* 9, no 2 (June 2019): 178–195.

Lebergott, Stanley. "Through the Blockade: The Profitability and Extent of Cotton Smuggling, 1861–1865." *Journal of Economic History* 41, no. 4 (December 1981): 867–888.

Lee, Matthew R., William B. Bankston, Timothy C. Hayes, and Shaun A. Thomas. "Revisiting the Southern Culture of Violence." *Sociological Quarterly* 48, no. 2 (2007): 253–275.

Legan, M. Scott. "Drugs for Louisiana: The Louisiana State Laboratory, 1864–1865." *Louisiana History: The Journal of the Louisiana Historical Association* 48, no. 2 (Spring 2007): 193–202.

Levine, Bruce. *The Fall of the House of Dixie: The Civil War and the Social Revolution That Transformed the South.* New York: Random House, 2013.

———. *Half Slave and Half Free: The Roots of the Civil War.* New York: Hill and Wang, 1992.

Libby, David J. *Slavery and Frontier Mississippi, 1720–1835.* Jackson: University Press of Mississippi, 2004.

Limerick, Patricia Nelson. *The Legacy of Conquest: The Unbroken Past of the American West.* New York: W. W. Norton, 1987.

Litwack, Leon. *Been in the Storm So Long: The Aftermath of Slavery.* New York: Knopf, 1979.

Lonn, Ella. *Salt as a Factor in the Confederacy.* New York: Walter Neale, 1933.

Malone, Ann Patton. "Searching for the Family and Household Structure of Rural Louisiana Slaves, 1810–1864." *Louisiana History: The Journal of the Louisiana Historical Association* 28, no. 4 (Autumn 1987): 357–379.

———. *Sweet Chariot: Slave Family and Household Structure in Nineteenth-Century Louisiana.* Chapel Hill: University of North Carolina Press, 1992.

Manning, Chandra. *Troubled Refuge: Struggling for Freedom in the Civil War.* New York: Knopf, 2016.

———. *What This Cruel War Was Over: Soldiers, Slavery, and the Civil War.* New York: Alfred Knopf, 2007.

Marion-Landais, George. "The Alfred Flournoy Jr. Letters to Theodosia, His Wife, 1861." *North Louisiana Historical Association Journal* 28, no. 2/3 (Spring/Summer 1997): 92–118.

Marler, Scott P. *The Merchant's Capital: New Orleans and the Political Economy of the Nineteenth-Century South.* Cambridge: Cambridge University Press, 2013.

Martel, Glenn. "Early Days in Northwest Louisiana." *Arkansas Historical Quarterly* 12, no. 2 (Summer 1953): 119–125.

Martin, Bonnie. "Slavery's Invisible Engine: Mortgaging Human Property." *Journal of Southern History* 76, no. 4 (November 2010): 1–50.

Martin, Jonathan D. *Divided Mastery: Slave Hiring in the American South.* Cambridge, MA: Harvard University Press, 2004.

Masur, Kate. "'A Rare Phenomenon of Philological Vegetation': The Word 'Contraband' and the Meanings of Emancipation in the United States." *Journal of American History* 93 (March 2007): 1050–1084.

Mayeaux, Steven. *Earthen Walls, Iron Men: Fort DeRussy, Louisiana, and the Defense of Red River.* Knoxville: University of Tennessee Press, 2007.

McBride, Dwight. *Impossible Witnesses: Truth, Abolitionism, and Slave Testimony.* New York: New York University Press, 2001.

McClelland, Peter. *Sowing Modernity: America's First Agricultural Revolution.* Ithaca, NY: Cornell Press, 1997.

McCrary, Payton. *Abraham Lincoln and Reconstruction: The Louisiana Experiment.* Princeton, NJ: Princeton University Press, 1978.

McCurry, Stephanie. *Confederate Reckoning: Power and Politics in the Civil War South.* Cambridge, MA: Harvard University Press, 2010.

——. *Masters of Small Worlds: Yeoman Households, Gender Relations, and the Political Culture of the Antebellum South Carolina Low Country.* New York: Oxford University Press, 1995.

——. *Women's War: Fighting and Surviving the American Civil War.* Cambridge, MA: Harvard University Press, 2019.

McDonald, Roderick A. *The Economy and Material Culture of Slaves: Goods and Chattels on the Sugar Plantations of Jamaica and Louisiana.* Baton Rouge: Louisiana State University Press, 1993.

McLure, Mary Lilla. "The Election of 1860 in Louisiana." *Louisiana Historical Quarterly* 9 (October 1926): 601–702.

McLure, Mary Lilla, and J. Ed Howe. *The History of Shreveport and Shreveport Builders.* Shreveport, LA: Journal Print Company, 1937.

McNeilly, Donald P. *The Old South Frontier: Cotton Plantations and the Formation of Arkansas Society, 1819–1861.* Fayetteville: University of Arkansas Press, 2000.

Mears, Michelle M. *And Grace Will Lead Me Home: African American Freedmen Communities of Austin, Texas, 1865–1928.* Lubbock: Texas Technical University Press, 2009.

Meier, Kathryn M. "The Removal of the Great Raft from the Red River." *North Louisiana Historical Association Journal* 31, no. 2/3 (Spring/Summer 2000): 24–33.

Metzer, Jacob. "Rational Management, Modern Business Practices, and Economies of Scale in the Ante-Bellum Southern Plantations." *Exploration in Economic History* 12 (1975): 123–150.

Merrins, H. Roy, and George D. Terry. "Dying in Paradise: Malaria, Mortality, and the Perceptual Environment in Colonial South Carolina." *Journal of Southern History* 50, no. 4 (November 1984): 533–550.

Miciotto, R. J. "Shreveport's First Major Health Crisis: The Yellow Fever Epidemic of 1873." *North Louisiana Historical Association Journal* 4, no. 4 (Summer 1973): 111–118.

Miller, James David. *South by Southwest: Planter Emigration and Identity in the Slave South.* Charlottesville: University of Virginia Press, 2002.

Miller, Steven F. "Plantation Labor Organization and Slave Life on the Cotton Frontier: The Alabama–Mississippi Black Belt, 1815–1840." In *Cultivation and Culture,* ed. Berlin and Morgan, 155–169.

Moneyhon, Carl H. *Texas After the Civil War: The Struggle of Reconstructions.* College Station: Texas A&M University Press, 2004.

Moore, John Hebron. "Cotton Breeding in the Old South." *Agricultural History* 30, no. 3 (July 1956): 95–104.

———. *The Emergence of the Cotton Kingdom in the Old Southwest: Mississippi, 1770–1860*. Baton Rouge: Louisiana State University Press, 1988.

Morgan, Jennifer. *Laboring Women: Reproduction and Gender in New World Slavery.* Philadelphia: University of Pennsylvania Press, 2004.

Morgan, Philip D. "Task and Gang Systems: The Organization of Labor on New World Plantations." In *Work and Labor in Early America*, ed. Innes, 189–220.

Morris, Christopher. "The Articulation of Two Worlds: The Master–Slave Relationship Reconsidered." *Journal of American History* 85, no. 3 (December 1998): 982–1007.

———. *Becoming Southern: The Evolution of a Way of Life, Warren County and Vicksburg, Mississippi, 1770–1860*. New York: Oxford University Press, 1995.

———. *The Big Muddy: An Environmental History of the Mississippi and Its People from Hernando Desoto to Hurricane Katrina*. Oxford: Oxford University Press, 2012.

———. "Within the Slave Cabin: Violence in Mississippi Slave Families." In *Over the Threshold*, ed. Daniels and Kennedy, 268–286.

Morrison, Toni. *Playing in the Dark: Whiteness and the Literary Imagination*. New York: Vintage, 1993.

Mutti Burke, Diane. *On Slavery's Border: Missouri's Small-Slaveholding Households, 1815–1865*. Athens: University of Georgia Press, 2010.

Nash, Stephen. *A Massacre in Memphis: The Race Riot That Shook the Nation One Year After the Civil War*. New York: Hill & Wang, 2013.

———. *When the Yankees Came: Conflict and Chaos in the Occupied South, 1861–1865*. Chapel Hill: University of North Carolina Press, 1995.

Nelson, Scott Reynolds. *Iron Confederacies: Southern Railways, Klan Violence, and Reconstruction*. Chapel Hill: University of North Carolina Press, 1999.

———. "Who Put Their Capitalism in My Slavery?" *Journal of the Civil War Era* 5, no. 2 (June 2015): 289–310.

Noe, Kenneth. "Fateful Lightning: The Significance of Weather and Climate to Civil War History." In *The Blue, the Gray, and the Green*, ed. Drake, 16–33.

Numbers, Ronald L., and Todd L. Savitt, eds. *Science and Medicine in the Old South*. Baton Rouge: Louisiana State University Press, 1989.

Nystrom, Justin. *New Orleans After the Civil War: Race, Politics, and a New Birth of Freedom*. Baltimore: Johns Hopkins University Press, 2010.

Oakes, James. *Freedom National: The Destruction of Slavery in the United States, 1861–1865*. New York: W. W. Norton, 2014.

———. *The Ruling Race: A History of American Slaveholders*. New York: W. W. Norton, 1998.

——. *Slavery and Freedom: An Interpretation of the Old South.* New York: W. W. Norton, 1998.

O'Donovan, Susan. *Becoming Free in the Cotton South.* Cambridge, MA: Harvard University Press, 2007.

Olmstead, Alan L., and Paul W. Rhode. "Biological Innovation and Productivity Growth in the Antebellum Cotton Economy." *Journal of Economic History* 68, no. 4 (December 2008): 1123–1171.

——. "Productivity Growth and the Regional Dynamics of Antebellum Southern Development." NBER working paper no. 16494, October 2010, National Bureau of Economic Research. www.nber.org/papers/w16494.

Painter, Nell Irvin. *Exodusters: Black Migration to Kansas After Reconstruction.* 1977. Reprint, New York: W. W. Norton, 1992.

——. *The History of White People.* New York: W. W. Norton, 2010.

——. "Millenarian Aspects of the Exodus to Kansas of 1879." *Journal of Social History* 9 (Spring 1976): 331–338.

Pargas, Damian Alan. "In the Fields of a 'Strange Land': Enslaved Newcomers and the Adjustment to Cotton Cultivation in the Antebellum South." *Slavery & Abolition* 34, no 4 (2013): 562–578.

Parsons, Elaine Frantz. "Klan Skepticism and Denial in Reconstruction-Era Public Discourse." *Journal of Southern History* 77, no 1 (February 2011): 53–90.

——. *Ku-Klux: The Birth of the Klan During Reconstruction.* Chapel Hill: University of North Carolina Press, 2015.

——. "Midnight Rangers: Costume and Performance in the Reconstruction-Era Ku Klux Klan." *Journal of American History* 92, no 3 (December 2005): 811–836.

Penningroth, Dylan. *The Claims of Kinfolk: African American Property and Community in the Nineteenth Century South.* Chapel Hill, University of North Carolina Press, 2003.

Peoples, Morgan D. "'Kansas Fever' in North Louisiana." *Louisiana History: The Journal of the Louisiana Historical Association* 11, no. 2 (Spring 1970): 121–135.

Peyton, Rupert. "The Civil War Began and Ended in North Louisiana." *North Louisiana Historical Association Journal* 7, no. 2 (Winter 1976): 75–77.

Pfeifer, Michael J. "The Origins of Postbellum Lynching: Collective Violence in Reconstruction Louisiana." *Louisiana History: The Journal of the Louisiana Historical Association* 50, no. 2 (Spring 2009): 189–201.

——. *Rough Justice: Lynching and American Society 1874–1947.* Urbana: University of Illinois Press, 2004.

Phillips, Jason. *Diehard Rebels: The Confederate Culture of Invincibility.* Athens: University of Georgia Press, 2007.

——. "Rebels in War and Peace: Their Ethos and Its Impact." In *The Great Task Remaining Before Us,* ed. Cimbala and Miller, 154–172.

Pollard, Leslie J. "Aging and Slavery: A Gerontological Perspective." *Journal of Negro History* 66, no. 3 (Autumn 1981): 228–234.

Pritchett, Jonathan B., and Herman Freudenberger. "A Peculiar Sample: The Selection of Slaves for the New Orleans Market." *Journal of Economic History* 52, no. 1 (March 1992): 109–127.

Proctor, Bradley. "'From the cradle to the grave': Jim Williams, Black Manhood, and Militia Activism in Reconstruction South Carolina." *American Nineteenth Century History* 19, no. 1 (2017): 47–79.

———. "The K. K. Alphabet." *Journal of the Civil War Era* 8, no. 3 (September 2018): 455–487.

Putzi, Jennifer. *Identifying Marks: Race, Gender, and the Marked Body in Nineteenth-Century America.* Athens: University of Georgia Press, 2006.

Quigley, Paul. *Shifting Grounds: Nationalism and the American South, 1848–1865.* New York: Oxford University Press, 2012.

Rable, George. *But There Was No Peace: The Role of Violence in the Politics of Reconstruction.* 2nd ed. Athens: University of Georgia Press, 2007.

———. *Civil Wars: Women and the Crisis of Southern Nationalism.* Champaign: University of Illinois Press, 1989.

Ransom, Roger, and Richard Sutch. "Capitalists Without Capital: The Burden of Slavery and the Impact of Emancipation." *Agricultural History* 62, no. 3 (Summer 1988): 133–160.

———. "The Impact of the Civil War and of Emancipation on Southern Agriculture." *Explorations in Economic History* 12, no. 1 (January 1975): 1–28.

Reece, Robert. "Color Crit: Critical Race theory and the History and Future of Colorism in the United States." *Journal of Black Studies* 50, no. 1 (2018): 1–23.

———. "Whitewashing Slavery: Legacy of Slavery and White Social Outcomes." *Social Problems* 67, no. 2 (May 2020): 304–323.

Reidy, Joseph P. *From Slavery to Agrarian Capitalism in the Cotton Plantation South, Central Georgia, 1800–1880.* Chapel Hill: University of North Carolina Press, 1992.

———. "Obligation and Right: Patterns of Labor, Subsistence, and Exchange in the Cotton Belt of Georgia, 1790–1860." In *Cultivation and Culture,* ed. Berlin and Morgan, 138–154.

Richardson, Heather Cox. *How the South Won the Civil War: Oligarchy, Democracy, and the Continuing Fight for the South of America.* New York: Oxford University Press, 2020.

———. *To Make Men Free: A History of the Republican Party.* New York: Basic Books, 2014.

Roark, James L. *Masters Without Slaves: Southern Planters in the Civil War and Reconstruction.* New York: W. W. Norton, 1977.

Roberts, Alaina E. "A Different Forty Acres: Land, Kin, and Migration in the Late Nineteenth-Century West." *Journal of the Civil War Era* 10, no. 2 (June 2020): 213–232.

———. *I've Been Here All the While: Black Freedom on Native Land.* Philadelphia: University of Pennsylvania Press, 2021.

Roberts, Giselle. "The Confederate Belle: The Belle Ideal, Patriotic Womanhood, and Wartime Reality in Louisiana and Mississippi, 1861–1865." *Louisiana History: The Journal of the Louisiana Historical Association* 43, no. 2 (Spring 2002): 189–214.

Robertson, Henry. *The Red River Campaign and Its Toll: 69 Bloody Days in Louisiana, March–May 1864.* Jefferson, NC: McFarland Press, 2016.

Rockman, Seth. "The Future of Civil War Era Studies: Slavery and Capitalism." *Journal of the Civil War Era* 2, no. 1 (March 2012).

Rodrigue, John C. *Reconstruction in the Cane Fields: From Slavery to Free Labor in Louisiana's Sugar Parishes, 1862–1880.* Baton Rouge: Louisiana State University Press, 2001.

Roediger, David. *Working Toward Whiteness: How America's Immigrants Became White.* New York: Basic Books, 2006.

Rohrbough, Malcolm J. *The Land Office Business: The Settlement and Administration of American Public Lands, 1789–1837.* New York: Oxford University Press, 1968.

Roland, Charles P. "Louisiana and Secession." *Louisiana History: The Journal of the Louisiana Historical Association* 19, no. 4 (Autumn 1978): 389–399.

Rolinson, Mary. *Grassroots Garveyism: The Universal Negro Improvement Association in the Rural South, 1920–1927.* Chapel Hill: University of North Carolina Press, 2007.

Rosen, Hannah. *Terror in the Heart of Freedom: Citizenship, Sexual Violence, and the Meaning of Race in the Postemancipation South.* Chapel Hill: University of North Carolina Press, 2008.

Rosenthal, Caitlin C. "From Memory to Mastery: Accounting for Control in America, 1750–1880." *Enterprise & Society* 14, no. 4 (2013): 732–748.

Rothman, Adam. *Beyond Freedom's Reach: A Kidnapping in the Twilight of Slavery.* Cambridge, MA: Harvard University Press, 2015.

———. *Slave Country: American Expansion and the Origins of the Deep South.* Cambridge, MA: Harvard University Press, 2007.

Rothman, Joshua D. *Flush Times and Fever Dreams: A Story of Capitalism and Slavery in the Age of Jackson.* Athens: University of Georgia Press, 2012.

Rubin, Anne Sarah. *A Shattered Nation: The Rise and Fall of the Confederacy, 1861–1868.* Chapel Hill: University of North Carolina Press, 2005.

Sacher, John M. "'Our Interest and Destiny Are the Same': Gov. Thomas Overton

Moore and Confederate Loyalty." *Louisiana History: The Journal of the Louisiana Historical Association* 49, no 3 (Summer 2008): 261–286.

———. *A Perfect War of Politics: Parties, Politicians, and Democracy in Louisiana, 1824–1861.* Baton Rouge: Louisiana State University Press, 2003.

———. "'Twenty-Negro,' or Overseer Law: A Reconsideration." *Journal of the Civil War Era* 7, no 2 (June 2017), 269–292.

———. "'A Very Disagreeable Business': Confederate Conscription in Louisiana." *Civil War History* 53, no 2 (June 2007): 141–169.

Sanson, Jerry Purvis. "Rapides Parish, Louisiana, During the End of Reconstruction." *Louisiana History: The Journal of the Louisiana Historical Association* 27, no. 2 (Spring 1986): 167–182.

———. "White Man's Failure: The Rapides Parish 1874 Election." *Louisiana History: The Journal of the Louisiana Historical Association* 31, no. 1 (Winter 1990): 39–58.

Saville, Julie. *The Work of Reconstruction: From Slave to Wage Laborer in South Carolina, 1860–1870.* New York: Cambridge University Press, 1994.

Savitt, Todd L. "Black Health on the Plantation: Masters, Slaves, and Physicians." In *Science and Medicine in the Old South,* ed. Numbers and Savitt, 327–356.

———. *Medicine and Slavery: The Diseases and Health Care of Blacks in Antebellum Virginia.* Urbana: University of Illinois Press, 1978.

Savitt, Todd L., and James Harvey Young, eds. *Disease and Distinctiveness in the American South.* Knoxville: University of Tennessee Press, 1988.

Scarry, Elaine. *The Body in Pain: The Making and Unmaking of the World.* New York: Oxford University Press, 1985.

Schafer, Judith. "Details Are of a Most Revolting Character: Cruelty to Slaves as Seen in Appeals to the Supreme Court of Louisiana—Symposium on the Law of Slavery: Criminal and Civil Law of Slavery." *Chicago-Kent Law Review* 68, issue 3 (October 1992): 1283–1311.

Schwalm, Leslie A. *A Hard Fight for We: Women's Transition from Slavery to Freedom in South Carolina.* Chicago: University of Illinois Press, 1997.

Schwartz, Marie Jenkins. *Born in Bondage: Growing Up Enslaved in the Antebellum South.* Cambridge, MA: Harvard University Press, 2000.

Scott, Rebecca. *Degrees of Freedom: Louisiana and Cuba After Slavery.* New York: The Belknap Press of Harvard University Press, 2008.

———. "Discerning a Dignitary Offense: The Concept of Equal 'Public Rights' During Reconstruction." *Law and History Review* 38, no. 3 (August 2020): 519–553.

Seip, Terry L. "Slaves and Free Negroes in Alexandria, 1850–1860." *Louisiana History: The Journal of the Louisiana Historical Association* 10, no. 2 (Spring 1969): 147–165.

Sherrod, Ricky. *Plain Folk, Planters, and the Complexities of Southern Society: A Case*

Study of the Browns, Sherrods, Mannings, Sprowls, and Williamses of Nineteenth Century Northwest Louisiana. Nagadoches: Texas A&M Consortium, 2014.

Shoalmire, Jimmy G. "Carpetbagger Extraordinary: Marshall Harvey Twitchell, 1840–1905." PhD diss., Mississippi State University, 1969.

Schoen, Brian. "The Burdens and Opportunities of Interdependence: The Political Economies of the Planter Class." In *The Old South's Modern Worlds,* ed. Barnes, Schoen, and Towers, 66–85.

Sibler, Nina. *The Romance of Reunion: Northerners and the South, 1865–1900.* Chapel Hill, University of North Carolina Press, 1993.

Silkenat, David. *Moments of Despair: Suicide, Divorce, and Debt in Civil War Era North Carolina.* Chapel Hill: University of North Carolina Press, 2011.

———. *Raising the White Flag: How Surrender Defined the American Civil War.* Chapel Hill: University of North Carolina Press, 2019.

Sipress, Joel M. "From the Barrel of a Gun: The Politics of Murder in Grant Parish." *Louisiana History: The Journal of the Louisiana Historical Association* 42, no. 3 (Summer 2001): 303–321.

Simpson, Brooks. "Mission Impossible: Reconstruction Policy Reconsidered." *Journal of the Civil War Era* 6, no. 1 (March 2016): 85–102.

Smallwood, Stephanie. *Saltwater Slavery: A Middle Passage from Africa to American Diaspora.* Cambridge, MA: Harvard University Press, 2007.

Smangs, Mattias. "Doing Violence, Making Race: Southern Lynching and White Racial Group Formation." *American Journal of Sociology* 121, no 5 (March 2016): 1329–1374.

Smith, C. Wayne, and J. Tom Cothren, eds. *Cotton: Origin, History, Technology, and Production.* New York: John Wiley & Sons, 1999.

Smith, Mark M. *Debating Slavery: Economy and Society in the Antebellum American South.* New York: Cambridge University Press, 1998.

———. *Listening to Nineteenth-Century America.* Chapel Hill: University of North Carolina Press, 2001.

———. *Mastered by the Clock: Time, Slavery, and Freedom in the American South.* Chapel Hill: University of North Carolina Press, 1997.

Smith, Michael Thomas. "'For Love of Cotton': Nathaniel P. Banks, Union Strategy, and the Red River Campaign." *Louisiana History: The Journal of the Louisiana Historical Association* 51, no. 1 (Winter 2010): 5–26.

Smith, Myron J. Jr. *Tinclads in the Civil War: Union Light-Draught Gunboat Operations on Western Waters, 1862–1865.* Jefferson, NC: McFarland, 2010.

Smith, Solomon K. "The Freedmen's Bureau in Shreveport: The Struggle for Control of the Red River District." *Louisiana History: The Journal of the Louisiana Historical Association* 41, no. 4 (Autumn 2000): 435–465.

Snay, Mitchell. "Democracy and Race in the Late Reconstruction South: The White Leagues of Louisiana." In *Democracy and the American Civil War: Race and African Americans in the Nineteenth Century*, ed. Kevin Adams and Leonne Hudson. Kent, OH: Kent State University Press, 2016.

Sontag, Susan. *Regarding the Pain of Others*. New York: Picador, 2003.

Stanley, Amy. *From Bondage to Contract: Wage Labor, Marriage, and the Market in the Age of Slave Emancipation*. Cambridge, MA: Cambridge University Press, 1998.

Steckel, Richard H. "Birth Weights and Infant Mortality Among American Slaves." *Explorations in Economic History* 23, no. 2 (April 1986): 173–198.

———. "A Dreadful Childhood: The Excess Mortality of American Slaves." *Social Science History* 10, no. 4 (1986): 427–465.

———. "Fluctuations in a Dreadful Childhood: Synthetic Longitudinal Height Data, Relative Prices and Weather in the Short-Term Health of American Slaves." NBER working paper no. 10993, December 2004, National Bureau of Economic Research. www.nber.org/papers/w10993.

———. "'A Peculiar Population': The Nutrition, Health, and Mortality of American Slaves from Childhood to Maturity." *Journal of Economic History* 46, no. 3 (1986): 721–741.

———. "Slave Mortality: Analysis of Evidence from Plantation Records." *Social Science History* 3, no. 3/4 (1979): 86–114.

———. "Women, Work, and Health Under Plantation Slavery in the United States." In *More than Chattel*, ed. Gaspar and Hine, 43–60.

Stevenson, Brenda E. *Life in Black and White: Family and Community in the Slave South*. New York: Oxford University Press, 1996.

Stokes, Melvyn, and Stephen Conway, eds. *The Market Revolution in America: Social, Political, and Religious Expressions, 1800–1880*. Charlottesville: University Press of Virginia, 1996.

Stoll, Steven. *Larding the Lean Earth: Soil and Society in Nineteenth-Century America*. New York: Hill and Wang, 2002.

Stowe, Steven M. *Doctoring the South: Southern Physicians and Everyday Medicine in the Mid-Nineteenth Century*. Chapel Hill: University of North Carolina Press, 2004.

———. *Intimacy and Power in the Old South: Ritual in the Lives of the Planters*. Baltimore: Johns Hopkins University Press, 1987.

Streater, Kristen L. "'She-Rebels' on the Supply Line: Gender Conventions in Civil War Kentucky." In *Occupied Women*, ed. Whites and Long.

Sutherland, Daniel. "Looking for a Home: Louisiana Emigrants During the Civil War and Reconstruction." *Louisiana History: The Journal of the Louisiana Historical Association* 21, no. 4 (Autumn 1980): 341–359.

Tadman, Michael. "The Hidden History of Slave Trading in Antebellum South Carolina: John Springs III and Other 'Gentlemen Dealing in Slaves.'" *South Carolina Historical Magazine* 97, no 1 (January 1996): 6–29.

———. "The Interregional Slave Trade in the History and Myth-Making of the U.S. South." In *The Chattel Principle: Internal Slave Trades in the Americas,* ed. Walter Johnson. New Haven, CT: Yale University Press, 2004.

Taylor, Joe Gray. *Louisiana Reconstructed: 1863–1877.* Baton Rouge: Louisiana State University Press, 1974.

Tolnay, Stewart, and E. M. Beck. *A Festival of Violence: An Analysis of Southern Lynchings, 1882–1930.* Urbana: University of Illinois Press, 1995.

Tomich, Dale W. *Through the Prism of Slavery: Labor, Capital, and World Economy.* Lanham, MD: Rowman & Littlefield, 2004.

Trelease, Allen W. *White Terror: The Ku Klux Klan Conspiracy and Southern Reconstruction.* Baton Rouge: Louisiana State University Press, 1971.

Trouillot, Michel-Rolph. *Silencing the Past: Power and the Production of History.* Boston: Beacon Press, 1995.

Trudeau, Noah Andrew. "Red River Fiasco." *Naval History Magazine* 25, no. 6 (December 2011).

Tunnell, Ted. *Crucible of Reconstruction: War, Radicalism, and Race in Louisiana 1862–1877.* Baton Rouge: Louisiana State University Press, 1984.

———. *The Edge of the Sword: The Ordeal of Carpetbagger Marshall H. Twitchell in the Civil War and Reconstruction.* Baton Rouge: Louisiana State University Press, 2001.

Tyson, Carl Newton. *The Red River in Southwestern History.* Norman: University of Oklahoma Press, 1981.

Vandal, Gilles. "'Bloody Caddo': White Violence Against Blacks in a Louisiana Parish, 1865–1876." *Journal of Social History* 25, no. 2 (Winter 1991): 373–388.

———. "The Policy of Violence in Caddo Parish, 1865–1884." *Louisiana History: The Journal of the Louisiana Historical Association* 32, no. 2 (Spring 1991): 159–182.

———. "Property Offenses, Social Tension and Racial Antagonism in Post–Civil War Rural Louisiana." *Journal of Social History* 31, no. 1 (Autumn 1997): 127–153.

———. "Regulating Louisiana's Rural Areas: The Functions of Parish Jails, 1840–1885." *Louisiana History: The Journal of the Louisiana Historical Association* 42, no. 1 (Winter 2001): 59–92.

———. *Rethinking Southern Violence: Homicides in Post–Civil War Louisiana, 1866–1884.* Columbus: Ohio State University Press, 2000.

Varon, Elizabeth. *Appomattox: Victory, Defeat, and Freedom at the End of the Civil War.* New York: Oxford University Press, 2014.

Vlach, John Michael. *Back of the Big House: The Architecture of Plantation Slavery.* Chapel Hill: University of North Carolina Press, 1993.

Voegeli, V. Jacque. "A Rejected Alternative: Union Policy and the Relocation of Southern "Contrabands" at the Dawn of Emancipation." *Journal of Southern History* 69, no. 4 (November 2003): 765–790.

Waldrep, Christopher. *Roots of Disorder: Race and Criminal Justice in the American South, 1817–1880.* Urbana: University of Illinois Press, 1998.

Waldrep, Christopher, and Donald Nieman, eds. *Local Matters: Race, Crime, and Justice in the Nineteenth-Century South.* Athens: University of Georgia Press, 2001.

Walsh, Lorena S. "Boom-and-Bust Cycles in Chesapeake History." *William and Mary Quarterly* 68, no. 3 (July 2011): 387–392.

Wancho, Tom. "Slave Life on Plantations with a Focus on Natchitoches and the Surrounding Red River Area." *North Louisiana Historical Association Journal* 16, no. 2/3 (Spring/Summer 1985): 79–92.

Ward, Jason Morgan. *Hanging Bridge: Racial Violence and America's Civil Rights Century.* New York: Oxford University Press, 2016.

Warren, Christian. "Northern Chills, Southern Fevers: Race-Specific Mortality in American Cities, 1730–1900." *Journal of Southern History* 63, no. 1 (February 1997): 23–56.

Watson, Harry L. "Slavery and Development in a Duel Economy: The South and the Market Revolution." In *The Market Revolution in America,* ed. Stokes and Conway.

Webb, Allie Bayne Windham. "Organization and Activities of the Knights of the White Camelia in Louisiana, 1867–1869." *North Louisiana Historical Association Newsletter* 6, no. 4 (August 1966): 1–5.

West, Stephen A. "'A General Remodeling of Every Thing': Economy and Race in the Post-Emancipation South." In *Reconstructions,* ed. Brown, 10–39.

Wetta, Frank J. "'Bulldozing the Scalawags': Some Examples of the Persecution of Southern White Republicans in Louisiana During Reconstruction." *Louisiana History: The Journal of the Louisiana Historical Association* 21, no. 1 (Winter 1980): 43–58.

——. *The Louisiana Scalawags: Politics, Race, and Terrorism During the Civil War and Reconstruction.* Baton Rouge: Louisiana State University Press, 2012.

Weiner, Marli. *Mistresses and Slaves: Plantation Women in South Carolina, 1830–1880.* Chicago: University of Illinois Press, 1998.

White, Deborah Gray. *Ar'n't I a Woman?: Female Slaves in the Plantation South.* New York: W. W. Norton, 1985.

White, Howard A. *The Freedmen's Bureau in Louisiana.* Baton Rouge: Louisiana State University Press, 1970.

Whites, LeeAnn. *The Civil War as a Crisis in Gender: Augusta, Georgia, 1860–1890.* Athens: University of Georgia Press, 1995.

Whites, LeeAnn, and Alecia Long, eds. *Occupied Women: Gender and Military Oc-*

cupation and the American Civil War. Baton Rouge: Louisiana State University Press, 2009.

Whittington, G. P. "The History of Rapides Parish." *Louisiana Historical Quarterly* 16 (1933): 427–440.

———. *Rapides Parish Louisiana, A History.* Alexandria, LA: Colonial Dames in the State of Louisiana, 1970.

Wiener, Jonathan M. *Social Origins of the New South: Alabama, 1860–1885.* Baton Rouge: Louisiana State University Press, 1978.

Wikberg, Ron, E. J. Carder, and Floyd Webb. "Tragedy at Colfax." *The Angolite,* November/December 1989.

Williams, Kidada. *They Left Great Marks on Me: African American Testimonials of Racial Violence from Emancipation to World War One.* New York: New York University Press. 2012.

———. "The Wounds That Cried Out: Reckoning with African Americans' Testimonies of Trauma and Suffering from Night Riding." In *The World the Civil War Made,* ed. Downs and Masur, 159–182.

Williard, David. "Criminal Amnesty, State Courts, and the Reach of Reconstruction." *Journal of Southern History* 85, no 1 (February 2019): 105–136.

———. "Executions, Justice, and Reconciliation in North Carolina's Western Piedmont, 1865–67." *Journal of the Civil War Era* 2, no. 1 (March 2012): 31–57.

Winters, John D. *The Civil War in Louisiana.* Baton Rouge: Louisiana State University Press, 1963.

Wood, Betty. *Women's Work, Men's Work: The Informal Slave Economies of Lowcountry Georgia.* Athens: University of Georgia Press, 1995.

Woodman, Harold. "Post–Civil War Southern Agriculture and the Law." *American History* 53, no. 1 (January 1979): 319–337.

Woodruff, Nan Elizabeth. *American Congo: The African American Freedom Struggle in the Delta.* Cambridge, MA: Harvard University Press, 2003.

Woodward, C. Vann. *The Strange Career of Jim Crow.* 1955. Commemorative reprint, New York: Oxford University Press, 2001.

Wooster, Ralph A. "The Louisiana Secession Convention." *Louisiana Historical Quarterly* 34 (April 1951): 112–118.

Wright, Gavin. *The Political Economy of the Cotton South: Households, Markets, and Wealth in the Nineteenth Century.* New York: W. W. Norton, 1978.

———. *Slavery and American Economic Development.* Baton Rouge: Louisiana State University Press, 2006.

———. "Slavery and the Cotton Boom." *Explorations in Economic History* 12 (1975): 439–451.

Wright, Gavin, and Howard Kunreuther. "Cotton, Corn and Risk in the Nineteenth Century." *The Journal of Economic History* 35, no. 3 (September 1975): 526–551.

Wyatt-Brown, Bertram. *Southern Honor: Ethics and Behavior in the Old South*. 1982. Oxford: Oxford University Press, 2007.

Young, Jeffrey Robert. *Domesticating Slavery: The Master Class in Georgia and South Carolina, 1670–1837*. Chapel Hill: University of North Carolina Press, 1999.

———. "Ideology and Death on a Savannah River Rice Plantation, 1833–1867: Paternalism Amidst 'a Good Supply of Disease and Pain.'" *Journal of Southern History* 59, no. 4 (November 1993): 673–706.

Zuczek, Richard. *State of Rebellion: Reconstruction in South Carolina*. Columbia: University of South Carolina Press, 1996.

INDEX